SPORTS
in the
Western
World

SPORTS
in the
Western
World

WILLIAM J. BAKER

ROWMAN AND LITTLEFIELD
Totowa, N.J.

for
Christina, Cynthia, Clara, and Catherine:
four who know the score

Copyright © 1982 by Rowman and Littlefield

First published in the United States 1982 by Rowman and Littlefield, 81 Adams Drive, Totowa, New Jersey 07512.

Library of Congress Cataloging in Publication Data

Baker, William J. (William Joseph), 1938-
  Sports in the Western world.
  Bibliography: p.
  1. Sports—History. I. Title.
GV571.B25   796'.09   82-3669
ISBN 0-8476-7075-9   AACR2

Printed in the United States of America

CONTENTS

INTRODUCTION

Human beings cannot live by bread alone. They dream and they strive. Not merely for warmth do they take fire from the altar of the gods; curiosity is their glory and their pain. They climb mountains, cross uncharted seas, and explore outer space for reasons other than material benefit. They thrive on challenges. Seekers of laurels, they especially measure themselves in competition with fellow humans. Where there is no contest, they create one. From deep within, and from millennia past, comes the impulse for athletic competition.

This book is about the history of competitive sports in the Western world—from ancient religious ritual and simple tribal contests to highly organized modern spectacles. Mere leisurely play, exercises and programs for health, and the pleasures of hunting and fishing must find their chroniclers elsewhere. Here these noncompetitive activities are considered only as they relate to the numerous physical contests and games that go by the name of sports.

In each successive epoch of human history, sports are integrally related to the political and social structures dominant at the time. Often sports reflect divisions of power, wealth, and class; sometimes they erode those barriers. Always their form is dictated by the technology that happens to be available. References to the contextual forces that give sports a unique texture in each era are interspersed throughout this book, particularly in the introductions to each of the five parts.

Yet for all the particular forms that sports take from age to age, four groups of people remain constant to the narrative. First are the athletes and the games they play. Whether rough Roman gladiators or genteel golfers, medieval peasants or modern superstars, individual Greek competitors or modern teams, the players and their games stand at the heart of the drama.

Behind the athletes is a second group common to all ages: patrons who organize, govern, and promote athletic contests. Modern league officials and club owners have ancient counterparts in tribal priests and chieftains, kings, and wealthy benefactors. Even rustic folk games depended on the managerial skills of village elders, who perpetuated customs and enforced unwritten rules.

Spectators are another constant of sports. Competitive sport virtually always has an element of display: athletes playing before, if not to, a crowd of onlookers. In ancient Olympia no less than in the Roman Colosseum, for medieval tournaments and eighteenth-century boxing matches as well as the most recent Super Bowl, spectators vicariously enjoy the action, cheer their heroes, and intensify the drama by their vocal interest.

A fourth group, commentators, are always associated with sports. In the ancient past, sages, poets, and philosophers described and interpreted the meaning of sports for their day. Theologians received the commentator's baton in the Middle Ages, passing it on to pamphleteers and authors of books for small audiences in the pre-Industrial age. Newspaper reporters, radio announcers, and television commentators supply the latest in a long line of descriptive, analytical commentary on sporting events.

Like threads on a shuttle, patrons, spectators, and interpretative comments weave in and out of the story of sports in the Western world, always with reference to the athletes and their contests. The tapestry is large, but the fabric is uneven in quality. While scholars repair various flaws, this broad survey is intended for the general viewer who wants to know how certain sports began, the manner in which their origins and development fit into the larger historical picture, and why they have come to be what they are. Notes on sources and suggested readings are provided at the end of the text for those readers interested in exploring specific subjects more closely.

This book is written by an American, and toward the end focuses mostly on the American scene. Here modern sport is writ large: highly commercial, popular to the point of excess, and ambiguously related to the highest human values. If ancient Greece is considered the birthplace of organized athletics and Great Britain the cradle of modern games, today the United States is the examplar of the best and worst tendencies of modern sports.

For the making of this book, my colleagues Dave Smith, Bob Thomson, and Jerry Nadelhaft regularly contributed information. Friends Jack Berryman, Stephen Hardy, Jack Higgs, Ron Smith, and a careful Rowman and Littlefield copyeditor corrected many mistakes. Most of all, I am grateful to John DiMeglio for his critical eye and matchless fund of knowledge. Jean Day transformed a cluttered manuscript into clean copy. Encouragement from Tina, my companion for the long distance, allowed me to finish this course with a measure of grace and delight.

W. J. B.
Bangor, Maine
1982

PART ONE

From Ritual to Recreation: The Beginnings of Sport

Virtually every competitive sport in the modern world is a refinement of physical contests originating in ancient and medieval times. Taking their form largely from primitive hunting and warring activities necessary for survival, competitive games began primarily as religious rituals designed to win the favor of the gods or to honor the memories of heroic leaders. Over the centuries the sacred aspects diminished. But whether in front of tribal totems, at the Egyptian temples to Osiris, beside Greek altars to Zeus, before the Roman pantheon, under the Mohammedan banner to Allah, or in medieval Christian monasteries and church cloisters, sports evolved always in relation to religious ceremonies, holidays, and institutions.

Sports first took root in societies that were mostly rural and sparsely populated. Although large urban centers thrived in ancient China, India, and Mesopotamia, cities in the Western world were small and unstable. The largest Greek city-state, Athens, numbered barely 150,000 at its peak. The city of Rome mushroomed to more than a million inhabitants at the center of a sprawling empire, only to decline to fewer than 20,000 when the empire collapsed. By modern standards even medieval Venice, Paris, Amsterdam, and London were merely large commercial towns. By 1500 about ninety-five percent of the world's population still lived in villages and remote cottages. Sports therefore tended to be rustic, provincial activities, entirely different from one place to another. Based on local traditions rather than on any written rules, they were slow to change. Roman soldiers and feudal warriors, Mohammedan and Christian missionaries, and energetic sailors and merchants all carried new forms of physical exercise and contests to regions far removed from their places of origin, but the rural character of society kept most of the earliest games simple and resistant to formal organization.

Assumptions of social inequality also weighed heavily on the origins of sports. Primitive tribes enforced definite standards of status, age, and sex for participants in their various cultic games. Slaves and "barbarian" foreigners were excluded from the Greek athletic festivals; on the other hand, only slaves and criminals were forced into the Roman gladiatorial arenas. In medieval Europe, tournaments, jousts, and court tennis were reserved by law for feudal kings and aristocrats, while only peasants customarily played football, quoits, and early stick-and-ball games. A person's pastimes bespoke his social rank just as surely as did his speech, dress, and diet.

Excluded from war, politics, and business, women also played almost no part in early sports. Young girls participated in some of the primitive ritualistic games, and Greek women held Heraean games at Olympia as well as short-sprint contests at some of the other festivals, but sport originally was primarily all male. Aristocratic medieval women sat on their luxurious pedestals, while peasant females went into the fields to work alongside men. But none was welcomed on fields of competitive play.

The world of ancient and medieval man was indeed a man's world. It was a world in which tribal chieftains, emperors, kings, and feudal lords ruled over dependent, subservient masses, all geographically dispersed in small, remote units unconnected by any efficient means of transport or communication. It was a warrior's world and a priest's world. It was a world that gave birth to sports.

Chapter **1**

THE COMPETITIVE IMPULSE

"What's your secret, Yaz? What keeps you going after all these years?" a sportswriter recently asked Carl Yastrzemski, the veteran star of the Boston Red Sox. Within a month of the queries, Yastrzemski celebrated his fortieth birthday and collected the 3,000th base hit of his major league career. He was still going strong despite two damaged Achilles tendons and all the muscle strains and bruises common to athletes. What was the source of his endurance? Money? Fame? Loyalty to the team? "The competition," he explained. "Facing the pitcher one on one. Once you get into the batter's box, pride takes over. Nobody can help. Something inside keeps me going." Although Carl Yastrzemski is a modern American athlete, a product of a culture that sets a high premium on competition, his "something inside" is a competitive impulse that is as old as the human race.

Hunters and Warriors

It all began as a form of survival. Prehistoric man lacked the protective fins of the fish, and the sharp fangs, claws, horns, and spikes of other animals. To avoid extinction, he tempered strength with cunning, endurance with agility. He first ran, jumped, climbed, swam, and fought literally for his life. Over many millennia he devised weapons to balance the odds. Scarcely is it a mere coincidence that primitive stones, clubs, and spears form the elementary shape of modern athletic equipment: balls of all shapes and sizes, baseball and cricket bats, hockey sticks, and tennis rackets, as well as the discus and javelin, which have little changed over the centuries.

Born of necessity, hunting skills were nourished for more than a million years as the larger brain, language, and artistic skills took shape. Even the first art was grounded in the hunt. In what is now France and Spain, paleolithic hunters twenty to thirty thousand years ago sketched and painted pictures of bears, mammoths, bison, and reindeer on the walls and ceilings of their caves, perhaps as a kind of magical attempt to control their prey. Circumstance, experience, and habit determined early human behavior. For the care and protection of children, human beings banded together for mutual benefit. Hunters also learned to work cooperatively, especially when stalking big, dangerous, or fast game. In loosely coordinated groups they surrounded their prey and drove them into ravines, where they could be slaughtered. Teamwork, like physical ferocity, has its roots in the primitive experience.

From the beginning, however, some hunters distinguished themselves as superior to others, thus winning prominence within the tribe. Like the fish and animal kingdoms whence man had come and with whom he originally competed to survive, small human groups established their pecking order of power and prestige. Tribal honor as well as material benefit fell to the strongest, fastest, most efficient hunters. Until recently the men of the Bachiga tribe in East Africa hunted together, but the first individual to wound and kill the game received the accolades, plus the best meat for his family. For the successful modern athlete who wins social status and personal esteem on the one hand, material reward on the other, only the form—not the essence—of the primitive competitive impulse has changed.

Competition flourished most in those early societies that were "loosely" organized. Aggressive behavior was at its lowest when tribal relationships and individual roles were clearly defined. The arrival of new, strange individuals or marauding groups threatened the hierarchy. Their dominance challenged, those individuals at the top of the social order fought to retain their positions, while subordinates struggled to establish themselves above the newly arrived outsiders. Little wonder that competitive sport thrives most in societies where achievement rather than mere birth is the means to success and acclaim.

Like his primitive forebears, today's athlete stakes his claim to dominance in terms of physical space: he "establishes position" under the boards, "guards the plate," and "stands his ground." Once individual hunters banded together in a fixed territory, they claimed squatter's rights to their hunting grounds. Encroachment of other individuals or groups endangered the local food supply. Still today the backward Arapesh tribe of New Guinea has a word, *ano'in*, which is best translated as "rival," specifically referring to someone who has killed precious game or seized a woman in another's territory.

Healthy, able-bodied women, considered prizes of precious value, stimulated male competitive impulses to a fighting pitch. Within tribes men competed with each other for the women of their choice. The best hunters and warriors claimed the best wives. Tribes raided other tribes not for horses or weapons or tools, but for women. Today we still refer to a young man "winning a girl's hand" in marriage; in the early days the winning was literal.

Warrior skills and competitive games blended freely in primitive societies such as this Indian tribe in Florida, as illustrated in an etching by Jacque Le Moyne for Theodore de Bry, *America*, II, 1591.

Old English, Norse, and German words for "wedding party" can also be translated as "a race." The oldest surviving Greek legends are filled with episodes involving foot races, wrestling matches, and chariot races for the hand of a bride. Often the contest occurred between local men and a competitor from afar. Mating and the territorial urge went hand in hand.

Ancient territorial invasion understandably produced fear, which in turn provoked aggressive behavior. Like growling dogs, twittering birds, and bristling apes, early defenders of home and hearth first attempted to repel their foes by bluff and threat. Today's boxers grimacing and snarling at each other prior to their fight participate in an ancient ritual of intimidation. When all else failed, however, war followed—and with a vengeance. Added to the original simple tools of the huntsman's trade, the knife and bow and arrow expanded the warrior's arsenal.

Defense of territorial boundaries became all the more urgent once man the hunter became man the farmer about 10,000 years ago. Now he had property, not mere indefinite parts of the forest, to defend. A tent or hut, tools, seeds for the next planting, pottery for cooking, eating and drinking, domesticated animals—all required protection, as did the family and tribe itself. Neolithic man continued to hunt and with new zeal he defended his territory. The stronger the tribal, community ties, the greater was the honor given to the warriors who guarded them. Bathonga tribesmen in South Africa who distinguished themselves in battle were treated like young kings as they performed their victory dances in the presence of the tribal chieftain. Those warriors who flinched in the face of the enemy suffered the humiliation of having to crawl on their knees to fetch water for the village.

Still hunters and warriors despite their new agricultural, domesticated lifestyle, primitive men largely left the planting and harvesting of food to women, children, and the aged. The forest, not the plowed field, was the customary male habitat. Becoming more inventive, they devised rafts, boats, and canoes to traverse watery areas. Relatively slow afoot, they began to ride rather than slaughter horses. In northern climates they overcame winter snow and ice barriers by making crude skis, snowshoes, and ice skates from animal bones. From the deep bogs of Norway and Sweden and the remote Russian mountains of Siberia, ancient snowshoes and skis have been discovered. Carbon tests indicate that they are at least 4,000 to 5,000 years old. The first skiers tracked down game for their families until the summer harvest, and maneuvered across snowy mountains and frozen lakes to do battle with their adversaries.

Gods and Games

Even prehistoric man did not live by work and war alone. Returning home from the hunt or battle, he warmed his feet at the fire and spun his yarns in a language given to body motions as much as verbal skill. All the while, his children played, often making games of their elders' work. Boys' play in the remote Ammassalik Eskimo tribe of Greenland illustrates the point. While their fathers were away hunting and fishing, the boys made their own weapons and competed against each other in shooting arrows and throwing harpoons. When a boy became twelve years old, his father built him a kayak. At fifteen, sons joined fathers in the hunt for seals and whales. Children's games grew out of adult necessity, and the games in turn prepared the children for adulthood. It was a pattern common to primitive peoples throughout the Western world.

The evidence that children's games were the channel through which ancient hunting and warring practices began to be transformed into contests approximating modern sports simply does not hold up. The transition from elementary animallike competitiveness to the symbolic hunt and mock warfare that make up modern sport came from adults. From primitive religious fear and superstition arose rituals designed to placate the unknown powers that people called gods. In many of those rituals lay the actual beginnings of sport.

For all his enlarged brain power, early man remained insecure. He could see and fight animals and opposing tribesmen, but the invisible forces of nature, disease, and death filled him with dread and awe. To the primitive mind the universe seemed divided between opposite elements: health and sickness, warmth and cold, fertility and barrenness, life and death. As the fruit of agricultural labor increasingly supplemented early man's meat diet, polarities of summer and winter, rainfall and drought, entered his consciousness. Above all the antagonistic forces stood the awesome moon and sun, obviously crucial but dimly understood.

From this mythology of dual forces at war in the world, religious ritual emerged as an attempt to encourage the good and defeat the bad, to win the favor of the gods. Man's first formidable foe, the wilderness, provided him with his earliest gods: mountains, rivers, springs, rocks, and trees. Then came the deification of the beasts and snakes he contested. The snake is a symbol of cosmic evil in Genesis. Equally old are frescoes and vases retrieved from the ruins of Minoan Crete depicting acrobats on the backs of bulls, an ancient ceremonial rite supposedly pleasing to the gods. Bullfighting originally combined piety and courage: the bullfighter believed himself to be competing with, or sacrificing to, the gods. The origins of other bloodsports such as bearbaiting, bullrunning, and cockfighting also lay in religious ritual.

The agricultural revolution shifted the deities to the heavens, whence came rain and warmth for the growth of crops. First the moon and stars (female goddesses), then the sun (a male god) came to be seen as the source of life. From the Zulus of Africa to the Zuni Indians of North America, in South America as well as ancient Egypt, mythology explaining the origins of the moon and sun thrived. Given the spherical shape of both deities, people saw them in terms of huge round stones or balls.

In a myth common to both the Aztec and Inca Indians of Central and South America, twin brothers once challenged the gods to a ball game, only to lose the game and consequently their heads on the sacrificial block. The head of one of the brothers was placed in a tree, where a young virgin happened to pass. From the head spurted a stream of sperm, impregnating the girl. She bore male twins, who in turn challenged the gods to another ball game. Unlike their "father," the young twins won the game, whereupon the severed heads of the original losers ascended to the heavens and became the sun and the moon.

Primitive imagination produced ritualistic dances and chants, blood sacrifices, and ceremonial games designed to appease the gods. Throughout what is now Mexico, the Aztecs built stone courtyards in which they played ball games of serious intent. Periodically the losers were taken to a nearby temple and slain on an alter to the gods. On special holidays, the winners of the game were sacrificed, their hearts cut out and ceremoniously burned. Supposedly the fragrance of the best available manhood gave special pleasure to the nostrils of the Sun God, who thus was encouraged to grant fertile crops, good births, and victorious wars to his worshippers.

Less brutal but no less religious, ritualistic competition thrived in most of the ancient Indian cultures in the Western Hemisphere. For centuries the Zuni Indians of the American Southwest gathered annually at the winter solstice to sprinkle sacred meal around a ball. Then warriors stood back and threw darts made of sticks and feathers at it. The first to penetrate the ball walked forward, picked it up, held it heavenward, and offered prayers of thanksgiving that the rains would come soon.

Nearby Apache Indians made an even more elaborate ritual of a relay race between young males who had reached puberty, a kind of initiation rite. One team represented the sun, the other the moon, in a reenactment of their eternal race across the heavens. For three days before the event, the tribes celebrated with music, dances, and feasts, all the while planting fertility symbols such as pollen, small trees, ears of maize, and eagle feathers along the track.

Ancient Egyptians similarly sought the favor of their gods. All the earliest references to ball play in Egypt appear in religious texts recovered from pyramids built around 2300 to 2100 B.C. Fresco paintings from roughly the same period depict four seminude women paired off in a piggyback fashion, tossing balls back and forth. In another wall painting of a slightly later date, a pharaoh holds a stick in his right hand and a ball in his left. Facing him are two priests, who appear ready to catch the ball. An inscription proclaims that "the enemies are struck before them," presumably a reference to darkness, infertility, and death, as well as opposing armies.

During the spring, priests annually carried a bannerlike image of Osiris, the god of the fertile River Nile, from the temple and through town streets, then back toward the temple. Townsmen played the role of the evil forces of infertility and in mock-seriousness attempted to prevent the image of Osiris from returning to its rightful place. More a religious drama than sport, the rite was nevertheless not child's play. Opposing forces recklessly wielded heavy wooden clubs. According to a Greek observer, Herodotus, at one of these engagements around 450 B.C., "there was hard fighting with clubs, and heads were broken." They took their religious games seriously.

Heroes and Hero Worship

Originally staged as imitative rituals, various forms of physical exercise and games lent themselves to official state occasions honoring the pharaohs and visiting foreign dignitaries. On the walls of the tombs at Beni Hasan, dating from about 2000 to 1500 B.C., numerous illustrations depict a wide range of competitive sports such as wrestling, boxing, fencing, swimming, rowing, running, jumping, weight lifting, archery, and horseback riding. For single-stick fencing, a game popular with soldiers training for hand-to-hand combat, scattered literary evidence supplements visual images to convey the flavor of a contest that went beyond the bounds of religious ceremony.

Soldiers displayed their skills not only at fertility festivals but also at various state ceremonies in celebration of foreign tribute paid to Egyptian kings. First the contestants bowed to their spectator audience, a small assemblage of high officials. Then they turned to face each other, crossed their long sticks, and began the duel. With none of the mock-seriousness that characterized cultic ritual, they parried and thrust until one proved himself superior. The winner raised both arms to the acclaim of the spectators, but the loser bowed his head and covered his face in shame. Postfight or postgame differences in the behavior of winners and losers are ancient.

Of all the competitive activities pictured on the walls of Beni Hasan, wrestling is the most prominent. Virtually all the contestants are naked; a few

In a timeless, competitive ritual, Egyptian boxers sparred for advantage before delivering a body blow such as the one to the left of this stone-carved scene from the tomb of Khereuf, near Luxor, the ancient site of Thebes. (Courtesy of Jean Leiper.)

wore belts. The rules are unclear, but certainly the holds varied. Some wrestlers employ belt grips in Japanese sumo fashion; others display a catch-as-catch-can style of leg or knee pickups, body locks and lifts, hip rolls, arm locks, and various combinations of holds. A few inscriptions accompany the pictures, most representing shouts of encouragement from the audience. One warns against a foul: "Look out! You are in the presence of the Pharaoh, your master."

Pharaohs of course loom large in the history of ancient Egypt. Massive pyramids witness to their majestic authority. Inscriptions tell of their mighty deeds in war and diplomacy—and occasionally in sport. According to one inscription, Amenophis II, King of Egypt from 1438 to 1412 B.C., was a gifted warrior and an avid, able sportsman:

There was no one who could span his bow and none equalled him in running. Strong was his arm and he did not tire when he seized the oar and rowed at the stem of his boat as stroke for two hundred men. They stopped when they had only half a mile behind them. They were already exhausted and their limbs were tired and they were breathless. But his Majesty was strong with his twenty foot-long oar. He stopped and grounded his boat after he had rowed three miles without a pause. Faces beamed when they saw him doing this.

There was method in this early media hype. Primitive man had long idealized, then deified, their ancestors and powerful chieftains. The pharaohs came to be seen as the mediators between nature-gods and men, and in the end they acquired a kind of divinity accorded the gods who guaranteed order and fertility. Feared in life, the pharaohs were worshipped in death. No doubt the tales of their exploits—athletic as well as military—became embellished in the telling.

Throughout the ancient world—in Asia as well as the Near East, in Europe and the Americas—people worshipped dead ancestors and heroes with a fervor. Funeral feasts, music, and games celebrated the departed's vigor; annual festivals kept his memory alive. In Ireland, well beyond the edge of the world known to inhabitants of the Mediterranean basin, a dying Celtic chieftain charged his followers to gather every third year at Carmen, near Wexford, to celebrate "a fair of mourning to bear his name forever." For centuries the Carmen fair flourished, attracting people from all over Ireland and Scotland. Amid the buying and selling of goods, courts were held and laws enacted. The central attractions, however, were competitive games in honor of the heroic, godlike chieftain.

Similarly rooted in the hero worship of a departed tribal chief, the Tailteann Games originated around 1800 B.C. in County Meath. As at Carmen, Celtic tribesmen turned to the fields of competition, where running, jumping, wrestling, hammer throwing, and horse racing contests supposedly kept alive the dead chieftain's hearty spirit. Despite sparse firsthand evidence, one can surmise that throughout pre-Christian Europe ancestor worship and fertility rites combined to produce local fairs: convivial gatherings and contests of physical skill and strength.

Evidence is firm for the funeral games of the ancient Greeks. Homer's *Iliad* and *Odyssey*, the oldest surviving books in the Western world, written between 900 and 700 B.C., portray life and thought eleven centuries before the time of Christ. Funeral games appear in Book XXIII of the *Iliad* in honor of a Greek soldier, Patroclus, who was slain in combat before the gates of Troy. Patroclus's friend and commander, Achilles, proposed to "mourn him, for such is the due of the dead." Achilles provided "a sumptuous funeral feast" for the army around the body of Patroclus. The following day, Achilles laid the body on a huge stack of wood, surrounded it with four slaughtered horses and the bodies of twelve young Trojan captives executed for the occasion, and set the pyre on fire to burn throughout the night. At dawn Greek soldiers gathered the bones of Patroclus into a golden urn, then started to return to their siege positions around Troy. "But Achilles restrained them," according to Homer, "and seated the troops in a large open space where the funeral games were to be." A slain hero deserved no less.

Homer underscores the traditional character of funeral games by having various characters refer to earlier last rites for King Amarynceus, when his sons "put prizes up for games in his honor." Games supposedly gave pleasure to the wandering soul of the honored person. Vigorous contests affirmed life in the face of death. Certainly the funeral games were bathed in religious mythology. When a chariot racer dropped his whip, he reasoned that an angry Apollo knocked it out of his hand; he retrieved it thanks to the intervention of the goddess Athena. An archer supposedly missed his target because he had neglected to promise a grateful sacrifice to Apollo, and "Apollo therefore begrudged him a win." In a foot race against Ajax, Odysseus stormed down the final stretch praying to Athena, "O goddess, hear me, and come put more speed in my feet!"

Whatever their religious beliefs, athletes compete to win, to prove their superiority over others, and thus to lay claim to a kind of primitive immortality. While the soul of Patroclus fought its own battles on the banks of the River Styx, his surviving comrades participated in a timeless athletic drama wherein patrons, spectators, and athletes each played a part.

Classic Contests

Only rich, well-born Greeks competed in these early games. The initial and most important event by far was a chariot race. Then, in order, came boxing and wrestling matches, a foot race, a duel with spears, a discus throw, an archery match, and a javelin throw. Individual sports, not team competition, appealed to the Greeks.

Achilles, both the patron and referee of the games, provided prizes for winners of each contest: horses, mules, and oxen; bronze cooking caldrons and tripods, silver bowls, iron axes, and gold coins; armor, weapons, and women seized from Troy. To a charioteer who came in last, he gave a consolation prize because the loser's horses were the slowest in the field. He bestowed another prize on an aged onlooker, Nestor, "for now your days of boxing and wrestling are over, nor will you compete again in the javelin throw or footrace. The weight of years lies heavy upon you."

Soldiers all, the spectators at these funeral games displayed a range of emotions and behavior common to sporting crowds of all ages. During the chariot race the spectators peered across the plains, attempting to determine the leader, and placed bets on their favorites. They became "bored and restless" when a wrestling match dragged on indecisively, but were "gripped with amazement" at the skill of the winning archer, and watched the dangerous spear-duel in a mood of "gripping suspense." They laughed in derision when a discus thrower wobbled his discus "off a short way," but they became "wild with applause" when another contestant got off his throw "with tremendous force, as far as a herdsman can fling his short throwing-staff." Like modern partisans, these soldier-spectators added excitement to the games. As Odysseus threatened to pass Ajax in the foot race, they "shouted to urge Ajax in his all-out effort to win."

The athletes similarly appear wholly recognizable. Fitting the mold of the boastful boxer, Epeus threatened to "crush every bone in my crazy opponent's carcass and pound his flesh to a pulp!" His opponent's "nearest and dearest of kin," he warned, should "stand by in a body, that they may carry him off unconscious when I have finished with him." He backed up his boast with brawn. A fierce uppercut sent his opponent sprawling on his back in the sand, to be dragged off "dangling his head to one side and spitting out clots of blood."

Although of princely birth, these athletes hardly displayed gentlemanly sportsmanship once the games began. They played fiercely to win, assaulted opponents who broke the unwritten rules, and disputed questionable decisions by the referee. Chariot drivers, for example, competed with "the heart of each man throbbing wildly to win, and each of them shouted to urge his pair [of horses] on, as they flew through the dust on the plain." A youth zealous for victory dangerously passed an older driver on a track of ground narrowed by spring floods. Reining in his horses, the more experienced charioteer screamed, "Go on, damn you! Surely no mortal has fewer scruples than you." By the same token, few mortals wanted so badly to win.

This competitiveness is the source of the word "athlete." A Greek word derived from two terms best translated as "contest" and "prize," the athlete is one who competes for a reward of tangible or intangible value. Another Greek word for an athletic contest (and also for a military engagement) is *agon*, whence the word agony. At the earliest Greek games on record, athletes agonized to win prizes offered by a rich patron. In the words of Homer, wrestlers' backs "fairly creaked as they gripped each other hard with their hands and grappled for all they were worth, streaming with sweat and raising many a blood-livid welt on each other's ribs and shoulders, as both of them strained every muscle." Yet for all their agony, the ecstasy of victory evaded both contestants. Achilles finally called the match a draw and divided the prize.

In Book VIII of the *Odyssey*, Homer attended to other athletic contests. Struggling to return home from the Trojan wars, Odysseus was shipwrecked before finally stumbling onto the island of Phaiacia. A benign king, Alcinous, provided him with a ship and crew, then spread a banquet to send him off. A minstrel sang "stories of famous men," some of whom were Odysseus's departed friends and comrades. Tears welled up in the eyes of the old warrior, prompting King Alcinous to announce, "Look here, gentlemen! We have had enough of our feast now, enough of banquet's bosom-friend the harp! Let us go out and try our luck at games and sports, that our guest may report to his friends when he gets home how we beat the world at boxing and wrestling and jumping and running!"

A crowd gathered in a nearby field to watch local champions display their prowess. In the first contest, a footrace, runners "went tearing along over the course all in a bunch" before one drew away, proving himself "far and away the best." Then in quick succession came competitive matches in wrestling, broad jumping, discus throwing, and boxing. One of the participants, a son of King Alcinous, suggested that they find out from Odysseus if he had any athletic ability. He approached their guest: "Come along, sir, have a try at the games yourself, if you have any skill. Sport is the best way to fame for any man alive—what you can do with your arms and legs." Odysseus tried to beg off, but Phaiacian athletes baited him further. "Ah, well, sir," mocked one, "I do not see you as a fellow who goes in for games, though that is the way of the world. You strike me as the captain of a merchant ship, always thinking of your cargo and grasping for petty profits. You are not an athlete."

Rising to the bait, Odysseus seized a discus and flung it well beyond all the earlier marks. "Touch that if you can, young men!" he growled. "If you do, I think I'll follow it up with another as good or better. Does anyone else want to challenge me? Out with it then, and take me on. You have put my back up, and I don't care what it is—box, wrestle, run." No challenger stepped forward, and King Alcinous called an end to the games, escorted Odysseus back to the banquet hall for more festivities, then sped him on his homeward way.

One final contest remained for Odysseus, a kind of championship tournament in which his athletic and warrior skills blended in heroic victory. During his long absence from home, a number of suitors had taken over his palace, vying for the hand of his wife, Penelope. Arriving home disguised as a begger, Odysseus instructed his son and a few faithful servants to arrange an archery contest. His own great bow would serve as the instrument whereby a suitor could win Penelope by shooting an arrow through holes in the heads of twelve axes set in a straight line. None of the eager contestants even had the strength to bend the large bow, of course. Odysseus stepped forward and performed the feat, then ruthlessly slew his competitors.

Standing over his fallen foes, Odysseus summoned his son, Telemachos, "to the place of battle (*agon*), where the best men are proved," in order for his son to remember never to disgrace his ancestors. Thus did the odyssey of ancient man culminate in a contest of animal strength, cunning, and courage, a contest for honor as well as survival.

Chapter 2

ORGANIZED GREEK GAMES

The story of organized athletics in the ancient world is primarily the story of Greece. A land of sunshine, mild climate, and rugged mountains rimmed by sparkling seas, Greece spawned philosophers and civic leaders who placed equal value on physical activity and mental cultivation. A vast array of gymnasiums and palaestras (wrestling schools) served as training centers for athletes to prepare themselves to compete in stadiums situated in every major city-state.

For more than a thousand years athletic festivals were an important part of Greek life. Originally mixtures of religious ceremony and athletic competition, hundreds of local festivals were held each year throughout the country and in Greek colonies in Egypt, Sicily, and on the banks of the Bosporus. By the fifth century B.C. four major festivals dominated the scene, forming a kind of circuit for ambitious athletes. The Pythian Games, held every fourth year at the sacred site of Apollo in Delphi, crowned victory with a laurel wreath. The Isthmian Games at Corinth in honor of Poseidon, the god of the sea, were conducted every other year, providing a victor's wreath of pine from a nearby sacred grove. The Nemean Games at Nemea, honoring Zeus every second year, awarded a sacred wreath of celery. The oldest and most prestigious of all the festivals, the Olympic Games, bestowed the olive wreath every four years in honor of Zeus.

The Olympics were the Super Bowl, the World Cup, the Heavyweight Championship of Greek athletics. By Olympic standards were the other festivals judged; at Olympia the sweet "nectar of victory" filled athletes with self-esteem and accorded them public acclaim. For our understanding of Greek culture, its open, competitive spirit, its glory and its limits, the

Olympic Games reveal more perhaps than do all the speeches of Pericles, the dialogues of Plato, or the imperial conquests of Alexander the Great.

A Valley of Legend and Sweat

The Olympic Games originated in a most unlikely place. Far removed from Athens, Corinth, and Sparta, the teeming centers of Greek culture and power, Olympia was a little wooded valley in the remote district of Elis on the northwestern tip of Peloponnesus (the peninsula that makes up the southern half of Greece), where the tiny Cladeus River flowed into the sluggish Alpheus River on its way to the sea. Mount Olympus, a site readily associated with the gods, lay far to the northeast. Yet according to ancient lore, little Olympia was the place where gods and heroes mingled to accomplish feats worthy of immortal praise.

The origins of the Olympic Games are shrouded in mystery and legend. According to one yarn, Hercules founded the games in celebration of his matchless feats. Some Greeks insisted that their two mightiest gods, Zeus and Cronus, contested for dominance on the hills above Olympia, and that the games and religious ceremonies held later in the valley were begun in commemoration of Zeus's victory. Others clung to the legend of Pelops, who won his bride in a daring chariot escape. The girl's father was an expert with the spear, and according to tradition, thirteen suitors had met death while attempting to steal the daughter away. But Pelops was shrewd. He loosened the axle of his adversary's chariot, took off with his prize, and breathed a sigh of relief when his lover's father broke his neck in the ensuing crash. Although it was not a very "sporting" deed, supposedly on that hallowed ground Pelops instituted the games and religious sacrifices in celebration of his god-given victory.

Significantly, all these tales involve competition, physical aggressiveness, and triumph. The origins of the Olympic Games are unknown, but like most sporting activities in the ancient world, the competitive games associated with Olympia grew out of religious ceremonies and cultic practices. With all their emphasis on man and his achievements, the Greeks were extremely religious. Polytheists, they looked to particular gods for assistance and blessing in every sphere of life. To Artemis they appealed when hunting, to Poseidon when sailing the seas, to Aphrodite in matters of love. Most of all they feared the wrath and sought the favor of Zeus, the mightiest of the gods.

In prayers, processions, and sacrifices, the ancient Greeks sought diligently to appease their gods. Religious festivals, accompanied by feasts, music, dancing, and athletic contests, were scattered throughout the Greek world. About 1000 B.C. Olympia became a shrine to Zeus. In addition to their religious ceremonies, young Greeks competed athletically in honor of Zeus, himself reckoned to be a vigorous warrior god who cast his javelinlike thunderbolts from on high. Competitors at Olympia swore by Zeus that they would play fair and obey all the rules. When they broke their oaths, they were required to pay fines, which in turn were spent to erect statues to Zeus.

The actual date of the first competitive games at Olympia is unknown. But the year 776 B.C. stands as a milestone, for in that year the Greeks first recorded the name of the victor in a simple footrace. For a time the footrace—a sprint of about 200 meters—was the only event associated with the religious festival at Olympia. In 724 B.C., however, a "double race" (400 meters) was added, and in 720 B.C. a long-distance race of 4,800 meters became a fixture. Within the next hundred years other events were established: wrestling and the pentathlon in 708 B.C., boxing in 688 B.C., chariot races in 680 B.C., and boys' footraces, wrestling, and boxing between 632 and 616 B.C. Finally in 520 B.C. the Olympic program was completed with the introduction of a footrace in armor. For almost a thousand years the list of events remained essentially intact. Every four years, strong, young Greeks gathered to compete, to strive for the victory wreath of olive branches.

In the beginning, however, Olympia was a simple site unadorned with buildings. A few scattered stone altars to Zeus stood in the *altis*, the sacred grove. But no stadium existed, nor was any specific place set aside for the games. Competitive events were held in randomly selected open spaces, as near to the *altis* as possible. Not until about 550 B.C. were buildings constructed. Then a temple was erected and filled with a gigantic stone sculpture of Zeus. Treasure houses followed, designed to contain the gifts brought to Zeus. Next a council house was built to serve as the headquarters for the organizers of the games. Finally a hippodrome and stadium were constructed, the latter about 200 meters in length with embankments sloping upward on both sides, providing space for about 40,000 spectators. A gymnasium and palaestra completed the athletic complex.

In the spring of every fourth year three heralds departed from Olympia to traverse the Greek world, announcing the forthcoming games and declaring a "sacred truce." By the authority of Zeus, competitors and spectators making their way to Olympia were allowed to pass safely through the countryside, even in times of war. The athletes and their trainers arrived in Olympia a month before the games. First they had to prove their eligibility—that they were Greek, freeborn (not slaves), and without criminal records. Then they had to swear by Zeus that they had been in training for the previous ten months. Participation in the Olympic Games was no light-hearted matter. Strict judges supervised a grueling month-long training program in order to ensure the fitness of prospective competitors, and they arranged elimination heats for those events that had attracted an unusually large number of athletes. Occasionally during the training sessions an athlete became intimidated by the speed or brawn of his opposition and withdrew before the games began.

While the athletes sweated and grunted through their preparatory exercises, little Olympia and the surrounding countryside took on a carnival atmosphere. Spectators came from all directions, and official delegations from Greek city-states arrived with gifts for Zeus. Food and drink vendors did a brisk business, as did hawkers of souvenirs and pimps with their prostitutes. Jugglers, musicians, dancers, and magicians displayed their talents, and soothsayers dispensed their wisdom. Deafening noise and stifling dust added to the midsummer heat, making attendance at the Olympic Games something of an ordeal.

Until late in the history of the games, tiny Olympia was ill-prepared to cope with the crowds. A few springs and the nearby rivers provided water for drinking and bathing, but sanitation and planned water facilities were not available until the second century A.D. Flies were everywhere. As one first-century visitor complained, life at the Olympics would have been unbearably crude and unpleasant were it not for the excitement of the games themselves: "Do you not swelter? Are you not cramped and crowded? Do you not bathe badly? Are you not drenched whenever it rains? Do you not have your fill of tumult and shouting and other annoyances? But I fancy that you bear and endure it all by balancing it off against the memorable character of the spectacle."

The athletes fared little better. Although they ate well during their month's training, they, too, received scant provision for physical comfort. Housing, or the lack of it, was a main problem. Servants of wealthy spectators and official delegations pitched richly embroidered tents on the hillsides, but most athletes simply wrapped themselves in blankets, slept under the stars, and hoped it would not rain. Not until about 350 B.C. was housing provided for the athletes, and even then it was too spartan for comfort. Certainly nothing approximating a modern Olympic village was ever constructed. One can imagine that the athletes breathed a sigh of relief as the sun rose on the day that the games were to begin. Butterflies in the stomach were not nearly so bothersome as black flies on one's food and in one's hair.

Olympian Efforts

For three centuries after the first recorded Olympic victor in 776 B.C., the sequence and duration of the games fluctuated from Olympiad to Olympiad according to the whims of the judges. In 472 B.C., however, the games were reorganized and fixed into a pattern that remained virtually unchanged for the next eight hundred years. The duration of the entire festival was set at five days, with only two and a half days devoted to the games themselves. The first day was given to religious ceremony: oaths, prayers, sacrifices, and the singing of hymns. Some athletes presented gifts and offered prayers to the statues of past victors who had been deified, at the shrines of various patron gods, and especially to the several statues of Zeus.

On the second day the sports competition began. Spectators gathered at the hippodrome, a level, narrow field about 500 meters long, to witness the chariot race. Amid great fanfare, splendid two-wheeled chariots pulled by four horses lined up in staggered starting places. Here was the most costly and colorful of all the Olympic events, a signal to the world that the owners were men of great wealth. Their drivers, decked out in finely embroidered tunics, tensely awaited the start. They could scarcely afford to relax. Their course was not a rounded oval but rather around posts set at each end of the hippodrome about 400 meters apart, requiring 180-degree turns for twelve laps. Rules forbade swerving in front of an opponent, but bumps and crashes and even head-on collisions around the posts were inevitable. In one race only one of forty chariots finished intact.

As soon as the dust settled and battered chariots were removed from the hippodrome, single horses and their jockeys moved into starting positions. Riding without saddles or stirrups, the jockeys were nude. Even more than the charioteers, jockeys got little credit if they won. They were the hirelings of wealthy owners, whose names were recorded as the winners of the race. Even the olive crown was placed on the owner's head, not the jockey's.

The morning having been given to these equestrian events, the afternoon was devoted to an altogether different contest, the pentathlon. Spectators crowded onto the grassy slopes of the stadium. Except for a few marble slabs provided for the Olympic officials, no seats were ever built. Through a narrow passageway at one end of the stadium the competitors entered. Naked and bronzed by the sun, they more than any of the other contestants at Olympia represented the Greek ideal of physical beauty. Pentathletes had to be fast as well as strong, with muscles well proportioned and supple but not overdeveloped. "Beauty for a young man is to have a body trained to withstand fatigue in running and in the exercise of strength and at the same time to be agreeably presentable," wrote Aristotle. Those athletes who engaged in the pentathlon, he added, "are the most beautiful because they are fit both for exercises of speed and for those of strength." Little wonder that the pentathlon was the event that most inspired poets and sculptors of the day.

Like the modern decathlon, the pentathlon rewarded the versatile athlete. First he had to throw the discus, a round, flat object originally made of stone and later of bronze. Five throws were allowed, and only the longest counted. Next came the javelin throw. About six feet long, the javelin had a small leather loop attached near the center of gravity. The athlete inserted one or two fingers in the loop, wound the thong around the javelin, and thus obtained leverage to make the javelin spin in flight. In the third event, the standing broad jump, the athlete carried weights in his hands, swung them forward to shoulder height, and then down as he leaped. Made of stone or metal in the shape of small dumbbells, the weights both increased the distance and helped the jumper to keep his balance when landing. A 200-meter sprint and a wrestling contest were the last two events in the pentathlon, but they were often not held: The athlete who first won three of the five events was declared the victor without further contest.

As the sun set on that second day of the Olympic festival, attention turned from athletic competition to religious ceremony. In honor of the hero-god Pelops, a black ram was slain and offered as a burnt sacrifice—always as the midsummer full moon appeared above the *altis*. On the following morning were religious rites, followed by a magnificent procession of priests, Olympic judges, representatives from the Greek city-states, the athletes and their kinsmen, and trainers. All finally arrived at the altar of Zeus, where one hundred oxen were slain and their legs burned in homage to Zeus. The carcasses were cooked and eaten at the concluding banquet on the final day of the festival.

Athletes in the ancient Olympic Games competed in the nude. This young javelin thrower, from a painting on an Athenian cup of the late fifth century B.C., is using the leather finger-thong for distance and accuracy.

On the afternoon of the third day, the footraces were held: 200-meter sprints the length of the stadium, 400-meter dashes around a post and back, and long-distance runs of 4800 meters (twelve laps). Marble slabs provided leverage for quick starts, and a trumpet blast served as the starting signal. In the 400- and 4800-meter races there was much jostling and tripping as the runners narrowly rounded the post and struggled to seize the lead on the return sprint.

The fourth day of the festival brought on the "heavy" events: wrestling, boxing, the pancration, and armored footraces. The first three were especially violent, brutal contests of strength and will. There were few rules, no time limit, and no ring. More important, there were no weight limits, thus restricting top-level competitors to the largest, best-muscled, and toughest men to be found throughout Greece. In the wrestling contests biting and gouging were prohibited, but not much else. A wrestler won when he scored three falls, making his opponent touch the ground with his knees. Wrestlers therefore concentrated on holds on the upper part of the body and tripped their opponents when possible. The most famous of all Olympic athletes was Milo of Croton, who won the boys' wrestling event in 540 B.C., six successive senior Olympiads, and more than two dozen crowns in other Panhellenic festivals. A braggart in the Odysseus mold, Milo often boasted that no man ever brought him to his knees. Technically he was right, but in fact he lost his seventh and final attempt to win an Olympic crown when his younger opponent delayed and evaded until the aged Milo had to withdraw from fatigue.

Yet wrestling was mild exercise compared to boxing. Boxers wound heavy strips of leather around their hands and wrists, leaving the fingers free. They aimed primarily for the opponent's head or neck, rather than the body. Slapping with the open hand was permissible, and it was often done to divert the attention, cut the face, or close the eyes of the opposition. The fight went on without a break until one of the competitors was either exhausted or knocked out, or until one raised his right hand as a sign of defeat. Blood flowed freely. Scarcely an Olympic boxer finished his career without broken teeth, cauliflower ears, a scarred face, and a smashed nose. He was lucky if he did not have more serious eye, ear, and skull injuries.

As if boxing and wrestling were not brutal enough, the Greeks threw them together, added some judo, and came up with the contest most favored by spectators at Olympia—the pancration. Pancratiasts wore no leather thongs on the fists, but they could use their heads, elbows, and knees in addition to hands and feet. They could trip, hack, break fingers, pull noses and ears, and even apply a stranglehold until tapped on the back, the sign that the opponent had given up. In 564 B.C. a pancratiast who had won in two previous Olympics found himself in both a leg scissors grip and a stranglehold. Literally in the process of being choked to death, he frantically reached for one of his opponent's toes and broke it. As he gasped his final breath, his opponent, suffering excruciating pain, gave the signal of capitulation. So the strangled pancratiast was posthumously awarded the crown of victory, and in the central square of his native village a statue was erected in his honor.

After the deadly serious business of wrestling, boxing, and the pancration, the final Olympic contest added a farcical touch to the festival. The 400-meter footrace in armor pitted naked men clad only in helmets, shin guards, and shields, a fitting though ludicrous reminder of the military origins of most of the games. Although the armored footrace remained on the Olympic program from its introduction in 520 B.C. until the end, it was never a prestigious event. Apparently it provided comic relief at the end of a gory day.

The fifth and final day of the festival was devoted to a prize-giving ceremony, a service of thanksgiving to Zeus, and a sumptuous banquet at which the sacrificial animals were consumed. As the moon rose over Olympia, men ate and drank their fill. "And with the delightful feastings, the holy place was full of song," wrote Pindar in one of his Olympic odes, "tuned to the fashion of the victor's hymn of praise."

Beyond Mythology

Beyond the euphoria that Pindar referred to as "the whole fellowship of warriors" assembled at Olympia, some of the limited features of the Olympic Games should be noted. In the first place, the athletic program was narrowly confined to two equestrian contests, six track-and-field events, three physical-contact sports, and the armored footrace. From a modern point of view, conspicuously absent were relay races, hurdles, pole vaults, high jumps, running broad jumps, weight lifting, and shot puts. Nothing approximating a modern marathon ever appeared on the ancient Olympic program. In 490 B.C. a young Athenian named Pheidippides ran twenty-five miles from the plains of Marathon to Athens with news of a Greek military victory over the Persians. "Rejoice, we conquer," he announced, and then dropped dead from exertion. Never did the Greeks consider imitating such a strenuous folly in athletic competition.

Given the fact that Greece is a peninsula and half of it virtually an island, it is surprising to find no water sports such as swimming, diving, sailing, or rowing in the ancient Olympic program. More understandably, the absence of ice and snow made winter sports impossible. Less apparent was the reason for the lack of competitive ball games. In fact, the Greeks played a number of individual and team games of ball. At Sparta "ball player" and "youth" were synonymous. Special rooms called *sphairisteria* were set aside in the palaestra for games of handball; the rules and form of play have not survived, but apparently it was a competitive sport. Without doubt the Greeks played a kind of field hockey game. Sculptured figures and scattered literary references indicate that teams hit a small ball with curved sticks, each side striving (as one writer put it) "to be the first to drive the ball to the opposite end of the ground from that allotted to them." Most common of all competitive ball play in Greece, however, was the game of *episkyros*, a team sport in which opposing sides threw a ball back and forth "until one side drives the other back over their goal line."

Why, then, were no ball games ever played in the ancient Olympics? When the Olympics began in the eighth century B.C., most ball play was still mere exercise, keep-away games at most. Mentioned occasionally by Homer, they were played by women, children, and old men, but not by serious athletes. Not yet rough mock forms of combat, ball games were considered child's play compared to the warrior sports of chariot racing, javelin throwing, wrestling, and the like. By the time competitive ball play became respectable for adult males, the Olympic program was already set on its traditional course. Conservative officials refused to change. After all the necessary allowances for time, culture, and climate have been made, one still must conclude that the Olympic events were extremely limited in scope.

Another limitation of the Olympics that more tellingly reflected the mentality of ancient Greek society was the exclusion of women from the games. In that patriarchal world, matters of business, government, and warfare were reserved for men. A woman might attend the theater if accompanied by a man, but even in the home she lived in separate quarters. Except for the honorary presence of the priestess of Demeter, women were altogether excluded from the Olympic Games, as spectators as well as competitors. Apparently only one woman ever broke the taboo, and her ploy provoked a rule change. In 404 B.C. a mother who wanted to see her son box slipped into the stadium disguised as a trainer. But when the boy won his match, she leaped over the barrier to congratulate him and in so doing gave herself away. Horrified Olympic officials immediately laid down a new rule: trainers henceforward must appear in the stadium stark naked, like the athletes.

Barred from the Olympic Games, women held their own competitive contests at Olympia in honor of Hera, the sister-wife of Zeus. Their competition was largely in the form of footraces, wrestling, and chariot races. Apparently these Heraean Games even predated the Olympic Games as fertility rites representing an early matriarchal society. During the history of the Olympic Games, however, Olympic officials proved to be a highly conservative group of men committed primarily to maintaining a successful formula, thus inadvertently protecting traditional male interests. Their conservatism is best seen by comparison with the other major Panhellenic games. As Greek women increasingly became emancipated (primarily in the cities) toward the end of the pre-Christian era, short-distance races for girls were introduced as an integral part of the program in the Pythian, Isthmian, and Nemean Games.

Olympia's relation to the other festivals on the athletic "circuit" calls to mind another myth long entertained about athletes in the ancient world: Olympic victors received no cash prizes or other material rewards with their olive crowns; thus it would appear that they were purely amateur, competing for the honor of victory. The appearance was a mere shadow of reality. Throughout the history of the Olympics, only aristocrats could afford the horses and chariots for the equestrian events. For the first 300 years or so, the games were dominated by athletes from wealthy families who could afford trainers and coaches, a proper diet (plenty of meat), full-time training, and travel. Around 450 B.C., however, lower-class athletes began participating in the track-and-field and physical-contact sports. Financed by local patrons and public funds drawn from taxes on wealthy citizens, they ran and fought to bring honor to their city-states as well as to themselves. Their city-states, in turn, rewarded them with cash prizes, free food, and lodging. Therefore, although the Olympic Games paid no direct material rewards, they existed in a maze of commercial enterprise. A victory at Olympia dramatically raised an athlete's value as he went off to sell his talents and brawn for further competition at the Pythian, Isthmian, and Nemean Games. Whether or not he received money for his Olympic exploits is beside the point. Well paid for his full-time efforts, he was a professional athlete.

A sure sign of this professionalism was the emergence of athletic guilds in the second century B.C. Like today's unions or players' associations, the guilds originated on the principle of collective bargaining. And bargain they did: for the athletes' rights to have a say in the scheduling of games, travel arrangements, personal amenities, pensions, and old-age security in the form of serving as trainers and managers.

When Greek poets, philosophers, and playwrights turned a critical eye on the athletes of their day, they seldom attacked professionalism. They assumed, with Pindar, that "wealth patterned with prowess" roused a "deep ambition to range afar" in search of victory; such ambition seemed like "a transcendent star, the truest light for a man." Yet athletics were scarcely beyond criticism. For well-born, highly cultured Greeks, athletics appeared to be a lamentably easy way for lower-class citizens to rise quickly to affluence, then to fall back into poverty once the strength of youth waned. Slaves to physical regimen, athletes "neither learn how to live a good life, nor could they possibly do so," Euripides insisted. "In their prime they made a brilliant spectacle as they go about and are the pride of the state; but when bitter old age comes upon them, they become like old coats that have lost their resilience."

Worse still, the successful athlete had to specialize to such an extent that he made a poor soldier. "For what good wrestler, what swift runner, what man who has hurled a discus well, or planted a well delivered blow on another's jaw, had ever defended the city of his fathers because of winning a victor's crown?" Euripides rhetorically asked in the fifth century B.C. Later Greek and Roman critics of the "useless pleasures" of athletics were even more outspoken, but they could not improve on the pithiness of Euripides' query: "Do men fight with the enemy holding discuses in their hands, or through the line of shields do they launch blows with their fists, and so drive the enemy out of the country?"

Yet of all the barbs directed against Greek athletics, the most common had to do with the glorification of physical strength to the detriment of mental and spiritual values. To the philosopher and satirist Xenophanes, it was "not right to honor strength above excellent wisdom." Ridicule was a favorite weapon of the critics. "You simpleton," exclaimed Aesop to a wrestler who boasted that he had beaten his opponent because he was the stronger of the two, "what honor have you earned if, being the stronger, you prevailed over a weaker man? You might be tolerated if you were telling us that by skill you overcame a man who was superior to you in physical strength." Milo of Croton was the butt of numerous jokes and slurs on the mindlessness of the muscle-bound athlete. "What surpassing witlessness," declared a moralist when he heard that Milo carried the entire carcass of a bull around the stadium at Olympia before cutting it up and devouring it. Before it was slaughtered, the bull carried its own body with much less exertion than did Milo. "Yet the bull's mind was not worth anything—just about like Milo's." The image of the "dumb jock" is as old as athletics.

Greek Athletics and the Ancient World

The Olympic Games had an enormous impact on the ancient world. At the simplest level, they provided the Greeks with a calendar. By about 300 B.C.

The roughest of all the Olympic contests, the pancration, inspired an unknown Greek sculptor to produce this graceful marble statue, whose permanent home is the Uffizi Museum in Florence.

the common time reference was an Olympiad, that four-year interval between each festival. Events were dated from 776 B.C., the first recorded Olympiad; the first year of the 195th Olympiad corresponded with the first Christian year. In much of Western civilization the Christian calendar did not displace the Greek reckoning of time until about A.D. 440, after the 304th Olympiad.

The Olympics and Greek athletics in general also made a profound impression on Greek art. Had athletes and athletic motifs not inspired sculptors, pottery painters, and fresco makers, we would be much the poorer in our understanding of antiquity. Myron's fifth-century B.C. discus thrower *(Discobolus)* is probably the best known of ancient sculpture, but for artists famous and unknown alike, nude athletes running, jumping, throwing the discus, boxing, or wrestling were ideal subjects through which they could express their admiration of strength and symmetrical beauty. Yet they refrained from mere idealization. A large bronze statue of a boxer, possibly created by the Athenian sculptor Apollonius in the first century B.C., portrays not only a beautifully muscled body but also the gnarled hands, broken nose, and scarred face common to the sport. Vase and cup painters were even more realistic. Alongside their trim, finely proportioned athletes they painted gaunt charioteers, grossly overmuscled boxers, and pitifully fat gymnasts.

Over the centuries thousands of stone statues and inscriptions were erected in honor of Olympic victors. Many were set in Olympia itself, others in the central marketplace of the village or town represented by the athletes. One of the wonders of the ancient world was a magnificent statue of Zeus, made by Phidias of gold and silver seven times life size, in the temple to Zeus at Olympia. Phidias might well have blended his perceptions of a well-proportioned pentathlonist with a heavily muscled pancratiast as a composite model for his work. Zeus was the ideal athlete, just as the athlete was the ideal Greek male. Unfortunately, the statue was destroyed by later barbarian invaders.

In the thinking of Greek philosophers, too, athletics played an important part. The fifth-century B.C. poet Euripides looked upon the brawny professional—"a slave to his jaw and obedient to his belly"—and concluded that "there is nothing worse than the race of athletes." Yet his more famous contemporary, Socrates, saw the ideal behind the immediate form of athletics. "How very unlike an athlete you are in frame," Socrates once chided a young Athenian weakling. "But I am not an athlete," retorted the literal-minded youth. "You are not less of an athlete," shot back the wise Socrates, "than those who are going to contend at the Olympic games. Does the struggle for life with the enemy, which the Athenians will demand of you when circumstances require, seem to you to be a trifling contest?" For Socrates, the key words were *contend, struggle,* and *contest.* Moreover, for Socrates the athlete provided the model for the principle that "the body must bear its part in whatever men do; and in all the services required from the body, it is of the utmost importance to have it in the best possible condition."

Socrates' prize pupil, Plato, agreed fully with his master. Plato, in fact, trained under the best wrestling teacher in Athens and reportedly competed in the Isthmian games. Originally his name was Aristocles, but his wrestling teacher changed it to Plato, meaning "broad shouldered." In *The Republic,* Plato set up a dialogue with Socrates to argue logically that gymnastic exercise was the "twin sister" of the arts for "the improvement of the soul." His ideal was the body and mind "duly harmonized."

This sense of balance between the physical and the mental prompted the third of the great Greek philosophers, Aristotle, to devote several sections of his *Politics* to the training of children to be good Greek citizens. "What is wanted," he insisted, "is not the bodily condition of an athlete nor on the other hand a weak and invalid condition, but one that lies between the two." Coming to manhood a hundred years or so after Socrates, Aristotle was more critical of "the brutal element" involved in organized athletics. Yet he, too, held the Olympic victors in awe. He revised, corrected, and updated a list of Olympic champions compiled two centuries earlier by yet another philosopher, Hippias of Elis.

Critical as they were of overspecialized athletes, the great philosophers still did not reject athletics. For them, the association of body and mind was literally intimate: gymnasiums were places where men not only exercised, but gathered to hear the lectures of philosophers and itinerant orators. Plato's Academy and Aristotle's Lyceum in Athens were, in fact, gymnasiums, centers of training "for the body and the soul." Ironically, the terms "academy" and "lyceum" have come to refer solely to intellectual pursuits, wholly divorced from physical training.

To a lesser degree than art and philosophy, Greek poetry and drama bore the mark of athletics. Sophocles' play *Electra* thrilled fifth century B.C. Athenian audiences with an imaginative description of Orestes, the son of Agamemnon, competing in the Pythian Games at Delphi: "Like a shaft he sped from starting point to goal and back, and bore the crown of glorious victory." In a subsequent chariot race, however, Orestes recklessly cut a corner too sharply, was thrown from his battered chariot, and met a gory death. He was the original athlete dying young, in the thick of competition.

Less given to such tragic themes, several Greek poets also immortalized athletic victors. Throughout the fifth century B.C. especially, towns and wealthy individuals commissioned odes to be sung at their victory celebrations. Some of the greatest of Greek poets, such as Simonides and Bacchylides of Ceos, and Pindar of Thebes, produced a prodigious number of hymns in praise of athletes. Much of that material has been lost or destroyed, but of Pindar's work, forty-four odes survive: fourteen for Olympic victors, twelve for Pythian, eleven for Nemean, and seven for Isthmian. Pindar extolled the athlete's quest for victory:

> For if any man delights in expense and toil
> and sets in action high gifts shaped by the gods,
> And with him his destiny
> Plants the glory which he desires,
> Already he casts his anchor on the furthest edge of bliss,
> and the gods honor him.

Pindar sold his services to the highest bidder and tailored his odes accordingly. Of all the festivals, however, Olympia inspired him most:

> But, my heart, would you chant the glory of games,
> Look never beyond the sun by day
> For any star shining brighter through the deserted air,
> Nor any contest than Olympia greater to sing.

The Olympic Games and the athletic values they represented made their mark on Mediterranean societies other than Greece. Sports were an integral part of that larger package of Greek culture that edged and forced its way into the mainstream of life in Asia Minor, southern Italy, and northern Egypt. Long after the Greek city-states passed their zenith of political importance, foreign cities and towns continued to build stadiums, hippodromes, gymnasiums, and palaestras. In Jerusalem a gymnasium was established in 174 B.C., much to the disgust of orthodox Jews, who detested the nudity of Greek athletes and art. Some young Jewish athletes, beguiled by foreign ways, submitted themselves to cosmetic operations to conceal the fact that they had been circumcised.

The Etruscans incorporated Greek sports into their martial exercises and adopted Greek depictions of track-and-field events into their art. But of all the Mediterranean peoples who took and transformed Greek ways for their own ends, the Romans were the most important. Their enthusuasm for Greek sports was tempered with a passion for spectacle and military practicality. What the Romans did with Greek ideals has much to do with the decline and fall of athletics in the ancient world, a lamentable chapter in the history of sports.

Chapter **3**

THE DECLINE AND FALL OF ATHLETICS

When the first Olympic victor was recorded in 776 B.C., Rome was a mere farm community surrounded by warring tribes. By 500 B.C., as the athletic program at Olympia settled into a fixed, predictable pattern, the Romans were rising up against the rule of the Etruscans, their hostile neighbors to the north. Within two centuries Roman military might, administrative officials, language, and culture dominated all of Italy. Then began their imperial conquest of Sicily, Carthage, and Greece. By the end of the first century B.C., the Roman empire covered the entire rim of the Mediterranean, extending to the northern reaches of Britain, to the Danube in Europe, and east to the Caspian Sea.

Cultivated Romans looked to the Greeks for models of art and literature. They copied the Greeks unabashedly; much of the fine sculpture from the Golden Age of Greece, including Myron's *Discobolus*, survived only in Roman reproductions. Greek sports and games were a means of unifying eastern and western parts of the empire. But Greek games were too individualistic, too geared to the participants rather than to spectator appeal, paradoxically too openly competitive yet too tame for the Romans. Different taste and social purpose prompted the Romans to prefer sporting spectacles such as hippodrome "circuses" and gladiatorial combats.

Highly popular as forms of mass entertainment, the spectacles were never free of opposition—from Roman and Greek philosophers, and primarily from an ever-enlarging chorus of Christian critics. Yet as long as the Roman empire remained intact, the spectacles flourished.

The Roman Response to Greek Games

Competitive sport as practiced in Greek gymnasiums and palaestras did not appeal to the Romans. They preferred more mild exercise in a field or anteroom attached to their public baths, exercises designed more for merely working up a sweat before entering the baths than for the testing of one's skill or strength in physical contest. After lunch each day men went to the baths for games, conversation, or reading. Before the beginning of the Christian era there were two hundred baths available in Rome; within three centuries seven hundred more were constructed. Most were privately owned, but some of the larger ones were public. The emperors Nero, Titus, Trajan, Caracalla, Severus, and Diocletian all built public baths, charged a small fee, and met the balance of the cost of services and repair.

Near several of the larger baths, the Campus Martius, a large stretch of level ground beside the Tiber River, served as a playground for Roman citizens. In the *Aeneid*, Virgil told of men and boys going to the Campus to run, jump, and playfully wrestle. But the purpose of their exercises was more for health than for competition. Only spirited boys played an adaptation of the old Greek ball game of *episkyros*. More attractive to most Roman citizens were games in which a ball was thrown into the sky as high as possible, or hit with the open hand against a wall, keeping it in motion. Several players juggled two or more balls in the air. In a game called *trigon*, three players formed an equilateral triangle and passed two balls from one to another, attempting to confuse each other. The terms for the balls fill Latin literature: *harpastum*, a small ball stuffed with hair; *pila* or *paginica*, a larger ball stuffed with feathers; and *follis*, the largest ball, filled with air. All were used primarily for physical fitness and agility, preparatory to plunging into a cold, then hot, bath.

As early as 186 B.C., wealthy Roman citizens brought professional athletes from the Greek circuit to display their talents in Rome. Their efforts met with a mixed reception. Roman spectators were shocked to see young Greeks strip nude for the games; many left for home long before the games were finished. Yet Roman consuls and emperors became patrons of Greek games. During the first century B.C., Sulla, Pompey, and Julius Caesar all arranged Greek athletic contests in the Imperial City. Caesar Augustus (25 B.C.–A.D. 14) attempted to restore the old festivals in Greece, and to create new ones. In celebration of his military victory over Anthony and Cleopatra at Actium, he instituted an "Actian" festival to rival Olympia; in A.D. 2 he founded Greek games in Naples. His successor, Tiberius, actually participated in the Olympic Games in his youth, winning the four-horse chariot race.

The most eccentric of all the Roman emperors, Nero, was a mad enthusiast for Greek athletics. In A.D. 60 he instituted a festival in Rome and several years later (a non-Olympiad year) visited Olympia, insisting that special "Olympic Games" be held in his honor. He entered the competition in a specially designed musical event and won, of course. More dramatically, he drove a ten-horse chariot to victory. Mentally unbalanced, he was assassinated within a year of his return to Rome, and Olympic officials, probably with unbounded relief, struck his name from the victors' record.

The Romans juggled and played keep-away with various kinds of balls prior to entering their baths. This fresco from the Via Portuense in Rome is one of the few surviving pictorial representations of ancient ball-play.

Seeing political benefits in Greek festivals and games, Emperor Hadrian in A.D. 131 created new games at Athens as a means of linking the eastern and western sections of his empire. One of his administrators, Tiberius Atticus, probably the wealthiest man in the ancient world, oversaw Hadrian's designs and himself became a sports patron of no small importance. He paid for the rebuilding of the stadium in Athens, a magnificently spacious and stolid structure of marble that has lasted to the present day. An avid sports fan, Atticus went every four years to watch the Olympic Games. He was so distressed with the inadequate supply of drinking water at Olympia that he had an aqueduct constructed, leading from the river to a fine marble fountain. Olympia and the Greek athletic games were not without their rich, influential Roman patrons.

Nor did they lack Roman critics. Greek athletics, according to many articulate Romans, were a corrupting influence on Roman youths. Never able to accept the nudity of Greek athletes, some Romans demanded that discus throwers and runners, not to mention wrestlers and boxers, wear shorts. "To strip naked," insisted Cicero, "is the beginning of evil-doing." The gymnasiums where Greek athletes trained appeared to be centers of homosexuality. As one critic put it, the result of allowing Greek games was "that our young men should be corrupted by these outlandish importations into becoming devotees of the gymnasium, of luxury and of unnatural vice." Worst of all, if young Romans imitated Greek athletes, "they would be compelled to strip naked, put on boxing gloves, and practice that form of exercise instead of war and arms."

Here was the crux of the opposition: Greek athletics did not good Roman soldiers make. The steady expansion of the Roman empire meant continuous warfare, and in the process the Romans developed an attitude of grim seriousness. If an activity was not militarily practical, it was not worthwhile. Roman boys swam, ran, and wrestled in order to become physically and mentally tough for the ultimate purpose of serving in the legions. As individualistic, highly specialized Greek athletics contributed little to the making of obedient soldiers, they were discouraged.

More appealing to the Romans were the sports and games of the people who ruled the Italian peninsula before them, the Etruscans. Like the Greeks, the Etruscans threw the discus and javelin, wrestled, boxed, ran footraces, and raced in chariots. But being a warrior people, they amused themselves with the fiercest of all the games in the ancient world, gladiatorial bouts and animal fights. Roman sports derived more from the Etruscans than from the Greeks. Under the Romans sport became a show, a dramatic staged event for the purpose of diversion. The Latin word *ludi* was distinctly Roman. Whereas the Greek word for athletics, *agon,* meant a contest, *ludi* was a game in the sense of an amusement or entertainment. The same root word was used for players and actors in the theater: *ludiones*. It was a far cry from the Greek athletic ideal.

Bread and Games

The Romans developed their sports for reasons of their own. Like the Greek festivals, many of the Roman game days were based on ancient ceremonies devoted to the gods and heroic figures of the past. By 173 B.C. there were fifty-three public holidays on the Roman calendar. Emperor after emperor set aside special days for feasting and games to commemorate important events in their own lives and reigns. By A.D. 300 about 200 days were designated as public holidays, 175 of which were given to games and spectacles.

There was method in this holiday madness. The games served as a safety valve, a barrier against social unrest. During the reign of Augustus about 150,000 idlers inhabited the city of Rome, without work and supported totally at public expense. An equal number of workers finished their jobs each day at noon. Boredom threatened. Knowing that a people who yawn are as ripe for revolt as those who are hungry, Roman emperors and magistrates buttressed their own security by providing, in Juvenal's classic words, "bread and circuses." As one Roman writer said of the emperor Trajan, perhaps the most lavish provider of games and spectacles, "he well knew that the excellence of a government is shown no less in care for the amusements of the people than in serious matters, and that although the distribution of corn and money may satisfy the individual, spectacles are necessary for the contentment of the masses." Entertainment, in other words, was icing on the bread-cake.

One of the favorite spectacles was chariot racing. According to tradition, an early Etruscan king of Rome built the Circus Maximus, a long rectangle rounded at one end, in the heart of Rome. Gradually enlarged and embellished with statues, arches, and obelisks, the Circus Maximus served as the model for other hippodromes in Rome and throughout the empire. By the first century A.D. it was about 600 by 200 meters in size, with a three-tiered stadium holding about a quarter of a million spectators. It was by far the largest "circus" in Rome, but two others in the city itself and yet three more in nearby small towns provided abundant entertainment for Roman citizens.

A Roman chariot race was a spectacle of the first order, far more colorful and excitingly dangerous than those of ancient Olympia. The charioteers, mostly slaves, wore shining helmets and bright red, blue, green, or white tunics representing their respective owners. In their hands they wielded a whip, and in their belts they had a knife to "cut the traces" around their waists in case of accidents. Normally the race consisted of seven complete times around the oval, a course made all the more difficult by the long, narrow island down the middle of the raceway and the necessity of making sharp turns at the end. Especially in the races in which the two-wheeled chariots were drawn by four horses abreast, collisions frequently resulted in a frightful mangling of horses, chariots, and men.

The massive crowd of spectators apparently loved it. Betting heavily on the races, they applauded, cheered, cursed, and groaned according to the fate of the charioteer on whom they had placed their wager. From time to time the emperor and his family occupied the imperial box of marble seats, surrounded by senators and other dignitaries. Whenever the crowd became too agitated or bored, the emperor had bread and fruit passed throughout the stadium. Some emperors—Nero and Domitian especially—distributed a kind of raffle ticket for houses, farms, and ships. Distracted with the prospect of gifts, unruly crowds soon settled down.

In normal times more predictable distractions claimed their attention. Between the chariot races, horseback riders exhibited their acrobatic skills by jumping from horse to horse, lying sideways on a galloping steed, and seizing prizes from the ground while the horse ran at full speed. Greek athletic contests such as footraces and wrestling matches were sometimes introduced to break the monotony of horses and chariots, but they received little acclaim from the spectators. More to the Romans' liking was the occasional boxing match, with a piece of metal secured on the fists under leather thongs (the *caestus*) to ensure brutality and an abundant flow of blood. Bearbaiting and bullbaiting added to the circus atmosphere, while chariots pulled into position for the next race.

For sheer theatrical effect, sham naval battles (*naumachiae*) outdid the chariot races. First begun by Julius Caesar in a flooded basin on the edge of Rome, this unlikely extravaganza appealed to Augustus, who once presented

3000 fighters on an artificial lake; to Nero, whose affinity for the exotic knew no bounds; and especially to the Emperor Claudius, who in A.D. 52 required 19,000 slaves to engage in deadly hand-to-hand combat as ships pulled alongside each other. Fully armored, more men died by drowning than by the sword. Spectators, necessarily stationed at a great distance from the action, soon lost interest in the *naumachia*, which was apparently more the product of the emperiors' vanity than of crowd appeal. Still, even the Colosseum in Rome was constructed so that it could be flooded for these sham battles.

The Colosseum, or Flavian Amphitheater, was expressly designed for the entertainment of Roman citizens. Begun under the emperor Vespasian (A.D. 69–79) and completed by Titus in A.D. 80, it was a four-tiered oval similar to a modern football stadium. The material was of native stone, with seats of marble for dignitaries. Eighty entrances, two reserved for the emperor and his suite, allowed the gigantic bowl to be filled and emptied of spectators in a few minutes. Huge awnings protected spectators from the hot summer sun; jets of scented water spewed forth from numerous fountains to cool and clear the air. The arena itself, about 280 by 200 feet, was surrounded by a fifteen-foot wall topped by an iron grating. A layer of sand covered an immense wooden floor, parts of which could be raised and lowered for changes of scene. Beneath the floor were cages and walled chambers holding animals and men for the program of the day.

The atmosphere at the Colosseum was electrified on those frequent occasions when the emperor chose to attend the games. On thrones of ivory and gold the emperor and empress sat surrounded by their family and servants. Walls separated the lower classes from the aristocratic members of Roman society, but lower and upper classes, males and females, took advantage of the emperor's proximity to convey their opinions, grievances, and petitions—for the pardon of a prisoner or slave, for legal or political reform, or for a change in imperial policy. At noonday most of the spectators went below to eat lunch, occasionally to be fed by the order and bounty of the emperor. Bands of musicians performed during interludes and added drama to the arena's combat by providing crescendo sounds as the tempo increased. On special holidays, contests were held at night, with a circle of torches lowered over the arena, casting an appropriate touch of artificiality on the scene.

Artificial as were the trappings, the battles in the Colosseum were far from sham. In the mornings were the animal fights. From all over the Roman empire, elephants, bulls, tigers, lions, panthers, bears, boars, apes, and even crocodiles were brought to Rome to be exhibited, trained, and paraded in the amphitheater. Often they were provoked into fighting each other. In one day under Nero, four hundred tigers lashed into bulls and elephants. More popular, however, were the scenes where men and women were forced into mortal combat with lions, tigers, and panthers. Condemned criminals dressed in skins to resemble animals were thrown to hungry beasts half-starved for the occasion. Practical-minded Romans thus found a way to achieve two purposes with one spectable: to provide entertainment for an idle populace while at the same time disposing of the socially undesirable. Christians as well as thieves and murderers fell into the latter category.

Towering above all the other events in popularity were the gladiator contests, which were usually held in the afternoon following the morning's animal fights. Drawn from the ranks of war prisoners, condemned criminals, disobedient slaves, and the occasional adventurous volunteer, the gladiators trained under stern instructors, who made small fortunes by providing a steady supply of fresh meat for the Colosseum carnage. According to their different skills and whims, gladiators were assigned a variety of arms: a shield and sword, a buckler (small round shield) and dagger, a net and a short three-pronged spear (*trident*), or any combination of these. Gladiators always fought other gladiators, never against animals. If they displayed exceptional bravery, they might win their freedom immediately, but if they merely survived a battle without distinguishing themselves, they had to fight again and again. For three years they were required to perform, then to be released into slavery for a two-year probation before they were set free. Rare was the man who survived three years.

It was a grim business. On the eve of combat, the gladiators enjoyed a rich banquet. The condemned either gorged and drank themselves into insensibility or understandably suffered a loss of appetite altogether. The next morning they slept off their hangovers or fretted over their prospects while the animal fights sent roars of delight reverberating through the city. In the early afternoon the gladiators entered the arena in full uniform and armor, paraded before the crowd, and finally appeared in front of the emperor's box. Then the duels began. The crowd, about 50,000 on a good day, bet as wildly on the gladiators as they did on charioteers. Thus they cheered with delight when their man wounded and finally destroyed his opponent. As a gladiator crumpled and lay prostrate on the sandy ground, attendants rushed forward to remove the body and hastily turn over the blood-stained sand in readiness for the next event.

The crowd became most excited when one gladiator dealt a stunning but not a death-blow to his opponent. Standing with sword raised over his fallen foe, the victor turned to the emperor, who often consulted the crowd. If the conquered gladiator had fought bravely, the spectators raised their thumbs and waved their handkerchiefs, signaling mercy. If, on the other hand, the fallen fighter had performed poorly or cowardly, or if the crowd was in a bad mood, the stadium was filled with down-turned thumbs, calling upon the emperor to pass the death sentence. The victorious gladiator dealt his final blow and himself lived to fight, and probably to die, another day.

In the most brutal of all the gladiatorial contests, only one of a great number escaped alive at the end of the day. The slaughter began with two men facing each other. When one fell, another took his place, more often than not slaying the original victor, who by now was fatigued. On and on, a succession of gory fights to the death filled an entire afternoon. Admittedly this form of combat was exceptional. Usually it was held when a good number of murderers, robbers, and incendiaries were on hand, having been sentenced, literally, to "death in the games."

Except for such desperately hopeless criminals, however, the gladiator's profession was not without its rewards. His barracks was a closely guarded prison, but he was fed well, served by masseurs and expert physicians, and trained by the best teachers available. His public performances were surrounded by pomp and splendor, applause and excitement. The skillful gladiator became a hero. Boys scratched his name and drew his picture on street walls. Women openly admired his animal strength and sought his favor. If he was victorious over a long period, the number of his combats and victories was inscribed on his tomb. An inscription to a gladiator reveals both the bright and dark side of the story. Fellow gladiators composed and paid for the inscription: The man died at thirty, having fought in thirty-four combats. He survived thirty-three.

By the first and second centuries the passion for gladiatorial contests was as strong in provincial towns as in Rome itself. Spectacles relieved the monotony of provincial life; local magistrates and wealthy patrons fortified their authority by paying for the show. The most obscure, little Italian towns, some deeply hidden in the Apennines, had arenas and regularly filled them. Larger still were arenas in populous Capua and Verona, and in distant Roman colonies of Arles in southern Gaul (France), Carthage in northern Africa, Alexandria in Egypt, and Corinth and Athens in Greece.

The best evidence portraying the character and popularity of gladiatorial games comes from Pompeii, buried in volcanic ash when Mt. Vesuvius erupted in A.D. 79. Pompeii's population was approximately 20,000, and its amphitheater seated 20,000. Pompeii had its own school for the training of gladiators, many of whose arms, helmets, and shields have been recovered. When Vesuvius rained death on the town, four gladiators were shackled in chains, probably because they had earlier tried to escape or were considered too dangerous to roam freely within the compound. Centuries later their skeletons were uncovered, still in irons. In another room seventeen gladiators took futile refuge. Among them was a woman wearing costly jewels. In all probability, the purpose of her visit was not to display her finery.

Pompeii is famous for its graffiti, much of it descriptive or sentimental, some humorous or lewd. Gladiators figure in many of the 3,000 items that have survived. One gladiator named Celadus was designated "the maidens' sigh." In the inner courtyard of a house on one of the main streets, the names of thirty gladiators were scribbled with their weapons described and their victories numbered. Some avid fan was keeping a scorecard on local heroes. Several carved and painted announcements of forthcoming events feature musical, theatrical, and sports offerings. One inscription reads: "Thirty pairs of gladiators furnished by the city mayor . . . will fight at Pompeii on November 24, 25, and 26. Hooray for Maius! Bravo, Paris!" Maius was the mayor, Paris the leading local gladiator.

Perhaps the most revealing of all the Pompeii evidence is the bevy of crude sketches covering the walls of streets, private homes, and the gladiators' own barracks. Some are profiles of notable gladiators; most depict combatants struggling against each other. In one, a fallen gladiator extends his hand heavenward imploring the spectators for mercy; in another, a gladiator is dying facedown in the sand. Excitement and death were never far removed from each other in the Roman arena.

Voices of Opposition

Despite this carnage, for centuries there was little opposition to the games. The gladiators themselves, regimented and closely guarded, were scarcely able to register much effective protest to their own role in the spectacles. The one revolt worthy of the term was led by the slave-gladiator Spartacus in 73 B.C. With seventy comrades he escaped, took refuge in the crater of the volcano Vesuvius, and raised an army of about 70,000 fellow slaves from the farms of southern Italy. For two years they roamed free, pillaged towns and cities, and defeated two Roman armies sent to subdue them. Then dissension set in: Spartacus was determined to lead his men over the Alps out of Italy back to their homes in the north, but other leaders insisted on a march on Rome. Finally, in 71 B.C. they were crushed by a large, fresh Roman army. Spartacus was killed in combat; most of his fellow rebels were captured and crucified. Never again did any substantial gladiatorial revolt occur.

All the while, some outstanding Roman poets and philosophers defended the games as a means of making Roman citizens hardened for the necessities of war—training them for "noble wounds and the scorn of death." Cicero was of the opinion that "when guilty men are compelled to fight, no better discipline against suffering and death can be represented to the eye." In truth, the spectacles brutalized the Romans, blunted their sensibilities, and made life cheap. Even the reflective philosopher-emperor Marcus Aurelius showed no inclination to question the traditional role of his office in sponsoring and attending gladiatorial contests. While the masses let forth their bloodthirsty cheers, most intellectuals closeted themselves and rationalized the whole affair.

Class prejudice lay at the base of those rationalizations. Blood spilled in the arena was, after all, merely the "cheap gore" of common criminals, as Tacitus noted. Attitudes of class and taste, not compassion or humanistic considerations, prompted an occasional disparagement of the spectacles. Pliny the Younger, for example, deplored his contemporaries' craze for "so silly, so low, so uninteresting, so common an entertainment," and congratulated himself on being "insensible to these pleasures." Cicero was of the same elevated mind, especially when he observed upper-class Romans mingling with the lowborn masses at an animal fight: "What entertainment can possibly arise, to a refined and humanized spirit, from seeing a noble beast struck to the heart by its merciless hunter, or one of our own weak species cruelly mangled by an animal of far greater strength?"

Roman intellectuals were simply out of touch with the mass culture associated with the Colosseum; the theater, not the arena, was their *milieu*. Their pragmatic defenses of the spectacles smack of conventional wisdom rather than much firsthand experience. A day in the life of Seneca, the first-century philosopher, is illuminating. Once he went to the Colosseum during a noonday recess "expecting some fun, wit, and relaxation," only to be shocked to find men being thrown to the lions and gladiators slaying each other with abandon. The barbarity of the situation appeared all the more ludicrous because the stands were virtually empty of spectators. "I came home more greedy, more cruel and inhuman," Seneca later reflected. "Man, a sacred thing to man, is killed for sport and merriment." No humanist could argue with such an observation.

Some criticism of the games came from Greek quarters. By the first century A.D. gladiatorial contests were being held throughout Greece, particularly in the larger cities such as Athens and Corinth, which were colonized by the expanding Roman empire. In Corinth riots occurred when the Roman proconsul attempted to introduce Roman sports on a mass scale. When Athenians attempted to rival Corinth by establishing a gladiatorial show, the philosopher Demonax suggested that they first topple the altar to the god of Pity. Some Greeks saw that their old Panhellenic Nemean, Pythian, Isthmian, and Olympic Games, which were still held regularly, were being swamped by the mass appeal of the more gaudy Roman spectacles. Thus they cited the gladiatorial contests as a reason for regarding the Romans as barbarians *(barbaroi)*. Greek criticisms of Roman sports were largely the reaction of a people chafing at the demise of their native traditions under the heel of a foreign imperial power.

The only concerted, sustained, and ultimately effective voice of opposition to the Roman games came from a minority group, the early Christians. In part, their protest was a matter of practical self-defense. In the oldest extant Christian document outside the New Testament, Clement of Rome in A.D. 96 wrote to the Christian community at Corinth lamenting "the great multitude of the elect" who were being made "the victims of many tortures and outrages" in the arena. As Ignatius, the Bishop of Antioch, put it while on the way to his own martyrdom (c. A.D. 108), the Roman spectacle was one of the most "cruel tortures of the devil" with which Christians had to contend.

Christians seldom attacked the Greek games. Like St. Paul, they often referred to them as metaphors for the Christian experience: "running the race" of life, "striving" (agonizing) for excellence of character, "wrestling" with the forces of evil, "beating the air" (like boxers) in futile gestures, "winning the prize" of faith, taking on the victor's "crown of life." Roman sports and spectacles were another matter altogether. Beyond their fear of being persecuted in the arena, Christians opposed Roman sports for the same reasons they abstained from military service and theatrical productions. They abhorred the paganism, the cruel bloodshed, the worldly associations, and the subservience to temporal authorities that such activities entailed. Principle rather than mere self-preservation led Christians to speak out. Athenagoras, a leader of the Christian community in Athens, insisted that he and his comrades in the faith saw "little difference between watching a man being put to death and killing him." "So we have given up such spectacles," he concluded. Cyprian, the Bishop of Carthage, condemned the gladiatorial contests on the ground that "man is slaughtered that man may be gratified" and that in the arena "crime is not only permitted, but is taught." A little-known Christian spokesman, Tatian, more heatedly denounced the

Now a silent shell of its former self, the Roman Colosseum houses ghosts of deadly battles past. (From J. C. Stobart, *The Grandeur That Was Rome*, 1913.)

spectacle as "a cannibal banquet for the soul." As a concrete expression of their abhorrence of the Roman games, the young Church refused to allow voluntary professional gladiators to be baptized unless they renounced their participation in the arena, and excluded from communion those Christians who attended the games.

Of all the Christian attacks on the Roman games, Tertullian's treatise *On Spectacles*, written about A.D. 200, was the most hostile. Trained in Roman rhetoric and law, Tertullian was middle aged before his conversion to Christianity. Zealously he employed his gifts of logic and satire. He would have "nothing to do, in speech, sight, or hearing, with the madness of the circus" or "the savagery of the arena." The Roman spectacles, he insisted, had originated as pagan festivals, encouraged immoral gambling and prostitution, and thrived on a cruel "misuse of God's creation by God's creatures." For those Christians who argued that the games were not forbidden by Holy Writ, Tertullian had little patience: "If we can plead that cruelty is allowed us, if impiety, if brute savagery, by all means let us go to the amphitheater." Tertullian's concern was not for the pagan apologists of the games. His message was directed primarily at the Christian: "God forbid that *he* should need further teaching to hate the spectacle."

Tertullian's confidence in the power of his own logic was somewhat misplaced. The spectacles exercised a morbid fascination for Christians as well as for pagans, especially outside Rome, where the arena was less associated with Christian martyrdom. Following an edict of toleration in 313, Christianity unofficially became the dominant religion in the Roman empire. But still the spectacles flourished, although they underwent some modifications. Under Constantine condemned criminals ceased being forced into the arena as gladiators; later emperors removed the names of the old pagan gods from the list of festival days. Late in the fourth century an emperor in Constantinople forbade provincial governors to allow chariot races and gladiatorial events on Sunday. Yet concerned as he was "that no uproar from the spectacles may avert the Christian law's venerated mysteries," the emperor was scarcely bothered with the morality or social validity of the spectacles.

The End of the Games

Not until the early fifth century (about 404) were the gladiatorial fights abolished by official decree. Apparently, Christian conscience, nominal at best on the official level, had little to do with the demise of the spectacles. By the fifth century the Roman Empire was a hollow shell, an impoverished society no longer able to recruit war captives and wild animals for lavish amusements. Ceaseless administrative expansion and military expense had proved to be an intolerable drain on resources. Taxes and prices rose disastrously, trade declined, and prominent families left the cities for the simpler security of country life. Thus the spectacles, dependent on abundant wealth and a large urban population, declined in popularity.

In 330 Constantine moved his capital to Byzantium (which he renamed

Constantinople), where chariot races thrived as a form of political ceremony, factional rivalry, and public entertainment well into the Middle Ages, possibly as late as the twelfth century. The move to Constantinople divided the empire and made Rome even more vulnerable to assaults from barbarian marauders out of northern and central Europe. In 410 the once proud and mighty city of Rome fell to Alaric and his horde of Goths. The two prime symbols of the Roman games met their end. The Circus Maximus was dismantled, and the Colosseum was abandoned to become a crumbling, grim relic of an age past.

Parallel to the demise of the Roman games, a decline and fall of Greek athletes occurred at Olympia. It was a decline all the more dramatic because of the final blaze of glory the Olympic Games enjoyed in the second century A.D., when Hadrian's beneficent patronage, Tiberius Atticus's energetic building program, and a flood of Roman and Greek visitors singing the praises of Phidias's shrine to Zeus all added up to renewed interest in the games. At the same time, several outstanding commentators such as Lucian and Pausanias penned elaborately detailed observations on both past and contemporary Olympic exploits.

From that pinnacle of acclaim, the Olympic Games plummeted to the depths of uncertainty in the third century. The classic deities, in whose honor the games had originated and flourished, finally lost their hold on Greek minds, victims of rational philosophy, escapist mystery cults, and Christian theology. In the struggle for the Greek and Roman soul, the third century was a kind of ideological battleground. Anarchy reigned, and it was not merely spiritual. As the frontiers of the empire began constantly to be assaulted by barbarian tribes, no less than thirty-seven men within thirty-five years proclaimed themselves emperor. All the while, Rome's economic crisis daily grew more severe. Reflecting that age of disorder and uncertainty, the Olympic Games languished.

Olympia's remote location, earlier an asset, now became a liability. Games in larger, more accessible cities stole the attention of the sports-minded: other games, offering large cash prizes, lured the best athletes. The Panathenaic Games in Athens competed for preeminence. In Corinth, on the other hand, gladiatorial combats and wild-beast hunts even overshadowed the Greek athletics of Corinth's own Isthmian Games. Symbolic of Olympia's decline, official records of victors ceased being kept in A.D. 265. Some subsequent winners of the olive wreath are known, but only through inscriptions and scattered literary references. Fittingly, the last champion for whom there is evidence was not a Greek, but an Armenian boxer named Varaztad. Of royal blood, in 385 he triumphed at Olympia and later reigned for four years as King of Armenia at the behest of the Roman emperor.

Resistant to change in a changing world, the Olympic Games finally succumbed to the reforming zeal of Christians. Once they found representation in the emperor's palace, Christians insisted that all pagan temples should be closed and their ceremonies abolished by official decree. Constantine partially met their demands, discouraging but not forbidding pagan practices. His successors, however, ordered the closing of the temples and the cessation of non-Christian ritual throughout the empire. Olympia, a monument to Zeus, was inevitably affected; the Olympic Games were doomed to extinction. In 393–94 the religious rites associated with the games were discontinued. The games survived for a time, possibly until the mid-fifth century, but severed from their roots, they soon died from atrophy.

Throughout the fifth century migrating warrior tribes from the north passed through Olympia, defacing the temple to Zeus and shattering the statues to Greek gods and heroes. Nature finished off man's work of devastation. In 522 and 551 two great earthquakes leveled the temple and changed the course of the river Alpheus. The face of the Hill of Cronus cascaded into the valley, mixing with silt and water from the river to submerge Olympia under several feet of marshy sand and gravel. The fall of athletics in the ancient world was complete, buried by time and circumstance.

Chapter 4

MEDIEVAL PEOPLE
AT PLAY

During the Middle Ages (c. 500–1400), Roman frontier games and Islamic cultic rituals combined with native European customs to produce a richly varied pattern of popular pastimes. The dominant institution of the period, the Catholic Church, adapted various "pagan" rites for Christian worship. Many of those ceremonies featured a symbolic tossing of a ball back and forth as a dramatic representation of the struggle between good and evil. Playful dramatizations soon leaped the bounds of their religious origins. As the Church provided seasonal holidays and physical sites for play, ball games flourished in medieval Europe. By the twelfth century, peasants enjoyed numerous types of handball, football, and stick-and-ball games. No written rules existed; each game evolved differently from one place to another according to local custom and whim. But in the play of medieval peasants lay the roots of virtually every ball game known in the modern world.

In feudal Europe sports for the privileged few were altogether different from the pastimes enjoyed by the masses. Horse racing, organized hunting, and hawking distinguished the feudal aristocracy. Their wealth and social status depended on military might, and for competitive sport they devised the tournament as an adjunct to war. Mock combat in jousting and melees kept knights honed for battle. Of equal importance, the colorful drama of tournaments provided entertainment for the castle crowd.

As feudalism began to disintegrate, peasant games and pastimes clashed with the interests of the guardians of law and order. Church officials, monarchs, and town authorities all had reason to curtail popular sporting practices. The attempt to redirect the energies of the masses from play to more useful purposes began in the late Middle Ages.

The Baptism of Pagan Rites

At its extremity in the fourth century, the Roman Empire included most of Europe, the Middle East, and the northern coast of Africa. Magnificently straight roads linked distant frontiers with Rome. In regions previously ravaged by marauding tribes, chaos gave way to stability in the form of Roman authority, government, and law. Roman architecture appeared in the construction of private homes for administrative officials and tradesmen, soldiers' quarters, and public buildings, aqueducts, and monuments. Roman modes of dress, social customs, and amusements flourished in provincial towns throughout the empire.

Yet when the imperial troops were called home early in the fifth century in a futile attempt to protect the city of Rome, Roman civilization quickly withered in the provinces. Especially in Britain and northern Europe, the togas, baths, villas, and amphitheaters had been superimposed on conquered peoples; the Latin language and lifestyle had been signs of submission, not of indigenous growth. Alien, affecting only the upper crust of the native population, Roman culture disappeared shortly after the troops and imperial administrators departed.

Certainly the Romans left scarcely any sporting tradition in northern Europe. Themselves holding Greek athletics in low esteem, they did not bother to introduce competitive track-and-field sports. With native slave labor they constructed a few arenas and staged chariot races and gladiatorial contests for the amusement of resident officials, soldiers, and tradesmen, but by the sixth century the arenas had fallen into ruin and the games forgotten. Athletics and spectacles, which had long dominated the sporting scene in the Mediterranean basin, proved unadaptable to the rural, less highly developed societies of medieval Britain, France, the Germanies, and the Low Countries.

Ball games were another matter. Wherever possible, the Romans established baths. The towns of Bath (Aquae Salis) in England and Baden-Baden (Aquae Aureliae) in Germany were fashionable resorts of Roman officials. At frontier posts (such as Hadrian's Wall in Britain), soldiers gave as much attention to the construction of artificial bathing facilities as to fortifications. Preliminary ball play, *harpastum* and the like, warmed the blood and loosened the limbs before a plunge into the baths. In frigid northern climes, such "warmups" were even more useful than in balmy Rome. Moreover, soldiers in their spare time occasionally played their adapted versions of the old Greek competitive game of *episkyros*. Unintentionally, they introduced ball games to northern Europe.

Yet ball play, like the Latin language and customs, would probably have disappeared with the withering of the empire had not ball games struck a responsive chord in the north. In fact, such games had indigenous roots. Like most primitive societies, northern worshippers of Thor and Woden and their various regional counterparts established religious ceremonies on antagonistic, competitive principles: life overcoming death, light *versus* darkness. According to one tradition, ball games in northern France were ancient rituals invented by the Gauls in honor of the sun.

One form of ball play that apparently predated the Romans was the German game of *kegels,* a kind of competitive bowling in which wooden balls were used to knock over targets, or "pins." The Romans had played some form of bowling game that they had learned from Egypt, but both the earliest literary reference (in the third century) and the later use made of the game in Germany suggest a non-Roman source. Kegels was a favorite practice of medieval German monks and priests, who used the game as a religious object lesson. The target (kegel) represented the devil. If the bowler successfully knocked over "the devil," he was supposedly cleansed of his sins. Both in form and significance, the game smacks of ancient ritual rather than Roman play.

Irish hurling and Scottish shinty were unquestionably pre-Roman. The Roman legions never even went to Ireland, and after a few forays into southern Scotland, they decided that the Scots were not worth the bother. At any rate, Irish hurling was mentioned in annals, law codes, and hero tales many centuries before the Christian era. A stick-and-ball game roughly resembling modern field hockey, hurling was transplanted from northern Ireland to Scotland, where it took on a new name, shinty, and became extremely popular in the Highlands. The identical name of the stick used in both games, the camen, reflects the common origin. Quite possibly the many stick-and-ball games that became popular in medieval France and the Low Countries were similarly ancient, but neither literary nor archeological evidence has survived to unravel the mystery.

One of the earliest known descriptions of a ball game north of the Alps sounds strikingly similar to a Roman version of ball play. Around 470 the French bishop of Clermont organized a game for a festival in one of his churches—a game in which even the most prosperous and respectable inhabitants of the town formed two teams, each attempting to control the ball as long as possible, passing it from one teammate to another to keep it away from the opposition. For the bishop the game was "as true a friend to me as are my books"; it helped rid him of "that sluggishness which inevitably results from my sedentary occupation." Although the origins of the game are forever lost in the mists of time, it is reminiscent of Roman play.

In contrast to the scanty evidence of Roman influence on medieval ball games, the importance of the Moors is well documented. During the seventh century Mohammedans adopted the old Egyptian fertility rites into their newly founded religion. At the center of those ceremonies were ball-and-stick games symbolizing the annual return of spring, the growth of crops, and human fertility. As Mohammedans moved across northern Africa, they taught their rituals to their converts. In the early eighth century Moslems from northwest Africa, the Moors, crossed the narrow neck of the Mediterranean into Spain. After conquering Spain, they pushed north into the heart of France before finally being stopped near Tours in 732.

For several centuries the Moors ruled in Spain, Moslems tolerantly living alongside Christians. The ball rites of Islam, practiced in the spring of each year, naturally blended with the Christian Easter festivals of the Spanish people. Especially in the countryside, illiterate peasants had difficulty keeping the rituals of the two religions separate. Firmly established in Spain, the customs of Islam spread into southern and western France.

Christian Europe's acceptance of those pagan customs reflected the attitudes of the leading spokesmen of the Roman church. Long before the Moorish invasion, Augustine of Hippo, the outstanding theologian of the early Church, insisted that Christians "ought not to reject a good thing because it is pagan. God is the author of all things. To continue the good customs that have been practiced by idolators . . . is not to borrow from them; on the contrary, it is taking from them what is not theirs and giving it to God the real owner." As the Church pushed north to do battle with paganism, Pope Gregory in 601 advised his missionaries to leave pagan rituals and customs intact while changing their usage "from the worship of devils to the service of the true God." Like northern Christmas trees and yule logs, ritualistic ball games were baptized in the service of Christianity and thereby became an important feature of medieval Europe.

In France, especially, the ball became an integral part of Easter ceremonies. Annually on Easter Day in the city of Auerre, near Paris, colorfully garbed church officials formed a processional down the aisle of the church. Chanting a traditional liturgy, they danced to the music of an Easter hymn while passing a ball from person to person. At Vienne, near Lyon, the Archbishop initiated a game of ball following an Easter meal. The popular association of ball playing with Easter ceremonies was best indicated by the protest of a Paris theologian in 1165, who opposed such games at Poitiers and Rheims because he said they were simply old pagan customs. He was right of course, but few shared his alarm.

Not only did the Church adapt and unintentionally popularize ball games, it also provided both time and place for the playing of games. For hard-working medieval peasants, Sunday was a day set aside for worship, rest, and "re-creation" of strength. Yet no puritan pall hovered over Sundays. After the sermon and the sacraments in the morning, villagers lounged or played on Sunday afternoon. For youths, especially, re-creation meant recreation. Nor was recreation confined to Sunday afternoons. The church calendar of holidays, aligned with ancient seasonal patterns, granted festive occasions at Easter, during harvest season, and at Christmas. Throughout Europe this basic pattern was followed; in specific countries variations were added, such as numerous saints' days in Italy, and Shrove Tuesday (before Lent) and May Day in England. Blessed by church leaders, accepted by landlords, and sanctified by tradition, some of these seasonal breaks in labor ran for several days. Wine or ale, music, and dance accompanied the peasant games and frolic.

In that day before school yards, public parks, or playgrounds were available for sports and games, villagers usually played on the village green, a "commons" traditionally set aside for the grazing of cattle, the holding of fairs, and the playing of games. Yet some villages were without a commons, in which case the church yard or cloisters served the purposes of mass recreation. For expansive games such as football, land owned by the Church and rented to wealthy landlords was traditionally turned over to peasant sport before and after harvest. Like medieval drama, mass recreation originally depended on the parish church for its sustenance.

Ball Games Beyond the Cloister

Whatever the original mixture of foreign and native elements, European ball games were gradually removed from church ritual, to take their place in the mainstream of medieval life. The French game of *la soule*, or *choule*, for example, was well established by the twelfth century. At first invariably associated with Christian holidays, mostly Easter or Christmas, *la soule* was played with a leather-covered ball stuffed with hemp or wool. It was an aggressive, sometimes violent village game. Often the men of an entire village competed against those of a neighboring village in an attempt to drive the ball by hand, foot, or stick to the opponents' goal. Occasionally, single men teamed up against married men. The religious holiday provided a welcome break in the monotonous work of field and shop, and the ball game added to the festive occasion.

Although *la soule* or *choule* was usually a loosely structured game in which hands, feet, and sticks propelled the ball, variations in local customs produced several more narrowly defined versions. One, similar to the modern game of soccer in which only the feet touch the ball, was *la soule au pied*. Another was *shouler a la crosse*, a stick-and-ball game mentioned in a document of 1374 as an activity that existed "so long ago that no one remembers to the contrary." For some reason, the game soon lost its popularity in France. Lack of evidence prevents our knowing if it was similar to the North American Indian game of lacrosse. Yet it is altogether fitting that several centuries later a Frenchman gave the name of lacrosse to the Indian game, for in his own heritage a form of play approximating the Indian game existed. Within the same family of medieval French games, *jeu de mail* featured hitting a ball along the ground with a wooden stick, or "mallet." The game varied throughout France, but it usually involved individual participants aiming for targets. Even the name varied: In one area, it was called *paille maille*.

Transported to Scotland, *paille maille* retained its form but had its name changed to pell mell, or pall mall. A team version of that individualist stick-and-ball game also had a similar appearance, but different names, on each side of the English Channel. A famous French medieval woodcut depicts men with curve-ended sticks scrambling for a ball, a form of field hockey. Actually, the French name for the game has not come to light. In England, however, a strikingly similar game was called "cambuca" in some areas, "bandy" in others. An English chronicler of the twelfth century, William Fitzstephen, described London youths going after dinner "into the fields to play at the ball." They had "their ball, or baton [staff], in their hands" while the elders of the city came out on horseback "to see the sport of the young men, and to take part of the pleasure in beholding their agility." Small as the crowd of onlookers might have been, field hockey (or cambuca, or bandy, or whatever they called it) was the first spectator sport of which we have any record since the days of ancient Greece and Rome.

ı la mozt Abatu lame lı eftuer renoze
fes vaches garder ne pozra mes entendze

The ecclesiastical connection to medieval ball games is illustrated in this drawing from the margin of a Latin manuscript, the *Alexander Romance,* as a monk with bat in hand takes a ball from a nun. Are the figures to the right praying, censoring, or getting ready to catch the ball?

The term "hockey" was not widely used until centuries later. Yet even its origins are uncertain. The French word *hocquet* meant "shepherd's staff"; the Anglo-Saxon word *hoc* meant "hook." The term could have derived from either source. The game was similarly played both in medieval France and Britain, with native roots in both places (hurling and shinty in Britain, *la soule* in France) but with elements of varying styles transported from one place to another by traveling churchmen, tradesmen, and warrior knights. It was a "folk game" in that it was popular with the peasants and played according to local traditions rather than written rules.

Even more popular was the peasant game of football, another game common to medieval France and England. In fact, the connection of the French game of *soule* or *choule* to English football is suggested by the name of the game in Cornwall, the remote English county in the far southwest, which had intricate ecclesiastical and commercial ties with Brittany, the westernmost province in France. In Cornwall football was called *chole.* In Wales, on the other hand, it was called *knappan;* and in East Anglia, *camp ball.* This lack of a standard name for the common game of football reflects the character of the medieval world: local standards were paramount.

Like most of the medieval sports and games, the beginnings of English football are unclear. According to one folk tradition, fourth-century Roman legionnaires taught early Britons a game of football, only to lose the game to unlettered natives. But that yarn was based on later patriotic mythology rather than on reliable documents, as was the equally unlikely tale of Englishmen kicking a Dane's head and thus inventing a football game in the eleventh century. Not until the early fourteenth century is there a definite reference to "futball": a ban on the game by an English king. According to that ban, the game was so widespread that it could safely be conjectured that no later than the thirteenth century did the game come into prominence among the English peasants.

On Shrove Tuesday, a final celebration before the onset of Lenten austerity, local football games were played. At Derby, especially, teams from the two parishes of St. Peter's and All Saints squared off. The three miles of country-side separating the parishes constituted the "field" of play. The size of the teams was not fixed; anyone living in the parishes played. There were no written rules. The purpose of the game was simply to kick, carry, or throw the ball against the opponents' goal—a prominent gate in the parish of St. Peter's, an old waterwheel in All Saints' parish. Inspired by local pride and Shrovetide ale, villagers kicked, bit, and mauled each other. Some took the opportunity to even old scores.

In the nearby village of Ashbourne, geography dictated a slight variation on the Derby game. A stream ran down the middle of the village, requiring the footballers to tread water and run the risk of being ducked or nearly drowned as they forced the ball toward their opponents' goal. Getting wet was the least of their worries. Severe scratches and bruises were to be expected and occasionally arms and legs were broken. In 1280 and again in 1321 accidental deaths from sheathed knives were recorded. In their Shrove Tuesday football matches, English peasants exacted on each other a bit of the violence they unleashed on bulls, bears, and boars in periodic animal baitings.

Compared to football, games such as stoolball and bowls, or bowling, were mild exercises. Utterly simple, they were popular pastimes in the towns and villages of medieval England. Stoolball was originally a game played by milkmaidens who used a familiar implement, the milking stool, and a ball. One player stood in front of the stool while another threw the ball in an attempt to knock the stool over. At first the "batter" wielded no bat or stick, but rather used the hand. Every time she successfully defended the stool from a pitch, she scored a point. When the pitcher finally knocked over the stool, or caught the hit ball before it touched the ground, she changed places with the batter. Soon the game was played by boys as well as girls, adults as well as children. It was the basis of the games of rounders and cricket, and from rounders American baseball evolved many centuries later. Although modern baseball is primarily American, urban, and male, its roots are medieval, English, rural, and female.

Bowls was another popular peasant game. For a time English and French bowlers played in a manner similar to the German game of kegels. Two players, each with a wooden or stone ball, stood some distance apart and rolled the ball to knock over a cone or wooden "pin" placed at the opponent's feet. While German and Dutch bowlers stuck with the practice of "bowling over" the targets, English and French players developed another form of the game by rolling the ball to stop as near a target (another ball or coin) as possible. A bowling green still in use in Southampton dates back to 1299. A contemporary and even more intricate medieval version of English bowls and French *boule* was the Scottish game of curling, the sliding of smooth stones across ice, with a fine, skilled touch distinguishing winners from losers.

Sporting Life at the Top

Late in the Middle Ages, the peasant game of bowls was taken from rough grounds and rainy outdoors into the homes of the upper classes and there transformed into two new games. In their massive halls gentlemen devised the game of shovel-board (shuffleboard) by substituting flat pieces of wood for balls. They propelled them either by hand or with a blunt-ended stick. Transferred from the floor to a tabletop, the game was gradually altered into a gentlemanly pastime resembling pocket billiards. Actually the name came before the pockets: French in origin, the term billiards derived from *bille*, a stick or piece of wood.

Both billiards and shuffleboard were late-medieval refinements of rustic games. Earlier sporting activities of the feudal aristocracy were scarcely as refined or derivative. Invariably outdoors and active, they were pastimes distinctly different from the recreations enjoyed by the masses. Like the purchase of a new Cadillac, Rolls Royce, or Mercedes Benz today, the possession of a stable of fine horses distinguished the privileged few from the indigent masses in the Middle Ages. On horseback men of means traveled; on horseback they fought their wars; and on horseback they enjoyed most of their sports. Horse racing was a favorite pastime. Most races were informal responses to specific challenges; sometimes they were organized. In England a twelfth-century royal secretary observed boy riders "inspired with thoughts of applause, and in the hopes of victory, clap spurs to the willing horses, brandish their whips, and cheer them with their cries." The scene sounds strangely modern. Unique to the Middle Ages, however, were races arranged by kings and local barons, featuring armored knights on horseback.

Peasants of course could not afford horses. Yet from the stables they improvised a game of quoits by heating and bending old horseshoes into iron rings, throwing them toward an iron peg driven in the ground. When American frontiersmen centuries later altered the game of quoits into horseshoe pitching, they unknowingly returned to the medieval origins of the game.

Hunting and hawking on horseback were the exclusive pursuits of a privileged order. Much of the finer wild game, in fact, was legally forbidden the masses. Especially from the twelfth century onward, bears, foxes, and deer were the playthings of the feudal nobility, who followed their hounds on horseback. Birds of all kinds were at the mercy of the specially trained hawk, a prime symbol of noble rank. One of the most prestigious and highest-paid officers in the court of medieval French kings was the Grand Falconer, who always rode beside the king on casual jaunts as well as extended journeys, and even in battle.

A day on horseback, hunting and hawking, provided kings and noblemen welcome relief from the pressures of diplomacy and estate management. A joker, or court jester, provided after-dinner diversion in the castle, but for a quiet evening lords and ladies turned to dice and card games of chance, or to the ancient board games of draughts and chess, which reached their height of popularity during the Middle Ages. In pieces such as knights, kings, queens, bishops, and jokers, chess and card games retain the mark of upper-class medieval life.

Yet no sports or games epitomized the interests of the aristocracy in the Middle Ages as did the war games called tournaments. The nobility won and retained their privileged position through combat. They recruited and sometimes led their knights into battle on the side of (and occasionally against) their king. The entire feudal contract was a product of military necessity, and it depended on martial strength for its stability. Originally tournaments were life-and-death engagements on the field of battle, between knights of opposing camps. The victors carried off horses, armor, and weaponry as booty; defeated knights who survived the battle were taken as prisoners, for ransom or enforced service under their captors. In the beginning the word "tournament," from the French *tournoi*, had no connotations of pageantry or chivalrous sport, but rather merely referred to the wheeling motion of knights on horseback as they completed a charge and returned for another assault on their adversaries.

In time, however, tournaments became staged events, cloaked in colorful ceremonies. Several days before the contests, pavilions and galleries were erected, hung with the banners of the noble households represented in the tournament. Two days prior to the event, a dramatic parade of arms was held, with two barons inspecting all the arms and banners of the participants in order to prevent any deviation from the required standards. No one beneath the rank of knight could compete. On the appointed day, heralds ceremoniously cried out, "To achievement!" Each horseman then came forth from his pavilion, armed and ready for combat.

A tournament included two different forms of combat, melees and jousts. In a melee, any number of men fought on each side, wielding dull-edged swords in hand-to-hand combat. In the joust, only two men competed against each other, charging on horseback, with lances raised, down either side of a barrier in an attempt to unseat each other. As the jousting contest became stylized in the late-medieval period, a points system came into use. To unseat one's opponent was to win the unequivocal victory, but one scored a point by landing a clean blow to an opponent's metal breastplate, and two points by connecting with a shot to the head. Yet the gamesmanship of this combat activity scarcely stripped it of danger. Although a helmet, with visor lowered, protected the head and face, a well-aimed blow virtually took the head off. A knight often deliberately wore his helmet loose, hoping it would topple off and leave the head intact.

Jousts and melees were supposedly designed not to maim or kill knights, but deaths and severe wounds inevitably occurred. Melees, especially, could be savage, as horsemen charged into each other swinging recklessly with heavy, blunted swords. Occasionally sharpened swords were used to settle

Justs.

Knights held the center of the medieval jousting stage, but children mime them on horse-sticks and citizens take to aquatic versions of the joust in these illustrations from Joseph Strutt, *The Sports and Pastimes of the People of England*, 1903 ed.

private feuds. In 1249 a tournament near Cologne pitted a large number of knights against each other, and by the end of the day at least sixty were dead or dying—most from bloody wounds, some from being unhorsed and trampled to death, and a few from suffocation by dust. Not surprisingly, the joust, with its spectacular but less brutal hazards, gradually superseded the older melee in popularity.

By the fifteenth century, tournaments were a relic of the past, a traditional form of aristocratic entertainment on festive occasions, but no longer connected to the military life. The age of courtly chivalry, always something of a fabrication at best, was dead. Armor-piercing weapons and swifter combat maneuvers consigned the heavily armored knight on horseback to museums. Occasional revivals of jousting contests in sixteenth-century Europe had more to do with romantic inclinations and contrived entertainment than with the military realities of aristocratic life.

Even at the height of the tournament's popularity, its brutality caused the Church to view it with disapproval. Churchmen encouraged a milder equivalent of the joust, *quintain,* an ancient game in which a mounted competitor charged a target fixed on a tree or post in such a way that failure to strike it properly meant a swift retaliatory blow. In late-medieval England and Italy, especially, *quintain* was a popular pastime enjoyed by all ranks of society. Some "ran at the quintain" on foot, attempting to hit it squarely with their lance in order to avoid being struck on the back of the head as they passed. But the most interesting variation was water *quintain,* a favorite recreation on the Thames River each summer. Awkward falls and ducked competitors provided amusement for the common folk gathered on the banks. It was a far cry from the gaudy spectacle of tournaments, with knights in shining armor.

Royal ("real") tennis was a more serious but similarly nonviolent pastime of the upper classes during the late Middle Ages. First played in monastic and church cloisters by French monks, abbots, priests, and bishops, the original name was *le jeu de paume,* a game of handball. Players hit a small ball over a cord stretched across the center of the cloister, onto the walls and off the sloping roofs. Here was the origin not only of handball but also of various racket-and-ball games. Rackets came gradually into use. But first the bare hand gave way to a glove, then to a binding of cord across the palm, and finally to the use of a small wooden board and then a racket, strung with sheep's intestines, in the fifteenth century.

By then *le jeu de paume* had been discovered by Frenchmen outside church cloisters. According to one legend, a king visiting a monastery admired the game and copied it in his royal palace. Certainly it soon became a royal and aristocratic game, not always with the best effect. In 1316 King Louis X was "playing at *paume*" so hard that he drank too much afterward, took a chill, and died. In 1498 Charles VIII died of a hemorrhage after banging his head on the stone lintel of a low doorway when going down to watch a tennis match in the castle moat. Yet not all the early tennis stories have unhappy endings. In 1427 a young woman named Margot, who came from the countryside to Paris, displayed exceptional talent at *le jeu de paume.* She took on all comers, including men, and beat most of them with her unorthodox use of the back of the hand as well as the palm. As one chronicler of the day put it, "she played vigorously, dishonestly, and ably, exactly like a man."

While *le jeu de paume* made its way from French monasteries to royal and aristocratic courts, the game of *pelota* developed in the Basque provinces of northern Spain. From its beginning pelota was a generic name (from the Latin *pila:* ball) for a number of different competitive games wherein a ball was hit with a hand, glove, or racket across a cord or net, off the enclosed walls of the court. Because of the physical isolation of Basque villages, each village evolved its own version of pelota, ranging from simple handball to the more active and sophisticated *longue paume* (elongated glove). Pelota soon crossed the Pyrennes into southwestern France, where it blended with *le jeu de paume*. More important, it slowly spread into most of Spain, and from there to the New World as a forerunner of the modern *jai alai*.

In contrast to the limited dispersion of pelota, the French game of *jeu de paume* was quickly imitated in Italy, Germany, the Low Countries, and England. In England, especially, it became a favorite game of the court and aristocracy. Soon the name of the game became Anglicized to tennis, probably a corruption of the French word *tenez*, meaning "Play!" The scoring system, too, was adapted to English ways. For the French, four points won a game; in the hands of the English the scores of Love–15–30–40 became standard. "Love" apparently was an Anglicized version of *l'oeuf*, an egg or oval (zero). English kings and aristocrats traditionally bet a crown on each tennis match, and because a crown was worth sixty pence, each of the four points was designated as 15. The score of 40 of course was a contraction of 45.

Whatever the English did to the name and scoring of the French game, the Channel crossing of *le jeu de paume* worked to the advantage of at least one Frenchman. When Charles, Duke of Orleans, was taken hostage at the battle of Agincourt in 1415, he relieved the monotony of his English imprisonment by playing tennis with his prison guards. Perhaps it is fitting that in the end, even tennis, the most nonviolent of all the pastimes pursued by the aristocracy in the Middle Ages, served as consolation for a defeated warrior.

Masters versus Masses

Sports in medieval Europe reflected a divided society. There were the masters with their sports and pastimes, and the masses with theirs. Seldom did the twain meet. Insulated by wealth, law, moated castles, and military might, the ruling classes largely ignored the leisure activities of the peasantry, and even encouraged fun on religious festival days as a safety valve against social unrest. In the fourteenth and fifteenth centuries, however, Europe's masters decided that their interests were not best served by the sports and games that brought pleasure to the masses. Thus the Church, municipal officials, and monarchs, all for different reasons, began to prohibit certain popular pastimes.

The first wave of assault came from the Church, an ambivalent institution in which parish priests identified with the masses, while hierarchical heads had more in common with established authority. Displeased that its churchyards were being desecrated by footballers, the Synod of Exeter (in England) attempted in 1287 to regulate such activities. In 1303 a churchman in Lincolnshire denounced the playing of football on church property; shortly thereafter another English cleric wanted to banish "dancing, playing at quoits, bowling, tennis-playing, handball, football, stoolball, and all sorts of other games." Yet some local priests not only sympathized with the peasants, but joined them: in 1364 the Synod of Ely issued a decree forbidding its clergy from playing football.

In France, *la soule* fared little better. Adding to the moral denunciations of several of his predecessors, a French bishop in 1440 forbade the playing of that "dangerous and pernicious [game] because of the ill feeling, rancor and enmities, which in the guise of a recreative pleasure, accumulate in many hearts." Aristocratic tournaments of course escaped his censorious eye.

On a more practical level, some citizens detested popular sports and games because they disturbed the tranquility of the social order. In 1314 the mayor of London issued a proclamation reminding the citizens that in the absence of King Edward II, who had gone north to battle the Scots, it was necessary "strictly to keep the peace": "And whereas there is great uproar in the City, through certain tumults arising from great footballs in the fields of the public, from which many evils perchance may arise . . . , we do commend and do forbid, on the King's behalf, upon pain of imprisonment, that such games shall be practiced henceforth within the City." Similarly, King Charles VI of France in 1369 attempted to suppress *la soule* not only because of its physical dangers but also because it led to mob scenes.

Of all the motives that lay behind numerous late-medieval efforts to stop the peasantry from playing their games, a concern for military preparedness was paramount. Time spent on the playing fields meant time taken from the more useful practice of archery. Thus a mid-fourteenth-century Irish parliament in Kilkenny decreed that the common people "should work more with their bows and arrows and less at the game which men call hurling." But if Irish rulers felt the need to demand archery practice of their citizens, English and French kings had much more reason to do so: in 1338 England and France began the Hundred Years' War. In the midst of the war, King Charles V of France complained that too many of his countrymen were playing *jeu de paume* and "all the games that do nothing to teach the manly art of bearing arms."

At the battle of Crecy in 1346, English archers using the new longbow penetrated the armor of mounted Frenchmen with devastating effectiveness. Yet the English king, Edward III, was not one to rest on success. Only three years after Crecy he complained to the sheriff of London that "the skill of shooting with arrows is almost totally laid aside for the purpose of various useless and unlawful exercises." Football being the most "useless and unlawful" of all popular games, Edward commanded his sheriff to suppress it. Apparently his prohibition had little effect. Again in 1363 and 1365 he demanded that every able-bodied man "shall in his sports use bows and arrows or pellets and bolts," and forbade Englishmen "under pain of imprisonment to meddle in the hurling of stones, loggets and quoits, handballs, footballs . . . or other vain games."

Within the next fifty years English monarchs issued no less than five similar decrees, all to no avail. Football and "other idle games" had embedded themselves in the popular culture. References in the writings of John Wycliffe and Geoffrey Chaucer, and in a wood-carved misericord and stained-glass window in the late-medieval cathedral of Gloucester, testify to the popularity of ball games. According to a poet in the early sixteenth century, football served as a solace as well as a delight for disadvantaged, hard-working peasants:

> The sturdy plowman, lusty, strong and bold
> Overcometh the winter with driving the football,
> Forgetting labor and many a grievous fall.

In the face of moral preachments and official decrees, English common folk refused to relinquish their games. Even with the passing of feudalism they had few rights, but apparently they considered their freedom to play as an integral part of their birthright. Such stubborn pride that endures, no less than the competitive urge to win, is a recurring theme in the history of sports.

PART TWO

Sports in an Expanding World: From the Renaissance to the Industrial Revolution

As the medieval world gave way to the early modern age, sports rode the crest of an expansive, adventurous era of life and thought. It was an era of intellectual boldness begun when Renaissance artists and men of letters started looking at themselves, their world, and the universe in entirely new ways. Individualistic, secular attitudes led to a colossal outburst of scientific speculations in the sixteenth and seventeenth centuries. Fresh ideas undermined traditional values, expectations, and relationships. Sports and pastimes were inevitably affected. Old games were adapted and new ones created to satisfy appetites freshly whetted.

Yet the bridge to the modern sporting scene was bumpy. Still a prime concern of Western man, religion in the Protestant Reformation became all the more personal and contentious. Various new Protestant forms of belief opposed both old Catholic and new secular attitudes. Sports got caught up in an ideological maelstrom. During the brief but intense period of English Puritanism, especially, popular pastimes came under a barrage of criticism and prohibition.

Sports survived largely under the patronage of yet another set of newcomers to the scene—strong national monarchies. Long had kings been present in western Europe, of course. But always their authority had been held in check by an assertive Catholic Church and powerful nobles. Both barriers to monarchical sovereignty fell in the fifteenth and sixteenth centuries as the Church declined and then split wide open, and as aristocratic fortunes suffered the double blow of civil wars and inflationary economics. Their opponents having faltered, Spanish, French, and English kings prospered and devised new bureaucratic mechanisms of control. Moreover, they became avid sportsmen. Colorful jousts, horse races, court tennis, and yachting became badges of regal distinction. A tolerant, indulgent attitude toward plebian pleasures served to convey a benign image. In their enthusiastic pursuit and patronage of sport, royalty was a force that not even the Puritans could counter.

Under the banners of the new monarchies, Europeans literally expanded their horizons. Skilled, adventurous seamen made their way to Asia, Africa, and the Americas. Particularly in the Western Hemisphere, they discovered native peoples altogether different from themselves. Strange sports and games as well as foreign languages and habits confronted the first explorers. What they could not fathom, they destroyed. Conquering, they soon colonized, turning the Americas into a dumping ground for European people and customs. Little could they foresee that the dumping ground would quickly become an experiment station for the making of revolutionary new patterns of thought, politics, and sporting activities.

Gold and silver from the New World contributed to a remarkable expansion of the European economy. Already a revival of trade with the East, through prosperous Italian city-states, had financed the flowering of Renaissance art and literature—and, incidentally, sports. Now new wealth gathered from afar stimulated commerce and industry. Colonies provided raw materials as well as markets for European goods. Population grew steadily, as both an effect and cause of enterprise. Prosperity made further investment possible. Astride this binge in commercial expansion came the Industrial Revolution in the eighteenth century. Beginning in Britain, a mechanized textile industry stood in the vanguard of vast technological and social change. People eager for work and excitement crowded into cities. Never again would family patterns of work and play be the same. Urban life in industrial England and the United States revolutionized sports and popular pastimes.

Chapter **5**

THE DAY OF THE SCHOLAR ATHLETE

The Renaissance (c. 1400–1600) began in Italy, where city-states bustled with trade and a money economy. Italian scholars and artists rejected the theological and ascetic preoccupations of the late medieval Church in favor of more humanistic concerns. As they looked to ancient Greece and Rome for a rebirth of European culture, they were especially attracted to the Greek ideal of the harmonious unity of body and mind. They extolled versatility. The ideal "Renaissance man" was socially adept, sensitive to aesthetic values, skilled in weaponry, strong of body, and learned in letters. No single virtuoso achieved the ideal of course, but many individuals excelled in sports as well as the arts. It was the day of the scholar athlete.

While peasants doggedly pursued their traditional games and pastimes, Renaissance intellectuals defined the nature and value of aristocratic sports. All the while, courtiers pursued distinctive games and exercises "fit for gentlemen." Tennis was a favorite court game, but most gentlemanly sports involved a kind of mimic combat. Yet warrior athletes were scarcely confined to sixteenth-century Europe. Renaissance seaman discovered that sport was also "the little brother of war" among Indian societies in the distant Western Hemisphere.

A Rationale for Sports

The Renaissance was an elitist movement. The vast majority of Europeans read neither the ancient classics nor Petrarch, Erasmus, or Rabelais. The masses could not read. Nor did they appreciate the subtleties of Boccaccio's paintings, Da Vinci's designs, or Michelangelo's sculpture. Renaissance literature and art were for the literate, the affluent, the privileged. Even in northern Europe, where the Renaissance arrived later and with less adulation of the Greeks and Romans, religious humanists such as Erasmus and Thomas More lived with, wrote for, and spoke to a small segment of the upper crust of society.

For those privileged few, Renaissance humanists provided aristocratic sports with a philosophical basis, a rationale firmly planted in the soil of Renaissance thought. In the education of *"L'uomo universale,"* the whole man, physical as well as mental development was important. "Games and exercises which develop the muscular activities and the general carriage of the person should be encouraged by every teacher," insisted one humanist in step with his times. Serving as tutors in the courts of rich Italian nobles, fifteenth-century humanists such as Petrus Paulus Vergerius, Guarino da Verona, Vittorino da Feltre, Leone Batista Alberti, Mapheus Vegius, and Aeneas Sylvius Piccolomini (later Pope Pius II) not only pored over classical manuscripts but also extolled swimming, running, horseback riding, acrobatics, archery, swordplay, and wrestling. They wrote elaborate treatises declaring the complementary relation of sound minds and strong, healthy bodies.

Much of the Renaissance emphasis on physical training extended the old ideal of the knight in arms, with ancient Sparta rather than Athens as the model for the military virtues of skill and endurance. Yet few programs of physical activity were designed merely for soldiery. Renaissance humanists assumed that statecraft and life at court, too, would benefit from supervised exercises. In order for young gentlemen better to perform their "ordered tasks," Vergerius recommended "the sharp exertion of ball-play," some "recreation in hunting, hawking, or fishing," and frequent "recourse to music and to song." Physical activity ensured a healthy body. More important, it endowed one with dexterity, a lightness of limb and grace of movement pleasing to the eyes of courtly princes and ladies.

In *The Book of the Courtier,* published in 1528, Baldassare Castiglione condensed much of what earlier humanists had said and written on the subject, and he stamped it with his own experience. Having accompanied the Marquis of Mantua in a war against the Spaniards for the Kingdom of Naples, he knew war firsthand; having spent most of his life in the courts of Milan and Urbino, he had a firm grasp on the gracefulness and courtly manners necessary for success in that refined company. His ideal courtier was "well built and shapely of limb," an expert at swordplay, archery, and horsemanship, and a participant in "all bodily exercises that befit a man of war." The accomplished courtier would know how to swim, leap, run, and throw stones. He would play tennis, a game "very befitting a man at court" because it called forth "the quickness and suppleness of every member."

Castiglione's "Renaissance man" was most assuredly male. The last half of *The Courtier* trails off in a discourse on the ideal court lady and her role in encouraging her husband's display of excellence—perhaps the earliest call in history for female cheerleaders. Concluding with a section on the Renaissance gentleman's relation to his prince, *The Courtier* was quickly translated into Spanish, French, and English as a prescribed text for aristocratic manners—and physical activity—throughout Europe.

Only three years after the original publication of *The Book of the Courtier,* the first educational treatise ever published in the English language appeared. In good Renaissance fashion, Sir Thomas Elyot's *Book of the Governour* devoted several chapters to physical education. Although Elyot frowned on bowls, quoits, and football, games he deemed socially unworthy of a gentleman, he promoted running, swimming, and hunting with numerous examples from Greek and Roman literature, and cited fencing, archery, tennis, and dancing as exercises that made "the spirits of a man more strong and valiant."

During the second half of the sixteenth century several English humanists followed Elyot in promoting physical activity as an integral part of the education of the upper classes. All had the life of the monarchical court or the aristocratic household in mind, until Richard Mulcaster, the first headmaster of the Merchant Taylors School in London, introduced the unorthodox idea that schools, too, should involve themselves with physical as well as mental training. Mulcaster distinguished between those exercises intended for sport, those designed for martial training, and those that merely contributed to good health. But his advocacy of games, gymnastics, and other physical activities in the schools apparently made little impression on his contemporaries.

Of all the humanists who encouraged an integrated wholeness of body and mind, Roger Ascham, a tutor to the young Queen Elizabeth, provided the best summary, In *The Scholemaster: Shewing a Plain and Perfect Way of Teaching the Learned Languages* (1570), Ascham concluded simply: "Young gentlemen should use, and delight in all courtly exercises, and gentlemanlike pastimes." By 1600 Ascham's proposal had become commonplace. Especially in Italy and England, which were intricately connected by traveling scholars and thriving trade (as reflected in several of Shakespeare's plays with Italian settings and themes), young gentlemen strove to be more active than contemplative and physically adroit as well as learned.

Gentlemanly Exercises

What "courtly exercises and gentlemanlike pastimes" did they, in fact, pursue? While dancing and wrestling were conducted literally at court, in the gardens and fields of the nobility young men ran, jumped over hurdles, threw heavy bars or stones, and swam in nearby rivers. Occasionally these "exercises" prompted competition, but more to the nobility's liking were jousts, horse races, fencing, and archery, contests traditionally associated with warfare.

By the fifteenth century the old medieval style of war had undergone a dramatic change. The armor-piercing longbow, gunpowder, artillery, and new engineering skills conspired to make the armored knight obsolete. For a knight's armor to be thick enough to withstand firepower, the knight would have been too heavy for his horse and totally defenseless when knocked from the saddle. A heavily armored horseman in 1500 was an oddity, the stuff of which portraits, parades, and quaint gestures to the past were made.

Militarily obsolete, the knightly style provided sport for the Renaissance nobility. Italian townsmen dressed colorfully, wielded blunt swords, carried huge shields, and annually engaged in mimic battles reminiscent of the old melee, attempting to drive each other from the piazza. Less dangerous, although similarly modeled on the melee, was *giuco del ponte,* a game wherein armored combatants clashed on a bridge, shoving and swinging their narrow pointed shields in an effort to force the opposition to retreat from the center of the bridge. Rough as it was, ponte was nevertheless a controlled sport, a far cry from the medieval melee. In good gentlemanly fashion, it was cloaked in ceremony. A parade and banquet concluded the festivities.

Jousting tournaments were far more fashionable. For the new moneyed nobility of Italy, jousts provided an explicit association with the old warrior nobility. Little did it matter that from Petrarch onward men of letters denounced the joust as dangerous folly without basis in classical antiquity: "In what book do we read that Scipio or Caesar were skilled at the joust?" The Medicis, especially, poured vast sums into ornate trappings and rewards for victors at the tilt. Such extravagance made the tournaments of Renaissance Italy much more spectacular than those in northern Europe, but in England and France, too, the tournament enjoyed its final blaze of glory in the sixteenth century. In 1511 Henry VIII, the youthful, athletic king of England, arranged a three-day tournament in which he had a number of his leading nobles participate. Like his French counterpart, Francis I, Henry VIII frequently promoted jousting contests.

But physical danger and military irrelevance made jousting contests increasingly unattractive to young gentlemen. At the Field of the Cloth of Gold in 1520, where both Henry and Francis distinguished themselves at the tilt, a French knight was killed. Jousting met its sudden end in France after King Henry II died from a blow of the lance in 1559. The demise of the sport came less abruptly in England, largely because of the personal patronage of Henry VIII's daughter, Queen Elizabeth I. As she visited the country estates of her most powerful and richest nobles, tourneys were a customary part of the festivities arranged for her entertainment. By the end of the Elizabethan period, however, the tiltyards at Westminster, Hampton Court, and Greenwich were abandoned. Renaissance gentlemen found new and safer ways to exert their manhood, celebrate their virtuosity, and charm their ladies.

Horse racing was one. Despite the demise of the armored knight, the horse remained essential not only for mobility on the field of battle but also for transportation, the pleasures of hunting, and competitive sports. Henry VIII introduced a law requiring all men of rank to maintain a certain number of horses, the number varying according to one's station in life. Military readiness was the immediate motive; aristocratic sport was the end result. Henry himself employed a private trainer and jockeys for his horses, dressed them in velvet and silk, and paid a bonus for each victory. Races were usually private two-horse affairs, staged in a park or in the open countryside. But around 1540 a permanent race course with annual competition was established in Chester. There races were held every Shrove Tuesday, the very day that village commoners played their rough, plebeian game of football. The coincidence underscored the difference between the rich and the poor. Only the rich owned horses. As one Tudor Englishman shrewdly remarked, expert horsemanship was a sure sign of superior rank; it conveyed "a majesty and dread to inferior persons."

In Renaissance Italy a contest called *palio*, originally a race of armored knights on horseback through the towns of Tuscany, became a race on horseback, on foot, or in a boat. Boys of lowly origins ran or rowed "a *palio*," but the official competition on horseback was still reserved for sons of nobility. Held in honor of a patron saint, in memory of a notable military victory, or in celebration of the arrival of sacred relics to the city, the event was named after the banner (the *palio*) awarded to the winner of the race. Reflecting its aristocratic origin, the banner was made of expensive silk or velvet.

Much more on the order of a "courtly exercise," fencing was another sport practiced throughout Renaissance Europe. With the discarding of armor, the massive old double-handed sword gave way to a long thin-bladed rapier. Early fencing masters borrowed tricks from wrestling, such as a cut inside the knee or a blow between the eyes, but Italian masters first developed the effective use of the point, with the lunge, thus placing emphasis on speed, skill, and technique rather than brute force. Fencing was the only manly art in which all courtiers were trained. As early as the mid-fifteenth century, Italian masters were recognized throughout Europe. Their services were eagerly solicited and dearly bought. Under their tutelage guilds of fencing masters sprang up in Germany (1480), England (1540), and France (1570). In that day of frequent gentlemanly duels, fencing lessons were a practical necessity as well as a competitive sport.

Archery, on the other hand, became relegated to the sphere of sport alone. Although Henry VIII apparently had military readiness in mind when he issued three separate decrees requiring his subjects to practice archery, the longbow—once the staple weapon of English armies—went the way of knightly armor, superseded by the effectiveness of gunpowder and shot. Sir Thomas Elyot devoted an entire chapter in his *Book of the Governour* to archery because of its hunting and sporting possibilities, not its military usefulness. In 1546 Roger Ascham wrote an entire book, *Toxophilus*, extolling archery in familiar Renaissance terms: "How honest a pastime for the mind; how wholesome an exercise for the body; not vile for great men to use, not costly for poor men to sustain." In fact, the poorer classes had little inclination to practice archery except for its being a cheap and practical means of putting fresh meat on the table. Peasant boys played with bows and arrows, but archery as a formal sport was largely confined to the aristocracy.

Another form of mimic combat was the game of *calcio*. Unique to Italy, in style *calcio* was similar to the plebeian games of English football and French *soule*. In Italy, however, "rascals" were "not to be tolerated [on the teams], neither artificers, servants, nor low-born fellows." According to one contemporary, only "honorable soldiers, gentlemen, lords, and princes" were allowed to play. They played with purpose, a purpose in keeping with Renaissance ideals. As Cardinal Silvio Antoniano noted in 1584, *calcio* made young gentlemen "more erect and more eager, and enables them to meet sadness and depression with unruffled brow."

Annually in early spring, between Epiphany and Lent, *calcio* was played in

Italian *calcio* was a kind of football game surrounded by elaborate ceremony such as this pregame pageantry in the Piazza of St. Croce in Florence, as etched in *Memorie del Calcio Fiorentino*, 1688.

the piazzas of most Italian towns north of Rome. On a cobblestone field defined by a fence of wooden posts on one side and a ditch on the other, players kicked, carried, punched, and threw a leather ball filled with animal hair. The object of the game was to kick or punch the ball across the opponents' goal. Teams of twenty-seven men each, dressed in uniforms of red or green, competed vigorously to the accompaniment of trumpets and the shouts of spectators who filled every available window and balcony overlooking the piazza.

Combining pageantry and spirited competition, a game of *calcio* brought out the entire town. Both players and spectators took the game so seriously that not even a military crisis could disrupt play. In 1530 a match was scheduled in Florence, when a hostile army led by the Prince of Orange took up positions on the hill overlooking the city. While the crowd cheered their football heroes, enemy soldiers fired several cannon balls over the Piazza del Santa Croce, where the game was being played. Undaunted, the players simply turned, gave obscene gestures to the Prince of Orange and his troops, then resumed play. Gentlemen athletes did not take kindly to interruption.

Ancient and Royal Games

An exercise altogether different from the war games enjoyed by Renaissance courtiers, tennis nevertheless shared several characteristics with fencing, archery, and the like: it had its roots in the Middle Ages, it was a game largely reserved for the upper classes, and its popularity transcended national boundaries. References to tennis can be found in the writings of many of the masters of Renaissance literature: Erasmus, Sir Thomas More, Benvenuto Cellini, Rabelais, Montaigne, and Shakespeare. Castiglione merely stated the obvious when he noted that tennis was the game most "befitting a man at court." During the Renaissance, tennis became solidly fixed as the international "sport of kings"; its common name, "real tennis," referred to its royal associations.

Virtually every French king in the sixteenth century played the game. Francis I had an indoor tennis court built on his royal yacht. His successor, Henry II, ordered the building of tennis courts at the Louvre, where he played daily (according to one chronicler) "dressed all in white, wearing his doublet, a straw hat on his head," smashing the ball "heatedly but without any pomp, except when his servants lifted the cord for him." In 1571 King Charles IX granted a charter to a guild of tennis players and racket makers in Paris, designating tennis as "one of the most honorable, worthy and healthy exercises which princes, peers, gentlemen and other distinguished persons can undertake."

Kings and gentlemen in Tudor England were equally devoted to the game. Henry VIII owned seven rackets and was an avid player. Shortly after he received Hampton Court as a "gift" from Cardinal Thomas Wolsey, Henry had a tennis court erected there—the oldest in the world still in use. At the Palace of Westminster he supervised the construction of four new courts, two indoor and two outdoor. He played all comers—his court cronies, Lombard merchants, French hostages, and royal visitors. In 1523 he joined Charles V, the Emperor of the Holy Roman Empire, in a doubles match against the princes of Orange and Brandenburg.

The other outstanding and long-reigning Tudor monarch, Queen Elizabeth, refrained from playing tennis but loved to watch matches involving the leading nobles of the realm. By the late sixteenth century tennis was such a familiar, popular game among the English aristocracy that Shakespeare mentioned it six times in his plays. The most memorable reference is in *Henry V*, where Shakespeare has young Harry use tennis as a metaphor for England's struggle with France. Responding to a gift of tennis balls from the French Dauphin, Henry declared:

> When we have match'd our rackets to these balls,
> We will, in France, by God's grace, play a set
> Shall strike his father's crown into the hazard.

Rackets, in fact, were relatively new to the game. Although mentioned by Chaucer and a few writers in the fifteenth century, rackets did not come to be widely used until the sixteenth century. At Windsor in 1505 the newly crowned King of Castile, Phillip, played a match against the Marquis of Dorset. Phillip used a racket, while the Marquis used only his hand. Apparently the racket was coming to be seen as the more efficient means of play: the Marquis was given an advantage of fifteen points in deference to his backward style. As good Renaissance men, however, some players were more concerned with gracefulness than with efficiency. In a dialogue written by Erasmus in 1524, one character admitted that "no play is better to exercise all parts of the body than a game using the hand," but added that "we shall sweat less if we play with the racket." His opponent was not convinced: "Let us leave nets to fishermen; the game is prettier if played with the hands."

Rackets were not the only controversial item of equipment. Tennis balls also varied widely. According to custom, the balls were made of leather casings stuffed with feathers, human hair, or wool. In fact, makers of tennis balls stuffed them with whatever was at hand, provoking noble patrons to complain bitterly of the uneven quality. One French king, for example, decreed that the ball used on his royal courts must be filled with wool "and not containing sand, ground chalk, metal shavings, lime, bran, sawdust, ash, moss, powder, or earth." Balls too hard, too soft, or quickly misshapen provided ready excuses for royal losers.

Worse than these variations in equipment was the confusion caused by the many different rules in effect in each country. In Italy rules and styles of play varied even from town to town. This confusing situation prompted a monk from Farrara, Antonio Scaino da Salo, to publish a treatise on tennis in 1555. Much of the text was a philosophical assertion of tennis being "the most appropriate sport for the man of letters," but Scaino's intention was practical as well as philosophical. He established a rudimentary set of rules, a standard court size, a scoring system, and some principles of etiquette for the players. Soon translated into most European languages, the treatise was revised and expanded in 1592, and published again in 1632.

Scaino also described in elaborate detail the varieties of the game as played in Spain, the Low Countries, and the German states, as well as the Italian, French, and English versions of the game. Moreover, he observed that real tennis, although still primarily associated with the monarchies and nobility of Europe, was beginning to exert a strong appeal to merchants, students, and artisans, who usually played on new outdoor courts. Contemporaries agreed. "Here you may commonly see artisans, such as hatters and joiners, playing at tennis for a crown," wrote a French visitor to England in 1558. By 1600 every major town in France had several courts; in Paris alone there were about 250 indoor and more than a thousand outdoor courts. Little wonder that a Venetian ambassador remarked that "the French are born with rackets in their hands."

But at the height of its popularity in 1600, tennis declined rapidly. A sport involving relatively few players and spectators, tennis simply could not compete in the public marketplace. In the early seventeenth century many owners of courts in both England and France found it more profitable to rent them as theaters for plays and concerts, or as arenas for boxing, wrestling, and acrobatic exhibitions. By the mid-seventeenth century, tennis was a game once again almost totally divorced from the masses. Its brief moment of widespread popularity dulled its mystique as a royal sport, and even its appeal to the upper classes was greatly diminished.

Another ancient and royal game, golf, went a different route. Never rising to such heights of popularity, it did not fall so precipitously. Unlike tennis, golf was geographically confined to Holland, Scotland, and England. In fifteenth-century Scotland, especially, it was so much a commoner's game that Scottish kings repeatedly prohibited it along with football and other sports that supposedly interfered with the military useful practice of archery. Yet royal antipathy soon changed to enthusiasm. In the first decade of the sixteenth century King James IV ordered golf balls and clubs by the dozens; his daughter, Mary Queen of Scots, also played, as did many of her more affluent subjects. Following the Calvinist Reformation, Kirk sessions in St. Andrews, Perth, and Edinburgh regularly railed against golfers who illegally appeared on the links during the "time of preaching." Sunday morning golf is as old as the game itself.

Still clubbing the ball toward a post or tree instead of a hole in the ground, Dutch burghers pursued their own version of golf *(kolven)*. Because of much commercial interchange between Scotland and the Netherlands, however, the disparate styles tended to merge in the late-sixteenth century, with the Scottish style proving to be dominant. All the while, Englishmen remained indifferent to golf. Although one of the wives of Henry VIII once noted that the king's friends were "busy with the golf, for they take it for pastime," the game held little attraction for Englishmen until King James VI of Scotland took the English throne in 1603 (as the first Stuart king of England, James I). His attendants, Scottish noblemen all, established their headquarters at Blackheath, a wide expanse of land adjoining London. There they improvised a golf course, and occasionally they were joined by the king for a round of play. Bemused at this foreign importation, English nobles played only in order to ingratiate themselves with their Stuart monarch. Golf remained on the fringe of Renaissance sports, a quaint Scottish custom.

Even more remote and geographically isolated was the Irish game of hurling. From the standpoint of ancient and royal associations, hurling in fact far outshone golf and tennis. Kings and warrior-heroes such as Loingseach, Cuchullain, Finn MacCool, and Diarmuid lived in the annals of Irish legend as men who had proved their worth as hurling champions; the Hill of Tara, a site traditionally associated with Irish kings, harbored memories of many a vigorous hurling match. By the sixteenth century, however, Tara was a part of "the Pale," that area around Dublin inhabited and dominated by Anglo-Irish (primarily of English descent, although born in Ireland) lords who had imposed their "civilized" government and society on Irish natives. The game of hurling had long since passed to the common folk, and it was a favorite pastime of Irishmen to the West and South.

Anglo-Irish governors occasionally forbade "the hurling of the little ball with hooked sticks or staves," but normally stood aside, watched with fascination, and commented upon the rough play and wild runs of Irishmen "hurling to goals." Little did they know that their spectator role was being reenacted on a much grander scale elsewhere in the world. Like Ireland itself, hurling was far removed from the mainstream of Renaissance Europe. Even more distant were various games played by native Indians in the Western hemisphere.

Play Beyond the Pale

The story of the European discovery and early exploration of the Americas is a tale often told, a drama well known. The same restless spirit that prompted men of the Renaissance to redefine man in humanist terms also compelled them to extend the boundaries of the known world. Adventurous, inventive, courageous, greedy seamen stumbled upon continents sparsely populated by peoples altogether different from their own. As they exchanged goods and later engaged in war with native Americans, they encountered strange new forms of government, military tactics, religious practices, and social customs. New sports and games also claimed their attention.

The first adventurers who pushed inland were the Spanish *conquistadores*, led by Hernando Cortes. In what is now Mexico, the Spaniards encountered an Aztec culture with sophisticated calendars, numbering systems, hiero-glyphic writings, grand temples and pyramids, complex social structures, and thriving markets. The Aztecs freely danced, sang, and gambled wildly at board and dice games. Although advanced in material terms, they were ferocious warriors who conquered neighbors at will, took tribute and slaves, and used their captives in ritualistic systems of human sacrifice. They made sport of their fallen foes. Like the Romans, they regularly staged a kind of gladiatorial contest in which captured slaves were required to defend themselves with wooden clubs against expert warriors armed with spears—spears tipped with razor-sharp volcanic glass.

At first glance, a ball game played by the Aztecs seemed a far more refined sport. Teams played in an I-shaped courtyard enclosed by high stone walls. Set near the top of each of the two sidewalls was a stone or wooden ring, vertical to the ground, through which opponents attempted to knock a small, hard rubber ball made from nearby tropical trees. The feat was difficult because players were allowed to hit the ball only with their hips and thighs, not with hands or feet. Padded on their thighs and knees with leather aprons, the contestants threw themselves madly at the ball and onto the stone surface. Serious injuries were common. Yet only the ruling class played, and only priests and aristocrats were allowed to watch the competition. There was more to the game than met the eye.

It was, in fact, an ancient ritual, probably at least a thousand years old when the Spaniards arrived. The ball courts, set beside ceremonial buildings such as priests' quarters and temples, represented the world; the ball symbolized a heavenly body, the sun or the moon. Thus the game was promoted as a ritualistic struggle of light against darkness, life against death, not unlike ancient ball play in faraway Egypt. But the Aztecs gave a unique twist to the outcome of their games. Often the losers were sacrificed to the gods; occasionally even the winners were slain and burned on the high altar.

The Spaniards were horrified. Although their country was the leader (beginning in 1478) of the brutal Inquisition—an attempt to protect the Catholic faith by interrogating, torturing, and sometimes burning Jews, Moslems, and Protestants—wholesale human sacrifice at the hands of "pagan" Aztec priests was intolerable. When the Aztecs fell to Cortes and his troops in 1520–21, the ritualistic ball games were doomed. Cortes took a team of Aztec ball players with him back to Europe, to have them exhibit their skills in the court of Charles V. But all over Mexico the pagan temples were destroyed, and with them, the ball courts.

Spanish explorers in Florida discovered another game. In an open field rather than in an enclosed court, Indians placed a square made of wood strips on a tree or pole about twenty feet high. Opposing teams then attempted to hit the target with a rubber ball. The game was not connected to human sacrifice, so the Spanish left it alone.

French and English explorers, traders, and settlers also discovered numerous sports and games among North American Indians. Competitive running, wrestling, archery, swimming, and canoe racing were highly practical exercises. Several games entailed an elementary manipulation of the weapons of war. A favorite of almost every tribe in North America was a game in which warriors shot an arrow or threw a spear to the spot where they thought a round, rolling stone would stop. In the frozen north Indians played "snowsnake," competitive distant throws of spears, bones, or darts on snow and ice.

The utter simplicity of these games scarcely surprised the earliest explorers who made their way to the wilds of North America. Europeans assumed that the "uncivilized" inhabitants of the New World were simple and fun-loving as well as savage folk, with "diversions as simple as their manners." Such assumptions, however, were called into question when white men encoun-

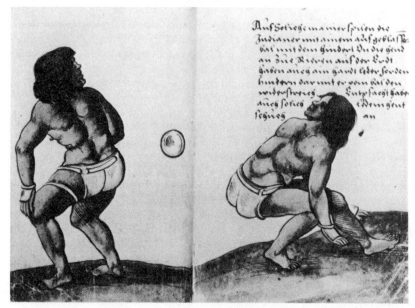

In the Aztec ball game, players controlled the ball mostly with their hips,
without the use of hands or feet. An Augsburg artist, Christoph Weiditz,
made these pen drawings of players before Charles V at Toledo, 1528.

tered Indian ball games that were in many particulars similar to games in the
Old World.

Among the Massachuset, Micmac, Narraganset, and Powhatan tribes of
the Algonquian nation, a game of football was far more "civilized" than the
peasant game played in rural England. In fact, it was a game similar to
modern soccer, in which tackling, tripping, and handling of the ball were
forbidden. "Their goals be a mile long, placed on the sands, which are even
as a board," observed an Englishman in Massachusetts in 1634; "their ball is
no bigger than a hand-ball, which sometimes they mount in the air with their
naked feet." The Algonquians took their game seriously but played without
malice. "They have great meetings of football playing," noted Roger Williams
in Rhode Island in 1643, "only in summer, town against town, upon some
broad sandy shore, free from stones, or upon some soft plot, because of their
naked feet, at which they have great stakings [i.e., bets], but seldom
quarrel." Indian football made English football look barbaric by comparison.

Another game recognizable to Europeans was the game of shinny, played
by virtually every Indian tribe in North America. With a wooden stick curved
at the bottom, both men and women competed in knocking a wooden or
buckskin ball across their opponents' goal line. Upon watching the Powhatan
tribe in Virginia play this game, an early English settler commented that it

was "much like that which [English] boys call bandy." It was also similar to English cambuca, Irish hurling, Scottish shinty, French *jeu de mail*, and Dutch *het kolven*. Stick-and-ball games were common in the Western world, in the Americas as well as Europe. While English and French explorers discovered them throughout North America, even Portuguese settlers in Argentina were finding yet another variation, *cheuca*, among the Araucano Indians.

The most distinctive of all the North American Indian games was rackets, or lacrosse, a ball game played with sticks netted on one end with strips of deer or squirrel skin. In their initial exposure to the game, some Europeans noted that the racket and ball resembled the equipment used in real tennis; but they quickly discovered that the Indian game was team rather than individual play, requiring strength and speed as well as quickness and skill. Aside from the coincidental similarity of equipment, Indian lacrosse was altogether different from the gentlemanly game of tennis. It was the favorite game of the Algonquians and Iroquois in Canada and the Northeast, the Dakotas in the upper Midwest, the Chinook and Salish tribes in the Northwest, and the Muskhogeans in the South. Each tribe, of course, had its own term for the game, but to the west and south Europeans called the game rackets, whereas in the north the term lacrosse was coined by a French Jesuit missionary, who observed that the stick with its small net at the top vaguely resembled a bishop's staff topped by a cross.

Most Indians used one racket, but the southern Cherokee, Choctaw, Muskogee, and Seminole tribes played with a racket in each hand. The object of the game was to pass and run with the ball embedded in the web of the racket, then to hurl it between two poles that served as the opponents' goal. Yet such bare description conceals the profound significance attached to the game by the Indians themselves. Lacrosse was a "little war," a mock military struggle in which warrior athletes tested their courage, endurance, and skill. The game was surrounded with religious ceremonies designed to obtain the favor of the gods who supposedly bestowed health and fertility on victorious tribes. When rival communities squared off on the field, life itself was at stake.

Baffled at the seriousness with which the Indians played their games, most Europeans viewed the ritualistic, warlike character of the games merely as a manifestation of the primitive appetites of an uncivilized people. Had those early invaders of North America known the history of Western civilization, however, they would have recognized their own past in the Indians' present. The ancient union of religious ritual and physical competition had long since evolved by way of classical and medieval activities into the secular sports and games of Renaissance Europe.

Chapter **6**

FROWNING PURITANS

The sun of Italian humanism shone dimly in the Gothic north. As Protestantism swept through Switzerland, Holland, England, Scotland, Scandinavia, and the Germanies, humanism was eclipsed by religious zeal. Particularly in those areas where Calvinist theology and ethical principles became established, old patterns of thought and behavior came under the censorious eye of reformers. Traditional sports and pastimes could scarcely escape scrutiny.

The most aggressive of all Calvin's followers, the English Puritans, sat in judgment not only on ecclesiastical forms and political practices, but also on many of the social customs of the English people. During the late sixteenth and early seventeenth centuries the Puritans railed against various "devilish pastimes." Recreation became a political issue. Finally, when the Puritans came to power in the mid-seventeenth century, they replaced preachment with legislation. Although they ultimately failed, they forced people to reassess the nature and worth of various games and pastimes. In North America as well as England, the age of Puritan prohibitions is an important chapter in the history of sports.

Seeds of Protest

The Renaissance in northern Europe was both later and different from the Italian Renaissance. In Switzerland, Germany, the Netherlands, and Britain, the Renaissance merged with the Protestant Reformation, producing a moral, religious tone in art, literature, and education. Compared to Petrarch and Dante, even Sir Thomas More's scholarship and statecraft, combined with Catholic piety, represented a throwback to the Middle Ages; the gothic style and subject matter of two dissimilar northern painters, Albrecht Dürer and Pieter Breughel, were far removed from the Renaissance world of Boccaccio, Michelangelo, and Da Vinci. Less infatuated with pagan antiquity, most northern humanists were, in fact, Christian humanists.

The Dutch scholar Desiderius Erasmus (1466–1536) is a good example. At the age of twenty he entered a monastery and there wrote an essay *On the Contempt of the World*, in which he asserted a most antihumanist distinction between body and soul: the body was "earthly, wild, slow, mortal, diseased, ignoble," while the soul was "heavenly, subtle, divine, immortal, noble." Erasmus's conclusion was monkish: "And so the happiness of the soul surpasses that of the body." He soon left the monastery and became critical of the monastic escape from the world. His questioning mind, scholarly commitment, and zeal for church reform represented the best in northern humanism. Yet Erasmus also epitomized the persistent religious strain in the Renaissance north of the Alps. For him and his fellow Christian humanists, the New Learning meant not only a love of "the liberal arts," preparation for the military "duties of life," and an acquaintance with "the rudiments of good manners," but also an opportunity to "absorb the seeds of piety."

Those "seeds of piety" were destined to become seeds of protest against sports and games in northern Europe. "We are not concerned with developing athletes," Erasmus once wrote, "but scholars and men competent to affairs, for whom we desire adequate constitution indeed, but not the physique of a Milo." Although his mind was fixed on the classics, Erasmus remained an ascetic at heart. Like most of the leading minds in northern Europe, Catholic as well as Protestant, he scarcely conceived of a harmonious development of body and mind.

Martin Luther was an exception to the rule. Himself a former monk, Luther was nevertheless a man of the soil, a rough-hewn individual who needed no Italian humanist or classical author to inform him that a sound mind and soul functioned best in a sound body. "It is the part of a Christian," Luther insisted, "to take care of his own body for the very purpose that, by its soundness and well-being, he may be enabled to labor, and to acquire and preserve property, for the aid of those who are in want that thus the stronger member may serve the weaker member, and we may be children of God . . . fulfilling the law of Christ." Obviously the religious motive was uppermost in Luther's idea of the physical life. He especially approved of the age-old German game of bowling (kegels), which reminded him of the Christian "knocking the Devil out of his ground."

No spoilsport, Luther urged his followers to pursue "honorable and useful modes of exercise" such as dancing, the "knightly sports" of fencing and archery, and the more physical demanding exercises of wrestling and gymnastics. Unfortunately his vision of the balanced integration of mind, body, and soul soon became fragmented. In the wake of the Reformation, Germans restructured their old burgher (town) and cathedral schools into a new kind of secondary school, the gymnasium, devoted to classical and religious studies and scarcely at all to physical exercise. Luther's point of view notwithstanding, the ancient union of body and mind underwent a divorce in the German gymnasium.

Of all the leaders of the Protestant Reformation who held, at best, an ambivalent attitude toward amusement and games, John Calvin was the most important. A classical scholar trained in the law, Calvin was a stern man with a stern faith. For him, God was sovereign in power and will; man was utterly depraved, destitute of intrinsic worth. Calvin made little distinction between body and soul; both were "thoroughly infected by the poison of sin." Applying his powers of logic and eloquence to the doctrine of the sovereignty of God, Calvin became the outstanding theologian of the Reformation. Because of his basic distrust of human motives, he became the most rigid disciplinarian of all the Reformers. In Geneva, Switzerland, from 1541 to 1564 he attempted to construct a "theocracy," a reign of godliness. Amusements and games took a beating.

In truth, Geneva was a center of debauchery before Calvin's arrival. Wild festivals, sexual looseness, drunkenness, robbery, homicide, and gambling were rife. In the course of twenty years Calvin and his followers banned about two hundred amusements and filled the stocks with public offenders. Knowing that he could not "forbid men all diversions," Calvin gave most attention "to those that are really bad." Prostitution, gambling, drinking, and dancing headed his list, followed closely by those games traditionally associated with gambling. For his educational academy, Calvin provided a weekly period for youthful recreation, but "in such a way that all silly sports be avoided." His definition of "silly sports" was never spelled out. Yet Calvin himself set an example in discrimination. According to contemporaries, he occasionally played at bowls and quoits. Unfortunately, the fine distinctions of the leader were lost on his followers.

Protestants from Germany, France, the Netherlands, Scotland, and England flocked to Calvin's Geneva. Some sought refuge from persecution, others hungered for a "purer" Protestant faith, but all found a confident, forceful mentor eager to dispense his views on the proper Christian creed and conduct. Most believed, as did Scottish reformer John Knox, that Geneva was "the most perfect school of Christ that ever was on earth since the days of the Apostles." English exiles, especially, drank deeply at the Calvinist fount. While about three hundred of their protestant comrades were being executed during the brief Catholic reaction under Mary Tudor ("Bloody Mary," 1554–57), hundreds of English refugees imbibed Calvin's doctrine firsthand and applauded his supervision of morals and manners.

At the accession of Queen Elizabeth, they returned to England zealously determined to win converts to their point of view, to cleanse the Church of England of all remaining vestiges of Catholic doctrine and practice, and to purge English society of its evil ways. Never a majority party in England, the Puritans were nevertheless destined to play havoc within the body politic and to sound a ringing indictment of numerous traditional amusements and pastimes.

Devilish Pastimes

The Puritans were certainly not the first Englishmen eager to curtail popular games. Two centuries earlier a combined effort of monarchs, church officials, and city administrators had, for various practical reasons, sought to stamp out football, quoits, and other peasant games. Early in the sixteenth century Henry VIII banned bowls and tennis for everyone except gentlemen. In 1531 humanist author Sir Thomas Elyot denounced football as a game of "beastly fury and extreme violence." Elyot of course was a spokesman for the courtly tradition, not for the masses. For him football was an exercise that should be "put into perpetual silence."

Yet football survived not only practical and moral assaults but also legal prohibitions. Earlier bans remained on the books, and a grand jury in Elizabethan Middlesex County formally indicted the leaders of a large group of "malefactors" who "assembled themselves unlawfully and played a certain unlawful game called football, by means of which unlawful game there was amongst them a great affray likely to result in homicides and serious accidents." Even the universities banned the game. An Oxford statute of 1555 forbade undergraduates from playing football, and in 1595 the Vice-Chancellor of Cambridge decreed that "the unscholarlike exercise of football and meetings tending to that end [must] henceforth utterly cease."

In the cities, especially, football was considered a disruptive game best prohibited. A London apprentice complained in 1592 that his master would not allow him "one hour for sport": "I must not strike a football in the street, but he will frown." And with good reason. Urban footballers not only interfered with commerce but also destroyed property. In 1608 the town council of Manchester complained that "a company of lewd and disordered persons" annually broke "many men's windows and glass at their pleasures." Threatening imprisonment of law breakers, the council banned the game.

Thus numerous non-Puritan members of the ruling class in England denounced football. James I banned it from his court and warned his son that football was a game "for laming" rather than for "making able" its participants. A common dislike of footballers was one of the few points on which James and the Puritans agreed.

In *The Anatomy of Abuses* (1581), an eloquent Puritan divine, Philip Stubbes, joined the establishment chorus in denouncing football as "a friendly kind of fight [rather] than play or recreation, a bloody and murdering practice [rather] than a fellowly sport or pastime." When he continued to assault football, however, Stubbes set himself apart from its non-Puritan critics. The Puritans objected to football, as they did to most popular sports and games, less from humanitarian, social, or legal motives than from a religious concern. "Any exercise," Stubbes continued, "which withdraws us from godliness, either upon the sabbath or any other day, is wicked, and to be forbidden." A serious, God-fearing people, the Puritans felt themselves chosen (elected) by God, commissioned to glorify God in every thought, word, and deed.

Football, like most recreation, failed the test. Most, in fact, flew in the face of the Puritan ideal of godliness. Virtually every competitive sport and game featured "stake money," a term referring to the stacking of coins beside the pole (stake) in a tennis match. "Honest recreations are meet for honest men, but carding and tennis players are not honest recreations," declared a Puritan

This seventeenth-century print depicts bullbaiting and bearbaiting, two of the popular pastimes opposed by the English Puritans. Notice that the bear seems to be winning the fray.

divine in 1579. It is surprising that his list was so short. The stakes were invariably high in fencing, bowling, cricket, football, wrestling, horse racing, and cockfights. Gambling on the outcome of games made for "profane exercises" in the Puritan's mind.

Gambling was an explicit "sin" calling for denunciation. On a more subtle level, the Puritans opposed the recreational life of the masses of Englishmen because it was geared to a seasonal cycle associated with the old Catholic church calendar. Various saints' days, the twelve days of Christmas, Plough Monday (the first Monday after Twelfth Day), Shrove Tuesday, Easter, May

Day, and Whitsuntide (forty days after Easter)—all were occasions for common folk to play football, stoolball, quoits, and bowls; to engage in dancing, boxing and wrestling matches, and running, jumping, and throwing contests; and to gamble on bull baits, bear baits, and cockfights. Even if the character of these activities had been acceptable, their ancient connection with pagan and Catholic festivities, smacking of popery and priestcraft, made them deplorable to the Puritans.

Of all the factors prompting the Puritans to denounce popular pastimes, their emphasis on a strict observance of the Christian Sabbath was the most prominent. Except for special holidays, Sunday was the only day of the week available for hard-working village folk to play. Traditionally, they went to church on Sunday morning, visited the pub at noon, went home to eat, then congregated on the village green to while away Sunday afternoon in play or idle chatter. To the Puritan, however, the whole of Sunday should have been devoted to private as well as public religious worship, study, and contemplation. "It is a notable abuse of many," lamented a pamphleteer, "to make the Lord's Day a set day of sport and pastime, which should be a day set apart for the worship of God and the increase of the duties of religion." Popular recreation and the misuse of the Sabbath came to be closely associated in the Puritan mind.

Even more closely did they associate traditional pastimes with frivolous delight in "carnal pleasures." In the Puritan equation, the active pursuit of pleasure meant a first step down the path of immorality, away from the portals of Heaven. The "wanton gestures" at May Day and parish festival dances seemed, to the censorious Puritan, to be "the storehouse and nursery of bastardy." One Puritan minister appointed himself the moral monitor of his flock, "testifying against their wakes or feasts, may-games, sports and plays, and shows, which trained up people to vanity and looseness, and led them from the fear of God." Like Calvin, the Puritans held a dark view of human nature; they feared the worst in men, and they usually found it.

Worst of all, sports fostered an idle and undisciplined way of life. For the Puritan, time was precious, work imperative. Play was not an end in itself, as it was for most Englishmen; rather, it was a means to the end of fulfilling one's call to work. Traditional recreations fell into the category of the most damning of all sins, idleness. William Perkins (1560–1602) best summed up the Puritan's indictment of popular sports and games when he denounced lazy and undisciplined folk "such as live by no calling, but spend their time in eating, drinking, sleeping, and sporting."

This Puritan hostility to customary recreations coincided with profound social changes in sixteenth- and seventeenth-century England. The enclosure movement, in which farm lands were fenced in and turned over to sheep grazing, took away many of the open fields on which peasants played their games. More important, enclosures forced villagers to move to new places—to distant farm land yet unaffected, or into towns where they might find work as servants or laborers. The old games had been a part of the fabric of village life, with oral rather than written rules, customary rather than formal ceremonies, all having survived largely unchanged for centuries simply because village life had remained stable. Economic change and population shifts undermined those traditions. The Puritan assault merely hastened the demise of many traditional amusements.

Politics at Play

Theoretically, the Puritan criticism of recreation included not only lower-class football, May Day games, and animal baitings, but also upper-class tennis, horse racing, and hunting. In practice, however, the Puritans were more severe in their opposition to public sports that included large numbers of participants than to private, individualistic sports and games. Aristocrats could easily engage in their activities privately; the pastimes of the masses were, of necessity, public. Thus the common folk felt the heavy hand of Puritan prohibition more keenly.

Those prohibitions also varied geographically. While Londoners continued to enjoy a thriving theater and Sunday sports, the Puritan successors of John Knox in Edinburgh closed the theaters and strictly forbade public play on the Sabbath. In the countryside, especially, the fate of festivals and games depended on the persuasion of local squires and priests. In East Anglia, a region heavily populated by Puritans (whence came Oliver Cromwell), traditional pastimes were severely curtailed.

Local influence was of utmost importance during the first half of the seventeenth century. Under the Tudors (1485–1603), the royal will was law, stamped with parliamentary approval and faithfully enforced in the most remote country village. Tudor monarchs carefully selected, groomed, and rewarded regional officials and local magistrates, thereby establishing a harmonious balance between central, provincial, and local administration. Under the Stuarts (1603 ff.), that cooperation broke down. From Scotland, James I was accustomed to ruling autocratically through court cronies. Parliamentary government irritated him. For James, politics meant simply the unfettered prerogatives of kingship, not the patient art of negotiation and compromise. Moreover, both James and his successor, Charles I, were forever tinged with Roman Catholic tendencies, scarcely a position to inspire confidence in regional and local officials who had heard of the inquisitionlike reign of "Bloody Mary" and lived through the crisis of the Spanish Armada. The situation was ripe for conflict.

Sport was a minor but symbolically central issue in the clash between Stuart monarchs and Puritan reformers. The two games that James brought with him from Scotland, golf and pall mall (a blending of golf and croquet), became exclusive pursuits of an exiled court. Like James's Scottish accent, they merely reminded Englishmen of his foreign roots. Worse still was the impression that his enthusiasm for horse racing made on the Puritans. James established Newmarket as the royal course and encouraged the reorganization of the races at Chester. Both towns soon became notorious centers of gambling and aristocratic frivolity.

Shortly after James moved from Edinburgh to London, an energetic royalist, Robert Dover, purchased an estate in the Cotswolds on the border separating Gloucestershire from Oxfordshire. Dover found that old village games in the Cotswolds had declined badly, largely the result of Puritan opposition. He set out single-handedly to revive them. Annually on Thursday and Friday of Whitsun week he sponsored "Olympick Games," turning over a large tract of his own land to cudgels, wrestling, quintain, leaping, footraces, handball, handling the pike, and pitching the bar and hammer. Even women's smock races were organized, with prizes awarded to all the winners.

Dover had a flair for the dramatic. Dressed in a colorful cloak with a gaudy feather in his hat, he rode about on a white horse, serving as master of ceremonies. He spared no expense. Dances and huge feasts surrounded the competitive events, and in order to attract the aristocracy, Dover staged chess matches, hare hunts, and horse races. Gambling flourished, of course. The entire scene was a defiant rejection of the Puritan point of view. In producing his Cotswold Games, Robert Dover made a political statement.

In 1618 the king took his own swipe at the Puritans. While visiting the county of Lancashire, he was given a petition protesting that local Puritan priests and magistrates were preventing common folk from enjoying their traditional "dancing, playing, and church-ales" on Sundays after church. Shortly thereafter James issued a royal proclamation entitled the *Declaration on Lawful Sports* (popularly known as *The King's Book of Sports*), in which he ordered that "no lawful recreation" should be hindered: "that after the end of divine service our good people be not disturbed . . . or discouraged from any lawful recreation such as dancing, either men or women, archery for men, leaping, vaulting or any other such harmless recreation." Bull baiting, bearbaiting, and bowling were still forbidden to the "commoner and meaner sort of people." But even May Day festivities were to be allowed on Sundays, so long as they represented no "impediment or neglect of Divine Service." The rebuke of the Puritans was thinly veiled.

But they were not easily silenced. Shortly after the death of James I in 1625, Charles I summoned Parliament for a grant to support a foreign expedition, only to have the House of Commons, now heavily Puritan, refuse to consider the king's request until they debated and passed "an Act for Punishing Divers Abuses committed on the Lord's Day, called Sunday." The question of Sunday sports, of course, was only a drop in a huge bucket of disagreement between king and Parliament. Larger issues of foreign policy, economic interests, political procedure, and ecclesiastical polity lay at the heart of the impasse. Yet the sports question epitomized mutual distrust and resentment. In 1633 Charles I had the *Declaration on Lawful Sports* expanded and reissued, decreeing that it should be read from every pulpit in the land. Numerous Puritan priests refused and were expelled from their parishes. One complied, but also read Scripture concerning the holy nature of the "Lord's Day," and concluded: "You have heard read, good people, both the commandment of God and the commandment of man. Obey which you please." Such advice was as seditious as it was courageous.

While the political positions of both the king and his Puritan critics hardened and became virtually irreconcilable, a quaint little volume entitled

Annalia Hubrensia appeared in 1636. It was a compilation of poems, anagrams, epigrams, and acrostics, the work of thirty-three different authors (including the poets Ben Johnson and Michael Drayton) extolling Robert Dover's Cotswold Games,

> That dost in these dull iron times revive
> The Golden Age's Glories.

In the final poem Dover himself defended his program of "innocent pastimes" against the Puritan accusation that it was "a wicked, horrid sin." Yet one contributor lamented that sports and games for the masses were being replaced by lectures and sermons. Traditional forms of recreation were "so reproved, traduced, condemned for vices, profane and heathenish, that now few dare set them afoot." Despite the attempt of Robert Dover, most pastimes were:

> Declined, if not deserted, so that now
> All public merriments, I know not how,
> Are questioned for their lawfulness.

The Puritan tide was approaching flood proportions. For eleven years Charles I refused to summon Parliament, but in 1640 the Puritans returned with a vengeance, impeaching and executing several of the king's leading ministers. In their articles of impeachment against Archbishop William Laud, they accused him of foisting Roman Catholic doctrine and liturgy upon the Church of England and promoting the 1633 edition of the *Declaration on Lawful Sports.* No doubt the Puritans saw a touch of divine retribution in that when Charles I, in 1641, first heard of the uprising in Ireland—one of several crises ultimately to plunge England into civil war—he was playing a round of golf on the links of Leith, near Edinburgh.

Led by Oliver Cromwell to victory in the war, the Puritans proceeded to execute the king and then to establish their own government. Finally they were in a position to abolish the old church festivals and to enforce their opposition to horse racing, cockfighting, bearbaiting, dancing, the stage, gambling, and desecration of the Sabbath. They banned maypoles, abolished Dover's Cotswold Games, and declared null and void the *Declaration on Lawful Sports.* In three successive acts of Parliament (1655–57) they prohibited Sunday amusements. To enforce their program, they divided England and Wales into eleven districts, over which stern army officers served as tax collectors and guardians of public morality.

They were not altogether successful. Maypoles appeared periodically as acts of defiance against Puritan rule. In 1656 some citizens of Maidstone reported boys and men playing football in the main street "to the disquiet and disturbance of the good people of this Commonwealth." Two years later, an official at Westminster School complained that studies were languishing because schoolboys were playing too much at games. Rigid prohibitions apparently provoked outright insubordination. According to one contemporary, in a villge in Essex "when the Book of Common Prayer was read the people did usually go out of church to play at football, and to the alehouse

THE HIGH BORNE PRINCE IAMES DVKE OF YORKE.
borne October : the 33. 3633.

Court tennis was one of the private pastimes that escaped censor by the Puritans. Although the game was in decline, it still attracted royal patrons such as young Prince James, Duke of York, the future King James II of England, shown here in a contemporary etching.

and there continued till they were drunk, and it was no matter if they were hanged."

Predictably, Puritan prohibitions against sports and games were enforced unevenly. Peasant activities such as maypole dances and bearbaits were squashed: They were public spectacles involving large crowds of people. Horse racing and bowling, on the other hand, continued unabated in the privacy of aristocratic estates. Cockfighting, the activity most given to gambling, went on largely untouched behind closed doors.

Even the public pastimes proved to be remarkably resilient. Although the Puritans controlled the government and laws of the land, they were a minority whose rigorous views remained unacceptable to the bulk of the population. Rural laborers continued to live their lives in terms of seasonal cycles, with periodic festivals and games compensating for times of intense labor. Puritanism was too urban in character, too austere, ever to be fully acceptable to that preindustrial society. Puritan prohibitions against sports and games were doomed to fail. In the end, only the Puritan Sunday established itself firmly in the lives of Englishmen, to become sacrosanct, free of sports and public amusements, until the twentieth century.

Puritans Abroad

Two years after King James I issued his *Declaration on Lawful Sports* as a political tract against the Puritans, a small body of discontented Englishmen boarded the *Mayflower* at Plymouth, bound for a new land, where they, not the king, might determine the laws, government, and social customs. The Zion in the wilderness of North America turned out to be an ordeal. Confronted with the barren soil, harsh climate, and physical isolation of Massachusetts, had the Pilgrims not possessed a body of opinion "in detestation of idleness," they would have been forced to create one. Forests had to be cleared, houses built, clothes made and mended, crops planted and harvested, game killed and preserved. With survival at stake, there was little time and less tolerance for laziness or frivolous play.

In their first Thanksgiving celebration, the Pilgrims feasted. But such relaxed moments were rare. Even hunting and fishing were practical necessities, scarcely "sport" in the Old World sense of the term. In New England idleness was deemed sinfully selfish. The General Court of the Massachusetts Bay Colony decreed that "no person, householder or other, shall spend his time idly or unprofitably, under pain of such punishment as the Court shall think meet to inflict." In England the Puritans were similarly outspoken, but they were unable to enforce their views against stubborn peasants and aristocrats. In New England they enforced them with fines, public floggings, and the stocks.

Early colonists in Virginia also found it necessary to stamp out idleness. At Jamestown, founded in 1607 (thirteen years before the Pilgrims landed in Massachusetts), disease, starvation, drought, and fire nearly destroyed the entire population within the first year. Unlike the Pilgrims, who were largely craftsmen, merchants, and peasant farmers, a number of the Virginia settlers were men of leisure from the upper echelons of English society, gentlemen unaccustomed to work. Apparently Captain John Smith's demand that colonists would have to work if they expected to eat was only partially successful. A new arrival at Jamestown in 1611 found the colony near starvation but happily playing bowls on the village green. Soon the governor of Jamestown banned any further bowling and "condemned to the gallery for three years" any citizen negligent of his duty. One of the first acts of the newly formed legislative assembly in 1619 was the banning of dice and card games, accompanied by the pronouncement that habitually idle persons would have to choose between work and the stocks.

Although the stark necessities of frontier life compelled the colonists both of Virginia and New England to take similar stands against idleness and impractical play, there was a fundamental difference. The Jamestown settlers forbade play as a temporary, expedient measure, whereas Pilgrim leaders dumped a heavy bag of moralistic prohibitions on the heads of New England colonists. Behind their ban against playful idleness always lay their views on the Sabbath, an association of sports and games with pagan or Catholic practices, a hatred of gambling, a fear of sexual immorality.

Old pastimes brought from the fields and villages of England had a difficult time surviving in the frigid Puritan atmosphere of New England. On Christmas Day in 1621 Governor William Bradford came across some newly arrived colonists in the streets of Plymouth "at play, openly, some pitching the bar and some at stool-ball, and such-like sports." He voiced his disapproval, but they countered that it was against their conscience to work on Christmas Day. He informed them that it was against *his* conscience to allow them to play. Idleness was not his only concern. His stern stance was directed as much against the recognition of Christmas, that old pagan, Catholic holiday, as against mere play.

Far more than games in the street, youths "dancing and frisking together" distressed the Pilgrim fathers. In their minds such frivolity smacked of the old May Day festivities; sexual indulgence ("bastardy") was one of their prime fears. In 1627 a lively character named Thomas Morton erected an eighty-foot pine pole that served as a maypole at Merry Mount, near Plymouth. He then invited neighboring colonists and Indians to join in the festivities of wine, dance, and song. Horrified, the Puritan governors sent a group of elders to investigate, and they promptly put an end to that "pagan merriment" by cutting down the maypole. Such imports from Stuart England had no place in the "ordering, & preservation & furtherance" of the Puritan theocracy in Massachusetts.

Nor did most of the old games. Early laws in Massachusetts, Rhode Island, and Connecticut banned dice, cards, quoits, bowls, ninepins, "or any other unlawful game in house, yard, garden, or backside." In 1650 even the innocuous game of shuffleboard was forbidden by a Connecticut law. Gambling as well as the frivolous misuse of time lay behind that prohibition. The banning of another game associated with gambling inspired the colonists to alter the game slightly in order to evade the law. With "nine-pin bowls" (skittles) forbidden, some Connecticut settlers merely added a pin and argued with the authorities that their new game of "*ten*-pin bowling" fell outside the prohibitory local ordinance. Thus was invented a distinctive American version of an ancient sport.

Many colonists in New England, in fact, turned a deaf ear to Puritan tirades against sports and games. Even at the height of the Great Migration, 1630–1640, only about one in four immigrants was a church member. The persistent railings of Puritan preachers against idleness, promiscuity, and religious indifference suggest that Puritan principles were as ineffectively enforced as they were zealously proclaimed. Once the colonists were established and securely buffered against cold and hunger, sermons against "idleness" lost their urgency. Ironically, Puritan strictures against sports and games fell most dramatically as a result of several civic occasions and work programs arranged by the Puritans themselves. Lecture days, military training (muster)sessions, election gatherings, house raisings, sheep shearings, log rollings, and husking bees all provided the opportunity for energetic youths to run, jump, wrestle, and play traditional games while their parents performed more serious duties.

Yet pockets of Puritan prohibitions against sports and games, dances and theaters, idleness and immorality, remained intact. The Puritan Sunday, protected by local "Blue Laws" (thus named because of the blue-colored paper on which Sunday activities were regulated in New Haven), was widely accepted and destined to last until the present day. But by the late seventeenth century the Puritan stronghold on old pastimes was broken. In 1686 a visitor to the town of Rowley, Massachusetts, watched "a great game of football" in which the players competed vigorously on a broad sandy beach. Even the most reviled of all the English games had safely made the transatlantic passage. In fact, the game and its players had improved. According to their English observer, the Rowley boys were not "so apt to trip up one another's heels and quarrel, as I have seen 'em in England."

Chapter 7

NEW STANDARDS FOR OLD SPORTS

As time and circumstances diminished negative attitudes toward sports in the American colonies, the Stuart Restoration produced a similar, more dramatic effect on sports and games in eighteenth-century England. Britons rich and poor reacted against the earlier repressive strictures of the Puritans. They enthusiastically returned to old field sports, embraced new water sports, and adapted traditional activities associated with country fairs, churchyards, and village greens to the new realities of town life produced by economic and population changes of the seventeenth century.

English monarchs and aristocrats became the prime patrons of sport, which provided them not only with pleasant diversion but also with occasions for gambling. Out of those gambling interests came a kind of revolution in sporting life. Rules, organization, and clubs flourished under aristocratic patronage, all motivated by the practical impulse to prevent unfair advantage in the placing of bets. Throughout the eighteenth century this quest for order continued, in America as well as England, bringing new standards to many of the old sports in the Western world.

The Restoration of Sports

The Puritan experiment in "godly government" having failed, in 1660 King Charles II returned from continental exile to reestablish the monarchy, the Anglican Church, and customary social activities. Like the theater and literature of the age, popular sports reflected the rough, bawdy life of the Restoration court. According to diarist Samuel Pepys, the king divided his affection between his sport and his mistresses. He was well provided with both.

Rustic customs and festivities thrived. Maypoles reappeared on village greens, often amid a debauched form of dance and revel. Bullbaiting, bearbaits, and dog and cockfights were renewed with a vengeance, degenerating into systematic butchery and wanton cruelty. Cockfights were especially brutal. In 1663 Pepys visited a cockpit in London and observed a "strange variety of people, from Parliament-men . . . to the poorest apprentices, bakers, brewers, butchers, draymen, and what not," all "swearing, cursing, and betting" as cocks were maimed or killed.

Traditional competitive games also revived. The old Cotswold Games commenced again, and frequent footraces were arranged in towns. King Charles himself sometimes attended such events, especially in spacious Hyde Park and in his own Windsor Park. In 1681 he and the Duke of Albemarle selected from their staffs of servants teams of twelve men each to engage in a wrestling match on a meadow near Windsor Castle. Heavy bets were laid, and the king's side lost. Then followed a fencing match, but yet again the king lost his stake money. Frustrated, his team challenged their opponents to a football match, only to finish with the same dismal results. King Charles seemed not to mind. According to one observer, "the king seemed highly pleased with the day's diversion."

Nor was he content to remain a mere spectator. In St. James's Park he constructed a new alley for the old Scottish game of pall mall, a site that soon came to be known as "the Mall." An enthusiastic bowler, he directed the drawing up of rules for the game in 1670. Fair play was hardly the issue. Charles was an inveterate gambler, as were most of his contemporaries. Until written rules were introduced, competition at bowls was always shrouded in what one player called "cunning, betting, crafty matching, and basely playing booty." Rules made the betting odds more even.

For most of those games that he played or patronized, the king was merely the most powerful and famous of a great number of sportsmen. Certainly bowls were enormously popular. Greens and alleys adjacent to taverns not only ensured good business but also made the game accessible to the masses. Aristocrats still kept their private alleys, but by 1700 enthusiasm for the game had reverted largely to the peasants and shopkeepers, with whom it had originated in the Middle Ages.

Tennis took an altogether different direction. Solidly associated with aristocratic opulence and vice, tennis waned in popularity throughout the seventeenth century. Even in France, its birthplace, the game declined so badly that by 1700 there were only ten tennis courts still in use in Paris, all of them run down. Yet Charles II momentarily revived the game in England. He had a new court built at Whitehall and flung open the doors to spectators. He basked in the crowd's adulation of his skills with the racket, but in fact he was an inconsistent player at best. Pepys observed that "open flattery" of the king was "a loathsome sight, though sometimes indeed, he did play very well, and deserved to be commended." Once Charles played the game so vigorously that he lost four and a half pounds in a single afternoon. Still, tennis remained largely confined to the royal court, and because Charles's successors lacked his ardor for the game, it almost vanished in the eighteenth century.

While restoring many of the traditional English sports and festivities, and briefly reviving the game of tennis, Charles II introduced some activities from the sporting life of the Continent. For ten years he and his royalist friends had lived in exile in Holland, and there on frozen canals they took to the use of a new piece of sporting equipment, iron skates. The English had long been avid ice-skaters on the frozen Thames and on the canals and bogs of the East Anglican fens, on crude brisquet-bones of oxen tied to their boots. The iron skate was a grand improvement, which provided for the "very pretty art" of ice-skating on the new canal in St. James's Park. According to one observer, numerous Londoners in the winter of 1662 enjoyed a "strange and wonderful dexterity . . . after the manner of the Hollanders." Ice-skating divided gentlemen and commoners. Whereas gentle folk skated for grace and poise, commoners strove more for speed and often introduced a competitive race at the end of a day's exercise on ice.

Summer water sports, too, brought the competitive impulses of Stuart Englishmen to the fore. Swimming and rowing races were annual features on the Thames and other rivers. While these impromptu events involved the common folk, Charles II introduced the more expensive sport of yachting. In Holland he had become infatuated with the sporting possibilities of the *jacht*, the Dutch term for cargo and passenger boats in the Low Country. Three months after Charles returned to the throne of England, the city of Amsterdam presented him with the *Mary*, a sixty-six-foot fast-sailing pleasure boat built originally for the Dutch East India Company. Other gifts and purchases provided the king with a personal fleet of speedy, highly maneuverable craft. Soon he began commissioning master craftsmen in England to build his yachts according to his own specifications.

Charles's brother, James, Duke of York (later King James II), was an equally enthusiastic yachtsman. In October 1661, the royal brothers staged a race on the Thames, from Greenwich to Gravesend and back. A wager was in order of course, and each put down one hundred guineas for this first yacht race ever held in Britain's waters. Both men handled their respective helms (in Pepys's words) "like common seamen." Nip-and-tuck for the first half of the race, Charles gradually pulled away on the return leg and stepped from his yacht at Greenwich to the applause of his subjects.

Of all his sporting enterprises, however, horse racing was Charles's first love. Near Windsor he had a private racecourse built, and he imported and bred the finest horses available. Under his patronage Newmarket also became a center of fashionable society. Every spring and autumn he removed his court, including his royal mistresses, to the little market town near Cambridge. Momentarily free of quarreling Parliaments and worries of finance and foreign policy, Charles played his role of horse owner, jockey, and gambler to the hilt. In 1671 he rode his own mount to victory against a field that included his illegitimate son, the Duke of Monmouth. That feat marked the end of an era. Shortly after Charles's death in 1685, professional jockeys began to be employed by owners eager for victory. By 1700 English gentlemen resigned themselves to riding only for transport, relaxation, or fox hunting.

The Quest for Order

The passing of the Stuart monarchy made little immediate difference in the patronage of the English turf. Both William of Orange, king of England from 1688 to 1702, and Queen Anne, 1702–14, were horse lovers. Despite his Dutch Calvinist background, William bet heavily at the track. More circumspect, Anne left her mark as a shrewd, businesslike owner, adding the famous Darley Arabian breed to the Godolphin Arabian and Byerly Turk stock and laying the foundation for the Royal Ascot, a course destined to be the most fashionable in the world. As the Hanoverian monarchs (the Georges) were much less interested in horsing matters, patronage in the eighteenth century passed into the hands of the gentry and titled nobility.

That transition from monarchical to aristocratic control of horse racing in Georgian England worked to the advantage of the sport. Prominent owners began to give form and rules to the turf. Scarcely motivated by any sense of sportsmanship, and certainly not by any enlightened zeal for reform, they were merely protecting their investments. Formal organization provided both predictability for their bets and expansion for potentially greater profits in prize money. In the seventeenth century one sportsman warned against "the knavery of the riders" and "the many subtilties and tricks" used to win races, prompting owners and jockeys to convene before each race to agree on the length of the course, the weights of the mounts, the number of heats, judges, and riding etiquette. By the early eighteenth century those agreements took the form of legal, written documents; by mid-century each course had codified its specific rules, thus removing the necessity of haggling for advantage.

Early in the century professional trainers appeared. The most famous was Tregonwell Frampton, an unscrupulous man who stopped at nothing to please his patrons with victory. His headquarters were at Newmarket; his patrons were four successive monarchs: William III, Anne, George I, and George II. By the time of his death in 1727, Frampton had amassed a small fortune from his hefty salary and wise wagers. More important, his efforts convinced horse owners that the key to success lay far more in the trainer than in the jockey.

The Jockey Club, created around 1750, was a grand misnomer. It was an organization of owners and breeders, all rich and many titled, who first agreed in a London coffeehouse to pool their efforts in governing the races at Newmarket. Heavily aristocratic, they soon exerted their influence throughout the horse-racing scene. They laid down rules of dress and behavior for jockeys; they appointed judges, starters, clerks, and other racing officials; they exacted penalties for offenders. In an age when Parliament, Church, and aristocratic manners were notoriously unreformed, those gentlemen running the Jockey Club were remarkably reform-minded. Yet there was no contradiction. While they controlled their rotten boroughs, manipulated church ap-

Several distinctive features of cricket in the eighteenth century can be seen in this contemporary sketch. The bats are slightly curved at the end, the bowler delivers the ball underarm, and the wicket is constructed of only two sticks stuck in the ground. Notice the scorekeeper sitting on the ground to the right of the batsman.

pointments, and persisted in their rustic, crude ways, aristocratic sportsmen brought reason and order to bear on the turf because it was in their own best interest to do so.

The *Racing Calendar*, first published by James Weatherby around 1770, became their official organ for publicizing rules and regulations, disseminating news of events, and regulating the annual schedule of meets. The schedule was no small item. As early as 1722 no less than 112 towns and cities in England held races regularly; by 1770 that number had greatly increased. Larger country towns arranged their races to coincide with local assizes (courts). By the end of the eighteenth century all the major race grounds in England had been established. The founding in 1766 of Tattersalls, an auction room that originally combined horse trading, clubbishness, and gambling, put the final aristocratic stamp of authority on all matters pertaining to the turf. Order reigned.

Yet the quest for order in eighteenth-century English sports was hardly confined to horse racing. Cricket enthusiasts, too, modified their game, agreed on a set of rules, and formed clubs, which acted as governing bodies.

During the seventeenth century cricket outgrew its peasant roots, attracting gentry and peers who often played alongside plebeians. Only the cockpit rivaled the cricket pitch as a place where the classes mingled. In the eighteenth century gentlemen became keen patrons of the game, often hiring plowmen, bailiffs, and coachmen primarily for their cricket abilities. Commoners were usually assigned the task of bowling, the most strenuous part of cricket.

Like horse racing, cricket matches served as occasions for high-stake gambling. In the spring of 1700 a London newspaper announced a "match at cricket," the best of five games to be played "on Clapham Common near Foxhall on Easter Monday next, for £10 a head each game and £20 the odd one." Organization of the game and codification of its rules proceeded apace. Early in the eighteenth century two gentlemanly umpires, one chosen by each side, officiated at most games. In 1727 some "Articles of Agreement" were drawn up to cover two important matches on which bets were heavy, but in 1744 a more all-embracing set of rules was applied to most all cricket matches. During the second half of the eighteenth century that rudimentary code was revised and expanded several times.

First popular in the rural southern counties of Kent, Sussex, and Hampshire, cricket spread quickly to London, then slowly to the west and north. The first club of any note was founded by a group of aristocratic patrons in the little Hampshire village of Hambledon, around 1750. In 1787, however, the far more powerful Marylebone Cricket Club was founded in London, destined to become the unofficial Mecca of cricket. In the same year a young Yorkshireman, Thomas Lord, arranged for the Marylebone club to play its games on a piece of nearby open land. By the end of the eighteenth century the M.C.C. and Lord's were interchangeably recognized as the administrative heart of the only game in Britain that bridged the gulf between the upper classes and the masses, north and south, town and countryside.

Of a far more limited appeal, golf nevertheless shared with cricket and horse racing the tendency to become organized and governed by written rules. Although the Blackheath Club was formed near London in 1766, golf remained primarily associated with Scotland. In 1744 some Leith golfers set up an annual tournament and formed the Honourable Company of Edinburgh Golfers. Ten years later a similar association, the Royal and Ancient Golf Club, was founded at St. Andrews. For its first tournament, it introduced a set of thirteen simple rules, the earliest written rules of golf. In 1764 the St. Andrews group established eighteen as the standard number of holes making up a round. Earlier there had been no uniformity: Leith originally had only five holes, which were later expanded to seven; the Blackheath links were established on an identical pattern, but a course at Prestwick had twelve holes, and St. Andrews earlier had twenty-two. As new clubs took to the idea that eighteen holes made a proper round of gold, they bore mute witness to the preeminence of the Royal and Ancient Golf Club of St. Andrews.

Still using little leather-covered balls packed with boiled feathers, Scottish golfers in the eighteenth century wielded clubs rough hewn from thorn trees bent by nature. They were an elite, geographically isolated group of men. Yet they, too, brought order and new standards to their game. Otherwise the rapid expansion of golf a century later probably never would have occurred.

Like golf, yachting in the British Isles in the eighteenth century was primarily the preserve of sportsmen in the so-called Celtic fringe. As interest in yachting waned in early Georgian England, wealthy Irish boatsmen took up the cause. In 1720 the Cork Water Club was founded by twenty-five prestigious Anglo-Irishmen, who dressed colorfully and practiced rigid naval formations but avoided competitive sailing. In 1765 they changed their name to the Royal Cork Yacht Club, an organization that still exists as the oldest yacht club in the world. Not until 1775 did a revival of the sport produce a similar club in England: the Cumberland Fleet, named after Henry Frederick, Duke of Cumberland. From that select group, which sponsored "water parties" on the Thames, several name changes and breakaway organizations finally resulted in the exclusive Royal Yacht Club (1820).

The Manly Arts of Self-Defense

Socially far removed from the refinements of yachting, golf, cricket, and horse racing, boxing in eighteenth-century Britain became organized for the first time in modern history. Since the demise of ancient Greek and Roman matches, for centuries spontaneous tests of prowess had been staged at local fairs and religious festivals throughout Europe. Especially popular in the west and north of England, traditional peasant pugilism seemed to be a combination of cockfighting and wrestling. Contestants pummeled and tugged at each other, hit below the belt, gouged with the thumbs, and kicked each other with nailed shoes. Cunning and brute strength determined the winner.

In early eighteenth-century England, however, pugilism became quite separate from wrestling. In London it became associated with swordplay and cudgeling (the two-handed use of a short, heavy stick: a cudgel or quarter-staff) as one of the "manly arts of self-defense." James Figg, an illiterate, unsophisticated young man from Oxfordshire, saw commercial possibilities in sharing his " knowledge on various combats with the foil, backsword, cudgel, and fist" with Londoners. As a self-designated "Master of the Noble Science of Defence," he opened a School of Arms near Oxford Road and exhibited his abilities at the annual Southwark Fair in southeast London. He attracted a large following, including the artist William Hogarth (who designed Figg's business cards), the politician Robert Walpole, the essayist Jonathan Swift, and the poet Alexander Pope. His public matches provided yet another occasion for gambling, prompting the wealthy Earl of Peterborough to support Figg's plans for the construction of a large exhibition hall in the heart of London, with a raised circular stage ("the ring") and seating space for several hundred spectators.

In most of his public appearances Figg only sparred at boxing and demonstrated his skills with the sword and quarterstaff, leaving the more serious fights to his pupils. In 1727, however, he was challenged by Ned Sutton, a

Greenwich pipe-maker. A packed crowd, including King George I and the young Prince of Wales, watched Figg make quick work of his challenger. In the sword duel, he drew first blood with a cut on Sutton's shoulder; in the boxing match, he floored his opponent with a blow above the heart; and with the quarterstaff he shattered Sutton's kneecap. Thus keeping his reputation intact as England's premier fighter, trainer, and promoter, Figg attracted numerous young men to his tutelage. For one, Bob Whittaker, he arranged the first recorded international boxing match, with an Italian challenger by the name of Carni. Early in the match Whittaker was knocked off the stage, but he returned "like a gamecock" to finish his opponent with a punch to the stomach.

At the end of the Whittaker-Carni program, Figg sparred with a promising young pupil from Bristol, Jack Broughton. Shortly thereafter the master retired, a rich man at the age of thirty-six. His success inspired a number of pupils to found academies of their own, but to none of them did the mantle of Figg fall as it did onto the broad shoulders of Jack Broughton. For fifteen years or so Broughton reigned as king of the ring in Britain. Assisted by yet another prominent patron, the Duke of Cumberland, he constructed a vast amphitheater on Oxford Road, near Figg's old smaller hall, effectively driving lesser academies out of business. More important, Broughton divorced boxing from its old alliance with swordplay and cudgeling and introduced the first set of written rules governing pugilistic contests.

Broughton's claim to the title of "the father of scientific boxing" began by way of a tragic accident. In a fierce fight in 1741, he and his opponent shoved, grappled, and struck each other for an interminably long session. Both were exhausted nearly to the point of collapse when Broughton finally finished the bout with a blow beneath the heart. It was a fatal blow. Severely shaken, Broughton swore that he would never fight again. Aristocratic backers talked him out of retirement, but Broughton returned to the ring only with the agreement that a set of rules would "be observed in all battles on the stage" of his amphitheater. Gambling interests lay in the background of that innovation, but ironically the most brutal of all competitive sports in eighteenth-century England arrived at a set of regulations because of humane rather than fiscal concerns.

Few in number, "Broughton's Rules" were revolutionary in character. They forbade hitting below the belt or when a man was down; they barred all wrestling holds beneath the waist; they broke up a bout into rounds, each round ending when a man went down or off the round stage; and they provided a thirty-second rest between rounds before each fighter had to "toe the mark" or "come up to scratch" in the center of the ring to avoid losing the match. Broughton's regulations of course, did not, tamper with the custom of bare-knuckle fighting. Although Broughton introduced gloves ("mufflers") for sparring and exhibitions, they were never used in official bouts. For many years the ring remained a raised circular platform, without ropes. Rounds, obviously uneven in length, could last thirty seconds or thirty minutes. And a fight still ended only when a man was knocked out or threw in the towel. With all their limitations, however, Broughton's rules governed English

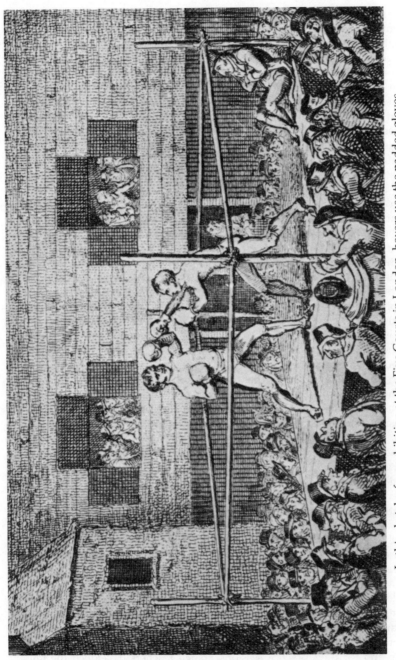

In this sketch of an exhibition at the Five Courts in London, boxers use the padded gloves that were customary only for exhibitions, not regular prize fights. Poles take the place of ropes, and a casual coach or second sits on the apron in the corner to the right. The caricatured spectators provide a comment on the sport. (From Trevor C. Wignall, *The Story of Boxing*, 1924.)

boxing for a hundred years and served as the basis for the London Prize-ring Rules of 1838 and the more sophisticated Queensbury Rules of 1867.

Broughton's ring career came to an unhappy end. In 1750 he unwisely accepted a challenge from a tough butcher of Bristol, Jack Stack, to fight for a large purse. Forty-six years old, Broughton nevertheless neglected to train for the bout. Long having reigned as the master of the ring, he confidently assumed that his ability would compensate for his age against the inexperienced Stack. He was sadly mistaken. Two minutes into the fight, Broughton received a stiff right between the eyes, a temporarily blinding blow. He struggled on but had to stop after fourteen minutes, unable to see his opponent. His patron, the Duke of Cumberland, lost a wager of £10,000. Infuriated, he accused Broughton of throwing the fight. Earlier the Duke had secured for Broughton appointment as Yeoman of the Guard to King George II; now he pushed an act through Parliament barring prizefights. With his amphitheater closed, Broughton went into seclusion. At his death in 1789, however, he was widely acclaimed as one of the great innovators of his day, and he was buried at Westminster Abbey alongside famous poets, soldiers, and kings.

For three decades after Broughton's departure, boxing suffered the double disadvantage of being legally banned and having a string of undistinguished champions. Advertised mostly by word of mouth, bouts continued to be held, usually in open fields. Authorities, bribed by local patrons, looked the other way. But not until the 1790s did skillful champions such as Daniel Mendoza and "Gentleman" John Jackson restore the reputation of the ring. Both followed the earlier examples of Figg and Broughton in setting up boxing schools in London. At the turn of the century no less a famous pupil than the poet Lord Byron looked to Jackson as a "friend and corporal master and pastor." Having flourished, waned, and revived, boxing by 1800 was once again established as a popular spectator sport. The first issue of Pierce Egan's *Boxiana* in 1812 and the founding of the Pugilistic Club in 1814 were evidence of the orderliness that the sport had achieved in the eighteenth century.

While boxing went its separate way, other "manly arts of defence" languished. No longer aligned with pugilism, swordplay and cudgeling lost their attractions for urban Englishmen in the eighteenth century. Only in the countryside did the use of the sword and quarterstaff continue. Fencing virtually vanished altogether in Britain, except in a few southern coastal towns such as Dover. The proximity to France was significant: Frenchmen had replaced the Italians and Spaniards as the fencing masters of Europe.

Even more than pugilism, fencing in the early eighteenth century was still considered both a sport and a means of practical defense. The breeches, stockings, and brocade coats worn at the court of Louis XIV had made the long rapier impractical. By 1700 gentlemen used lighter, shorter court swords to protect their person or honor. Successful defense required practice, of course, and for their practice sessions French teachers developed the foil, similar in size to the court sword but with a blunt point. As bloodletting duels became less common, the foil gradually became the dominant instrument in the making of a courtly sport.

As an elite company of fencing enthusiasts watches, Chevalier d'Eon, the leading fencing instructor of the day, lunges toward his opponent in Henry Angelo's Fencing Academy in London, as depicted in a water color by Thomas Rowlandson, 1791.

In the eighteenth century French fencing masters introduced two major innovations. The first had to do with style, a stance and technique of attack easily recognizable by modern practitioners of the art. Fencers placed themselves in the "on guard" position with the free hand balancing the weight on the rear foot, and with the head well back. They were taught never to aim for the opponent's head; only a hit to the right breast was valid. The attacker had the "right of way" until his movement was thwarted ("parried"), whereupon his opponent launched a counterattack ("riposte").

This technique was designed as much for safety as for grace. The risk of injury to the eyes was always present, a danger only minimized, not eradicated, by the backward tilting of the hand and designation of the breast as the target. A further innovation dealt specifically with this problem. About 1780 a French master named La Boessière invented the mask and required his pupils to use it, thus encouraging more vigorous, complex swordplay without danger of serious injury.

Like other organized sports of the period, fencing was primarily promoted by local clubs. Courtly and aristocratic as it was, however, fencing never evolved a controlling body similar to horse racing's Jockey Club, cricket's Marylebone Cricket Club, or golf's Royal and Ancient Club in Scotland. As the influence of the French language, philosophy, and courtly style spread throughout the upper reaches of European society, fencing styles varied according to each master's eccentricities and indigenous traditions. Yet in its technical innovations, if not in its organization, fencing shared with its sporting contemporaries the orderly, rationalizing tendencies of the age.

Sport in Colonial America

Three thousand miles removed from Europe, settlers along the eastern seaboard of North America applied rules and organization to their sports in a manner remarkably similar to the Old World from which they had emigrated. No less than their countrymen who remained at home, gentlemanly English colonists gambled wildly on sporting contests, especially at horse races and cockfights, and were therefore compelled to bring order to their sports as a means of providing predictability to their bets.

They followed the lead of the mother country in matters of sports as well as dress, manners, and government: "New Market" was a favorite name for race tracks all along the seaboard, from New York to South Carolina, and rules for tracks and the formation of jockey clubs in England prompted similar innovations in the colonies. More important, the task of creating a new civilization in the wilderness—clearing the forests, coming to terms with native Indians, building towns, creating the means of transport and communication, and establishing a stable government—entailed a quest for orderliness and control. The colonists' organization of their sports was merely an extension of their more fundamental need to organize their society in an alien situation.

The geography of colonial sports reflected the varied origins of the settlers. In New Netherlands (soon renamed New York) amusements included summer boat racing, ninepins (skittles), winter sleighing, ice skating, and the distinctive Dutch form of golf. In early New England, Maryland, and Virginia, the old English games of cricket and football were common sights. By 1700 local prohibitions were few, except as they pertained to Sunday sports. Although the descendants of the Puritans in Massachusetts took slowly to the prospect of sports and games, even they ceased making official pronouncements such as the one endorsed in 1716 by Philadelphia Quakers against "such as run races, either on horseback or on foot, laying wagers, or use any gaming or needless and vain sports and pastimes."

Neither puritanical prohibitions nor gentlemanly regulations affected sports in the mountainous back country of Virginia and the Carolinas, where footraces, cudgeling matches, and wrestling contests were the favorite sports of clannish Scotch-Irish settlers. Wrestling matches were so notoriously brutal that the Assembly of Virginia passed several laws against maiming "by gouging, plunking or putting out an eye, biting, kicking or stomping upon" one's opponent. Such restrictions were largely ignored in the backcountry. Late in the eighteenth century an Englishman in the vicinity of Charlottesville witnessed a "boxing match" in which the contestants entered "into an agreement, whether all advantages are allowable, which are biting, gouging, and (if I may so term it) Abelarding each other." An English boxing match, by comparison, was "humanity itself, compared with the Virginian mode of fighting." Geographically isolated, mountain settlers established their own rules, which were few.

The sporting scene in the more "civilized" coastal region of America was altogether different. Royal officials and their subordinates from England filled the posts of colonial governments and brought with them the desire to establish standards for fashionable gentlemanly sports in the New World. Richard Nicolls, governor of New York from 1664 to 1667, is a good example. Largely under his patronage, a racetrack was built in 1670 on Salisbury Plains, the present site of Garden City, attracting spectators and gamblers from all around, especially from Manhattan Island. One of Nicolls's successors, Governor William Burnet (1720–28), was the compleat sportsman. Combining Dutch and English traditions, he bowled, played golf and cricket, fenced, and frequently attended horse races.

Largely because of their different social structure and climate, Virginians and South Carolinians took to the turf with even greater enthusiasm. Wealthy owners of plantations harvesting tobacco in Virginia and rice (and later indigo) in South Carolina had the financial means to promote this expensive sport. Moreover, Southern society was rural, dependent on the horse for transportation, and in need of frequent social gatherings for companionship. A milder climate allowed outdoor sports the year round. As one Virginian noted in 1724, "The Common planters leading easy lives don't much admire labor, or any manly exercise, except horse racing, nor diversion, except cockfighting, in which some greatly delight."

Actually the cockpit, usually connected to the tavern and exclusive of women, never attained full respectability. In some quarters it was avoided because it fostered an uneasy mixing of the classes. The poorest farm laborer or black slave could own and train a cock for combat; certainly the poor sat beside the rich, "jowl to jowl," as spectators at cockfights. Horse racing, on the other hand, was legally and financially reserved as a sport for gentlemen.

During the first half of the eighteenth century the character of horse races changed. Earlier, they were straight sprints for about a quarter of a mile in a field near a church, courthouse, or tavern. Usually the owner wagered and rode his own steed against another owner. By mid-century that amateur sort of spontaneous competition was a thing of the past in the plantation regions. Mile-long oval tracks became the vogue, with the old "quarter-races" consigned to the mountainous backcountry areas of western Virginia, Carolina, Tennessee, and Kentucky. Jockeys, often small but sinewy black slaves, rode the mounts. Informal arrangements gave way to regularly scheduled programs, "subscription" races in which the winner's purse was paid both from membership dues and entry fees.

These changes occurred most rapidly between 1730 and 1750, a period in which the tobacco trade in Virginia and Maryland and rice production in South Carolina boomed. In the 1740s Carolina indigo planters also began reaping huge profits. Apparently those planters applied their organizational skills to their sport as well as business. Certainly their increased affluence allowed them to gamble more heavily, prompting them to protect their bets by bringing order to the turf.

Because of the manner in which they organized their estates, Carolina planters had more leisure time than did their Virginia counterparts. From May to November of each year they moved family and servants to Charleston in order to enjoy the pleasures of the theater, club life, dancing, dinner parties, and the turf. In 1735 a group of those prominent planters joined with wealthy Charleston merchants in creating an informal jockey club to supervise the schedule and regulations of the newly built York Race Course. Soon three new race tracks were built in or near Charleston; after 1743 races were held regularly each month the year round, offering prizes to the winners. Women as well as men frequented the races, thereby adding an air of respectability. The establishment of the elite Carolina Jockey Club in 1758 gave the scene a stamp of authoritative orderliness.

Lacking a metropolitan center the size of Charleston, Virginians turned to their capital, Williamsburg, or to Annapolis, Maryland, where a jockey club was formed in 1745. Mostly they remained on their plantations, with only an occasional foray to a racing town. They put their energies and investments into the raising of thoroughbred studs. Between 1730 and 1774 about fifty English stallions of the select Byerley Turk, Darby Arabian, and Godolphin Arabian lines were imported to Virginia. By the time of the American Revolution, virtually every large plantation in the Tidewater region possessed a stud farm. "Surprising as it may appear," an English visitor wrote home from the Annapolis spring races in 1770, "I assure you there are few meetings in England better attended or where more capital horses are exhibited."

Yet that expansive era was at its end. With the coming of the Revolution, the Continental Congress in 1774 urged colonists to promote economically practical agriculture and industry, and to discourage "horse racing and other expensive diversions and entertainments." The war itself played havoc with the turf. Many fine horses were killed in battle. Loyalist owners of stud farms and racing stables had their property confiscated or destroyed; those loyalists who fled to England sold their racing interests to the highest bidder, usually for a pittance.

The revival of the turf in post-Revolutionary America was marked by some important geographical shifts. In 1788 a new Virginia Jockey Club was founded, not in tiny out-of-the-way Williamsburg, but rather in the more populous, centrally located Richmond, the new capital. In 1802 a Jockey Club was founded and the National Course built in Washington, D.C., obviously to cater to the nation's legislators. Even more important as an indicator of the future shape of horse racing, and of the westward expansion of the youthful nation itself, in 1797 a jockey club was formed in Lexington, Kentucky; in the following year the first circular track west of the Alleghenies was built. The grip of the eastern seaboard had been broken.

Yet the East continued to dominate American life in terms of finance, government, and culture, just as England remained for many years the fount of American economic and cultural growth. A clear-sighted prophet in 1800 might well have foreseen a century of transatlantic interdependence between Great Britain and the United States, a shifting scene in which sports and games reflected features both common and unique to the respective nations. The transatlantic quest for order in traditional sports and games, as in colonial relations, was past; the age of enterprise was at hand.

Chapter 8

THE BIRTH OF MASS LEISURE

Early in the French Revolution, rebellious representatives of the French masses were barred by King Louis XVI from their usual meeting place at Versailles. On 20 June 1789 they assembled at an indoor royal tennis court, where they solemnly agreed not to disband until they had given France a constitution. The "Tennis-Court Oath" set the French Revolution in motion. Given birth in a very old aristocratic place of play, radical new ideas of liberty, equality, and fraternity undermined traditional governments, attitudes, and patterns of life. The French Revolution also unleashed the potent force of nationalism, which was to exert profound influence on sports in the West.

Greater still was the impact of the Industrial Revolution. Beginning with the harnessing of steam and the mechanization of the textile industry in England, the Industrial Revolution altered the social landscape throughout the West. Industrialism created a new kind of citizen (factory worker) in a new kind of society (urban). First in Britain and the United States, then in western Europe, and much later even to the far reaches of Russia, the rapid growth of cities created the need for new housing, sanitation facilities, food supply, transportation, law enforcement, and government. Close on the heels of these practical necessities came the demand for new types of recreation as the Industrial Revolution gave birth to mass leisure.

Nationalistic Sportsman

In the course of the nineteenth century, gymnastics came to be an important part of the program of physical activity for city youths and adults alike. Particularly in urban America, where German and Scandinavian immigrants introduced their various forms of gymnastic exercise, many winter afternoons were spent at rope climbing, on parallel bars, or with groups responding in unison to the directions of a gymnastic instructor.

The gymnastic movement was deeply rooted in eighteenth-century European thought and life. During the age of the Enlightenment, the body became the object of scientific interest. Philosophers and men of medicine turned their attention to questions of anatomy, physiology, health, and human motion. Rousseau's call for men to "return to nature" meant not only delight in mountains, woods, and streams, but also an enthusiastic sense of individualistic physical self-expression. For Rousseau, "our limbs, our senses, and our bodily organs" were "the tools of the intellect." "Would you cultivate your pupil's intelligence," he argued in *Emile*, "cultivate the strength it is meant to control. Give his body constant exercise, make it strong and healthy, in order to make him good and wise."

What Rousseau asserted, others put into practice. German schoolmasters Johann Bernhard Basedow, Gerhard Vieth, and Christian G. Salzmann forged the way in promoting physical exercise as an integral part of their educational programs. Yet another German, Johann Friedrich GutsMuth (1749–1837), is popularly regarded as the "grandfather" of modern physical education. For fifty years he taught and wrote numerous books and pamphlets asserting the importance of games and gymnastic activity in the school curriculum. His seminal *Gymnastics for Youth* (1793) went through several revisions and foreign translations. For decades it was considered the bible of gymnasts.

GutsMuths's program of running, jumping, vaulting, and balancing, along with his apparatus of hanging ladders, climbing masts, rope ladders, and wooden horses, were all duplicated in a private gymnasium in Copenhagen in 1799, the first of its kind, separate from a school, in modern Europe. The creator was Franz Nachtegall; by 1805 he had 150 pupils, adults as well as children. One of those pupils, Per Henrik Ling, was from Sweden. An avid student of Scandinavian languages, literature, and history, Ling returned home to the University of Lund as lecturer in Norse literature and history. He wrote poems and essays extolling the glories of Swedish life. He also served as a fencing master and introduced gymnastics to his university students.

The acknowledged founder of Swedish gymnastics, Ling actually altered the form of exercises he had learned from the writings of GutsMuth and the example of Nachtegall. In his opinion German apparatus was cumbersome and the exercises unnecessarily complicated. Ling favored freer movement "for overcoming awkwardness and stiffness," movements "more easily adaptable to the bodily peculiarities of individuals." Thus he dispensed with the heavier German equipment and devised some new, simpler items. Yet Ling, far more than his German or Danish tutors, promoted group exercise with an entire class following the command of an instructor. His motive was clear: "The execution of gymnastics at the word of command reenforces the effect of strictly military drill." For all their philosophical theory and athletic enthusiasm, the founders of European gymnastics turned their programs over to schemes of military preparation.

In 1804, as Napoleon and his Grand Army raised anxieties throughout Europe, the Danish government appointed Nachtegall the director of a new Military Gymnastic Institute for the training of army officers. Danish gymnastics thus became, and remained for decades, primarily military in character. So did Swedish gymnastics. In 1808 Russian armies conquered the whole of Finland, stripping Sweden of one-third of her territories. A romantic patriot, Ling rushed to his country's defense, offering his gymnastic program as a means of building the moral and physical fiber of Swedish youth. In 1814 he became the director of the Royal Central Institute of Gymnastics in Stockholm, a post he held for the last twenty-five years of his life. Fittingly, his first classes were held in a gymnasium made from an abandoned cannon factory.

Of all the gymnasts caught up in the swirl of historical events in the early nineteenth century, the most important was a German, Friedrich Ludwig Jahn (1778–1852). Generally considered "the father of German gymnastics," he was first and foremost a passionate nationalist, a liberal advocate of personal freedom and political self-government. When the Prussian army met defeat at the hands of Napoleon in 1806, he bowed his head in shame. He took heart from philosopher Johann Gottlieb Fichte's *Addresses to the German Nation,* delivered at Berlin in 1807–8, a ringing affirmation of pride in the heritage, character, and destiny of the German people. Actually there was no German state at the time; "Germany" was a conglomeration of about three hundred sovereign principalities and independent cities, with Prussia the only unit representing any substantial size and strength. Prussia's recent defeat merely underscored for Jahn and his fellow nationalists the need for a unified, independent German state.

For Jahn, the future of Germany lay in her youth; but her youth, he believed, had been stultified by classical education, the pursuit of mental development to the exclusion of physical activity. In 1810 he began teaching in a boys' school in which Wednesdays and Saturday afternoons were given to walks in the countryside with the teachers. Jahn encouraged his boys to run, climb trees, throw sticks and stones at targets, and jump over barriers. Conversant with the considerable body of literature on gymnastics, within the year he transformed these simple, informal activities into a program of exercise on crudely built horizontal bars, climbing poles, ladders, and ropes. All were set on a playground *(Turnplatz)* on the outskirts of Berlin, an area quickly enlarged to include a running track, jumping ditches, parallel bars, vaulting horses, and various climbing devices. Adults turned out in large numbers to watch. Soon they too began to participate.

In 1813 Jahn joined the Prussian army in the War of Liberation against Napoleon, but the *Turnplatz* continued to thrive. Turner (gymnastic) societies sprang up throughout Prussia and in other German states after the publication of Jahn's *German Gymnastics* in 1816. The *Turnvereine* were egalitarian: Jahn urged uniforms to diminish class distinctions. Even more apparent was the patriotic element. Jahn delivered inspirational talks, led group-singing of patriotic songs, scheduled demonstrations on important German holidays, and awarded badges bearing significant dates in German history.

Following the peace settlement at the Congress of Vienna (1814–15), Germany remained divided under the reactionary rule of Prince Clemens von Metternich, an Austrian. Metternich suspected the Turners as a body of potential revolutionaries, particularly when Turners led in forming a new organization of university students, the Burschenschaften, to agitate for liberal and patriotic goals. In 1819 a Turner, Karl Sand, assassinated one of Metternich's cronies. Although Jahn had nothing directly to do with the murder, he was immediately arrested and the Turnvereine was abolished by decree. Jahn remained in jail only briefly, but never again did he actively lead the Turner movement.

Officially banned for twenty years, German gymnastics not only survived, but flourished. Yet they underwent a subtle change. Under a far less liberal, more authoritarian leader, Adolph Spiess, gymnastics in the 1840s were made a part of the Prussian school curriculum. Required, not voluntary, Spiess's program aimed for discipline and obedience in the child, rather than spontaneous, informal exercise. Jahn had been orderly but not rigid. By mid-century his motto of "frisch, frei, frölich, fromm" (bold, free, joyous, and pious) was lost amid regulations. Perhaps the best symbol of the change could be seen in the new physical setting where gymastics were practiced. The open-air Turnplatz was largely abandoned in favor of indoor gymnasiums. When the Turners went indoors, they minimized games, footraces, and leaping, contenting themselves with formal exercises on their apparatus.

That change contributed to the survival of gymnastics in nineteenth-century urban centers, where a large, old downtown building could be converted into a gymnasium easier than an open tract of land could be found. Moreover, indoor gymnasiums provided protection from the wintry blast of snow and ice, thus allowing wholesome exercise the year round for those timid city folk who cared little for outdoor winter sports. Ironically, for all their romantic infatuation with nature, German and Scandinavian founders of the gymnastics movement created a sport peculiarly suited to the artifices of indoor, urban life.

Scarcely adaptable to the indoors, the Highland Games in Scotland were, like continental gymnastics, an early nineteenth-century product of romantic nationalism. Actually they were ancient folk games, banned after the abortive Jacobite uprising of 1745, then revived as a part of the emergence of Scottish nationalism, best represented by the folk literature of Sir Walter Scott. Around the turn of the century numerous local Highland Societies were formed, and in 1832 the "clans" gathered at Braemar for music, dancing, and frolic. Traditional Highland Games formed the core of the festivities: throwing the hammer, putting the stone, tossing the caber, pole vaulting, footraces, jumping contests, and a tug o' war. Novelty events such as sack races, three-legged races, and "wheelbarrow" races added interest to the occasion; kilts, bagpipes, and distinctive brogues provided color. After 1832 the Highland Games at Braemar became a regular fixture on the Scottish calendar of events.

Thus at the outset of the nineteenth century, two distinctive kinds of sporting activities came into being. One essentially new but with vague connections to ancient Greece (gymnastics), the other ancient but revived and standardized (the Highland Games), both were conceived in the womb of romantic nationalism. Both were destined to become badges of ethnic identity for German, Scandinavian, and Scottish immigrants who made their way to the cities of North America.

England's Revolution in Sports and Pastimes

In 1800 England's leading romantic writer and future Poet Laureate, William Wordsworth, noted in the preface to his *Lyrical Ballads* "the increasing accumulation of men in cities, where the uniformity of their occupations produces a craving for extraordinary incident, which the rapid communication of intelligence hourly satisfies." Even to a recluse like Wordsworth, the social effects of the Industrial Revolution were apparent.

In the Midlands and north of England, especially, accessible coal and metals encouraged entrepreneurs to build large factories, transforming former small towns such as Manchester, Birmingham, Sheffield, Bradford, Bolton, and Leeds into sprawling industrial cities. Liverpool, a port city through which raw cotton passed on its way to the mills and returned as finished cloth, similarly mushroomed. Between 1801 and 1851 Manchester grew from 50,000 to almost 400,000, Birmingham from 73,000 to 250,000, and Liverpool from 77,000 to 400,000 inhabitants. The census of 1851 revealed that more people in Britain lived in cities than in the countryside—the first predominantly urban nation in history.

Most of that urban expansion came as a result of migration from rural villages. Forced off the land by enclosures and mechanized competition, farm laborers and domestic craftsmen turned to factory employment. Others voluntarily made their way to the cities seeking work and physical security. Most soon found factory labor and town life tedious, and they sought diversion. In Wordsworth's words, they needed to satisfy "a craving for extraordinary incident." For him, "the rapid communication of intelligence" meant books and museums, lectures and theaters, music and art. But industrial laborers lived on a different plane. In the pubs, not in halls of high culture, they found respite from factory routine and impersonal machines. In addition to food, drink, and good company, in the pubs they found games from the villages of their youth: bowls, billiards, and quoits.

Except for bowls, all these pub sports were indoor activities, played mostly during evening hours with a glass of ale in hand. Outdoor sports and games were at a premium. Open space was simply not available in most industrial towns. In 1833 a Londoner lamented that workers were "expelled from field to field, and deprived of all play-places." But the situation was far worse in northern cities, which had grown with little regard for parks and playgrounds near working-class housing areas. Even when a piece of land became available, a captain of industry inevitably bought and covered it with yet another profit-making factory. Until urban transportation came into being in the second half of the nineteenth century, allowing workers to leave their crowded ghettos to find space and clean air on the outskirts of town, common folk had no fields on which to play even if they could find the time.

Time, or the lack of it, was also a major restriction. The customary twelve to fourteen-hour work day, six days a week, left little time for play. Public sports on Sunday were forbidden by law, and it was just as well: Sundays were necessarily a day of rest, to retrieve one's strength for the workweek ahead. Moreover, the old calendar of religious, seasonal holidays—when villagers traditionally played their outdoor games—underwent a drastic reduction in the new industrial society. By 1834 there were only eight half-day holidays in England. Young boys who worked alongside their fathers in the mills could well complain, as one did to a factory examiner in 1836, that there was "never any time to play."

In addition to the relative absence of time and space was the prohibitory attitude of the ruling classes. Simultaneous with the Industrial Revolution, puritanism revived in the form of the Wesleyan and Evangelical movements. Like the Puritans of old, these morally upright reformers looked on most popular sports and amusements as agents of violence, gambling, and sexual immorality. The Evangelicals led in the suppression of age-old village blood sports such as animal baiting and cockfighting. In the cities, parsons and Bible societies joined forces with employers and police forces to "civilize" the working class, to strip them of their rustic ways and instill in them a sense of decency and discipline. This grinding work ethnic and dismal lack of opportunity to play prompted William Howitt in 1840 to comment on "a mighty revolution" that was taking place "in the sports and pastimes of the common people."

The fate of football, the one game always associated with common people, epitomized the revolution to which Howitt referred. What earlier prohibitions of monarchs, Puritans, and rural magistrates failed to accomplish, urban life almost achieved: the total abolition of the game. Without written rules, the old peasant game varied from village to village according to local tradition. When former farm laborers became factory workers in the city, they had no unifying traditions on which to call. Moreover, the village versions of football required open fields and country lanes. Most important, football crowds were a far greater threat to property and civil order in the cities than they had ever been in the countryside.

At Derby, where football had always thrived, a correspondent to the local newspaper in 1844 referred to it as a "relic of barbarism" that was "wholly inconsistent with the intelligence and the spirit of improvement which now characterize the people of Derby." In the following year the annual match at Derby was prohibited by law. Ironically, while legal ordinances and the more general conditions of urban life removed football from the hands of the common people, it was being adopted and becoming a favorite sport in most of the elite "public" (private) schools of England, by boys tidily removed by distance and protected by ancient walls from the industrial masses.

Physically and legally barred from playing their traditional games, urban workers turned to spectator sports. Despite their rigid, heavy work schedule, they had some time to spare in addition to the eight official half-day holidays and election days. Workers even created their own holiday, "St. Monday," when they refused to go to the factory but instead stayed at home to recover from a weekend drinking spree. Also, there were periods of involuntary leisure, when a downward turn in the economic cycle resulted in workers being temporarily laid off.

Aside from the pub, consolations were few until the second half of the century. Pedestrian (walking or running) contests occasionally provided diversion. Patronized earlier by gentlemen in the countryside, competitors by 1850 were usually sponsored by tavern owners who awarded prizes and placed bets on the races. On most holidays and many St. Mondays, urban workers lined the streets of industrial towns to cheer on their favorites, mostly men from their own class. Respectable citizens looked on the whole affair as a nuisance; from time to time police cracked down with charges of obstruction, trespass, breach of the peace, and vagrancy. But pedestrianism, one of the few sports available in the industrial cities, nevertheless flourished in the first half of the nineteenth century.

So did horse racing, but for different reasons. Patronized and defended by the aristocracy against reformers, horse racing in the 1840s even received the backing of a committee in the House of Lords as a sport "in accordance with a long-established national taste, because it serves to bring together for a common object, vast bodies of people in different parts of the country, and to promote intercourse between different classes of society." In fact, the mingling of the classes was minimal. The turf remained the stronghold of aristocratic patronage and lifestyle, but it attracted the urban proletariat in ever-increasing numbers. By 1850 the spectators at races in Manchester, Newcastle, and Doncaster were predominantly working class.

Rowing was another traditional upper-class sport. The masses of course had nothing to do with the boat clubs founded at Eton, Westminster, and other public schools in the early years of the century, nor with the "bumping races" that began at the two ancient universities, Oxford and Cambridge, in the 1820s. Few laborers witnessed the first Oxford-Cambridge University Boat Race at Henley in 1829, but when the race became an annual event on the Thames after 1839, the number of common folk lining the banks of the river grew each year.

Cricket was the only ball game available for urban workers to watch in the first half of the nineteenth century. They hardly noticed that the game itself was undergoing important changes, such as the side-arm ("round-arm") delivery from the bowler replacing the underarm motion, the invention of leg pads and gloves for batters, and the altering of the bat from a slightly curved end to a straight, flat surface. They merely turned out to watch the games when they could, especially in the 1840s when William Clarke, a cricketer from Nottinghamshire, organized an "All-England XI" to tour the country playing exhibition games against local town and county teams. Yet cricket was much too gentlemanly, too slow and time-consuming, ever to become that popular with working people pressed for time.

Wrestling and boxing matches were much more to their liking. In the 1830s and 1840s wrestlers left the remote counties of Devon, Cornwall, Cumberland, and Westmorland to make their way to the larger industrial cities, where they could reap financial rewards for demonstrating their prowess. Men, women, and children watched the contests, gambled on the outcome,

Engaging in one of the few spectator sports available to city dwellers early in the Industrial Revolution, rowers heave-ho to the cheers from the banks in this pen drawing in G. A. Hutchinson, *Outdoor Games and Recreations*, 1892.

and vicariously participated in the excitement of competition. A staple of village life, wrestling matches in the cities probably reminded adult workers of their simpler youth.

With the abolition of blood sports involving animals, boxing might well have become a substitute spectacle, equally violent and raucous. But as gentlemen had ceased publicly patronizing the ring, boxing was banned by law. Matches nevertheless continued to be held on the outskirts of towns, usually near railway lines, which allowed industrial workers to attend. It was a seedy business, rowdy and heavily male, with vast sums of money wagered. Largely ignored by the press, "champions" of the period were more local than national, mediocre pawns in the hands of gambling interests.

One exception was Tom Sayers, a fisherman and bricklayer from Brighton, who came to ring prominence in the 1850s. Only five feet, eight inches tall and weighing less than 160 pounds, Sayers beat every opponent in sight, all the while promoting himself as a dandy. In 1860 he met his match in John C. Heenan, an Irish-American five inches taller and thirty pounds heavier. Patriotic overtones prompted the press to publicize the match, and a huge crowd of rich and poor showed up near the village of Farnborough for the match. Early in the contest Sayers broke a bone in his right arm, but within the next hour he virtually closed Heenan's left eye with left-handed punches.

For more than two hours the fighters mauled each other. With Sayers near collapse on the ropes, someone cut the ropes, bedlam broke loose, and the referee declared the bout a draw. It was a fitting anticlimax to a period sadly lacking in wholesome pastimes.

The Search for Excitement in Antebellum America

Like traditional English villagers, Americans in the rural South and on the western frontier blended work and play, necessity and pleasure. Living by the seasons rather than the clock, their chopping bees, plowing matches, and husking bees served practical purposes, but at the same time they relieved tedium, overcame isolation, and allowed the display of skill, speed, and endurance. Shooting matches such as "driving the nail," "stuffing the candle," or aiming at more ordinary targets were mere sporting extensions of ordinary life. Certainly horseshoes, similar to the Old World game of quoits, was an amusement directly related to everyday experience.

While rural Americans adapted old games and created new ones to suit their rustic environment, the rapid growth of towns and cities set the stage for an altogether different sporting scene. In 1820 only twelve population centers (all, with the exception of New Orleans, on the eastern seaboard) numbered 10,000 or more; by 1860 no less than 101 claimed 10,000 inhabitants, with eight exceeding the 100,000 mark. Totals unimpressive compared to the huge industrial cities of England, these figures nevertheless represent a dramatic ratio of growth. Inland commercial centers such as Pittsburgh, Cincinnati, Detroit, Cleveland, Louisville, and St. Louis tripled or quadrupled during the first half of the century. By 1860 still only one out of every six Americans lived in cities, but urban growth was as irreversible in its tendency as it was profound in its effect.

Ultimately the effect was similar to the English pattern. Like their British counterparts, urban Americans could not live by work alone. While the unemployed—some newly arrived without jobs, others out of work from necessity or choice—sought the solace of crowds and amusements, factory laborers, business clerks, and shopkeepers also sought recreational relief from their onerous routine. Yet most American cities were essentially different from those in the industrial Midlands and north of England. Except for the factory centers in the Northeast, they were less solidly industrial, more mixed at their economic base. Commerce blended with small, varied industries, all with an eye to meeting the distinctive needs of both the settled East and the expanding West. Moreover, the structure of society in American cities was less fixed, more aggressively fluid. Master-servant, employer-employee relations ceaselessly shifted. In a cash rather than class society, the demand for urban recreation and amusement brought a ready response from entrepreneurs eager to provide goods.

Like upper-class Victorian Englishmen, morally earnest reformers in the northeastern corner of the United States believed that a program of self-improvement was the answer to spare time. Thus they sponsored public

A large crowd cheers the horses Peytona and Fashion in their race for a prize of $20,000 at the Union Course on Long Island, 13 May 1845, from a lithograph by Nathaniel Currier.

libraries and reading groups, and in 1826 founded the Lyceum movement for the support of lectures on artistic, literary, and scientific subjects. The Lyceum system spread rapidly into the Midwest; by 1831 no less than 900 local lyceums were organized under a central agency.

Keenly supported by affluent, respectable citizens, the Lyceum hardly appealed to the masses. Nor did the theater, although it also thrived and attracted all classes of people in growing towns and cities. More geared to the taste of the urban masses were diversions such as variety and minstrel shows, amusement parks, public dance halls, concert saloons, and the circus. With one hand on the public pulse and the other open to be filled with dollar bills, Phineas T. Barnum combined freak shows, acrobatics, riding and tumbling acts, trained animals, and slapstick comedy to give the public what they wanted. Yet they wanted more than mere extravaganza. From 1830 to 1860, especially, urban dwellers turned out in increasingly large numbers to watch several kinds of traditional sporting events.

Except in New England, horse racing flourished in towns and cities throughout the country. In 1830 about fifty major horse races were scheduled regularly; by 1839 the number had jumped to 153. New York, Washington, Louisville, Cincinnati, and New Orleans were the prime centers of turf activity, but even in the booming town of Nashville, President Andrew Jackson, an enthusiastic patron of the track, noted "the greatest concourse of people I ever saw assembled, unless in an army." Three periodicals, John S. Skinner's *American Farmer* and *The American Turf Register and Sporting Magazine*, founded in 1819 and in 1829 respectively, and William T. Porter's *The Spirit of the Times*, begun in 1831, fanned the flame of enthusiasm. Although avoided by upright middle-class folk, the race track in the 1830s enjoyed a heyday.

Two factors conspired quickly to diminish its appeal. The Panic of 1837, a collapse of bank loans, commercial credit, and railway investments, hit the horse-racing industry hard. Facing financial ruin, many wealthy owners closed their stud farms and sold their thoroughbreds. In the 1840s numerous races ceased; by 1850 three out of every four tracks that had operated in 1840 had gone out of business. Yet scarce money was not the only reason for the collapse of horse racing. Trotting races stole the show.

A distinctive American creation, trotting races suited the times. A trotting rig and horse were far less expensive to buy, train, and maintain than was a thoroughbred racehorse. Moreover, trotting races were not so associated with gambling as was horse racing. Respectable middle-class folk could now attend the races without loss of reputation. Sponsors for this new form of entertainment extolled its democratic virtue as a sport "open to every one who keeps a horse for his own driving . . . , the butcher, the baker, or the farmer." It was supposedly as American as apple pie: "Trotting, in America, is the people's sport, the people's pastime, and consequently is, and will be, supported by the people."

Another kind of race supported by urban people was the "pedestrian," or footrace. At first young men competed spontaneously on city streets, with a rider on horseback opening a lane through the crowd. As large numbers of

Trotting (harness) races were a distinctive American creation and a highly popular spectator sport on the eve of the Civil War. A lithograph by Nathaniel Currier captures the action at the Union Course on Long Island, 5 June 1855.

spectators began turning out for the excitement, however, the races were removed to enclosed racetracks, where admission could be charged. Cash prizes were offered the contestants, usually for besting a field of opponents, sometimes for beating the clock. In New York City in 1835 a purse of $1,000 was offered to any man who could run a ten-mile course in less than an hour. Almost 30,000 spectators watched as only one of the nine starters finished the course in time. The crowd applauded wildly as the winner leaped on a horse and rode triumphantly around the track.

Pedestrian races appealed to both sexes and all ages, classes, and colors of people. As a newspaper journalist in New Orleans noted, a fifteen-mile footrace in 1850 "drew together the most miscellaneous crowd of men, women, and children, loafers, wharf rats, Fourierites, Agrarians, gentlemen, niggers, vagabonds, and outside barbarians, that have rejoiced in fresh air and the sight of green fields, since the day when Adam mounted his first pair of breeches!" With no baseball, football, or basketball stars yet on the scene, professional pedestrians were the sports heroes in antebellum America. In a style of showmanship recently practiced by Muhammad Ali, they advertised themselves, taunted their opponents, and challenged each other in a manner conducive to box-office success. Brightly colored shirts and shoes complemented colorful nicknames by which the better runners were known in most of the major cities: "American Deer," "Boston Buck," "Bunker Hill Boy," "Welsh Bantam," and "Worcester Pet." Sport as show biz is no recent development.

Even the most unlikely of all sports for spectator appeal, yachting, attracted a great deal of attention in the press. Since the early days of the century, small-boat sailing and racing had been popular on the Hudson River. In 1844 Commodore John C. Stevens, "the father of American yachting," led in the founding of the exclusive New York Yacht Club. In the following year a regatta was held at Nahant, Massachusetts, and became an annual event. In 1849 the Southern Yacht Club was established near New Orleans. As a stamp of validation on all this upper-class enthusiasm for yachting, Stevens in 1851 won the One Hundred Guineas Cup race in England, sponsored by the Royal Yacht Squadron. In honor of his specially built schooner, the *America*, the New York Yacht Club in 1857 established an annual international race, the America's Cup. Like the American nation, American yachting was coming of age. Yet yachting was an impossible sport for mass participation or spectator appeal. However much the press publicized the sport, races were necessarily held on the open seas or up wide rivers, and yacht clubs were exclusive fraternities of wealthy merchants, businessmen, and manufacturers in seaport towns.

Just as trotting races emerged as a popular offshoot from thoroughbred racing, competitive rowing became the aquatic spectator sport for the masses barred by physical and financial distance from yachting. In the 1830s and 1840s rowing clubs proliferated in New York, Boston, Philadelphia, Baltimore, Charleston, and New Orleans. Colleges and universities followed suit: Yale in 1843, Harvard in 1844, and the University of Pennsylvania in 1854 formed boating clubs, and began intercollegiate competition in the early 1850s. By mid-century the rowing fever had spread north to Portland, Maine, and west to Pittsburgh, Chicago, Milwaukee, and St. Louis.

At first, amateur boat clubs were socially exclusive, like yacht clubs. In the terms of the constitution of the Castle Garden Amateur Boat Club, membership was restricted to "young men of the highest respectability" who would "combine with pleasure the utmost propriety of conduct." But compared to a schooner, a rowing hull was cheap to purchase and maintain, easy to master, and adaptable to short distances on narrow waterways. Unlike yachting, rowing required physical strength and stamina, gifts not reserved to young men of wealth. Especially in those inland towns and cities where the social exclusivity of yacht clubs was not established, men of plebeian origins rowed with and against those of "the highest respectability."

Between 1830 and 1860 rowing races were one of the most popular of all spectator sports in urban America, rivaled only by the professional pedestrian races. As early as 1824 a boat race in New York Harbor attracted about 50,000 spectators, many of whom surrounded the winning crew as they made their way to the Park Theater, where they received a trophy and $1,000 in prize money. For a rowing regatta in 1839 in Newburgh, New York, people crowded into windows, covered the housetops adjacent to the river, and filled sloops and steamboats along the route, straining to get a view of the race. For participants and spectators alike, the sport of rowing attracted a cross section of city life.

Hardly could the same be said for boxing. At the outset of the nineteenth century, American pugilism was dominated by two black champions, Bill

Richmond and Tom Molineaux. In 1810–11 Molineaux twice lost to the British champion, Tom Cribb, the first time only because of an unfair delay after he had Cribb knocked senseless. Within the decade, Molineaux died, alcoholic and penniless. As the antislavery question brought matters of race to the fore, the ring became closed to black fighters, and prizefighting declined in popularity. It was of course a brutal sport. Despite the use of Broughton's Rules, deaths and serious injuries often resulted from bare-knuckle pummelings. In the 1840s, however, many working-class English and Irish immigrants took to the ring in hopes of profit or acclaim. The names of the leading boxers of the period tell the story of immigrant aspirations: James Burke, Sam O'Rourke, "Yankee" Sullivan, John Morrissey, Tom Hyer, and John C. Heenan.

In most American cities local ordinances banned prizefights, forcing boxers, promoters, and spectators to move to a wooded area on the outskirts of town, or across a river or nearby lake. From New York City, for example, spectators regularly boarded steamboats to Staten Island or to Westchester, beyond the reach of the authorities. For a championship fight in 1849, a boatload of militia broke up a gathering on Staten Island, driving them to a distant secluded area on Maryland's Eastern Shore. According to one New York journalist, prizefighting was "one of the most fashionable abominations of our loafer ridden city," but in fact the violent, corrupt, and clandestine character of boxing forbade its becoming a popular, much less respectable, spectator sport.

Exercise in the City

With horse racing in decline and boxing corrupt, the range of spectator sports in antebellum America was pitifully narrow. For the steady stream of migrants from outlying rural areas and the hordes of immigrants from abroad, only trotting, professional footraces, and competitive rowing were available. Little wonder that the masses turned to freak shows for diversion and to the saloons for solace. Nor is one surprised to find that the two most popular participant sports of the period were games originally associated with drinking parlors.

One was ten-pin bowling. By 1840 about 200 bowling alleys were to be found in New York City alone, representing only a slight exaggeration of the game's widespread popularity. As in colonial days, many alleys were located within or adjacent to saloons and taverns. As the more respectable elements of urban society sought amusement and exercise, however, new alleys (often with rules against drinking) were built. Soon the game became a fashionable pastime, for women as well as men. Especially appealing to those urban citizens who led a sedentary life, bowling was a favorite noon-hour amusement of clerks and secretaries.

Until mid-century the length of bowling lanes, the size of balls and pins, and the method of keeping score varied widely from place to place. But even before a standard style and set of rules were established, bowling alleys took on a uniform appearance of polished lanes made of narrow wooden boards, side gutters in which the ball was returned to the bowler, and a young boy stationed above the pit to set up the pins and return the ball. Crowds flocking to such alleys provoked a foreigner to remark in 1849 that of all "species of [participant] sports," bowling was "the national one in America."

Billiards was its only rival. Like bowling, billiards in colonial America was a tavern activity, but by the nineteenth century it appealed to all classes. In the 1820s Charles Francis Adams played it while an undergraduate at Harvard, considering it "the most delightful of all mere amusements." By the 1830s and 1840s many affluent Americans played billiards in their own homes or in private men's clubs. The masses of necessity played in public parlors: all male gatherings, mostly still in taverns where drinking and gambling were rife. Despite (or because of) the sex barrier, billiard rooms were filled during the decade prior to the Civil War. Like professional pedestrians and boxers, professional billiard masters toured the country exhibiting their skills and challenging local talent. In 1859 the first "national championship" tournament was held in Detroit; amid the fashionable audience were even a few ladies.

Yet neither billiards nor bowling could retain its peak of popularity. The reputations of both remained tainted with the smoke-filled liquor rooms of their origins; both remained predominantly male pursuits. More important, neither game was physically vigorous enough to attract city youths seeking an outlet for their animal energies. The future lay with active outdoor recreation untainted with saloon life, games attractive to women as well as men. These were the characteristics of those individual and organized team sports that claimed America's attention after the Civil War.

Post–Civil War developments, however, built on prewar foundations, not the least of which was a movement to provide public parks and playing fields in the cities. Before the mid-nineteenth century Boston and Philadelphia were the only major cities with open space available to their citizens. In 1850 the Massachusetts Medical Society issued a clarion call for public parks: "Open spaces would afford to the artisan and the poorer classes the advantages of fresh air and exercise, in their occasional hours of leisure." Confined to what Edward Everett called "tasteless and soulless dissipations which are called amusements," urban Americans were notoriously gaunt and physically unfit. Yankee intellectuals such as Thomas Wentworth Higginson and Oliver Wendell Holmes repeatedly lamented the state of "stiff-jointed, soft-muscled, paste-complexioned youth," middle class and poor alike. Public playing fields promised to better the situation.

In the 1850s New Haven, Hartford, Providence, Brooklyn, Baltimore, Cincinnatti, St. Louis, New Orleans, and San Francisco all created public parks. In 1858 Frederick Law Olmsted's design for a fifty-acre Central Park in New York City was accepted, not merely as an enlightened provision of recreational space but also "as a necessary sanitary provision" and "as a great preventative of crime and vice." Whatever the mixed motive of health and social control, the mid-century public park movement encouraged crowded tenement dwellers to turn out to walk, picnic, hold footraces, kick footballs, play cricket and baseball games, and ice-skate in winter.

Two immigrant groups especially benefited from this increase in the availability of space in the cities. In 1836 some immigrant Scotsmen gathered at the Elysian Fields in Hoboken, New Jersey, "to renew the sports of their native land." The old Highland Games in the United States took on the name of the Caledonian (Scottish) Games. In the 1850s Caledonian Clubs were formed in Boston, New York, Philadelphia, and Newark, all sponsoring annual festive gatherings of music, dance, and athletic contests. In 1858 the New York club charged twenty-five cents admission to the games. The turnout was so large that they doubled the price the next year. As the sympathetic editor of a New York newspaper commented, "These are the kind of manly pastimes that give not only health and vigor to the frame, but place a large share of contentment in the mind, and make men fond of the soil on which they are enjoyed." Like so many of the sports in nineteenth-century America, the Caledonian Games combined exercise, spectator pleasures, reminiscences of the Old Country from which the games came, and patriotic adaptation of the immigrants' new life in America.

German gymnastics also fit that pattern. Introduced in Massachusetts during the 1820s by three German exiles, Karl Beck, Karl Frollen, and Franz Lieber, elaborate apparatus for running, vaulting, and climbing was first set up out of doors. True to the tradition of "Father Jahn," gymnastics before the Civil War were more often playground than indoor activities. Non-Germans watched with fascination. Although some participated, the American Turners remained heavily ethnic, particularly after the unsuccessful German revolt of 1848 sent thousands of new refugees to American shores. In virtually every major American city, from Boston to San Francisco, by 1860 about 150 Turner societies represented 10,000 members. Soon gymnastics went indoors and broadened its appeal to people other than German-Americans. But on the eve of the Civil War, it was still very German and largely open-air.

In summary, the birth of mass leisure proved to be painful, and its early growth was awkward and difficult. Of the restricted number of sports available, most catered exclusively to certain ethnic, social, and financial interests. Despite improvements, limitations on free time and available space persisted. Not until the second half of the nineteenth century did mass leisure grow into robust maturity.

PART THREE

Teams Take the Field: The Emergence of Team Sports in the Nineteenth Century

The French painter Eugène Delacroix captured the spirit of the nineteenth century in his romantic *Liberty Leading the People*. Liberty is a woman of goddess proportions. The People range from affluent middle class to the laboring poor, from the young to the very old. All appear confident but determined. All are militantly moving forward to claim the rights of full citizenship. They are people for whom the combined effects of industrialization and the French Revolution have broken the grip long held on European society by priests, kings, and aristocrats. For the first time ever, the masses began to concern themselves with politics, economic and social policies, education, and recreational activities of their own choosing.

In sheer numbers the ranks of common folk enlarged dramatically—from about 193 million Europeans in 1800 to 423 million by 1900. Over the course of the century the population of England and Wales alone leaped from 9 million to 32 million. The greatest numerical growth occurred during the second half of the century, when diets and sanitation improved and fewer wars claimed civilian lives. Despite even the frightful losses of the American Civil War, the population of the United States grew from 32 million in 1860 to 75 million in 1900.

Many of those new Americans were immigrants from Europe, people literally on the move seeking better lives for themselves. An average of 400,000 Europeans annually emigrated during the second half of the nineteenth century. More than half took cheap steamship passage to North America; others went mostly to South America and Australia. Yet emigration was only one aspect of the mass movement of people. Exodus from the countryside into the cities, begun early in the Industrial Revolution, accelerated. By 1900 city dwellers accounted for about three-quarters of all British citizens, more than half of the German population, and just under half of traditionally rural France. Even the United States, with a western frontier still largely unsettled, doubled its urban population within the three decades following the Civil War.

Economic opportunity was by no means the sole magnet drawing people from the countryside. Cities offered variety, excitement, and anonymity. But freedom from the restrictions of rural family and village life soon proved to be a mixed blessing. The cost of urban independence was a loss of ties that came from shared assumptions and common experience. City schools, churches, social and civic groups, and labor unions satisfied some of the need to be part of a well-defined community. Sports clubs and teams served similar functions. Sponsored by clubs, schools, and universities, numerous new team sports became organized as antidotes to the individualistic tendencies of modern city life.

Team sports also reflected the nationalistic, patriotic tendencies of the age. Individuals found a sense of self-importance as parts of a larger whole—a nation, club, or team. As one youngster in the novel *Tom Brown's Schooldays* (1857) said of the team game of cricket, "The discipline and reliance in one another which it teaches is so valuable, I think. It ought to be an unselfish game. It merges the individual in the eleven; he doesn't play that he may win, but that his side may." Tom Brown heartily agreed: "That's very true and that's why football and cricket, now one comes to think of it, are such much better games than fives or hare and hounds, or any others where the object is to come in first or to win for oneself and not that one's side may win." Although individual sports also became highly organized in the second half of the nineteenth century, team sports peculiarly suited the temper of the times.

Moreover, team sports appealed to city spectators repelled by the brutalities of the prize ring, and bored by the lack of variety offered by footraces, boat races, and horse races. The fast, intricate movements of soccer, rugby, and American football presented a kind of coordinated complexity akin to the character of city life. Spacious cricket and baseball fields, on the other hand, evoked pleasant pastoral images reminiscent of the recent rural past. Seldom absent from the history of sports, spectators in the nineteenth century became a central feature of the sporting scene.

Most modern organized team and individual sports originated in Victorian England, just at the time when the British Empire stretched to the four corners of the earth. Sport as well as commerce followed the flag to distant places such as South Africa, India, New Zealand, and Canada. In a less orderly fashion, British industrial advisers, merchants, sailors, and tourists enthusiastically introduced their sports around the world—to Hungarians as well as Frenchmen, in Russia as well as the United States. Britain's imperial involvement in world affairs facilitated the rapid geographical spread of sports in the late nineteenth century.

In industrialized Britain and the United States, especially, several factors coalesced to encourage sports participation and spectatorship. Rising wages and a shortened workweek (half-day Saturdays at first) allowed laborers to make their way to new parks, playgrounds, and sports fields. City tram systems, first drawn by horses and later by electricity, provided transportation. Cheap train service carried both players and spectators to games in other cities. Newspapers exploited innovative print technology to publicize forthcoming events, and then they gave instant reportage by means of new telegraph and telephone systems. Editors soon discovered that more sports coverage meant higher circulation figures, particularly with the arrival of yet another nineteenth-century invention, photography. By 1900 some sportswriters were pecking away at a new contraption called a typewriter.

Technological advances also played a major role in sports equipment. Tougher iron and steel went into the making of goals for soccer, rugby and American football, ice hockey, and basketball, and for golf clubs, ice skates, bicycle frames, gymnastic equipment, spiked shoes, and face masks, not to mention the construction of sturdy stadiums. Vulcanized rubber provided resilient, air-filled balls of all shapes and sizes and pneumatic tires for bicycles and harness-racing rigs. Mechanical sewing machines turned out uniforms at a pace and low cost never before possible; new synthetic dyes added touches of color to the fabrics. Most important of all, perhaps, was the invention of the incandescent light bulb. By the mid-1880s indoor gymnasiums and sports arenas began scheduling evening prizefights, gymnastic classes, wrestling matches, and pedestrian contests under electric lights rather than by the earlier inadequate, foul-smelling gas lamps and torches. Outdoor night games lay several decades in the future, but by 1900 electric lights had revolutionized the social life of the cities. Amid all the strategic factors affecting sports in the nineteenth century, technology stood tall.

Chapter **9**

VARIETIES OF
FOOTBALL

Of all the team sports that became organized in the nineteenth century, football was the most international in appeal and diverse in form. Nourished in England's prestigious "public" (private) schools, the old plebeian game split into two distinct styles of play. Association (soccer) football featured kicking and controlling the ball with the feet, without the use of hands; rugby football entailed handling as well as kicking, tackling as well as running with the ball. These distinctions emerged slowly, amid much controversy, and in the end appealed to quite different segments of British society. The simpler of the two games, soccer, attracted mass participation and spectator audiences. Especially in the industrial Midlands and northern England, professional soccer became a spectacle of unrivaled popularity. During the last decade of the century, some northern rugby teams also went professional, but the rugby game remained largely a middle-class and aristocratic sport dominated by the elite public schools and universities and their graduates.

Made in Britain, both games were quickly exported. Rugby became established largely in British colonies throughout the Empire, but soccer spread like wildfire in all of Europe and South America. By 1900 soccer football was well on the way to becoming the most internationally popular game in the world. For a brief time it was the dominant campus game in the United States, only to be replaced momentarily by the rugby code, then transformed into a unique American version of football. From the outset the varieties of football were numerous.

Schoolboy Games

While restrictions of space, time, and local ordinances kept common folk from playing their traditional game of football in England's newly industrialized towns, schoolboys at institutions such as Eton, Harrow, Westminster, Winchester, Charterhouse, Shrewsbury, and Rugby made the game their own. Called "public schools" because they had been founded in the distant past as charitable institutions for the education of bright but poor boys, these schools by the turn of the nineteenth century were anything but public. Rich parents happily paid large sums to have their sons exposed to the niceties of Latin and Greek, the advantages of useful connections, and the possibilities of maturation in a loosely structured environment. Life at the public schools was coarse and often brutal. Discipline was lax. Boys mostly governed themselves by means of their own pecking order of authority: older boys bullied newcomers mercilessly. On the playing fields as well as in the dormitories, the future leaders of England learned to exert their personalities and thus to wield power over the younger, weaker, or more timid members of their society.

Games admirably served those purposes. In the early autumn and late spring, boys rowed and played cricket. For the major part of the school year, however, their attention turned to football. Each school, physically isolated from the others, developed its own style and rules of play, usually in accordance with the grounds available. The two London schools, Westminster and Charterhouse, had only long brick-covered cloisters. Their football games therefore featured much pushing and shoving but no tackling; "dribbling" (controlling the ball with the feet) but no long, high kicks; some handling but no passing of the ball. At Winchester, too, rough and constricted grounds dictated a controlled kicking game. A perennially muddy field set in a basin at Harrow made for an even slower game with a large, heavy ball. Slower still was the Eton "Wall Game," played on a field 120 yards long and only 6 yards wide, with a brick wall forming one of the sidelines. About twenty boys on each team shoved, kicked, and clawed for the ball, attempting to propel it to the "goal": a small garden door at one end of the field, an old tree stump at the other. Appropriately, the knotted mass of bodies was called a "bully."

At Rugby School, where more spacious, lush fields were available for play, an altogether different style of football evolved. According to legend, a young Rugbeian named William Webb Ellis in 1823 seized the ball in his hands and ran with it, thus inventing the distinctive game of Rugby football. In truth, that account is misleading. Well before 1823 Rugby boys customarily caught the ball in midair and kicked it back to their opponents, but not until the late 1830s did the running and tackling style of Rugby play become common. In *Tom Brown's Schooldays* (1857), Thomas Hughes penned a famous description of football as he and his Rugby mates played it around 1840. Massive teams struggled in the "scrum," pushing and "hacking" (kicking each other's shins), cracking skulls on skulls, flailing elbows into ribs. Rugby football still had a long way to go before it became a game of dash and spectacular runs.

The headmaster of Rugby School from 1828 to 1842, Dr. Thomas Arnold unintentionally encouraged the distinctive Rugby game. Intent on reforming the old lax and aristocratic nature of the public school, Arnold welcomed sons of professional and business families. He forbade traditional aristocratic field sports such as hunting, shooting, and fishing (which in fact meant poaching from the fields and streams of farmers in the Rugby area), replacing them with team sports. A contemporary headmaster of Shrewsbury School, Samuel Butler, denounced football as a game "more fit for farm boys and labourers than young gentlemen," but at Dr. Arnold's Rugby School football was encouraged as a means of instilling manly virtues. Geographically removed from the other public schools, Rugby boys devised a unique style of "running in" with the ball for a "touchdown." By the early 1840s their game was commonly acknowledged as an odd deviant of the football being played elsewhere.

While Rugby went its own way, Eton schoolboys came up with a new "Field Game" of football. Necessity forced the invention. In 1827 the rough Wall Game at Eton produced a free-for-all, and Eton's officials banned the Wall Game for ten years. Not to be denied their play, Eton schoolboys turned to a nearby open field and invented a wide-open game in which more kicking and running for the ball replaced the old thickly massed "bully." By 1840 Eton, Harrow, and all the other public schools except Rugby played a style of football roughly equivalent to the future soccer game. Yet all these various forms of football were confined to intraschool competition. Not until the 1850s, when a network of railways made travel easy, did teams represent their schools in competition with other schools.

At Oxford and Cambridge, where cricket, rowing, and field hockey were the traditional university sports, chaos reigned when boys turned to the football field. "The result was dire confusion," according to one contemporary, "as every man played the rules he had been accustomed to at his public school." Before each game, captains of the opposing teams had to negotiate the number of men per team, whether or not handling and running with the ball would be allowed, whether hacking and holding were permissible, and on and on. More time was spent negotiating the rules than in playing the game itself.

A codification of the rules was necessary. In 1845 a group of Rugby boys produced the first-ever written rules for football. Three years later a group of fourteen Cambridge undergraduates spent seven hours debating a set of "Cambridge Rules." According to one participant, "the Eton man howled at the Rugby man for handling the ball." Outnumbered Old Rugbeians momentarily had to play a style of game totally different from their schoolboy days. The handwriting was on the wall: Rugby football was simply unacceptable to the majority of footballers in mid-nineteenth-century England. In the 1850s public school and university graduates founded several football clubs in Sheffield and London; except for the Blackheath and Harlequin clubs (London), all played the Eton and Harrow kind of kicking game.

Finally in 1863 the impasse became fixed. While American Union and Confederate armies clashed three thousand miles away, English footballers fought their own serious though less dangerous version of civil war. On 26 October 1863 captains and representatives of several London and suburban clubs met to form the Football Association "for the regulation of the game of football." According to the rules agreed upon by the majority, no player

A crowd rings the field as the scrum-half waits for the ball to emerge from the scrum in this English rugby match. In this sketch from Montague Shearman, *Athletics and Football*, 1889, note the referee in bowler hat, with cane in hand.

could run with the ball. No tripping, hacking, holding, or pushing would be tolerated, and throwing or passing the ball to another player was forbidden. Actually, some handling of the ball was still permissible: "If a player makes a fair catch, he shall be entitled to a free kick, provided he claims it by making a mark with his heel at once." Not until 1870 did the Football Association altogether abolish touching the ball with the hands.

Despite further refinements, however, the year 1863 is a red-letter date in the history of football, for in that year was formed the first national organization and the first set of rules governing the game throughout an entire country. The term Football Association soon became abbreviated to "Assoc.," whence came the word "soccer." Most important, the rules laid down by the Football Association decisively alienated the advocates of the "carrying game," preventing a single, all-inclusive game of football in Britain and the world.

In 1871 the rugby equivalent of the Football Association, the Rugby Football Union, was formed. Two London clubs, Blackheath and Richmond, organized the meeting of twenty-two club representatives. They took only two hours to reach an agreement on the principles and title of their group, which has remained the central authority of rugby football in Britain to the present. Within two months of the formation of the Rugby Football Union, an English team played its first international match against Scotland; during the following decade Irish and Welsh international teams began competing. Similarly prestigious, the annual university match between Oxford and Cambridge began in 1872.

During the 1870s the Rugby Football Union abolished "hacking," reduced the size of teams to the now standard number of fifteen, and began counting points for touchdowns ("tries") as well as field goals. In the 1880s the style of the game changed dramatically, from a sluggish mauling in the scrum to exciting open maneuvers and sharp passes (laterals). Yet the social basis of the game remained the same: respectably middle and upper class. Whereas Dr. Arnold of Rugby granted team sports an important but subordinate role in the inculcation of gentlemanly Christian character, headmasters of late-Victorian public schools turned games into a fetish. With the expansive British Empire beckoning public-school-trained army officers and administrators, Greek verbs and Latin authors paled beside the manly courage that one supposedly learned on the football field. Thus the rugby game remained faithful to its schoolboy, amateur, upper-class roots. Association football took an altogether different turn.

Football Mania

For a time, gentlemen of leisure dominated the Football Association as well as the Rugby Football Union. During the 1870s the two leading soccer figures, first as players and then as officers on the F.A. governing committee, were C. W. Alcock and A. F. Kinnaird. Alcock was a Harrow man, a quick, agile athlete, and an energetic writer who explained and extolled Association football. A red-bearded Old Etonian, Kinnaird was a fierce competitor on the field and a shrewd negotiator on matters of policy; he was a future banker, peer, and Lord High Commissioner of the Church of Scotland.

This upper-class leadership reflected the composition of the dominant teams in the 1870s. In 1872 the first F.A. Cup (championship) was won by the Wanderers, a team totally composed of public school and university men. Between 1872 and 1882 the Wanderers claimed five cups, the Old Etonians two, and other similar "old boy" organizations the remaining four. Yet their days in the limelight were numbered. C. W. Alcock said more than he intended when he observed in the *Football Annual* for 1878: "What was ten or fifteen years ago the recreation of a few has now become the pursuit of thousands." Soon thousands of common people seized the game of soccer football out of the hands of the privileged few and made it their own. During the last quarter of the nineteenth century, soccer became the "people's game."

Increased leisure time, extra spending money, and new public facilities made the takeover possible. Once mid-century legislation limited the working hours of women and children in textile factories, aggressive labor unions set to work on shortening the traditional six-day work week of male adults. By the 1870s most factories, mines, and workshops closed down at noon on Saturday. Simultaneously, wages handsomely increased for most British laborers. New city trams furnished cheap and easy transportation to newly established public parks in town, or to open fields beyond the suburbs. Saturday afternoon became a time of family outings for picnics and games.

Soccer was a game made to order. Compared to rugby football, soccer was a simple game of few rules, requiring little practice, coaching, or study. Cricket was similarly attractive, but cricket required a certain kind of ball, a bat, and wickets. Soccer could be played with any kind of ball, even with a round piece of wood or tin can. Most important, people of all ages, sizes, and abilities could play. Quickness and agility, not brute strength, counted most on the soccer field, but even the slowest and most awkward player could derive pleasure from it. More than any other team sport in Victorian England, soccer was (as one journalist put it) a "democratic game . . . within easy reach of absolutely everyone."

From casual, fun-filled play came organized teams. When the F.A. Cup competition was established in 1871, only fifty clubs belonged to the Association; by 1900 almost 10,000 had joined. Most traced their roots to the 1870s and 1880s. Some, like Burnley, Derby County, Sheffield Wednesday, and Tottenham Hotspur, were offshoots of cricket clubs. Many others originated in churches, local branches of the YMCA, or temperance societies. Both Aston Villa and the Bolton Wanderers originated in 1874 as church teams; from 1875 to 1880 Birmingham City, Everton, Burnley, and Wolverhampton clubs were formed out of similar religious and philanthropic organizations. Local schools also fielded teams, such as the Blackburn Rovers, Leicester City, and Sunderland. The names Stoke City, Manchester United, Arsenal, and West Ham United betray their origins at the hands of industrial workers and labor organizers eager to play. Except for London-based Tottenham Hotspur, Arsenal, and West Ham United, all these new clubs sprang up in the industrial Midlands and northern England, where a massive growth of population had occurred in the nineteenth century.

Southern gentlemanly organizers of the Football Association might well have taken alarm when an obscure club from the Lancashire mill town of Darwen reached the fourth round of eliminations for the F.A. Cup in 1879. Not one of Darwen's players could claim even a white-collar occupation, much less a public-school background. All were young working men from local factories whose incomes were so marginal that they had to solicit public contributions in order to pay their train fares to London for a playoff game against Old Etonians, their social opposites. Unfortunately, the game ended in a draw, 5–5. Darwen returned home, passed the hat once more, and made their way back to London the following week. Perverse were the furies that produced yet another draw, 2–2. Finally on their third expensive trek to London, Darwen succumbed. Yet in defeat they served notice of a new and vigorous working-class participation in the game to the north, beyond the pale of southern refinement.

Four years later the promise was fulfilled. The Cup Final of 1883 pitted the Blackburn Olympics against another team of Old Etonians. Captained by a master plumber, the Blackburn squad included three weavers, a spinner, a dental assistant, a picture framer, and an iron-foundry worker. They beat the upper-class Old Etonians in overtime. The dike was broken, never to be repaired. From 1883 to 1914 northern working-class teams won every F. A. Cup except one. Even the one exception, the Tottenham Hotspurs who won the Cup in 1901, was a team comprised of three Englishmen from the industrial north, five Scotsmen, two Welshmen, and an Irishman.

In the rise of those northern clubs lay the origins of professional soccer. Working-class footballers were simply unable to take time off their jobs to practice and travel unless their expenses were paid. Even expenses were forbidden by the amateur officers of the Football Association, but payments soon went under the table. In semiprofessional fashion northern footballers went from one town to another taking employment for their football as well as for their industrial skills. Scotsmen especially capitalized on this arrangement. Jobs were scarce in Scotland, and Scottish footballers happily crossed the border to sell their services to the highest bidder in northern England. They offered a fast-paced team concept of short, accurate passes, a style vastly different and far more effective than the traditional English pattern of individualistic ball control and field-length "dribbling." Like recent American baseball players in Japan, Scottish footballers were recruited and paid handsomely.

London officers of the Football Association avoided the issue as long as they could. In 1884, however, William Sudell of Preston, whose northern team was in the Cup finals, publicly admitted that he paid not only his players' expenses but also small salaries. While other northern owners and players gave understanding nods, howls of protest arose from southern public-school quarters. F.A. officials threatened to ban the Preston team from further championship play, but Sudell in turn called a meeting of Lancashire clubs to form a breakaway professional organization. Led by C. W. Alcock, the F.A. committee reluctantly backed down. One Old Boy declared that it was "degrading for respectable men to play with professionals"; Alcock countered that it was hardly "immoral to work for a living." Following a long and heated debate, in 1885 the Football Association reached a compromise, whereby separate amateur and professional leagues could operate within the same organization.

The day of competitive amateur soccer, at the national level, was past. One team, the Corinthians, was formed by selecting the best players from all the leading amateur clubs in London, and they survived into the twentieth century as a team of amateurs who could beat most professional squads. But they were exceptional. As a rule, amateur clubs soon found that they could no longer compete successfully with the professionals. Most refused to try; some doggedly persisted, but with dismal success. At the turn of the century public-school amateurs established their own F. A. Amateur Cup, only to languish in mediocrity and low crowd appeal. For soccer excellence and spectator excitement, one had to look to the industrial north, where soccer became a business.

Factory owners, rich with their industrial profits, applied their managerial skills to the game, pumping expanding profits into new stadiums, equipment, uniforms, and salaries. The heavier the investment, the less could they afford to continue in the traditional amateur pattern of scheduling impromptu games during the season leading up to the more orderly Cup playoffs. Thus in 1888 they enthusiastically endorsed a proposal by William McGregor, director of the Aston Villa (Birmingham) club, for a number of professional teams to organize themselves into a Football League for the purpose of regularly scheduling home and away games. Twelve teams joined—six from the northern county of Lancashire, six others from Midlands counties, none from London. Following suit, the Irish League was formed in 1890 and the Scottish League in 1891. Finally, in 1894 teams from London and counties to the south formed the Southern League.

Spectators flocked to the stadiums in droves to see their favorite teams, especially in the industrial cities. Professional soccer matches provided color and excitement for an otherwise drab existence of factory routine and cramped working-class ghettos. Only nightly pubs and music halls competed with Saturday afternoon football for laborers' entertainment. Workers who had recently come to the city from rural villages found a feeling of identity as they gathered and cheered "their" team with their fellow workers. For Cup Finals in London they also traveled *en masse* by train, singing songs, wearing colorful scarves, drinking, and generally delighting in the new-found comradeship. Attendance figures bear witness to the football mania that swept the country toward the end of the nineteenth century. From the 2,000 spectators who watched the first F. A. Cup Final in 1872, the number jumped to 25,000 in 1892, and to more than 110,000 in 1901.

Little wonder that the game attracted working-class players. Not only would they be paid for playing a game they enjoyed; a professional football career also offered a chance of social recognition. In class-structured Victorian England, politics, commerce, and higher education were beyond the reach of sons of mill workers and miners. On the football field, on the other hand, they could compete on even terms regardless of background or wealth, even to the extent of soundly defeating the old upper-class amateur teams.

Yet salaries were low by modern standards. By 1900 the average wage of a professional soccer player was nearly two pounds a week, about the same as a skilled artisan, but the inflated salaries of a few exceptional players hid the fact that younger, lesser known footballers received a pittance for their efforts. Worse still, after professionalism became publicly accepted, owners legislated stern managerial policies. Once a player signed with a club, he was registered on its books by the Football Association, thereby forfeiting his right to bargain for a better contract with any other club until his owner granted an official release. Like American baseball owners with their "reserve clause," professional soccer owners ruled with an iron hand.

In tightening their grip they squeezed the old public-school originators of soccer right out of their places of authority. In the early 1890s rugby football appeared to be headed in a similar direction. Although not as popular as soccer, rugby also appealed to northern working-class communities. Taking a cue from their soccer counterparts, several Yorkshire rugby clubs in 1893 submitted a formal request to the Rugby Football Union that "players be allowed compensation for bona fide loss of time." But rugby officials, incensed at the turn taken by Association football, dug in their heels. In 1894 they declared that professionalism was "contrary to the true interest of the game and its spirit" and announced that "only clubs composed entirely of amateurs shall be eligible for membership" in the R.F.U. At an impasse, twenty representatives of northern rugby clubs gathered at Huddersfield, a mill town situated between the industrial centers of Manchester and Leeds; in August 1895 they formed the Northern Rugby Football Union.

That northern professional branch of rugby football (soon renamed the Rugby Football League, a name that still holds) altered the rules and style of the game to make it faster and more attractive to paying customers. But while amateur rugby continued to thrive in the public schools, the universities, and Old-Boy clubs in London and the southern counties, professional rugby remained provincially isolated in northern industrial towns. At the end of the nineteenth century English football—soccer as well as rugby—accurately reflected a nation socially divided. On just one point did the upper classes and the masses resemble each other. They all fiercely defended and zealously promoted their respective versions of football.

The American Way

American football might well have gone the soccer route. Certainly the first intercollegiate contest, between Princeton and Rutgers in New Brunswick, New Jersey, in 1869, was primarily a kicking game with no holding or tripping allowed. The ball was round and could be punched with the fist, but goals were scored only by propelling the ball between sticks stuck in the ground several yards apart at each end of the field. As several hundred spectators stood along the sidelines or straddled a fence running along one side of the field, Rutgers won the historic match, 6–4, then hosted their rival neighbors at a postgame dinner.

Like Association football in England, the Princeton-Rutgers match represented both a culmination and a compromise of earlier diverse traditions. Since the early years of the nineteenth century, various styles of football had been played in colleges and major cities throughout the Northeast. Competition on college campuses was mostly confined to annual spirited encounters between sophomores and freshmen, with local custom rather than written codes determining the rules of play. Yet a general uniformity prevailed among the activities of Princeton, Rutgers, Columbia, and Yale footballers. All played a soccerlike game. With little disagreement over their respective rules, Yale beat Columbia, 3–0, in 1872 and in the following year lost 3–0 to Princeton. When an Eton team visited New Haven in December 1873, Yale men took to the authentic Association game with ease. They beat their English guests 2–1.

That Eton team did not visit Boston, and it was just as well, for the "Boston game" featured kicking but also allowed holding as well as some handling and carrying of the ball. A local schoolboy game, it was picked up by Harvard undergraduates early in the nineteenth century, providing an annual "Bloody Monday" bash in which freshmen were initiated into the collegiate scene. Like rugby football in England, the Boston game was an odd variant of most football being played in the United States in the early 1870s. But the Boston game achieved something that the rugby code never accomplished. It quickly swallowed up the soccer game, launching American football in a direction radically different from any other game in the world.

Far more important than the Princeton-Rutgers match of 1869 was an encounter between McGill University and Harvard in 1874. A center of English learning and influence in Montreal, McGill played according to the Rugby Union code. Hearing that the Boston game was similar to its own, McGill challenged Harvard to two matches, one to be played in Montreal by Harvard's rules, the other in Cambridge by McGill's rules. Harvard officials refused to allow their undergraduates time off from school to travel so far for such an apparent frivolity, so both games were played in Cambridge. Surprisingly, the Harvard team did well, winning the first game and tying the second. More important, they liked the rougher, more complex rugby version better than their own. Prior to the arrival of the McGill team, the editor of Harvard's campus newspaper berated rugby rules as "wholly unscientific and unsuitable to colleges." After witnessing both games, however, he did an about-face. "Football will be a popular game here in the future," he rightly predicted. "The Rugby game is in much better favor than the somewhat sleepy game now played by our men."

Little Tufts College nearby immediately adopted the rugby code (possibly after seeing the McGill-Harvard game) and beat Harvard at the game in the early summer of 1875. That autumn Harvard and Yale agreed to a set of "concessionary rules," which blended rugby and soccer rules, with the rugby style dominant. For the inaugural match in their century-long rivalry, Yale wore dark trousers, blue shirts, and yellow caps; Harvard took the field in white knee breeches and caps, with crimson shirts and stockings. The game was held in New Haven, and about 2,000 people paid fifty cents apiece to watch the Crimsons beat the Blues. Not for another fifteen years did Harvard top Yale on the football field.

The rugby game overwhelmed soccer on college campuses. Within the year both Columbia and Princeton took up rugby, and on 23 November 1876 some Princeton men invited representatives from Harvard, Yale, and Columbia to join them in Springfield, Massachusetts, to organize an Intercollegiate Football Association. All agreed in general to the rules established by the English Rugby Football Union in 1871, but debate raged over particulars, such as the size of teams and a system of scoring. Yale insisted on teams of eleven, the size of a soccer squad; Harvard, Princeton, and Columbia held out for the more traditional rugby number of fifteen players per team. Everyone assumed that touchdowns should count considerably less than field goals, but Yale and Columbia argued that field goals alone should determine the winner. Harvard and Princeton wanted three touchdowns to equal one goal; the group compromised on a placement or dropkick being worth four touchdowns. Otherwise, English rugby standards prevailed. The old round rubber ball was replaced by an oval, leather-cased one. The length of the game was set at two forty-five-minute halves, and the size of the field was fixed at 140 yards by 70 yards. In the same year that Americans celebrated the

Centennial anniversary of their independence from Great Britain, the nation's leading educational institutions adopted a game that was peculiarly British in form and appeal.

It did not long survive. During the season of 1879, Princeton developed a technique of "guarding the runner" by stationing a man on either side of the person carrying the ball, thereby providing a kind of passive interference. Of dubious legality according to Rugby Union rules, this innovation was a harbinger of much more radical changes to come. They came mostly from the fertile mind of a Yale man, Walter C. Camp. A seventeen-year-old freshman halfback in the first Yale-Harvard game of 1876, Camp was a versatile athlete without peer. For four years as an undergraduate and two as a medical student, he competed at the intercollegiate level in baseball, rowing, swimming, and track and field. Next he mastered the new game of lawn tennis. In the best sense of the word, he was an amateur: a lover of sports for their intrinsic excitement and satisfaction. For a decade or so after graduation he coached Yale's football team, largely on an informal, unpaid basis, while working his way from salesman to the presidency of the New Haven Clock Company. From 1878 until his death in 1925, he was a member of every annual football rules convention. There he won the unrivaled title of "the father of American football." Observant and imaginative, he first conceived and then promoted most of the basic innovations that turned rugby into an American game.

Camp's affiliation with a clock company was a fitting coincidence, for he embarked upon revisions of the rugby game largely because it seemed to him to be disorderly and unpredictable. His earliest proposals for change were relatively minor. As a brash nineteen-year-old member of Yale's delegation to the second annual meeting of the Intercollegiate Football Association in 1878, he argued for the reduction of the size of teams from fifteen to the more manageable number of eleven, a team size long demanded by Yale men. Voted down, Camp returned the following year with the same proposal, plus the unconventional idea that the rugby practice of touching down the ball behind one's goal in order to get a free kick should be counted as a "safety," a score for the defending team. Again his motions were rejected.

Yet Camp's restless, empirical mind was already concocting the first major departure from the rugby game. The scrum, a mass of bodies interlocked at the arms with everyone attempting to heel the ball backwards to a scrum half, seemed to Camp a most chaotic, unreasonable way to deal with the ball after a runner was tackled. An offensive attack was too quickly, fortuitously, thrown on the defensive, preventing well-planned tactics and coordinated momentum. At the annual convention in 1880 Camp submitted his newest and most revolutionary proposal: to replace the mass scrum with a "scrimmage" in which the man tackled with the ball would get to his feet and kick or heel the ball back to a "quarterback," thus allowing prolonged possession and strategic maneuvers.

So thorough was Camp's rationale that the assembly unanimously accepted the change. It also capitulated to his earlier insistence that the size of teams be reduced to eleven men, and then further agreed that the field dimensions should be changed from 140 by 70 yards to 110 by 53 yards. American football was never the same again. In the creation of a "scrimmage," Camp set the American game on its way toward a distinctive "line of scrimmage," a center "snapping" (handing rather than kicking) the ball back to the quarterback, and the first of all backfield alignments, the T formation with two halfbacks. Soon a system of designed "plays," called out in code by the quarterback, became common. Yet the path to the present was not smooth. Innovation created problems that required further changes.

At first the scrimmage was disastrous. Camp envisaged sustained offensive maneuvers the entire length of the field; instead, he got boring possession football. Teams quickly learned that by refraining altogether from the staple ingredient of rugby football, punting for position, they could hold onto the ball interminably and thus prevent their opponents from having the opportunity to score. Camp himself played (as a postgraduate student, which was then permissible) in two of the dullest matches imaginable against Princeton in 1880 and 1881. Both ended in scoreless draws. In the 1881 game Princeton controlled the ball for the entire first half, Yale for the whole of the second half. Spectators and players alike clamored for a solution to this dilemma.

Camp set his mind to the task and came up with yet another fundamental divergence of the American game from its rugby roots: a system of "downs," in which the team possessing the ball had three attempts to advance the ball five yards (or, quaintly, lose ten yards), or turn it over to the other team. The rules convention of 1882 heard, applauded, and accepted this proposal. Five-yard stripes suddenly appeared on football fields. Not until 1906 did the designated five yards get doubled to ten; finally, in 1912 the present system of four downs to gain ten yards became fixed.

Walter Camp's final contribution to the making of American football was a new scoring system, introduced first in 1883 and revised the following year. According to the 1884 agreement, a field goal (dropkick) scored five points, a touchdown four points, a conversion (goal after touchdown) two points, and a safety two points. Until the early years of the twentieth century, the old rugby tradition of placing a premium on the expert kicker remained intact. Yet a basic contradiction existed between the scoring system and the actual style of play. From 1885 to 1905 American football was a mild form of trench warfare, a game of brute force with little finesse. Harvard officials momentarily banned the game in 1884, denouncing it as "brutal, demoralizing to teams and spectators, and extremely dangerous." It was to become far worse before it improved.

Two tactical developments in the 1880s added immeasurably to the roughness of the game. First, the old Princeton technique of "guarding the runner" against tackles from the side evolved into undisguised interference, with the blockers in front of (as well as beside) the ball carrier. From that tactic came another, the infamous "V trick." As in rugby, a man kicking off could either kick the ball deep to the opposition or merely touch the ball lightly with his foot, pick it up, and pass it back to one of his own teammates. From the latter option the V trick emerged as a kind of human wedge, with one man tucked inside just behind the point blocker to receive the toss from the kickoff man. In juggernaut fashion they charged the opposition. In 1892 Harvard added another, rougher, wrinkle: the "flying wedge" was the V trick accelerated. Beginning twenty or thirty yards away, players forming the wedge timed their forward surge to be at full speed when they received the ball. So many injuries resulted from these tactics that they were effectively prohibited by a rule that has survived to the present. In 1894 the rules committee decreed that the ball must travel at least ten yards on the kickoff unless it is touched by an opponent.

Yet brutal formations from scrimmage went unchecked. Ends, tackles, and guards dropped back from the line of scrimmage in order to get a running start at the stationary defense linemen. The "turtleback" and "revolving tandem" formations massed the offensive team in an oval, bent over with the ball carrier in their midst. At the snap of the ball they rolled their oval right or left, trying to spring the runner loose. One of the masterminds who designed these mass assaults was Amos Alonzo Stagg. A Yale player under Walter Camp's tutelage, Stagg coached briefly at little Springfield College (1890–91), then moved to the University of Chicago, where he produced several powerhouse teams over forty years. Although he would later devise new backfield shifts and imaginative pass patterns to open up the game, as a young coach in the 1890s he was constricted by the fashions and rules of his day.

Rule changes in 1896, limiting movement before the ball was in play and requiring at least five men on the line of scrimmage, did not solve the problem. Numerous injuries, a few deaths, and too many slugging matches on the field of play caused several colleges, such as Marquette, to abolish the game. State legislators in Indiana, Nebraska, and Georgia nearly prohibited football by law. The editor of the *Nation* attempted to put the problem in perspective: "The spirit of the American youth, as of the American man, is to win, to 'get there,' by fair means or foul; and the lack of moral scruple which prevades the struggles of the business world meets with temptations equally irresistible in the miniature contests of the football field." The so-called gilded age of late nineteenth-century America was, in fact, an age of conflict. New urban values clashed with traditional rural perspectives; labor challenged capital; West battled East for political dominance. At home and abroad brute force dominated.

Football also had its gilded side. A glamorous spectacle, it attracted ever-increasing crowds of spectators. Only 2,000 people viewed the first Harvard-Yale game in 1875; more than 22,000 cheered Crimson and Blue heroes in 1900. The annual Thanksgiving Day game became the most important event on the collegiate calendar. In 1896 the *Chicago Tribune* estimated that no fewer than 5,000 football games were played on "turkey day." Included in that number were new powers such as the universities of Pennsylvania and Chicago, Cornell, the universities of Michigan, Minnesota, and Wisconsin, and numerous small colleges such as Lafayette, Centre, Carlisle, Transylva-

W.C.Rhodes G.W.Woodruff W.W.Heffelfinger C.O.Gill F.W.Wallace W.T.Bull
A.A.Stagg J.McClung W.C.Wurtenberg W.H.Corbin W.P.Graves
CAPTAIN

This Yale football team of 1888 scored 698 points while holding its opponents scoreless. At the center of the back row is W. W. "Pudge" Heffelfinger, perennial All-American. Note that the team has only eleven players, as no substitutes were allowed. (Courtesy of Yale University.)

nia, Beloit, and Washington and Lee. By the 1890s a number of natural rivalries were already becoming annual events: Army versus Navy, Minnesota versus Wisconsin, and Georgia versus Georgia Tech.

Yet the Big Three remained dominant to the end of the century. Perennial encounters between Harvard, Yale, and Princeton were grand social events as well as athletic contests. On the field, Yale won the laurels. From 1876 through 1900 Yale teams won 231 games, lost 10, and tied 11. In their grandest season of all, the Blues in 1888 outscored their thirteen opponents 698–0, a record that will likely be forever unbroken. Walter Camp, then a sales manager for the New Haven Clock Company, was their spare-time coach. William H. Corbin, a tough center who sported a handlebar moustache, was their captain. At left end was Alonzo Stagg, at the time a divinity student; at right guard was George Woodruff, later a famous, innovative coach who constructed a 65–1 record at the University of Pennsylvania from 1894 to 1898. Most impressive of all, however, was a freshman guard, the legendary William Walter ("Pudge") Heffelfinger.

Heffelfinger was physically large for his day. In 1888 he stood about six feet two inches tall and weighed 190 pounds. The team average was only 163 pounds. In the team photograph of 1888 he towers over his older teammates, and he was still a growing boy. Larger still were his fabled feats. Ferocious blocks and wild-man tackles won him All-American accolades for four consecutive years. Like Paul Bunyan in the lore of northern woodsmen, Pudge Heffelfinger stands larger than life in the annals of early American football. Significantly, he was a rugged lineman, not a flashy back. He and his game were made for each other.

Unlike English soccer and rugby, American football barely had a hint of professionalism before 1900. A few "professional" teams in little Pennsylvania and Ohio towns were in fact semiprofessionals who flexed their muscles in ragtag fashion to earn a few extra dollars for beer money. They represented a backwater, not the mainstream, of the American game. Collegians ruled the day. Despite the violence and ponderous tenor of their game in that era before the creation of the forward pass, theirs was an age of innocence. Team captains, not paid coaches, called the shots. Raw strength and determination, not tricky plays, distinguished Saturday's heroes.

Durable Exports

While restless, imaginative Americans totally revised the rugby game, both rugby and soccer football made their way intact to the far reaches of the globe. Britain's late-Victorian football mania coincided with the great age of empire, when British naval and commercial interests dominated the world. Not surprisingly, the rugby game caught on best in those areas of the British Empire where upper-class army officers and civil servants exerted political and cultural control over native populations. Soccer, on the other hand, mostly thrived in ports frequented by English sailors and in foreign cities where English businessmen, engineers, and artisans lived and worked. Both games proved to be durable exports.

In distant New Zealand, a colony far removed geographically but strikingly similar to Britain in cultural terms, soccer football was introduced by public-school emigrés in the 1860s. In 1870, however, Charles John Munro, the son of the Speaker of New Zealand's House of Representatives, finished his public-school education in England, returned to his home in Nelson, and enthusiastically propagated the game of rugby football that he had come to love. In May 1870 the first football match ever to be held in New Zealand under the rugby code was played in Nelson, and from there the rugby game spread quickly to Wellington, Auckland, Dunedin, Canterbury, and Otago. By 1882 about 78 rugby clubs flourished in New Zealand. Eight years later the number had jumped to 700, partly inspired by the first tour ever conducted by a British international rugby team, composed of English, Scottish, and Welsh players. In 1892 the New Zealand Rugby Football Union was founded.

In another of Britain's "white dominions," South Africa, rugby football was first played by British troops stationed in Cape Town in 1875. Quickly the game became popular among British and Dutch colonists. In Kimberley, in 1889, the South African Rugby Football Board was formed, and in 1891 the

Prime Minister of Cape Colony, Cecil Rhodes, dipped into his diamond fortune to defray the costs of a tour by a British international rugby team in South Africa. Composed of players from England and Scotland, several of whom were graduates of Cambridge University, the British team won all sixteen matches played against South African teams. Yet in defeat the colonists learned better how to play the game from a team representing its place of origin. The elite, upper-class traditions of rugby football were highly attractive to the South African white ruling classes.

British immigrants to Canada began playing rugby football in the early 1870s; otherwise McGill University players could not have introduced the game to impressionable Harvard boys in 1874. Rugby especially flourished in Canadian cities with a strong English flavor, such as Toronto and Kingston, but severe winters hampered play except on the West Coast in the mild Vancouver area, where rugby became a staple club sport. Difficulties of another kind hindered the growth of rugby football in Argentina, the one South American country where the game made any appreciable impact. Introduced by British engineers who were constructing railways near Buenos Aires in the 1880s, rugby clubs became so widespread that the Argentina Rugby Union was formed in 1899. Because of its geographical isolation, however, rugby remained an eccentric pocket of Argentine upper-class play. The masses of South America preferred the simpler game of soccer.

Rugby also fared poorly in Europe. By 1900 a few university student clubs in Germany played the game, as did some resident Englishmen and French students in Paris and the provincial universities. But only in the southwest of France, around Bordeaux, did clubs promote rugby football enthusiastically. In Bayonne it was introduced by a Scottish player, Alfred Russell, who went to Bayonne to study French and stayed to teach rugby. Early in the twentieth century, a French resident of Bayonne visited Wales and brought back the imaginative Welsh style of passing and open-field play. The flair with which French internationals still play the game derives largely from Scottish and Welsh, not English, influence.

Rugby's limited appeal in France, however, accurately reflects its lack of attraction for all of Europe. Most French sports of the era were for the rich and well-bred; rugby football was even more so. It was, according to one contemporary, "the preserve of an elite," whereas soccer was "essentially popular." As in England, the much simpler and inexpensive game, soccer football, took Europe by storm during the last two decades of the nineteenth century.

In a most unlikely place, Switzerland, the first soccer football clubs were established on the Continent. Apparently English boys attending private Swiss schools led in the formation of Le Chatelaine of Geneva in 1869, the St. Gallen Football Club in 1879, and the Grasshoppers of Zurich in 1886. All the while, English sailors, technicians, clerks, and laborers were founding organizations such as the Le Havre Athletic Club (1872), the English Football Club in Copenhagen (1879), and the English Football Club of Dresden (1890). From the Atlantic to the Danube, from the Baltic to the Mediterranean, the spread of soccer football followed a common pattern. Introduced by visiting or resident Englishmen, who largely made up the early organized teams and at first headed the administrative national associations, the game soon developed local roots. Clubs proliferated and Cup competition and touring English teams stimulated spectator interest.

Professionalism soon followed. Austria and Italy are good examples. In the early 1890s a large colony of English expatriates in Vienna formed two clubs, First Vienna and Vienna Cricket and Football Club. In 1894 they began competing against each other in soccer. One of the first native Austrians admitted into the Vienna Cricket and Football Club was Hugo Meisl, destined to be acknowledged as "the father of Austrian soccer" because of his coaching and organizing skills. An English employee of the Thomas Cook Travel Agency in Vienna, a man named Nicholson, became the first president of the Austrian Football Union.

Simultaneous in time and similar in pattern, Italian football began when English residents formed the Genoa Cricket and Football Club and the Palermo Football and Cricket Club in the early 1890s. Both played some cricket but mostly soccer. In 1896 the Genoa club first accepted Italians into membership. Within a year the famous Juventus Football Club was founded in Turin, based largely on the work of Edoardo Bosio, an Italian businessman who commuted frequently to London and returned from each trip with English equipment, knowledge, and enthusiasm for soccer football. In 1898 the Federazione Italiana di Football was formed, providing Italian footballers with a governing body for their game, which was fast becoming popular.

Germans, too, took to soccer football. The first club on record, the English Football Club of Dresden (1890), was obviously composed mostly of emigrant Britons, but within the decade two Schricker brothers and a fellow countryman named Bensemann vigorously promoted the sport. They helped finance a tour of British amateur and professional footballers to Germany in 1899. Two years later they arranged for a German team to play exhibition games in England.

In the larger cities of central Europe the game began to flourish. In the 1890s an emigrant Scotsman, John Dick, who had played professionally for Woolwich Arsenal in London, formed a football club in Prague. Still further afield, some Lancashire textile engineers employed as advisers in a factory near Moscow taught the soccer game to their Russian hosts. Envisaging soccer as an antidote to revolutionary activity among their workers, Russian industrialists welcomed the game. Shortly after the turn of the century, however, both they and Tsarist officials began to fear that private football clubs and unruly crowds might foster rather than prevent political activism. Although popular both as a participant and spectator sport among Russian laborers, soccer football barely survived east of the Urals during the two decades prior to World War I.

South Americans were as enthusiastic as the Russians were ambivalent. Of all the Latin American countries, only Argentina saw soccer refuse to take root in the late nineteenth and early twentieth century. In 1893 English businessmen in Buenos Aires led in the formation of the first national Football Association in the Western Hemisphere, but the popularity of the rugby game relegated soccer to an inferior position until a later mass immigration of Italians swamped the rugby crowd. Yet Argentina was the exception that proved the rule: Englishmen introducing soccer in Latin America everywhere met with an overwhelmingly positive response from native Latins.

Uruguay, destined to be the site of the first World Cup competition in 1930, was first introduced to soccer football by an English professor at Montevideo in the 1880s. In 1891 four British workmen employed by Uruguayan Central Railways formed a cricket club, which in fact played more soccer than cricket, and soon produced one of the most prestigious teams in all of Latin America, Penarol. The Uruguayan Football Association was established in 1900. Simultaneously, soccer seeds quickly took root in Brazil, the future base of the famous Pelé. A Royal Navy squadron played and taught soccer to the residents of Rio de Janeiro in 1884. More important, a son of English parents in São Paulo, Charles Miller, studied in England and returned to Brazil in 1894 with soccer in his blood. He formed several clubs in São Paulo, mostly composed of resident Britons. In 1898 the local Mackenzie College became the first football club to feature native Brazilian talent. By 1900 both São Paulo and Rio de Janeiro sponsored separate leagues. Firmly based in Brazil, Uruguay, and Chile (whose Football Federation was founded in 1895), Latin American soccer catapulted into the twentieth century as the dominant spectator sport in the southern half of the Western Hemisphere.

Soccer in South America and Europe succeeded largely because it encountered no competition from other team sports. Aztec ceremonial ball games, Italian *calcio*, and French *soule* were relics of the past, mostly forgotten. The vast majority of countries did not even have memories of popular ball games. Soccer claimed uncontested territory. In those areas of the world where a lively ball-playing tradition existed prior to the introduction of soccer, however, the story was somewhat different. Football in nineteenth-century Ireland illustrates the point.

Although not as ancient as Ireland's stick-and-ball game of hurling, Gaelic football had a long, vigorous history. In the sixteenth century it was known as "football with the great (large) ball." In the seventeenth century Gaelic football was roughly similar to the old English peasant game in which kicking, handling, running with the ball, and tackling were indiscriminately mixed. By the mid-nineteenth century that rough-and-tumble game was especially popular in rural countries throughout southern and western Ireland. Unlike much of the rest of the world, Ireland was no blank tablet on which English team sports could make their mark unopposed.

At Trinity College, Dublin, rugby football was introduced in 1856; in anglophile Belfast the first rugby club was formed twelve years later. Northern and southern Rugby Unions appeared shortly thereafter and finally joined forces in a Combined Irish Rugby Union in 1881. Later arriving, soccer football was more dramatic in its expansion. In 1880 a group of Belfast businessmen founded the Irish Football Association. In the following year they established the Irish Cup, and in 1882 they organized the first international match with England. Badly beaten, 13–0, Irish soccer footballers nevertheless established the game as a popular spectator sport in populous Belfast. In 1886 open professionalism capitalized on crowd appeal, and in 1890 the Irish equivalent of England's professional Football League, the Irish League, was founded.

Outside of Ulster and a large colony of resident Englishmen in Dublin, however, soccer as well as rugby football suffered a distinct disadvantage. They were *English* games. To many Irish nationalists they were, like the English language, manners, and institutions, symbolic of England's imperial dominance of Irish political and cultural life. During the 1870s and 1880s violent secret societies and eloquent Irish politicians campaigned for Irish independence. Sports took on political significance. In 1884 a nationalist newspaper, *United Ireland*, called upon "the Irish people to take the management of their games into their own hands." Their native games were hurling and Gaelic football, not soccer, rugby, or cricket. As a part of Ireland's reaction against English rule, the Gaelic Athletic Association was founded in 1884 for "the preservation and cultivation of [Ireland's] national pastimes."

They met with mixed success. In Belfast and Dublin both soccer and rugby football continued to attract large crowds. In rural counties, however, hurling and Gaelic football dominated the sporting calendar. At first glance, modern Gaelic football looks like a combination of rugby and soccer; in fact, it is an old Irish game that late in the nineteenth century took on rules and a distinct form of running, tackling, passing, punching, and kicking for goals either into a soccerlike net or over a rugbylike set of uprights.

In distant Australia, Irish immigrants (many of whom originally left the British Isles as involuntary political prisoners, exiled by English authorities) propagated their Gaelic games. Yet another variety of football emerged. Australian Rules football is a composite of Gaelic, rugby, and soccer football, with some improvisations of its own. It is the only football game in the world played on an oval-shaped field. To American viewers the game seems to be a wild, chaotic affair, but in truth Australian Rules and American football have one fundamental point in common: they both refused, finally, to become carbon copies of English soccer or rugby.

Chapter 10

BATS, BALLS, AND BUSINESS

Hardly anyone can doubt that American football is an adaptation of the British game of rugby. The pedigree of American baseball, however, is a matter of some dispute. According to popular legend, baseball was invented by Abner Doubleday in Cooperstown, New York, in 1839. Unfortunately, that myth is built on the most shaky of evidence. It became established in the early twentieth century—almost three-quarters of a century after the time when the game supposedly began—as an expression of American anti-British nationalism. The origins of baseball are more complex, and far more interesting, than the Doubleday story would lead one to believe.

Like English soccer, American baseball began as an organized form of gentlemanly competition, but it soon became a popular game with the masses. Mass spectator interest quickly turned the "national game" into a professional sport. During the last quarter of the nineteenth century, organized baseball expanded dramatically, producing management-player conflicts common to the big business of the era. All the while, baseball's transatlantic cousin, English cricket, also became consolidated as a popular team sport. A new style of play, better grounds and organization, and the emergence of several outstanding players all combined to make first-class cricket a central feature of late-Victorian life. In a fashion uniquely English, amateur and professional cricketers participated together without the one ever rooting out the other.

Gentlemen and Players

On the eve of the Civil War, cricket was the most popular of all organized team sports in the United States. English immigrants brought the game with them, especially to large cities such as Boston, New York, and Philadelphia. In 1857 twelve representatives from cricket clubs as far away as Albany and Philadelphia convened at the Astor House in New York City to form the United States Central Club, an American equivalent of the Marylebone Cricket Club in London. According to one commentator, cricket was "the leading game played out of doors" in the United States in 1858, "the favorite game of the country village and the country town, as well as the larger commercial cities." In the following year a cricket match between a visiting English team and a local team at the Elysian Fields in Hoboken, New Jersey, drew a crowd of 25,000, requiring extra ferries to carry people over from Manhattan.

Yet the enthusiasm surrounding that cricket match was misleading. Scattered throughout the American past was another, simpler kind of bat-and-ball game. A derivation of the old English games of stool-ball and "old-cat," the game of rounders was traditionally played by children on a field with four stones or posts set on a square, which runners traversed clockwise. As far back as 1700, in both England and colonial America, it was sometimes known as "base," "base ball," or "goal ball." The batter was "out" when he missed three swings, hit the ball foul, had a batted ball caught before it hit the ground, or was struck by the ball while he was running the bases. Rounders was a far more active game than cricket. Batters and fielders ran more; a batter quickly relinquished his place to another; teams frequently changed from offense to defense and back again. Compared to cricket, rounders was also a relatively brief game. It was ideally suited for active children.

And for active Americans. According to diarists of the day, soldiers played "base" on 7 April 1778 at Valley Forge, and in 1786 Princeton undergraduates played "baste ball" on the campus. Throughout the Northeast, boys played on village greens while their elders attended town meetings. Not surprisingly, the name "town ball" became common. Yet the forms and rules of town ball, or base ball, varied according to local customs. By the early nineteenth century, two dominant versions had emerged. The older "Massachusetts game" featured bases (usually poles) on an oblong pattern; after the batter hit the ball, fielders scrambled to retrieve it and threw it at the runner to "plug" or "soak" him before he safely reached a base. The "New York game," on the other hand, set the bases on a square and required fielders to touch the base or runner with the ball rather than throwing it at him.

Beginning in 1842, a group of affluent merchants, professional men, and white-collar clerks began playing the New York game regularly on a vacant lot at 27th Street and Fourth Avenue in Manhattan. In 1845 a member of the group, Alexander Cartwright, suggested that they form a baseball club. Restricting their membership to forty, they charged annual dues of $5.00 each, held a banquet after each game, and levied strict fines against any ungentlemanly conduct, such as swearing, disobeying the captain, or disputing an umpire's decision. They were an elite social clique as well as a sports club. Common laborers, poor immigrants, or black Americans need not have applied for membership. America's first organized baseball team, the Knickerbockers, prided themselves on being exclusively "gentlemen."

To keep order on the field of play, Alexander Cartwright drew up a rudimentary set of rules. He set flat bases (not poles) at ninety feet apart in a diamond-shaped layout, with a pitching "box" forty-five feet from "home plate"; he limited teams to nine players, forbade throwing the ball at a runner, and designated twenty-one "aces" (runs) as the number necessary to win a game. Alexander Cartwright, not Abner Doubleday, is the "father" of American baseball. Unfortunately, the father did not stay around to see his child develop into manhood. In 1850 Cartwright left for Hawaii and never returned.

Decked out in blue woolen pantaloons, white flannel shirts, and straw hats, the Knickerbockers spawned imitators who soon began issuing challenges for games. On 19 June 1846 the Knicks played their first game against another club, the New Yorkers, to whom they curiously lost, 23–1. Baseball clubs quickly became the rage. By the mid-1850s the Knickerbockers, Gothams, Eagles, Empires, Mutuals, and Metropolitans in Manhattan, and the Excelsiors, Putnams, Eckfords, and Atlantics in Brooklyn engaged in spirited competition. By 1858 about fifty clubs regularly played in the metropolitan area of New York City, and already clubs were being formed in upper New York State, in major cities such as Cleveland, Detroit, and Chicago, and in Maryland, Delaware, and Pennsylvania.

In New England, too, baseball clubs first took shape in the 1850s. The Boston Olympics, founded in 1854, led the way, and in 1857 representatives of ten clubs met in Dedham, Massachusetts, to form the Massachusetts Association of Base Ball Players. Predictably, they agreed to compete according to the "Massachusetts rules" to which they were accustomed. The first intercollegiate baseball game, on 1 July 1859 between Amherst and Williams, was played under the Massachusetts rules; Amherst won, 73–32, in twenty-six innings. Not until after the Civil War did the New York rules become established in New England's urban centers. In rural areas, features of the Massachusetts game survived well into the twentieth century.

Organization proceeded apace in New York City. In 1858 delegates from twenty-two clubs convened to form the National Association of Base Ball Players; it elected six officers and a committee to draft a constitution. Quickly the group became national in authority as well as in name. Within its first year membership more than doubled as five new clubs from upstate New York and four from New Jersey joined. For thirteen years delegates and officers met annually to revise rules, settle disputes, and generally to govern the game of baseball.

Except for a new provision of a nine-inning game to replace the traditional twenty-one "aces," the game itself largely remained faithful to the rules established by Alexander Cartwright in 1845. Foul balls caught on the first bounce still put a man out; pitchers continued tossing the ball in a stiff-armed underhand motion; batters still called for their favorite high or low pitch and swung only at pitches they liked. In time, of course, all these rules and styles would be altered, largely for the purpose of crowd appeal. But from the beginning baseball was a conservative game, slow to change.

Beyond the rules and style of play, however, the founding of the National Association signaled a profound change that had already occurred. Not one of the original six officers of the National Association came from the old Knickerbocker club. The brief day of gentlemanly dominance was past. As New York and Brooklyn shipwrights, mechanics, firemen, policemen, teachers, and bartenders organized their own baseball clubs, the "Base Ball Fever" celebrated in a popular song of 1857 was a popular, democratic fever:

> Our merchants have to close their stores
> The clerks away are staying,
> Contractors too, can do no work,
> Their hands are all out playing.

Simple and inexpensive, the old English game of rounders lent itself to the playful impulses of clerks and laborers no less than to merchants and contractors.

Yet baseball was not solely derived from rounders: it was a hybrid of rounders and cricket. From rounders baseball took its rudimentary "diamond" design and the practice of running around bases, but from the more highly organized game of cricket it borrowed the idea of a fixed number of players on each team, a vocabulary ("batsman," "playing the field," and the like), and an umpire to whose authority players deferred. More important, from cricket baseball took its spirit, its code of sportsmanship. Despite baseball's subsequent history of seedy characters, petty power struggles, and numerous scandals, it retained the indelible stamp of its gentlemanly cricket origins: the ideal, if not always the reality, of fair play.

Baseball became a distinctive Yankee game in part because of the innovative efforts of English immigrants in the United States. One, Henry Chadwick, became baseball's first notable journalist, author, and editor. He invented the box score, and for the first half-century of organized baseball he constantly demanded "gentlemanly demeanor" on the field. Another English immigrant, a man named Wright, left England in 1835 and for years played for the St. George Cricket Club on State Island. Three of his sons became outstanding baseball players. The eldest, Harry Wright, at first bowled (pitched) for New York cricket clubs, then launched a baseball career in which he played, managed, and promoted the game into the national limelight. Sometimes called "the father of professional baseball," Wright nevertheless retained his English cricketer's sense of amateur delight in the game.

A National Game

Because of its widespread popularity, baseball could scarcely remain amateur for very long. The constitution of the National Association sternly forbade pay for play, gambling on games, and players jumping from one team to another. Yet in the same year that organization was formed, some New York teams began charging admission to games, with the players dividing the gate

"The American National Game of Baseball," a print by Currier and Ives in 1866, shows the pitcher tossing the ball underhand to a batter whose hands are widely spread on the bat. The catcher is without a mask or body protection, the basemen hug their bases, and the umpire stands off to the right of home plate. Spectators have their eyes glued to the action on the field, but players for the team at bat seem most intent on posing for the artist.

receipts. Winning teams drew the largest crowds, so teams competed for the services of the better players by offering money under the table. Outstanding pitchers, especially, were in great demand. Thomas Wentworth Higginson, a Boston preacher and essayist, said more then he knew when he suggested in 1858 that baseball was "our indigenous American game . . . whose briskness and unceasing activity are perhaps more congenial . . . to our national character, than the comparative deliberations of cricket." Baseball satisifed not only America's love of brisk activity, but also its acquisitive tendencies. On the eve of the Civil War, increasing crowds and players' willingness to turn a fast buck all pointed to professionalism.

The Civil War momentarily retarded the growth of baseball. As men took up arms, they laid down their bats and balls. Yet Yankee soldiers took their game with them, played it in army camps, and taught it to friends and foes alike. Imprisoned Union soldiers occasionally challenged their Confederate captors to baseball contests. A painting immortalizes such an event in Salisbury, North Carolina, in 1862. According to a documentary source, a game on Christmas Day, 1862, at Hilton Head, South Carolina, attracted the attention of an entire army base of 40,000 men. Before the war eccentric versions of town ball were played in places such as Charleston and New Orleans; after the war the "New York rules" uniformly governed play in much of the South as well as the North, in the West as well as the East. The Civil War contributed mightily to the geographical diffusion of baseball.

On a more subtle level, the Civil War caused Americans to recognize baseball as their "national game" in contrast to cricket, the Englishman's game. Sport reflected diplomacy. When the war began, support for the Confederacy was strong in Britain, especially among the ruling aristocracy. The English government declared itself neutral and allowed Confederate representatives to borrow money, buy arms, and build ships in Britain. Throughout the war the influential London *Times* editorially backed the Confederate cause, infuriating Union politicians and newspapermen. The northern press was rabidly anti-British. American sport got caught up in that patriotic fervor. In 1862 a Brooklyn newspaper shrewdly observed that cricket would never again be "in much vogue with the Americans," not only because cricket was too slow a game but also because it was "not an *American* game, but purely an *English* game." Sour Anglo-American relations during the Civil War helped to spoil cricket's chances for popularity in the United States.

As the war ground to an end in the spring of 1865, some Philadelphians met to reorganize their Old Olympian Cricket Club, which had been disbanded during the war. "At first, it was hard work," wrote one member of the club, "[because] the baseball mania was just beginning to spread, and no one would join a cricket club." Most of the older, socially prominent members returned to their cricket club, but younger men turned to baseball. The generation gap was significant. Baseball appealed both to youthful patriotism and to youthful energy.

In the wake of the Civil War a baseball mania swept the nation. A game between the New York Mutuals and the Brooklyn Atlantics in the late summer of 1865 attracted about 20,000 spectators, a record for that era. More important, baseball quickly became the dominant summer pastime in small towns, villages, and rural crossroads throughout the United States, and the favorite topic of winter conversation around hot stoves in country stores. During the decade following the Civil War, baseball became a rural and small-town game as well as a city pastime, a national rather than a regional mania.

In 1865 a convention of the National Association of Base Ball Players attracted representatives of ninety-one clubs, nearly double the highest prewar figure. In the following year the number more than doubled again, to 202 clubs from seventeen different states. By 1867 the annual convention was so large and unwieldy that the officers of the Association changed the constitution to allow only representatives from state associations to attend the annual conference.

The professional question quickly reasserted itself. In 1866 the Philadelphia Athletics openly paid three players $20 each per week, but for most teams the payments remained secret or disguised. In a fashion that has come to be known as semiprofessional, players were supposedly paid to work, but actually they were paid to play baseball. Large industries and affluent merchants carried baseball players on their payrolls; politicians paid them at public expense. William Marcy Tweed, the notorious boss of Tammany Hall, was also the president of the New York Mutuals (1860–71). He placed virtually all his Mutuals on the New York City payroll as clerks and streetsweepers. According to one estimate, Tweedism in baseball cost New York City taxpayers $30,000 annually. Baseballers in Washington, D.C., similarly enjoyed an easy ride during the corrupt first term (1869–72) of President Ulysses S. Grant. As one critic noted, the United States Treasury Department was "the real birthplace of professional base ball in Washington."

In that postwar society, where public scruples were at a premium, enterprising baseball players often cooperated with gamblers in fixing ("hippodroming") games. They also frequently "revolved" from one team to another in response to the highest bidder. William Fischer, for example, agreed to play for the Philadelphia Athletics, who gave him a suit of clothes, paid for his room and board, got him a job, and gave him $115 as a bonus for signing. Yet Fischer remained in Philadelphia for only a few days. Wearing his new clothes and keeping his bonus, he left to take a better offer from the Chicago Cubs.

The first admittedly all-professional club was the Cincinnati Red Stockings of 1869. Their manager, Harry Wright, raided clubs in Washington, New York, and Brooklyn to obtain the best players, and he ended up with only one Cincinnati native on his ten-man squad. Salaries ranged from $800 to $1,400 for the starting team, with the one substitute drawing $600 for the season. The total payroll was $9,300. The Red Stockings traveled throughout the Northeast, then returned home briefly before launching a trip to the West Coast. In all, they won fifty-six games and tied one in 1869. They were Cincinnati's darlings. "Glory, they've advertised the city," exclaimed one proud and grateful resident, "advertised us, sir, and helped our business."

Their season in the sun was brief. Throughout the next season, fans stayed home and the club lost money. As the owners drastically cut salaries, Harry Wright took his best players with him to Boston, where he established another dynasty. Having robbed Cincinnati's roster, he even stole their nickname. The modern Boston Red Sox and Cincinnati Reds take their nicknames from an age of chicanery and ruthless competition.

Wright's move to Boston coincided with a crisis in the old National Association. Irritated with rampant professionalism, amateurs withdrew to form their own organization, and in March 1871 ten professional clubs formed the new National Association of Professional Base Ball Players. From the outset, the organization was unstable. Gambling, hippodroming, and revolving continued unchecked. Each club arranged its own schedule, but toward the end of each season the clubs that were losing money simply refused to travel afar to fulfill their commitments. Clubs rose and fell rapidly. Within the five years of the Association's existence, twenty-five different clubs came and went as members; eleven teams survived only one year.

A nationwide economic depression, beginning in 1873, added to the problem. Few clubs made money. The most successful of all, Boston, lost $3,000 in 1872, netted less than $1,000 in 1873 and 1874, and finally netted only $3,000 in 1875 despite an outstanding record of 71–8. While indirect investment nearly doubled between 1865 and 1878, a narrow profit margin and a high risk of loss cooled the ardor of potential investors in the baseball enterprise. As the season of 1875 came to a close, negotiations were under-way to restructure the professional game, taking control away from the players and putting it in the hands of owners.

Yet professional teams represented only one aspect of the national game. Years later Clarence Darrow recalled growing up in a small Ohio town in the 1870s, playing baseball as if it were the "one unalloyed joy in life." Darrow and his schoolmates were shocked when they heard that professionals moved from team to team playing the game for money rather than for local pride. In young Darrow's Ohio, fierce rivalry between neighboring towns was played out on the diamond. Ohio was a microcosm of small-town America. "The game is truly a national one," observed the popular *Spirit of the Times* in 1873: "In every little town and hamlet throughout the country we find a ball club, generally two, bitter rivals, at it with hammer and tongs, ding-dong the entire summer, as though all creation depended on the defeat of the other crowd, and then away goes a challenge—to the next town, and from there to the next, and so on."

On college campuses, too, baseball flourished. For a decade or so before football became established as the autumn sport, baseball dominated the autumn as well as the spring portion of the academic year. In 1873 the son of a future president of the United States, Rutherford B. Hayes, wrote to his father that he dreaded leaving college because he might not then be able to play baseball. "The love of other boys for smoking, chewing, drinking, skating, and swimming," he concluded, "in my case is all concentrated on ballplaying." From its earliest years, the national game meant wholesome, popular activity as well as professional spectacle.

Baseball Business

In 1876 the first of the two present major leagues, the National League, was founded. Replacing the short-lived National Association of Professional Base Ball Players, the full name of the new organization was the National League of Professional Base Ball Clubs. The new title accurately conveyed the essence of the change. For the first time club owners, directors, and administrative staffs separated the management of the game from the playing of it. In the age of Rockefeller, Carnegie, Vanderbilt, Gould, Pillsbury, Armour, and Swift, baseball also spawned its investment barons.

Foremost was William A. Hulbert, a Chicago businessman. Representing a new breed of baseball magnate, Hulbert never played the game; financial and civic interests rather than sporting enthusiasm attracted him to baseball. In 1870 he became a charter stockholder of the newly founded Chicago White Stockings, and soon he became president of the club. At the end of the season of 1875, he collaborated with a Chicago journalist, Lewis Meacham, in outlining the inadequacies of the player-controlled Association. Player control of the game, he insisted, produced inflated salaries, team jumping, gambling scandals, team imbalance, and uncompleted schedules, all resulting in tepid spectator interest and subsequent losses at the gate. Hulbert's remedy was simple. He proposed that a "closed corporation" of baseball owners impose discipline and order on the game.

Before he made his move, Hulbert covered his own base. In 1875 he raided the championship Boston Red Stockings team of its four best players, and the Philadelphia Athletics of one. From Boston he got a gem of a young pitcher, Albert G. Spalding, whom he immediately installed as playing manager and team captain. Like Hulbert, Spalding was an astute businessman. Upon arriving in Chicago, he opened a sporting-goods store primarily to sell "all kinds of base ball goods." He equipped his own team, of course, and shortly after the founding of the National League gained a monopoly for the furnishing of the league's official balls, as well as the exclusive rights to publish the league's first informational and statistical record, the *Base Ball Guide*. Spalding's sporting-goods investment quickly outweighed his commitment to playing the game. A millionaire by his early thirties, he was living proof of the profitable marriage of sport and business. He fully supported Hulbert's efforts to establish baseball on a firm business basis.

Spalding applauded the formation of the National League as a means of giving management the upper hand in "the irrepressible conflict between Labor and Capital." Yet regional as well as financial interests lay in the background of the new organization. Recovering quickly from its great fire of 1872, Chicago mushroomed both in size and importance as the commercial center of the Midwest. Civic leaders such as William A. Hulbert resented the political and cultural dominance of Philadelphia, New York, and Boston, a dominance symbolized in the control of professional baseball by eastern clubs. Acting on his resentment of those "Eastern cusses," Hulbert late in 1875 secretly invited baseball owners from Louisville, Cincinnati, and St.

Louis to meet with Chicago officials to devise a new professional baseball league. The group convened in Louisville, drafted a constitution, and then (in early February 1876) presented their plan to four eastern clubs. The charter members of the National League represented Boston, Hartford, New York, and Philadelphia in the East; Chicago, Cincinnati, Louisville, and St. Louis in the West.

They agreed to protect their "territorial rights" by having only one club per city and forbidding league members from playing any nonleague teams. Each club paid annual dues of $100, ten times the amount levied by the old National Association. The constitution provided for a central office, and for governance of league affairs by a five-man board of directors selected by the owners, one of whom served as president of the league. Predictably, no player representatives were allowed on the board.

According to the preamble of the constitution, the purpose of the National League was to "encourage, foster, and elevate" the game by making it "respectable and honorable." As a first move in that direction, league officials constructed a seventy-game schedule for each club, and they dealt severely with an old problem that had long plagued professional baseball: the reluctance of losing teams to finish their schedules at the end of the season. In 1876 the Philadelphia Athletics and New York Mutuals were expelled from the league for refusing to make a final western tour. Then the owners turned to more visible signs of respectability. In order to attract a higher class of spectators, they banned gambling and the selling of beer at the ball park; to raise the image of the game, they forbade Sunday contests. For better discipline on the field, they created a paid corps of umpires (a departure from the traditional use of local amateur arbiters) and ruled that only the captain of a team could dispute the umpire's decision.

Like their counterparts in American industry, National League owners imposed a stern discipline on their workers, the players. Ruthlessly they cut salaries, required players to pay for their own uniforms, and charged fifty cents a day for expenses on road trips. In 1877 they banned four Louisville players for life for throwing a game. Nor was their control of players limited to public affairs. In 1880 they announced that players would be barred "from play and from pay" for "insubordination or misconduct of any kind." Albert Spalding, who took over the presidency of the Chicago club following the death of Hulbert in 1882, required his players to sign a pledge of total abstinence from beer, wine, and whiskey, then hired a private detective to trail suspected offenders. Threats of fines and suspensions were written into contracts. Players who protested were blacklisted. At one point in the early 1880s, thirty-four players and one umpire were blacklisted.

Of all the measures taken by owners to discipline their players, the creation of a "reserve clause" was the most important in its long-term effect on professional baseball. Determined to prevent players from moving freely from one team to another in quest of higher salaries, owners in 1879 secretly agreed among themselves that each owner would designate his best five players as "reserved property," off limits to other owners. Soon the arrangement became public knowledge. In 1883 the number of reserved players per club was extended to eleven and in 1887 to fourteen. In that day of small squads, fourteen players included virtually the entire team.

Written into every player's contract, the reserve clause meant that only the club owner could terminate the contract. A player could no longer bargain annually with other clubs. His owner might sell his contract or release him outright, but if a player refused to come to terms with his own club, he simply had to quit baseball altogether. From the owner's point of view, the reserve clause was deemed a necessity. As William A. Hulbert candidly admitted, it was a "business coalition . . . , a perfectly just and proper stroke of business." Certainly it was consistent with the practice of big business in late nineteenth-century America.

As in the industrial sphere, however, the abuse of managerial authority provoked worker resistance. Rules governing personal conduct were irritants to rough and boisterous youths. Fines, suspensions, blacklisting, and the reserve clause were barely tolerable. But the imposition, in 1885, of a salary ceiling of $2,000 proved to be the final straw. In the autumn of 1885 a kind of players' union, the Brotherhood of Professional Base Ball Players, was formed to work for the abolition of the salary ceiling, a modification of the reserve clause, and generally for a more active voice in determining the terms of employment as professional athletes.

John Montgomery Ward, a most unusual baseballer, led the rebellion. In a day when most players were barely literate, Ward held a bachelor's degree from Pennsylvania State College and a law degree from Columbia University, earning the latter as a part-time student while playing for the New York Giants. He had begun his baseball career as an outstanding pitcher for Providence, where in 1879 he achieved a phenomenal 44–18 record. Shortly thereafter he injured his arm, switched to the infield, mastered switch-hitting, and became the captain of the Giants. Handsome and dashing, he also became a prominent figure on the New York social scene, marrying a beautiful, well-known actress. In terms of money and status, Ward had little to gain from leading his baseball teammates in their stand against the owners. But lead them he did. Within a year of its formation, the Brotherhood numbered more than a hundred members, well over half of all major league players.

Adamantly refusing to enter into serious negotiations with their players, the owners intimidated newspaper editors into discrediting the Brotherhood, bribed hesitant players, and threatened to fire the "hot-headed anarchists" who led the rebellion. Ward and his comrades refused to be intimidated. For four years they pushed their points, and in several states they took the reserve clause to court. Legal decisions went consistently in their favor, against the reserve clause, but were not enforced. Finally, in 1890 the players faced a fateful decision: to strike or to form a league of their own in competition with the National League. They chose the latter course. They were not even union-minded men, much less anarchists.

A throwback to the earlier days of player-controlled baseball, the Players League was a grand but brief experiment in owner-player cooperation, featuring shared profits as well as governance. Unlike the old National

Association, however, the Players League had to compete with an established, better-financed rival. The season of 1890 was a catastrophe for all concerned. Although the Players League lost only half as much money as did the National League, the latter had sufficient capital to survive and to buy off both investors and players from the rebel organization. The folding of the Players League prompted John Montgomery Ward to utter one of his few truisms: "Baseball is a business, not simply a sport."

Yet despite the big-business orientation of major league owners, baseball remained a shaky business right up to the end of the nineteenth century. The Players League was only one of several new leagues that rose to challenge the monopoly of major-league owners. The most successful of all those rivals, the American Association, lasted for nine seasons (1883–91). It charged a lower admission price, sold beer at games, and allowed games on Sundays. With those Association clubs, the League owners reached an accommodation. In exchange for major-league status, Association officials agreed not to raid National League teams of their players. More important, they provided opposition for a series of postseason playoff games, forerunners of the modern World Series. Yet even that early version of the World Series reflected the experimental, fumbling character of the baseball business in the late nineteenth century. At first League and Association champions played for the best of five games, then several times for the best of seven, and once scheduled fifteen games scattered in most all the cities represented by the two bodies. Not surprisingly, spectator interest dwindled to a ridiculously low level.

Amid all the organizational and personnel strife, several players emerged as popular American heroes. Adrian "Cap" Anson, a burly, boisterous farmboy from Iowa, enjoyed a long and illustrious career (1871–98) as a player and manager with the Chicago White Stockings. One of his players, Mike "King" Kelly, was as spectacular on the base paths as he was in the batter's box, and in 1887 he was sold to the Boston club for the record price of $10,000. William "Buck" Ewing was a fiery catcher for the New York Giants, drawing the top salary of the day, $5000. In the 1890s William "Wee Willie" Keeler ignited the fans in Baltimore, especially in 1897 when he hit safely in forty-four consecutive games. The first famous spray hitter, Keeler had a simple formula: "Keep your eye clear and hit'em where they ain't."

Free spirits all, each of these superstars had a nickname, a sure sign of notoriety. They were also all white. Shortly after the Civil War the amateur National Association of Base Ball Players banned blacks. For a time the new professional leagues put more stock on winning games than on the color of players' skin, opening the door in the 1870s and early 1880s for several blacks to compete on northern major and minor league clubs. In the late 1880s, however, the color line was drawn in baseball as in all American society, more by a tacit, unwritten agreement of white owners and players than by explicit legislation. The infamous separate-but-equal clause in the *Plessy v. Ferguson* decision of 1896 simply put a legal stamp of approval on Jim Crow reality. Segregated baseball was no worse, though no better, than the society of which it was a part.

Except for its lily-white personnel, baseball at the close of the nineteenth century bore a striking resemblance to the modern game. The ball was not as lively as the one now used, requiring more scientific hitting and strategic maneuvers on the base paths. But by 1900 the pitcher threw overhand, sixty feet and six inches from the batter. Catchers stationed themselves immediately behind the plate, used a heavy mitt, and wore a mask and protective armor. Most defensive men wore gloves, admittedly small and frail by today's standards. Then, as now, journalists wrote colorful accounts of games, filled with jargon and usually partial to the home team. Setting American sport on it way toward the modern statistical fetish, journalists also dutifully recorded and daily publicized each player's batting, fielding, and pitching statistics. Yet baseball at the end of the nineteenth century was in a bad way. In 1900 the *New York Times* observed that "rowdyism by the players on the field, syndicalism among the club owners, poor umpiring, and talk of rival organizations . . . are the principal causes accountable for baseball's decline." As Americans entered the twentieth century, the future of their national game hung in the balance.

Graceful Cricket

While American baseball suffered birth pangs and the traumas of early adolescence in the second half of the nineteenth century, English cricket capitalized on its longer history by smoothing out its rough spots and entering a stage of maturity universally acknowledged as its "golden age" in the late Victorian and Edwardian eras. In 1900 English cricket was more organizationally sound and widely popular than ever before.

Some smoothing, both literal and figurative, was necessary. According to the reminiscences of one old cricketer, matches at the game's premier grounds, Lord's, in the 1850s and 1860s were "mostly of no interest [to anyone] except the players themselves." The physical state of the field symbolized the nature of the game at mid-century: "Lord's was a heavy clay and badly drained, and the outfielding was always rough and treacherous," according to one contemporary. "There were no boundaries—except the pavilion—no stands or fixed seats of any kind, nothing but the small old pavilion and a line of loose benches running part of the way round the ground." London's other major cricket ground, the Oval (founded in 1845 in Kennington as the headquarters of the Surrey County Cricket Club), was little better.

Increased spectator interest first brought rope boundaries and stands to Lord's for the Eton vs. Harrow match of 1866, and other grounds soon followed Lord's example. More intrinsically useful to the game was the work of diligent groundkeepers in smoothing those "rough and treacherous" fields on which cricket was played. Requiring special attention was the area called "the wicket," the stretch of ground on which the ball was pitched by the bowler. In 1887 a spectator at Lord's observed "a beautiful wicket . . . as true as a die, without an atom to choose at either end." Although such a "true" (or "plumb") wicket was merely the work of careful groundsmen, in fact the physical change came as a result of a major tactical innovation: overarm bowling. The condition of the ground was important, of course, because the ball normally hit the ground before reaching the batter.

From the old underhand bowling, a kind of sidearm motion evolved in the first half of the nineteenth century, and in the 1860s it gave way to the much faster overhand delivery. According to the rules established in 1835 by the governing Marylebone Cricket Club, the ball had to be released at a level below the shoulder. But many bowlers ignored the rule without penalty. In 1862 a crisis arose when Edgar Willsher, a left-hander from Kent, flagrantly bowled overhand in a match at the Oval. The umpire called "no ball"—an illegal pitch—five times in a row. Frustrated, Willsher finally threw the ball to the ground, and he and his entire team stalked off the field. Negotiating their return, officials agreed to a new, more lenient umpire, and on the following day Willsher resumed his unorthodox delivery.

In 1864 (two decades before overhand pitching was allowed in American baseball), the rules of cricket were changed to permit the overhead motion, but with a clause requiring that "the ball must be bowled; if thrown or jerked, the umpire shall call 'no ball'." Thus the stiff-arm style of the cricket bowler was forever to be different from the more flexible delivery of a baseball pitcher. Cricketers' dress also became distinctive in the 1860s and 1870s. The "bowler hat," a round, narrow-brim adaptation from tall beaver-skin hats, gave way to little caps with narrow front bills; white buckskins replaced black shoes and brown boots; older uniforms of black, blue, or red shirts and white trousers were replaced by all-white shirts and trousers.

More important than these matters of style and appearance was the emergence of county teams and intercounty competition. Traditionally a village game, with neighboring villages occasionally forming teams and playing each other, cricket broadened its organizational scope once the railways made distant travel possible. Yet it remained true to its rural roots by forming new teams according to county affiliations rather than city or town ties. By 1860 Sussex, Kent, and Surrey fielded representative teams, and within the next two decades another dozen or so counties selected their best players to compete for the County Championship. Rules of player eligibility were agreed upon in 1873; in 1887 a County Cricket Council was formed, and three years later all the county teams were divided into first, second, and third divisions, with intricate provisions for promotion into a higher division or relegation to a lower.

Concurrent with the development of the County Championship was the emergence of first-class international cricket. After the All-England tour of Canada and the United States in 1859, unpredictable autumn weather, the onset of the Civil War, and the subsequent rapid rise of baseball all conspired to dampen English enthusiasm for further tours to North America. Instead, they turned to Australia, the English colony where cricket thrived most. Beginning in 1861, English teams regularly visited Australia, consistently coming away the victor. Finally in 1878 an Australian team reciprocated, shocking a large audience at Lord's with a victory over a team representing the Marylebone Cricket Club.

The first official Test Match was held at the Oval in 1880. About 20,000 spectators attended both days to watch the Australians push England to the limit before admitting defeat. In the first Test Match in Australia, in 1881, England won yet again. The following year, back at the Oval, was another story. Having trained hard, the Australians arrived in a serious mood—too serious for old English cricketers' tastes. For ten weeks or so the Australians lost only a handful of numerous exhibition matches. In the Test Match, however, they fell behind early. Rain interrupted play for half of the second day, but once play was resumed the Australians edged up, evening the score by mid-afternoon. Partisan English spectators fidgeted, sensing disaster. One dropped dead of a heart attack; another, it was said, gnawed pieces out of his umbrella handle with his bare teeth. All to no avail. The Australians carried the match, serving notice of their arrival as top-flight cricket competitors.

Out of that English defeat of 1882 came the traditional victor's symbol of the England-Australia Test Match: "the Ashes." Shortly after the match, the *Sporting Times* ran a mock obituary notice "in affectionate remembrance of English cricket, which died at the Oval on 29th August 1882." Supposedly the body would be cremated "and the Ashes taken to Australia." The notice tickled the fancy of two English dames, who presented an "Ashes Urn" in honor of the rivalry. Though the urn was to remain always in the pavilion at Lord's, the victor in the Test Match "wins the Ashes." By the end of the nineteenth century, national teams from India, South Africa, New Zealand, and the West Indies were playing against All-England teams, but the struggle for "the Ashes" always provided the best cricket in the world.

Of all the individual players in that late-Victorian world of cricket, William Gilbert Grace was the best and by far the most famous. He was England's first nationally recognized sports hero, a superstar by modern standards. In a long career of first-class cricket that spanned the entire final third of the century, he collected 54,896 runs, 2,864 wickets, and 126 centuries (100 runs in one turn at bat), a phenomenal record comparable to the exploits of the best of baseball's greats. Prior to Grace, bowlers had dominated the game; he transformed batting into a science. Quick, efficient, and strong at the stumps, he often remained with bat in hand, giving bowlers fits for an entire afternoon.

Neither on nor off the field could Grace ever be mistaken for someone else. He was portly and sported a huge beard. Easy to photograph and easier to caricature, his dominating image sold copy for the *Times* as well as the *Sporting Times*, for *Punch* as well as the yellow press. A native of Gloucestershire, he first played in a county match in 1862, at the age of fourteen, against Devonshire. By 1870 his feats were legendary, as he dominated County Championships and international Test matches over the years. At his death in 1915 he was rightly described as "the best known of all Englishmen." Certainly the Disraelis, Gladstones, Salisburys, and Balfours of the day scarcely rivaled his public acclaim.

Despite his profession as a country doctor, Grace refused to read more than was absolutely necessary, for fear of straining his eyes. To the end of his

England's most famous cricket player of all time, W. G. Grace, was heavy of body and beard, as here seen in an engraving by W. Spielmeyer for *The English Illustrated Magazine*, 1890.

playing days, his batting eye never failed him. But his legs did. Always stocky, in the end he was grossly overweight, unable to run out his still substantial hits. In 1891 he injured a knee and had to sit out almost the entire season. He was over forty, and his career seemed finished. He returned the following year, however, resumed his assault on bowlers, and in 1895 began the season by staying at bat for an entire day against a Kent team, finishing the month of May with 1,016 runs and the season with 2,346. Journalists understandably tempted the gods of late-Victorian propriety by referring to him as "Amazing Grace," the title of a popular Evangelical hymn. Finally at the end of the season of 1899 he retired at the age of fifty-one from his Gloucestershire and All-England captaincies to manage a newly formed London Country Club.

A Gentleman (amateur) rather than a Player (professional), Grace nevertheless made a substantial fortune from testimonials, endorsements, and exhibition fees. Yet when he left the game, the custodians of cricket etiquette still made a sharp division between amateurs and professionals. When teams traveled, Gentlemen and Players stayed in different hotels; they dressed in separate rooms and even continued to enter the field through different gates. Although cricket was a "national" game that cut across lines of class and region, it retained its class distinctions well into the twentieth century.

By 1900 new stars had appeared in the persons of J. S. Ranjitsinhji, an India-born Cambridge graduate who broke many of Grace's records, though he never won commensurate esteem and public affection, and young John Berry ("Jack") Hobbs, destined to collect an aggregate of 61,237 runs, a mark that has never been broken. At the turn of the century, amateurs in the public schools, universities, and country houses played a larger part in the game than ever before or since. Unlike American baseball, cricket entered the twentieth century firmly established and eminently respectable.

Chapter 11

BOYS OF WINTER

Until the recent construction of indoor ice-hockey rinks, tennis courts, and stadiums, sport was organized along predictable seasonal and geographical lines. In frigid northern climes the turning of autumn leaves signaled not only the early completion of the football season but also the exchange of baseball, cricket, tennis, and golf equipment for skis, toboggans, and ice skates. Like ancient seasonal rituals of play, basketball and gymnastic seasons followed close on the heels of the last football game.

The organization of most of these winter sports occurred in the second half of the nineteenth century simultaneous with the emergence of organized baseball and football. As people learned to play on summer fields of green, they carried their competitive impulses on to snow-covered hills and ice-bound lakes and rivers. In the process they invented a new game, ice hockey, a winter adaptation of field hockey. For some, the rigors of the frozen outdoors had little appeal. The old gaslight and the newly invented incandescent bulb enabled a small but enthusiastic band to enjoy billiards and bowling, and the masses to watch commercial pedestrian races. Gymnasts also went indoors, in gyms provided by athletic clubs, schools, and the philanthropic Young Men's (and Women's) Christian Association.

In the YMCA two new winter team games, basketball and volleyball, were created specifically to cope with the sports vacuum that existed between the end of the football season and the spring renewal of baseball. By the end of the nineteenth century, northerners had little excuse to hibernate and fatten like bears during the winter months.

On Snow and Ice

Of all competitive winter sports, curling was the first to be organized. Having originated centuries earlier on the frozen canals of Holland and the lakes of

Scotland, it was a game similar to English bowls, with players sliding a round, slightly flattened granite stone toward a designated spot on the ice. In eighteenth-century Scotland neighboring villages annually gathered for festive events called "bonspiels," featuring curling matches. Rules of the games varied widely from village to village and even more from county to county. The formation of the Royal Caledonian Curling Club in 1838 provided a common set of rules. To the present day the Royal Caledonian remains the parent organization of curling throughout the world.

Scottish immigrants introduced curling to Canada, leading to the formation of the Royal Montreal Curling Club in 1807. Shortly thereafter clubs also formed in Kingston and Toronto, and in 1832 the first American curling club was founded at Orchard Lake, Michigan. By mid-century bonspiels were common throughout central Canada; in 1866 the Chatham Club organized a match against a combined Detroit-Pontiac team. In the 1870s clubs and bonspiels proliferated in upper New York state, west to Manitoba and Saskatchewan, and east to the Canadian Scottish enclave of Nova Scotia. In 1880 a notable enthusiast, the Governor General of Canada, Lord Dufferin, established the Governor General's trophy, a silver cup, for the curling champions of Canada. Four years later a New Yorker, Robert Gordon, donated a trophy to promote competition between the United States and Canada.

Curling was not confined to Scotland, Canada, and the icy regions of the United States, however. Scottish engineers and travelers established the game in Scandinavia and central Europe. Now largely considered a quaint game enjoyed mostly by older men, curling in the second half of the nineteenth century enjoyed a golden age of popularity. In many northern towns it was the only winter sport. Young and old alike competed for local honors until the turn of the century, when youths turned to the thrills and vigorous exercise of new ski slopes and ice-hockey rinks.

Long an essential mode of transportation in Scandinavia and Finland, skiing became an organized competitive sport in the nineteenth century. Ski carnivals in Norwegian towns featured cross-country runs and jumping contests. Skiers still used the single long pole for balance, but improved bindings held the heel as well as the ball of the foot on the skis, allowing sharp twists and turns. New maneuvers took their names from the towns where the techniques first became popular: Telemark was the home of Sondre Nordheim, who perfected the S-turn, and the "Christiania" derives its name from the ancient site of Oslo. In the 1860s slalom (a Norwegian dialect term for downhill tracks in the snow) races were regularly scheduled in the vicinity of Oslo, and an annual cross-country race of more than a hundred miles began between Telemark and Oslo. Finally, in 1883 the Norwegian Ski Association was formed, the first of its kind in Europe.

Norway's severe climate and terrain made for better winter sports than for year-round jobs. Like the Scots, restless Norwegians migrated to fairer fields abroad, especially to the gold fields of Australia and California. A decade before the founding of the Norwegian Ski Association, immigrants in Australia formed the Kiandra Ski Club, which survives to the present as the oldest

In "Ice Boats on the Hudson," a lithograph by Currier and Ives, sailboats on ski-like runners keep pace with a train down the frozen Hudson River.

of all ski clubs. In the California Sierras bearded Scandinavian miners careened downhill for bets and lager beer, silver dollars, and gold-mine claims. By the end of the century competitive events regularly attracted paying spectators and offered cash prizes in Alta, Utah; Aspen, Colorado; Ishpeming, Michigan; Revelstoke, Canada; and Berlin, New Hampshire.

In the 1890s skiing became the rage in Europe, particularly in the Swiss, German, and Austrian alps. For the inconsistent depths of snow on steep Alpine slopes, Matthias Zdarsky, an Austrian army officer, designed a short grooveless ski with steel bindings, replaced the long single stick with two short ones, and invented a kind of giant slalom technique with a low crouch. By 1900 Scandinavia's gift to the sporting world had been adapted to the unique conditions of Europe and North America, ready to blossom as a genuinely popular sport with the coming of automobile travel and mechanized ski lifts.

More elite than skiing, ice yachting was a winter adaptation of rich summer yachtsmen in Holland, Scandinavia, Finland, northern Germany, Canada and the northeastern United States in the nineteenth century. Some of the early ice yachts were huge, requiring crews of several men. One, built in 1870 by Commodore John Roosevelt for winter play on the frozen Hudson River, measured sixty-nine feet in length. But Roosevelt's extravagance quickly became a dinosaur. For reasons of economy and speed, most sportsmen streamlined their winter crafts to carry only one or two occupants.

Ice yachting especially flourished in the Hudson River Valley, where the

Poughkeepsie Ice Yacht Club was established in 1865; five years later a larger, more exclusive Hudson River Ice Yacht Club was formed. Annual competitive races began in 1881. From Poughkeepsie yachtsmen traveled eight miles downriver to a stakeboat and back, at speeds exceeding a hundred miles an hour. Such speed entailed some danger. In one disaster a runner caught a crack in the ice, throwing the driver into the path of another yacht. He was killed instantly.

Crowds gathered on the frozen shores of the Hudson to watch these races, but for mass outdoor winter exercise, ice-skating sufficed. The pastime was hardly new. For centuries inhabitants of the icy regions of Europe and North America strapped bone and iron runners on their shoes with strips of leather to enjoy casual frolics on the ice. In the nineteenth century, however, the leisurely pastime became a competitive sport. Of no small importance was a new skate that clipped onto the boot, invented by a Philadelphian in 1850, increasing both agility and speed on the ice.

The first notable figure skater was Jackson Haines from Chicago. A trained professional dancer, Haines developed a spectacular twirling technique on skates. In 1864 he went abroad, astonished Europeans by dancing and gliding to waltz music, and thereby established an international figure-skating style. One of his best pupils was Louis Rubenstein, a Canadian who dominated "fancy" skating in North America in the 1880s. Two Scandinavians, Ulrich Salchow of Sweden and Axel Paulsen of Norway, perfected jumps that are still associated with their names.

Frozen ponds in new city parks lent themselves to figure-skating exhibitions as well as family outings. One of the first used, in 1858, was in Central Park in New York City; within a decade Toronto, Montreal, London, and Zurich all offered similar pleasures. In 1876 the first indoor rink with artificially frozen ice, the Glaciarium, was built in London. It was tiny, only forty feet long and twenty-four feet wide, but it provided galleries for spectators and walls decorated with Swiss Alpine scenes painted by a Parisian artist. Within three years of the opening of the Glaciarium, imitations appeared in Manchester and Southport. Although all were too small for speed-skating, they were ideal for figure-skating contests.

Still a fine art at best, the judging of figure-skating competitors was arbitrary until national skating associations in England (1879), the United States (1886), Canada (1888), and most European countries devised systems of scoring for proficiency and style. National bodies also arranged speed-skating rules and tournaments. In 1885 the first official international competition was held in Hamburg, Germany; the next was in Slikkerveer, Holland, in 1887. American competitors were determined, as was one young man from Newburgh, New York, "to conquer Europe on steel." None succeeded until 1890, when Joseph F. Donoghue carried away all the laurels from the first international contest held in England.

Donoghue was exceptional. As a rule, competitive skating (especially for speed) at the turn of the century continued to be dominated by Europeans. For years neither the American nor the Canadian national skating associations joined the International Skating Union, founded in 1892 and represented by Austria, Germany, England, Holland, Hungary, and Sweden. Yet North American isolation was primarily a matter of geographical distance rather than disinterest. Throughout Canada and the northern border of the United States, winter outdoor sports boomed in the second half of the nineteenth century.

Hockey on the Brain

The earliest Indian inhabitants of North American played lacrosse the year round. The Winnebago tribe in Wisconsin, for example, not only competed in a spring festival game but also after the winter hunt. Indians everywhere played darts, dice, and guessing games on long winter evenings, but more hardy young warriors spent entire afternoons playing lacrosse on frozen rivers or lakes. Indians in the Canadian Northwest traditionally took to icy lacrosse fields after the winter hunts as well as during the summer.

Until the mid-nineteenth century, English settlers in Canada left lacrosse to the Indians. In 1842, however, members of the new Olympic Athletic Club of Montreal began competing against nearby Indian teams. At first the Anglo-Canadians were so inept that the Indians allowed them to field two or three extra players in order to even the competition. Finally, in 1851 a white team recorded its first victory against an Indian side, and in the decade of the 1850s several new Anglo-Canadian lacrosse clubs were formed. They quickly made the game their own. Dr. W. George Beer, the supposed "father of lacrosse," drew up a set of rules and specifications for field and equipment. In 1867, the year of Canadian Confederation, a convention of several clubs in Kingston established the National Lacrosse Association; in the same year lacrosse was designated as Canada's "official" national game.

Never in the history of colonization was a native treasure seized so quickly and decisively. In 1880 the National Lacrosse Association ruled that only amateurs could play lacrosse, effectively barring Indians (who customarily played for cash prizes) from competing in the national championships. Indians banded together to form their own Indian World Championship, but the games of Anglo-Canadians received most of the press attention. Contests against new teams from the northeastern United States heightened public interest. During the second half of the nineteenth century, lacrosse was undoubtedly the most popular team sport in Canada.

Departing from the former Indian pattern of year-round play, Anglo-Canadians confined their lacrosse competition to summer and autumn. Occasionally they experimented with winter contests, but with unsatisfactory results. In the 1870s several lacrosse matches on the indoor Victoria Rink in Montreal produced more broken windows than goals. Outdoors on frozen lakes, lacrosse on ice skates proved as awkward as did similar attempts to play winter soccer, cricket, and baseball. Short Canadian summers left a large part of the year in need of an appropriate team sport. Ice hockey filled the bill.

Centuries earlier, Dutchmen played with sticks and little balls on ice, but North American ice hockey came from Britain, where field-hockey games variously known as hurley, shinty, or bandy adapted easily to ice. On the windswept frozen canals and ponds of the Fens in East Anglia, that adaptation took place long before Canadian ice hockey began. East Anglians played with curved sticks and a small, round, flat object, and called their game by the old Tudor term, bandy. In 1860 some Fensmen exhibited their aggressive skills on the ice of Crystal Palace in London. Had freezing cold spells in England not been punctuated with warming thaws, ice hockey probably would have become a distinctively English rather than Canadian game.

No one knows the precise time and place of the beginning of ice hockey in Canada. Various claims have been made for the provinces of Ontario, Quebec, and Nova Scotia, all placing the origins of the game in the first half of the nineteenth century. According to an official report of the Amateur Hockey Association of Canada, released in 1941, the first recorded game was played in the winter of 1855 in Kingston, Ontario, by English troops attached to a regiment of the Royal Canadian Rifles. But anyone familiar with the "official" committee accounts of the origins of games such as English rugby and American baseball instinctively leaves the subject open to doubt. Ultimately, the exact date and place of the first game, or games, are unimportant. More to the point, the fast and rough game of ice hockey became firmly established in the second half of the nineteenth century as Canada's premier winter sport.

Montreal was the center of the game's early development. Two energetic McGill University students, W. F. Robertson and R. F. Smith, were the earliest visible patrons. Apparently they never saw an ice-hockey or bandy match until they played in one of their own making. Visiting England in the summer of 1879, Robertson witnessed several field-hockey contests, saw the possibilities of adapting the game to ice, and returned home to work with Smith in devising a new winter sport for McGill students. In the winter of 1879–80 they led in the formation of the McGill University Hockey Club and created the "McGill Rules," which came to be commonly accepted. To prevent the round rubber field-hockey ball from bouncing wildly on ice, they decided to use a square rubber "puck." They agreed on nine players for each side and banned all forward passing of the puck.

Shortly after the creation of the McGill Rules, an annual Carnival Week in Montreal featured an ice-hockey tournament between four Montreal teams: the Victorias, the Montreal Amateur Athletic Association, the Crystals, and McGill. By the 1890s nearly a hundred amateur clubs regularly competed against each other in the vicinity of Montreal.

From Montreal the game spread rapidly in all directions. In 1885 another McGill student athlete, A. P. Low, introduced ice hockey in the Ottawa area. In the same year the first league was formed in Kingston, composed of Queen's University, the Kingston Athletics, the Royal Military College, and the Kingston Hockey Club. Within a decade local teams and leagues formed in Regina, Calgary, and Vancouver. Ice hockey was especially popular in frigid Winnipeg, where the Manitoba and Northwestern Amateur Hockey Association formed in 1892 and sent an all-star team to win nine of eleven matches in Kingston, Montreal, and Quebec.

Just as surely as baseball earlier made its way north across the Canadian-American border, ice hockey quickly caught on in the northwestern United States. In 1893 Yale and Johns Hopkins universities took it up as an intramural sport. Three years later four amateur teams in New York City formed the United States Amateur Hockey League. Teams in Boston and Pittsburgh followed suit, and in 1898 Brown scrubbed Harvard, 6–0, at Boston's Franklin Park rink in the first intercollegiate ice-hockey match ever held in the United States.

In a manner further similar to baseball, ice hockey early became a professional sport. In 1903 the first all-professional team was founded in Portage Lake, Michigan. Within the decade professional leagues emerged in both Ontario and British Columbia. Nor was the popularity of the game confined to North America. In 1908 amateur clubs from France, Belgium, Switzerland, and Great Britain followed the leadership of a Frenchman named Magnus in forming the Ligue Internationale de Hockey sur Glace, now known as the International Ice Hockey Federation.

Despite all its organizational expansion and vigor, ice hockey to the end of the nineteenth century remained a remarkably simple and unsophisticated game. It was almost always played outdoors between snowbanks or on rinks made for skating or curling. Without boards lining the sides or ends of rinks, pucks often got lost in the snow. Likely as not, the puck was made of wood rather than hard rubber. The goal consisted of four-feet-high sticks frozen in the ice six feet apart without crossbars or nets. Players wore no gloves or pads, and they stayed on the ice for the entire game unless injured. Early goalies wore no leg pads or chest protectors, and certainly no masks. Finally, in 1896 a goalie for a Winnipeg team took the ice in Montreal amid howls of protest: he was wearing cricket pads to protect his shins. In 1900 hockey adopted another practical piece of equipment. A Montreal fan brought fish nets with him from Australia to drape around the goal sticks, thereby providing a more certain judgment on shots at goal.

Spectators bring color and excitement to sporting events. For the sake of spectator appeal, officials often change schedules and even styles of play. In early Canadian ice hockey, however, fans contributed materially to the game. The addition of goal nets is one example; the creation of the Stanley Cup is another. During his five-year tenure as Governor General of Canada, Sir Frederick Arthur Stanley became an enthusiastic spectator at ice-hockey matches. Upon his return home to England in 1893, he paid ten guineas to a London silversmith for a silver bowl with an interior finish of gold set on an ebony base, then donated the "Stanley Cup" as an "outward or visible sign of the championship" of Canadian ice hockey. At the outset, the cup was passed from one amateur champion to another; in 1910 it was taken over by the National Hockey Association, a professional league, and it remains today as the oldest and one of the most coveted of all awards for professional athletes in North America.

For the first Stanley Cup in 1894 the Montreal Amateur Athletic Association defeated the Ottawa Capitals, 3–1, on an outdoor rink. About 5,000 spectators braved the cold to watch. The ethnic composition of the teams

In this sketch from *Harper's Young People*, 1884, boys are using bent wooden sticks, a round ball, and strapped-on skates for a vigorous informal game of ice hockey.

reflected the character of ice hockey in the late nineteenth century. Every single player spoke English; for years not one French-Canadian played on a Stanley Cup championship team. Like American football and baseball, ice hockey was rooted in the English tradition of team sports, but by 1900 it was adapting to its new environment in a manner uniquely North American. It was destined soon to replace lacrosse as Canada's unofficial national game. An elderly skater best summed up the situation when, in 1892, he was unable to gain access to his local rink because of a prolonged hockey match. Too many Canadian youths, he complained, had "hockey on the brain."

Moving Indoors

To avoid the wind and cold, many North Americans sought their diversions indoors. In fact, they adapted outdoor ice-skating into a new form of pleasant exercise, roller-skating. In 1863 an American inventor, James L. Plimpton, took out a patent for a skate with four wooden wheels set in pairs. During the 1870s, businessmen in Canada and the United States, and afar in Great Britain and on the Continent, turned old warehouses and abandoned factories into roller-skating rinks. They then hired bands and rented out skates to provide a convivial atmosphere for city youths and adults hungry for mild winter activity. In good American fashion, however, even roller-skating soon produced a competitive game. Roller polo, actually a kind of ice hockey on roller skates, enjoyed a brief but widespread popularity in the 1880s. Seven midwestern cities in 1882 formed an indoor "roller polo" league.

Less vigorous winter sportsmen turned to the numerous bowling alleys and billiard parlors built before the Civil War. Billiards remained a male-dominated game tainted with liquor and gambling associations, but ten-pin and duck-pin bowling increasingly appealed to women as well. According to one reporter, bowling during the second half of the nineteenth century fostered "a more perfect *entente cordial* between the sexes." A sure sign of respectability and popularity, the American Bowling Congress was founded in 1895 to standardize rules, equipment, and competitive matches.

More on the order of a spectacle rather than participant sport, pedestrianism went indoors after the Civil War. Shrewd promoters rightly reasoned that indoor races during the winter months would face less competition from other diversions than did outdoor summer contests. In Canada and the United States, and to a lesser extent in England (where milder winter weather allowed outdoor competition), indoor walking races became highly commercial during the 1870s. Outstanding American competitors such as Edward Payson Weston and Frank Hart (one of the few blacks in the sport) raced for both distance and time. Six days, from Monday through Saturday, was the favorite term of duration for walk-as-you-can races. In 1874 Weston made $5,000 at the American Institute Building in New York City, as he barely failed to walk 500 miles in six days.

Attracted by the delights of drink and gambling, spectators came and went, usually always returning for the sixth and final day of the races. In 1881 a large field of walkers competed on a sawdust track in the American

Institute Building, with the winner covering 567 miles in six days. As he neared the finish, 4,000 spectators crammed into the stands to cheer. In grueling, often ludicrous contests of pedestrians walking backwards, carrying anvils in their hands, or pushing wheelbarrows mile after mile, pedestrianism turned into a kind of circus for amusement-starved city folk during the winter months.

An ancient form of competition, wrestling, first became organized on a professional, international basis in the late nineteenth century. In old opera houses, new music halls, and traveling circuses, wrestlers competed in one of two styles: Graeco-Roman, which forbade tripping holds beneath the waist, and "catch-as-catch-can," with no holds barred. Unlike the farce that goes by the name of modern professional wrestling, most matches were authentic contests. In 1881 a crowd of 2,000 spectators at New York's Terrace Garden Theater watched William Muldoon and Clarence Whistler grapple for seven hours, with neither man able to pin the other. Finally at 4 A.M. the proprietors cut off the gaslights and sent the crowd home. Muldoon, an Irish-American policeman on the New York City force, claimed the American championship for fifteen years, from 1880 to 1895. He traveled widely (often with John L. Sullivan, the boxing champion) and beat the best that Britain, France, and Spain had to offer. When Muldoon retired, two Europeans, George Hackenschmidt and Eugen Sandow became the most popular international attractions.

Both Sandow and Hackenschmidt began as weight lifters, another form of sport spectacle that emerged during the second half of the nineteenth century. As ancient as running and wrestling, weight lifting also became modernized as a kind of circus entertainment for city dwellers in search of diversion. Of all the exhibitionists of the era, Louis Cyr of Quebec was the most famous. Carrying more than 300 pounds on a frame less than six feet tall, Cyr once lifted a platform holding eighteen men, whose aggregate weight was 4,300 pounds. While circus strong men pumped barbells and dumbbells, Cyr attached a chain and ring to a weight of 588 pounds, then lifted it with one finger. A consummate showman, he wore his blond hair unusually long. "It's attractive when exhibiting," he candidly explained.

Urban crowds willing to pay for such exhibitions led to the transformation of many old amateur sports into professional displays in the nineteenth century. Yet the impulse to watch sporting events was only one side of the story of indoor winter amusements. City people needed more than vicarious tests of strength and skill. For the more affluent, old outdoor games of Irish handball and English rackets (racquets) and squash were taken into new indoor courts in the mid-nineteenth century. Shortly after the founding of a London racket club in 1853, British officers stationed in Montreal, Hamilton, Quebec, and Halifax introduced indoor racquet-and-ball play to Canadians, and from the Montreal Rackets Club the game quickly spread south to New York, Philadelphia, Boston, Chicago, and Detroit. Yet winter rackets, squash, and handball were for the chosen few who could afford the fees of private club membership. The urban masses in search of winter indoor exercise turned to an institution that was a distinct child of nineteenth-century city life, the gymnasium.

Although some early exercise rooms in the United States were called gymnasiums, until mid-century a gymnasium was usually a field or park set aside for outdoor exercises. In 1852 an indoor gym was constructed in Hesse, one of the German states where Adolph Spiess made gymnastics an integral part of the school curriculum. In order to promote gymnastics the year round, even in the northernmost latitudes of Europe, advocates of both the German and Swedish systems built indoor gymnasiums with equipment appropriate to their respective styles. In the United States, too, immigrant German *turners* raised private capital to construct indoor gymnasiums in numerous towns and cities.

Athletic clubs, although primarily devoted to outdoor track, field, and water competition, quickly joined the craze for indoor gyms. The London Athletic Club, founded in 1866, the New York Athletic Club (1868), and the Hungarian Athletic Club in Budapest (1875) were geographically distant from each other but similarly intent on providing indoor winter facilities as well as outdoor competitive events for their members. The founders of the New York Athletic Cub, Bill Curtis and Henry Buermeyer, devised indoor exercise rooms before their "club" even had a name, and long before the NYAC made its mark in track and water meets. Tenants in a large apartment at 200 Sixth Avenue and 14th Street in New York, Curtis and Buermeyer in 1866 converted their parlor into a small gymnasium with pulleys, dumbbells, and exercise bars, and they turned their bedroom into a boxing ring. Their athletic club was firmly, if humbly, set on a course of winter exercise for "feats of strength and pugilistic aptitude."

But athletic clubs in the nineteenth century tended to be ethnically exclusive and financially beyond the reach of most people. A far more popular provider of indoor gymnasiums was an unlikely institution, the Young Men's Christian Association. Founded in England in 1844 by George Williams, originally the YMCA was purely an evangelistic religious body. It spread throughout the world but was strongest in Canada and the United States. In the early 1860s it began seriously to deal with "the whole man": the physical as well as spiritual well-being of city youths. In 1864 the directors of the organization decided to include physical recreation in all YMCAs, and in 1869 local branches in New York and San Francisco simultaneously built the first YMCA gymsiums in the United States. Within only four years, YMCA gyms in North America numbered almost 400, with about half of them employing physical-education directors. As the YMCA spearheaded the "muscular Christianity" movement, churches followed suit. In 1875 Park Church in Elmira, New York, built the first church gym, and by the end of the century a number of large, prominent churches in the United States and Canada opened gym floors during the week.

Gymnasiums in churches were largely confined to North America; gymnasiums in schools and universities knew no geographical bounds in the Western world. Several decades before American schools built gyms, German and Scandinavian enthusiasts made gymnastics an integral, often compulsory part of European student life. At mid-century, gymnastic institutes sprang up in central and eastern Europe for the training of professional physical-education teachers. For Europeans plagued by international tensions and threats of war, gymnastic exercise was ideal for physical training and military preparedness. It was a badge of nationalistic patriotism in nations as diverse as Germany, Denmark, Greece, and France. The most famous of all nationalist organizations based on gymnastics was the Sokol, founded in 1862 in Prague, Bohemia (Czechoslovakia). The leader of the movement, Miroslav Tyrs, admired the ancient Greeks, loved his native land, and required his pupils to pledge allegiance to brotherhood and country. At first the Sokol catered solely to males, but in 1869 a womens' and girls' branch was created. Beginning in 1882 national festivals gathered Sokol members from all over Bohemia to Prague for dramatic displays of gymnastic skills and massive formations set to patriotic music and rhetoric. As they required gymnastics of all pupils in the schools, Bohemians were little different from other Europeans. With no ball-playing tradition competing for students' attention until the late nineteenth century, German apparatus and Swedish calisthenic exercises blended to form the core of physical culture in schools and universities throughout Europe.

In England, on the other hand, gymnastics were slow to catch on in the schools. Several Swedish masters opened private gymnasiums in mid-nineteenth-century London, and in 1858 Archibald Maclaren established a gym in Oxford. But the English were much more interested in outdoor competitive ball games than in indoor exercises. In 1885 some educators attempted to make physical education compulsory in the elementary schools, but local, insular resistance prevented it until the early twentieth century.

A harsh winter climate and the presence of numerous German and Scandinavian immigrants in the northern United States made for a different story in American school and university circles. By 1860 Harvard, Yale, and Amherst had indoor gyms. Physical educators such as Dio Lewis, Edward Hitchcock, Dudley Allen Sargent, and Catharine Beecher (an early champion of female participation in gymnastics) eclectically combined German and Swedish systems with innovations of their own. In 1880 a national convention of *turners* voted to campaign for compulsory gymnastics in the public schools, and shortly thereafter the newly founded American Association for the Advancement of Physical Education passed a similar resolution. By 1900 gymnastics were a part of the school curriculum in more than fifty of the larger cities in the United States.

From the beginning, however, gymnastic exercise was only one of many indoor activities made possible by the gymnasium. Fencing equipment, padded boxing gloves, and wrestling mats were all put to good use in the gym. Courts for handball, racquets, and squash appeared in the larger gymnasiums. During the last quarter of the nineteenth century, athletic clubs, YMCAs, YWCAs, and universities built indoor swimming pools. By century's end, the options for indoor play were numerous.

Naismith's New Game

Following on the heels of autumn football, winter gym activities soon lost their savor for Americans. Gymnastic work on bars and ropes was fine for health-giving exercise and body-building strength, but it lacked the competitive element so deeply ingrained in American life. Combative sports such as boxing, wrestling, and fencing, on the other hand, were too individualistic for athletes who had become accustomed to the delights of spirited team play in football and baseball. To fill the winter vacuum, a few Americans turned to water polo, a game invented around 1870 in Britain. An adaptation of soccer football, water polo ("football-in-the-water") was a vigorous, rough team sport. Had indoor swimming pools been sufficiently available in the 1870s and 1880s, water polo might well have become popular in the United States. But pool facilities were few until the turn of the century, leaving Americans to their own wits to devise a competitive team game to fill their winter hours.

They tried "indoor baseball." Limitations of space on the gym floor called for shorter bases, underarm pitching, a broomstick for a bat, and a boxing glove wrapped in twine, which could not be hit as hard or far as a real baseball. In 1887 George W. Hancock, a member of the Farragut Boat Club in Chicago, drew up a set of rules and popularized the game. Here was the beginning of the now popular outdoor game of softball, but for many Americans in the late nineteenth century it was so tame compared to baseball that it was dubbed "kitten ball" or "mush ball." Originally it appealed more to children and women than to adult males. Entering the final decade of the century, Americans keenly felt the need for a popular indoor team sport.

No one confronted the problem more directly than did the staff and students at a new International YMCA Training School in Springfield, Massachusetts. In 1891 YMCA directors from all over the United States convened at Springfield for a summer school of theoretical and practical study of physical education. To a man, they reported that gymnastics were losing their appeal to American youths familiar with the excitement of baseball and football games. In a faculty seminar in the autumn of 1891, the director of the school, Luther Gulick, explored the need for a game that would be easy to play indoors under artificial light. Set to work on the problem, various members of the staff merely created new pieces of gymnastic apparatus and devised new forms of exercises, innovations that soon lost their novelty even among the students at Springfield.

Gulick then turned to one of his youngest and most imaginative instructors, James B. Naismith. Born in Almonte, Ontario, in 1861, Naismith was a graduate of McGill University, where he played rugby football for seven years while studying for undergraduate and divinity degrees. During his last year of theological training, however, he decided that "there might be other effective ways of doing good besides preaching." A Muscular Christian incarnate, he entered the Springfield training college in the autumn of 1890, the very year that Amos Alonzo Stagg first organized a football team for the college. Stagg placed Naismith at center because, as he explained, Naismith could do "the meanest things in the most gentlemanly manner." After a year of study, the gentlemanly Naismith became an instructor at the school.

Charged by Gulick to invent an attractive indoor game, Naismith first tried several forms of tag, then introduced a soccer ball for various keep-away games. Initial enthusiasm quickly turned to boredom, prompting Naismith to modify soccer, lacrosse, and American football for indoor play. They proved to be too rough and destructive for indoors, however. Naismith decided that only a game involving a ball and goals had a chance for popularity. Finally, two weeks before the Christmas break in 1891, he came up with the idea of setting a goal on a horizontal plane above the players, thereby forcing them to lob the ball rather than kick or hit it into the goal.

To prevent tussles on the gym floor, Naismith decided to use a ball that could not be hidden from view. Thus he rejected the use of a baseball and a rugby football, and chose instead a soccer ball. For the size and shape of goals, however, Naismith had to improvise. He asked the superintendent of buildings if he had two boxes about eighteenth inches square. None could be found, but the superintendent remembered "two old peach baskets down in the store room, if they will do you any good." Only this freakish circumstance prevented the present game of basketball from being called "boxball." Naismith nailed the peach baskets onto the lower rail of the balcony at each end of the gym. Then he tacked thirteen rules for the game on the bulletin board and anxiously awaited the outcome. Initial student impression was not promising. When the first member of the class arrived, read the rules, and saw the peach baskets, he dubiously muttered, "Huh! Another new game!"

And a new game it was. Naismith's first five rules sharply distinguished the style of play from all other ball games, especially those involving physical contact. Players could throw the ball in any direction, but they could not strike it with the fist, hold it against the body, or run with it. The crucial fifth rule banned "shouldering, holding, pushing, tripping, or striking" one's opponent. Infringement of this rule constituted a foul, with three team fouls between goals counting as a goal. When a player committed a second foul, he was sent to the sidelines until the next goal was scored, and an infraction with "evident intent to injure" meant disqualification for the entire game, with no substitute allowed. To enforce these rules, Naismith designated an umpire to call fouls and disqualify players if necessary, and a referee to serve as the supreme arbiter on matters of scoring, out-of-bound balls, and time-keeping. A game was divided into two fifteen-minute halves, with a five-minute rest in between.

So much for the rules. Practicality determined many features of the game. With eighteen men in the class, nine played on each side. For several years the number of players was unlimited. Shortly after the game became established at Springfield, a physical-education instructor at Cornell University, Edward Hitchcock, introduced it to a class of a hundred. Fifty enthusiastic players on each team created turmoil, though. In 1895 the problem was overcome by limiting each team to five players.

Equipment similarly evolved in response to practical necessity. At first a ladder was used to retrieve the ball from the peach baskets. Then boys in the balconies did the job, and soon some innovative soul drilled a hole in the bottom of the basket and used a pole to punch the ball up and out. Within a year or so after the game began, round iron rims with heavy woven-wire baskets replaced the peach baskets, but still the basket held the ball after each goal; a chain ran over a pulley to the bottom of the wire net, to open it and let the ball drop free. In 1893 bottomless cord nets became standard equipment.

In 1894 an official basketball slightly larger than a soccer ball came into use,

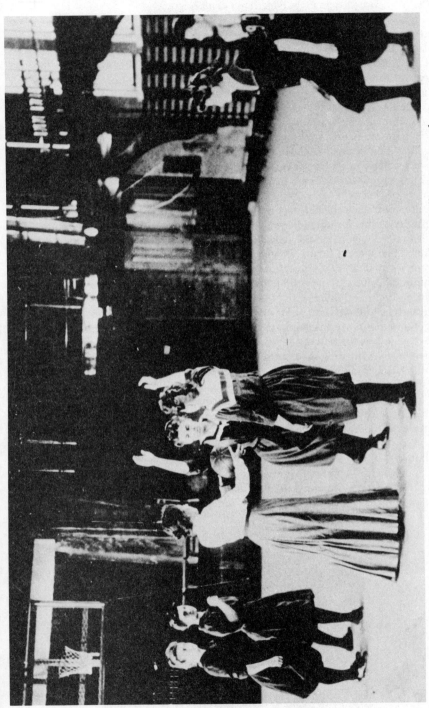

Scarcely more than a year after James B. Naismith created the game of basketball, women students at Smith College in Northampton, Massachusetts, were playing. Miss Senda Berenson, in long dress, served as coach and referee. Note the basket set somewhat awry on a wire screen. (Courtesy of the Basketball Hall of Fame.)

first manufactured by the Overman Wheel Company of Chicopee Falls, Massachusetts. Then came the construction of heavy wire-screen backboards in 1895, to prevent balcony partisans from deflecting shots away from the goals. The weight and mesh of the wire varied so widely from gym to gym that the home team enjoyed an inordinate advantage, bringing on standard wooden backboards by the turn of the century. Also by 1900 dribbling (bouncing) the ball became a common tactic. Naismith originally envisaged only a passing and "shooting" game, but players quickly learned that they could obtain better angles for their maneuvers if they bounced the ball once or twice before shooting or passing off to a teammate.

These rapid changes in techniques and equipment reflected the lively nature of Naismith's new game. As Springfield men in long pants enthusiastically competed against each other, the game quickly spread beyond the confines of the Springfield gym. A YMCA paper, *The Triangle*, publicized the rules and development of basketball to every branch of the YMCA in the United States and Canada. Within three years of Naismith's invention, teams were formed at the universities of Chicago and Iowa and at Stanford, Vanderbilt, and Yale; by 1897 about sixty athletic clubs sponsored teams. During the first decade of the twentieth century, intercollegiate eastern and western leagues were formed, and interleague competition began in 1909.

Within months of the beginning of the men's game, women began playing. Basketball was the first active team sport for women. Smith College fielded a team in 1893, dividing the floor into three sections. One of the earliest female enthusiasts, Maude Sherman, took a husband with her game. She and Naismith were married in June 1894.

In the same month one of Naismith's better pupils, William G. Morgan, graduated from Springfield and took a position as the physical-education director at the YMCA in Holyoke, Massachusetts. As a basketball teacher, he soon confronted the need for a game for middle-aged businessmen, for whom basketball was too exhausting. Thus in 1895 he formulated the game of "minionette," soon to be known as volleyball, the last of several competitive team sports invented in the nineteenth century whereby men and women overcame the constrictions of winter.

Chapter **12**

INDIVIDUALISM, RUGGED AND REFINED

Had Charles Darwin cared about sports, he might well have observed that many of the sports of his day would have to adapt or become extinct. In sport, as in the animal world, only the "fittest" survive. The demise of the ancient Greek games, Roman gladiatorial spectacles, and medieval tournaments proved that those sports that do not (or cannot) adjust to new circumstances are soon relegated to the museum of historical artifacts. The story of football, on the other hand, is a classic example of survival by adaptation. As urban congestion and new moral sensibilities could no longer support the anarchistic brutality of the rural game, footballers constructed rules, confined their game to a limited playing area, and made it socially indispensable as a new form of urban entertainment.

Ancient individual sports similarly changed in the nineteenth century. No longer could boxing survive as a shady, coarse affair supported only by gambling interests; no longer could horse racing depend solely upon aristocratic patronage. Both adapted. Boxing produced a figure of international prominence in the flamboyant person of John L. Sullivan, "civilized" itself by the introduction of a more rational set of rules, and by the end of the century began realizing the commercial importance of a cleaner image. Horse racing also began to capitalize on the potential of a mass audience, and in the process it became transformed into a modern spectacle.

For more refined citizens of the Western world, several ancient aristocratic games were adapted to the privacy of middle-class lawns and clubs. Croquet, archery, badminton, lawn tennis, and golf set the well-to-do apart from the masses just as surely as did income and education. These "new" games provided both leisure activity and organized competition. The species of sport that adapted well to the marketplace of nineteenth-century life did not merely survive; they thrived.

The Last of the Bare-Knuckle Breed

Arguably the most ancient form of physical contest, pugilism was undoubtedly the most rugged and controversial of all individual sports in the nineteenth century. For three decades following the famous Heenan-Sayers fight in 1860, prizefighters continued to throw and pummel each other around the ring in the bare-knuckle, few-holds-barred style sanctioned by the London Prize Ring Rules of 1838. In an attempt to "civilize" the sport, the Marquis of Queensbury, an English aristocrat, lent his name and patronage to a new set of rules. The Queensbury Rules of 1867 called for the use of padded gloves, the abolition of holding and wrestling, rounds of three minutes each with a minute's rest between, and a count of ten seconds over a fallen fighter. But for years only young gentlemanly members of athletic clubs adhered to the Queensbury Rules. Professional prizefighters persisted in their traditional rougher mode.

Sponsors and spectators, too, were notoriously rough. Gamblers arranged most bouts, and gambling enthusiasts set the rowdy ringside tone. Liquor and profanity flowed freely. Postfight crowds were a menace. Once on the mud flats of Hoboken, New Jersey, the supporters of a popular defeated fighter "took possession of every beer saloon along the road to the ferries," according to a local journalist, "and made Hoboken a place for decent people to avoid until a late hour in the morning."

Legally banned, the fight game tested the mettle of policemen. In Britain, the birthplace of organized boxing, Victorian "bobbies" cracked down on fighters and patrons alike in remote villages and little railway towns. Stern English judges slapped heavy fines and prison terms on offenders. In the 1860s and 1870s English "champions" Tom Allen, Jem Mace, and Joe Goss emigrated to the United States to ply their trade. The much larger, more heterogeneous character of American society made for an uneven enforcement of the law. Local police could be bribed more easily; bouts could be moved secretly across the Canadian border or held in one of the hundreds of little depot towns along the endless miles of American railroads. Until late in the century, "championship" fights were scheduled in unmemorable sites such as Busenbark Station, Ohio; Cold Spring, Indiana; Bay St. Louis, Mississippi; Kennerville, Louisiana; and Pacific City, Iowa. The greatest fighter of the era, John L. Sullivan, clandestinely met his first real test in 1881 against a New York thug, Johnny Flood, under gaslights on a barge tied up at a Yonkers dock.

Until Sullivan, the idea of a "championship" was a farce. Between 1860 and 1900 weight divisions—middleweight, welterweight, lightweight, featherweight, and bantamweight—became recognized, but most matchmakers still disregarded weight differences. Hungry Irish immigrants such as Joe Coburn, Mike McCoole, and Paddy Ryan brawled and bluffed their way to prominence. Ryan, the best of the lot, reigned for just two years, 1880–82, before relinquishing his title to a fellow Irish-American, the great John L. Sullivan.

Born in Roxbury, Massachusetts, of hardy Irish parentage from counties Kerry and Roscommon, John Lawrence Sullivan was an extraordinary individual. For a year and a half he attended Boston College, where he excelled in drama and rhetoric in preparation for fulfilling his mother's dream of his entering the priesthood. Yet baseball and boxing interested him more, causing him to withdraw from college, take up work as a plumber and tinsmith, play semiprofessional baseball, and engage in exhibition boxing matches in Boston's Opera House. Promoters recognized a good thing and booked "the Boston Strong Boy" for exhibitions in Cincinnati and New York City. In 1880 Sullivan turned professional, making quick work of several early opponents. By February 1882 he was ready to take on the champion, Paddy Ryan.

The bout was scheduled for New Orleans, a city famous for its flexible laws and social gaiety. While Sullivan and Ryan trained, however, newspaper journalists publicized the fight in such sensational terms that officials became alarmed at the prospect of bad publicity for their city. On the eve of the bout, they forbade it within the precincts of New Orleans, forcing the fighters and a special train loaded with sporting enthusiasts to move across the state line to remote little Mississippi City, Mississippi. There, fighting under the London Prize Ring Rules, Sullivan pulverized Ryan, finishing him off for good in the ninth round. "When Sullivan hit me," Ryan reportedly later commented, "I thought a telegraph pole had been shoved against me endways."

Despite the low reputation of boxing, Sullivan was America's first authentic sports celebrity. Journalists dogged his steps, eager to quote every colorful quip and boastful yarn that came from his mouth. He gave them a steady stream of copy and in the end created an image bigger than life. His exploits were in fact dramatic and his appetites enormous. A notorious drinker and woman chaser, he turned his fame into fortune. During a fourteen-year career, he made just over $100,000 in the ring, and in the same period he pocketed more than $1 million from theatrical tours and lectures. On the vaudeville circuit his showmanship flowered. He challenged all comers, offering handsome sums of money to any man who could last four rounds. Exhibitions in England and Australia made him internationally famous.

The first popular sports hero in the United States, the "Great John L." was the last of the bare-knuckle champions. Of seventeen bare-knuckle challengers for the crown, only Charlie Mitchell, the English champion, pushed him to the limit. In 1888 they squared away in a muddy, rain-drenched ring on the private estate of Baron Rothchild in Chantilly, France, and battered each other for more than three hours before both agreed to a draw in the thirty-ninth round. In the following year Sullivan fought Jake Kilrain in the last heavyweight championship fight held under the London Prize Ring Rules. Under a scorching sun they met in a rickety wooden arena set up in a clearing

John L. Sullivan, heavyweight boxing champion from 1882 to 1892,
was America's first notable sports
hero. Here is the Great John L. in
his prime, as photographed by
John Wood of New York City in
1885.

in the woods near Richburg, Mississippi, with the bout lasting more than two
hours before Kilrain's seconds threw in the sponge at the end of the seventy-
fifth round. Sullivan seemed invincible.

Appearances were misleading. For three years following the Kilrain bout,
Sullivan entered the ring only for exhibition matches. The outstanding
challenger of the day was Peter Jackson, an Australian black, but Sullivan
adamantly refused to fight "a member of the colored race." He also refused to
train. The vaudeville circuit, late-night carousing, and barroom sprees took
their toll. Sullivan's sturdy 5'11" frame, accustomed to carrying 195 pounds of
firm muscle, tottered under the weight of 220 pounds. Thirty-four years old
in 1892, the Boston Strong Boy had become a soft middle-aged man.

In another Irish-American, James J. Corbett, he met his opposite. A former
bank clerk from San Francisco, Corbett packed a trim 184 pounds on a 6'1"

frame. He lived cleanly, spoke modestly, and prided himself on polished manners. He was "Gentleman Jim," a new kind of professional boxer. Possessing no murderous punch like Sullivan's, Corbett was nimble of foot and quick with feint and jab. Sullivan dubbed him a mere "fancy dude"; following their encounter on 7 September 1892, the world acclaimed him the new heavyweight champion of the world.

The fight was held in the indoor Olympic Club of New Orleans, a tribute to the popular acceptance of professional boxing. For the first time ever in a championship match, the Queensbury Rules prevailed. Padded five-ounce gloves probably helped Corbett absorb Sullivan's powerful blows, but in fact few of the blows landed. Corbett bobbed and weaved, jabbed and clinched; Sullivan rushed and swung wildly, tired quickly, and finally sank glassy-eyed to the floor for the count of ten in the twenty-first round. According to one reporter, Corbett's finishing left hook was "audible throughout the house," but Sullivan's end was actually the result more of fatigue than of a knockout punch. His defeat signaled the passing of an old order.

While the American public slowly absorbed the shock, Sullivan resumed his vaudeville antics to make yet another fortune, and before his death in 1918 he even renounced his beloved whiskey bottle in favor of temperance lectures. Meanwhile, Corbett met and defeated several challengers to the title, until he fell victim to a vicious blow to the stomach by Bob Fitzsimmons in 1897. Weighing only 167 pounds, Fitzsimmons had already won the middleweight title in 1891; his defeat of Corbett made him the first man ever to hold two division titles simultaneously. His claim to the heavyweight crown, however, did not last long. In 1899 he gave away forty pounds to an inexperienced but muscular James Jeffries, and in the eleventh round fell under a barrage of blows.

Of far greater importance than the parade of victors and vanquished were the internal changes that overtook boxing at the turn of the century. There was no turning back from the new Queensbury Rules first employed in the Sullivan-Corbett title bout of 1892. While the Queensbury code broke matches into three-minute rounds, it still set no limit on the number of rounds. Victory went to the man who could endure the longest. Within the decade, that practice changed. By 1900 each bout terminated at a fixed number of rounds agreed upon previously by the fighters and their handlers, and if no knockout occurred, the referee decided the victor.

These alterations of form coincided with changes in the legality of the sport. Previously banned by law everywhere, boxing was finally made legal in New York in 1896 and in Nevada in 1897. Three years later the New York legislature momentarily removed its sanction, leaving the legality of the fight game to be clarified in the early years of the century. Yet by 1900 two things were certain. First, the center of prizefight activity had shifted from Great Britain to the United States, where commercial enterprise and immigrant ambitions coalesced to produce lively ring encounters. Second, the day of the bare-knuckle breed was decisively past. In Abingdon, Massachusetts, rotund John L. Sullivan lived out his life as a mythical giant, a legend of a bygone era.

The New Turf Crowd

Like boxing, age-old racing sports flourished during the second half of the nineteenth century. Aquatic sports remained exclusive. Resumed in 1870 after the disruption of the Civil War, the America's Cup was held spasmodically whenever prosperous English yachtsmen challenged the American trophy holders. English crews attempted to win the cup nine times before 1900, and nine times they failed. At century's end (1899), Thomas Lipton, an Irish millionaire tea merchant, made the first of five unsuccessful bids to win the America's Cup in his specially constructed *Shamrock*. Yet yachting was by no means confined to Anglo-American competition. French, Dutch, and German clubs thrived, and in distant Russia clubs founded in St. Petersburg (1860) and Moscow (1867) set the standards for about forty similar Russian groups established by 1898. Despite widespread upper-class enthusiasm for the sport, however, yachting continued as always to be financially distant from mass interest.

Rowing, on the other hand, lost much of the public attention it had enjoyed at mid-century. For England's annual Oxford–Cambridge University Match, spectators still lined the banks of the Thames, and occasional international challenges from Harvard and Yale crews stirred journalistic attention. But as newer, more attractive team sports emerged in Britain and the United States, rowing contests between elite English and American university students created fewer and fewer ripples in the public consciousness. In Germany and France, the other Western nations where competitive rowing most took hold in the late nineteenth century, private male clubs conducted their river races largely ignored by the public at large.

Of all the traditional racing sports, organized horse racing grew most in the nineteenth century. Beyond its early British and American foundations, the turf expanded throughout Europe and Latin America. In France it was first officially sponsored in 1833 with the founding of the Société d'Encouragement pour l'Amélioration des Races de Chevaux en France. French patrons originally imported studs, rules, and official jockey colors from England, not to mention terms such as *le turf, le sweepstake,* and even *le betting room*. By mid-century, Longchamps, a magnificent track near Paris, became the center of turf activity in France.

Miming the British pattern, the French nevertheless contributed a key ingredient to organized horse racing. In 1865 a Parisian chemist and perfume vendor, Pierre Oller, invented a new gambling system, *pari-mutuel*, as a corrective to shady bookmakers. Meaning "between ourselves," *pari-mutuel* was a scheme in which bettors pooled their money, with the winners splitting the total balance after Ollard collected a five-percent commission. An obvious ploy to avoid the odds-system arbitrarily devised by bookmakers, *pari-mutuel* was operated by machines. Quickly it became the only legal form of track gambling in France. In the 1870s it was introduced to tracks throughout the Western world, but it was a controversial item. Needless to say, bookmakers vehemently opposed it.

Other European nations followed the French in establishing organized horse racing. In 1867 a jockey club was first founded in Prussia and in 1881 in Italy, where tracks in Rome and Milan stirred ancient memories of equestrian contests. By 1900 virtually every European capital held its own derby in imitation of the English turf. Far away in the southern part of the Western Hemisphere, English colonies in Argentina and Brazil eagerly promoted the sport, and tracks subsequently appeared in Chile, Colombia, Peru, Uruguay, Venezuela, Panama, and Mexico. To the north, Canada's most prestigious turf fixture, the race for the Queen's Plate, began in Toronto in 1860, and from Halifax to Vancouver summer social festivities centered on horse races.

All this geographical expansion coincided with profound structural changes in the character of the sport in Britain and the United States. Once a local, exclusive pastime of aristocratic Britons, horse racing in Victorian England became a commercially profitable spectacle appealing to people of all ranks. The crucial new factor that did most to bring about this change was the railway, which not only allowed spectators to travel afar easily and cheaply but also provided the means for owners to move their horses quickly from one track to another. Increased crowds prompted track organizers to enclose their tracks with fences, install turnstiles, and charge admission. Growing profits in turn provided larger stakes for the contestants, thus encouraging patrons to enter their horses in more events than ever seemed feasible in the old days of gentlemanly contests for mere honor and plate trophies.

Sandown Park on the outskirts of London was Britain's first successful experiment in making the track commercially profitable. Enclosed in 1875, Sandown Park served as a model for numerous tracks, old and new, in the last quarter of the century. Two new groups of spectators, women and common laborers, signaled a radical departure from the previous all-male, upper-class crowd at the track. Factory hands especially were finally coming to enjoy the benefits of an industrial economy: physical mobility, some time free from work, and money to spend on things other than the bare necessities of life. As half-day Saturdays became the norm for factory operatives, racing organizers rushed to arrange races on Saturday afternoons (the day traditionally left open for aristocratic owners to transport horses back to their training grounds). By 1900 remote Doncaster to the north and elite Newmarket in East Anglia had opened their gates to hordes of common folk who came by train to place their bets and cheer the horses of their choice.

Compared to the United States, however, British commercialization was minimal. Already in the 1840s and 1850s many American track owners had enclosed their tracks to charge admission to pedestrian contests, horse races, and harness races. Ambitious promoters enjoyed a field day in post–Civil War America. One was John Morrissey, a former prizefighter, who in 1864 opened a track in Saratoga Springs, New York, catering to that summer resort's fashionable society. Two years later Jerome Park opened in Westchester County, just north of New York City, and within the decade Monmouth Park in New Jersey, Pimlico in Baltimore, Churchill Downs in Louisville, and the Fair Grounds in New Orleans headed a list of dozens of new tracks. The inaugural running of the Kentucky Derby in 1875 completed the American turf trinity later to be called the Triple Crown: the Derby, the Preakness (at Pimlico), and the Belmont Stakes.

As in Britain, only wealthy Americans such as Leonard W. Jerome, William R. Travers, and August Belmont could breed horses and promote track activities. But even more than their Victorian counterparts, the post–Civil War American track fraternity transformed the turf into a popular commercial enterprise. The development of horse racing in New Orleans is a case in point. At the end of the Civil War, the elite Metaire Jockey Club (founded in 1838) controlled turf matters. Ostensibly, it opened its gates to the general public, but it charged two dollars for daily admission and thereby ensured that only the more affluent, "respectable" citizens could attend. Moreover, the club strictly divided the stands into three sections—one for male club members, another for women, and a third for the public at large. Representing old, established wealth, the officers of the Metaire Club still looked on horse racing as a pastime pursued by gentlemen *for* gentlemen.

Younger members dissented. Wanting to establish the track on better business principles, in 1871 they broke away and formed a rival group, the Louisiana Jockey Club. They then purchased a decrepit antebellum track, the Union Course, changed its name to the Fair Grounds, and constructed a new three-tiered grandstand with a seating capacity of 5,000. Although they continued to segregate spectators along lines of social class and sex, they lowered the price of general admission to one dollar and allowed spectators into the infield for only fifty cents.

As a further attraction, the new club provided for small bets by replacing large-sum auction pools with the "Paris Mutual Pools," which received minimum bets of five dollars. As one local journalist noted, the new *parimutuel* system was "especially adapted to the requirements of that class of pygmy speculators who are inclined to sing small at the pool box." Small bets and low admission fees combined to draw huge crowds. Even during the financial depression of the 1870s, capacity crowds often filled the stands, and for special races the infield spectators swelled the total to 20,000.

In the 1890s yet another new organization, the Crescent City Jockey Club, removed the segregating barriers altogether, charged men only fifty cents admission and admitted women free of charge. With an eye to commerce, it also built a restaurant, a press box near the finish line, and a special room for journalists beneath the stands. Since it catered to publicity and numbers rather than to social snobbery, the track in New Orleans epitomized the general American tendency to change horse racing from an exclusive pastime of the rich and well-bred to a commercially profitable sport that appealed to a mass-spectator audience.

Commercialism worked to the advantage of jockeys. Traditionally attached to single owners, early jockeys were poorly paid and seldom recognized. Prior to 1800 few (even the winners) were mentioned in press accounts. But gamblers, professional and amateur alike, knew that the better jockeys produced more winners, so they insisted on knowing who was riding before they placed their bets. Thus jockeys not only became visible but also quickly learned to barter their services from owner to owner for specific races. In Britain, boys and small, wiry men of working-class origins rode their way to financial security, as did Irish immigrants and blacks in nineteenth-century America.

Less bound by traditional attitudes of social deference, American jockeys exercised their new bargaining power more effectively than did British jockeys. More important, they were less hesitant to innovate in their riding techniques, and in the 1890s came up with a new style of horsemanship. Rather than hold long reins and sit upright in the saddle with their legs dangling down in long stirrups, they experimented with short reins and stirrups while crouching forward on the horse's neck, thereby lessening the wind resistance and giving a better distribution of weight on the horse. Todhunter ("Tod") Sloan, the American jockey who popularized this new technique, was met with howls of derision when he first raced in England in 1897. He answered his critics by simply compiling an overwhelming record of victories. Reluctantly, the insular British ceased dubbing him "a monkey-on-a-stick," because their own jockeys had to adapt or forever be defeated.

In truth, despite all their similarities of new commercial emphasis and popular appeal, the track scenes in Britain and the United States were vastly different. Americans outdid the British in selling the turf to a mass market, but the basic difference was not simply a matter of degrees. British patrons were of a different kind from the Americans. For centuries the fine horse had been an emblem of aristocratic status, a status based more on birth than on mere wealth, hedged round by innumerable unwritten customs, public ceremonies, and conservative attitudes. Try as they might, Americans could never produce an Ascot, which was (and still is) as much a social scene as a sporting event, or even a Newmarket, which bred and trained aristocratic assumptions as well as thoroughbred horseflesh. All the money of Saratoga Springs and Newport, Rhode Island, did not an Old World gentleman make. Nor did polo, show jumping, foxhunting, and all the other gentlemanly horsemanship of the British aristocracy ever gracefully make the transatlantic passage.

At a more obvious level, differences existed in the kinds of races popular in Britain and the United States. The steeplechase, for example, originated in England and Ireland, and it remained a favorite British variation on the more predictable dash around a circular track. In the 1870s American turf patrons imported English trainers and riders to teach "hurdle racing," but American jockeys simply never mastered the art. Numerous horse fatalities and jockey injuries prompted one critic to denounce the steeplechase as a senseless sport "surpassing in brutality a Spanish bull fight." Highly popular in Britain, the steeplechase in the United States remained forever foreign, a novelty at best.

Harness racing, on the other hand, never caught on in Britain, but in America it built on its antebellum respectability to expand dramatically after the Civil War. Even in rural small towns, the Grange sponsored harness races at state and county fairs. In 1870 the National Association for the Promotion of the Interests of the American Trotting Turf was formed, and shortly thereafter the *Trotting Register* was begun. By 1886 about 800 tracks held regular harness races. Foreign visitors in the nineteenth century often commented on this unique innovation.

The Lawn Set

For all its commercial investment and popular appeal, the track forever remained suspect in the eyes of respectable middle-class folk. Rumors of fixed races surfaced regularly, and gambling thrived openly. Unprincipled rich owners, unlettered jockeys, and uncouth spectators were common stereotypes. Like the prizefight ring, the turf was tainted with the smell of bad money and loose morals.

Respectable people found better things to do. Some attended football, cricket, or baseball games. Most turned to outdoor games that could be played in the privacy of their own grounds or social clubs. As Thorstein Veblen observed in *The Theory of the Leisure Class* (1899), "the lawn, or the close-cropped yard or park" appealed especially "to the taste of the well-to-do classes." Lawn and club games such as croquet, archery, badminton, and lawn tennis conspicuously served the purposes of middle-class affluence and respectability. All these activities were suitable for family participation, particularly for the newly emancipated woman. All evolving from ancient forms of play and competition, they provided both leisurely pastime and sporting rivalry for well-to-do westerners.

Croquet enjoyed the earliest popularity. A modernized version of the old French game of *le jeu de maille*, croquet was a favorite pastime of retired British army officers in Pau, France, following the Napoleonic Wars. In 1857 John Jaques manufactured the first set of equipment and composed a rudimentary set of rules. On the tidy suburban lawns of Victorian England, the game flourished. In 1867 the first championship tournament was held at Evesham, Worcestershire, and three years later moved to the new all-England Croquet Club at Wimbledon, where a group of croquet buffs drew up a set of rules and specifications that survive with few alterations to the present.

Shortly after the Civil War, croquet became the rage in the United States. According to *The Nation* (1866), "Of all the epidemics that have swept over our land, the swiftest and most infectious is croquet." For Americans eager to learn and display the manners of good society, croquet was a boon: "Grace in holding and using the mallet, easy and pleasing attitudes in playing, promptness in taking your turn, and gentlemanly and ladylike manners generally throughout the game, are points which it is unnecessary for us to enlarge on," observed the editor of an early American book of rules.

Most of all, like no other game at the time, croquet provided good family fun. Courtships ripened between the wickets on late summer afternoons. Croquet revolutionized the relation of women to sport. Emerging from their stuffy parlors and confined domestic roles, women learned first to play and then to compete with men in outdoor exercise. So great was the vogue of croquet in the 1870s that manufacturers could not fill orders for equipment fast enough.

Archery, another genteel sport, similarly attracted women participants. From the beginning, Britain's Grand National Archery Society (1861) and the National Archery Association of America (1870) included both male and female members. As archery became highly popular at private girls' schools, *Harper's Weekly* reported that "ladies and gentlemen from the cultured circles of society" competed in a large tournament in Chicago.

Yet widespread enthusiasm for archery, as for croquet, was short-lived. The novelty soon wore off. American men turned to a more exclusively male kind of target sport, rifle shooting, and in 1871 founded the National Rifle Association. By the time of the founding of the American National Croquet Association in 1882 and the British Croquet Association in 1896, the game had passed its zenith of popularity. The original appeal of archery and croquet—their gentle, sociable qualities—proved to be liabilities. Except for the occasional lawn party, only the old and the very young chose to play croquet instead of more vigorous new lawn games.

Badminton, for example, became highly popular in the English suburbs and seaside resorts in the 1870s. The game derived from an old exercise called battledore and shuttlecock, in which children wielded light wooden paddles to keep a feathered cork in the air. Around 1870 a strung racket and net began to be used, especially at the Duke of Beaufort's estate, Badminton, in Gloucestershire, where the name of the game originated. In 1873 the first badminton club was formed at Bath, a favorite resort for wealthy Britons.

At first three to five people played on each side of the net, the men in their Prince Albert suits and starched shirts, the women in long dresses, corsets, bustles, and high-buttoned shoes. Originally set indoors, the courts were in the shape of an hourglass, narrower at the net than at the four corners in order for the massive doors of Victorian salons to open in the center of the room beside the net. The court was not made rectangular until 1901. Also by the turn of the century the game was being played more on outdoor lawns than in indoor salons, under rules laid down by the Badminton Association, founded in 1893 in the seacoast town of Southsea, Hampshire.

Except in distant India, where British army officers promoted the game at leisurely lawn parties on humid afternoons, badminton never became popular outside the British Isles. It was introduced in the United States in the late 1870s, and in 1879 the Badminton Club of New York City was founded. But most wealthy Americans looked upon badminton as an inferior version of another new and much faster, more versatile racket-and-net game, lawn tennis.

Like many sports, lawn tennis has a popular myth of instant creation: Major Walter Clopton Wingfield supposedly invented the game in 1873. In truth, however, lawn tennis is yet another English middle-class adaptation of an ancient royal game, "real" tennis. In the egalitarian age of the nineteenth century, the expensive indoor courts and aristocratic exclusiveness of real tennis made it as anachronistic as the traditional monarchies with which it was associated. More accessible was an outdoor game played with rackets and a cork ball. In a French version, *la longue paume*, and its English equivalent, "field tennis," players hit the ball over the net into the prescribed area rather than off indoor ceilings and walls in the old real tennis fashion. Once a rubber ball came into use during the Victorian era, tennis on grass became all the more attractive. Lawn tennis was more of an evolution than an invention.

In 1858 Major T. H. Gem, a clerk to the magistrates in Birmingham, England, and his Spanish friend, J. B. Perera, set up a net and established boundary lines on the back lawn of Gem's home in Edgbaston, a suburb of Birmingham, to the amusement of gawking neighbors. For years they played there, using the scoring system of the old royal game. In 1872 they joined with two local doctors to form the first lawn-tennis club at the Manor House in nearby Leamington Spa.

Major Wingfield's contribution to the early development of the game was both more eccentric and more widely publicized than Gem's. In 1873, to a gathering of upper-class friends at a house party in Nantclwyd Hall, Wales, Wingfield introduced equipment and a set of rules for a "new" game that he called "sphairistiké." He proposed a scoring system based on the old game of rackets rather than on royal tennis. Apparently having come in contact with badminton, he laid out the court in an hourglass design, with the net five feet from the ground at the posts. For a "serving box" he drew a small diamond-shaped box on each side of the net, in which the server had to stand. Never did a supposed "father" of a sport produce a design so unlike the finished product.

In 1874 Wingfield attempted to patent his "new and improved" version of "the ancient game of tennis," and in several articles and pamphlets propagated his scheme to the Victorian reading public. He struck a responsive chord in people tired of the tameness of croquet, archery, and badminton. In 1876 the essayist and playwright Oscar Wilde visited friends in Nottinghamshire and reported "some very pleasant garden parties and any amount of lawn tennis."

Yet early converts to lawn tennis were by no means uncritical of the details of Wingfield's game. In 1875 wealthy members of the All-England Croquet Club set aside an area for lawn tennis and badminton and immediately formed a subcommittee to codify the rules of tennis. Within two years they radically reshaped Wingfield's design. First they agreed to drop the name "sphairistiké" in favor of the simpler term, lawn tennis. Then they adopted a rectangular court in place of the hourglass shape, and the scoring system of real tennis (15–30–40) rather than rackets. Lowering the net to three feet, three inches at the center, they put the server back on the base line; to compensate for the increased distance, they allowed an extra serve if the first was not successful. Finally, they covered Wingfield's hollow rubber ball with white flannel for better control, an innovation of John Meyer Heathcote. By 1877 the rules and form of lawn tennis were largely fixed in a fashion that has remained intact to the present.

So was its oldest competitive tournament, Wimbledon. Adding "Tennis" to its name, the All-England Croquet Club sponsored the first Wimbledon matches in 1877. Twenty-two players competed for a trophy valued at twenty-five guineas. For the final championship match, won by Spencer W. Gore, 200 spectators looked on. The growth of the crowd for subsequent Wimbledon tournaments tells the story of the instant popularity of the game. Within one year the number of spectators jumped to 700 for the final, then to 1,100 in 1879, and to 3,500 by 1885. Never again did Wimbledon officials have to fear low turnouts at center court. As the crowds increased, the program enlarged. Women's singles were added in 1884; in the same year the men's doubles, begun at Oxford in 1879, moved to Wimbledon. Finally, in 1899 an unofficial women's doubles championship entered the picture, and in the following year mixed doubles completed the program.

The quality of play also increased rapidly during those early years. For the first Wimbledon, S. W. Gore won by methodically serving, charging the net, and slamming the ball back away from his opponents. In the following year, however, he was beaten by an opponent who consistently lobbed the ball over his head, thus popularizing a rather dreary lob game from the baselines. Not until the emergence in the early 1880s of the sparkling Renshaw brothers, William and Ernest, did the era of "pat ball" end. Dominating both the men's singles and doubles throughout the decade, the Renshaws perfected the hard, deep volley. Added to the overhead serve, which became standard for men (not women) in the late 1870s, the volley made the game a test of stamina as well as skill. From the beginning, Wimbledon displayed the best tennis in the world.

Lest Wimbledon obscure the social importance of lawn tennis in Victorian England, however, one must hasten to add that it was merely the competitive reflection of a widely popular pastime of middle-class Englishmen. As one commented in 1890, "A lawn, a racket, a soft ball, a net, a pot of paint, and an active member of either sex, here are all the materials needed for lawn tennis, and every country house and most suburban villas can supply them."

By the time Scottish and Irish tournaments began in 1878–79, Frenchmen were already taking to the game with a zeal befitting a people who were the early masters of royal tennis. In 1875 courts appeared in Paris and Cannes, the latter amid a colony of summer English visitors. Unable to grow grass that would endure the pounding of tennis feet, the French developed clay courts *(terra battue)*, particularly on the fine sands of the Riviera. The French championship, still the world's premier clay-court event, began in 1891.

One young Frenchman, destined to become the first notable star in the illustrious French galaxy of tennis, learned the game firsthand in England. Max Décugis spent eight years studying English and lawn tennis at a boys' school near Twickenham, entered several English tournaments before he was sixteen, and then returned home to launch a career in which he won twenty-eight French titles in men's singles and doubles championship tournaments.

In 1893, two years after the founding of the French championships, a similar tournament was held in a German Baltic seacoast town, Bad Homburg, where English Victorians vacationed. The pattern repeated itself all over Europe in the 1890s. On Dutch asphalt courts at the Hague, at St. Moritz in the Swiss Alps, at Marienbad in the Hapsburg Empire, and in St.

A well-dressed crowd of spectators ringing the court at Newport, Rhode Island, reflects the elite character of lawn tennis, as recorded by a photographer for *Harper's Young People,* 1892.

Petersburg on the Neva, wherever Englishmen visited or worked they carried their tennis equipment and met with an enthusiastic response from upper-class Europeans.

Within a year of Wingfield's patent, lawn tennis was introduced in Toronto. Members of the elite Toronto Lawn Tennis Club were elected by secret ballot, and they paid a high fee to keep their membership exclusive. Similar new clubs formed in most Canadian cities in the 1870s and 1880s. Lawn tennis, for Anglo-Canadians, meant yet another piece of England transposed to the wilds of North America. "It is almost impossible to believe that I am not dreaming," wrote one English visitor to Victoria in 1887. "Sitting by the open window, the drowsy summer air comes in off the sea and fans my forehead; from the lawn outside I can hear 'Well played', 'Love thirty', 'Deuce', and other scraps of tennis jargon from lips of English men and women." In the early 1890s Canada's Lawn Tennis Association was formed, and it immediately began to arrange tournaments.

Legend has it that lawn tennis came to the United States at the hands of Mary Ewing Outerbridge, a New York socialite. Supposedly, in the spring of 1874 Miss Outerbridge vacationed in Bermuda, became infatuated with tennis as played there by British garrison officers, and arranged for a set of equipment to accompany her back to Staten Island. No doubt the story is true, but certainly the transatlantic passage of lawn tennis was less simple than the solitary act of one individual. Courts established in the summer of 1874 in Nahant, Massachusetts, and Newport, Rhode Island, suggest that Yankee tourists in England probably saw and read about lawn tennis, and returned home with the game in hand. Moreover, the Outerbridge story ignores the fact that the first lawn tennis club founded in the United States, in 1876, was in New Orleans rather than New York or even New England. Given the traditional French character of New Orleans, lawn tennis might well have been introduced there by French rather than British enthusiasts.

Whatever the manner of its geographical dispersion, the game caught on quickly in wealthy American circles. The formation of the United States National Lawn Tennis Association in 1881 gave order to the rules and administration of the game. The home of that new organization, the posh Newport Casino Club, hosted annual men's championship tournaments. Richard Sears, a Bostonian, won the first seven singles titles. Teamed with Dr. James Dwight, one of the notable early American patrons of the sport, Sears also dominated the first several years of the doubles championship.

From the outset, American women enthusiastically played lawn tennis. It was "a game in which the elements of exercise and competition are combined," as a writer for *Outing* magazine noted, and was "the one athletic game which women may enjoy without being subjected to sundry insinuations of rompishness." In 1887 the Philadelphia Cricket Club organized a women's tournament, which was officially recognized two years later by the Lawn Tennis Association. Early women competitors held their rackets in one hand and picked up their long skirts with the other. They served underhand, patting the ball back and forth over the net with hardly a thought for hard volleying. Only as their skirts became progressively shorter did they pursue a more active style, a style that in turn hastened the streamlining of their garb.

Even more than today, wealth in the nineteenth century meant physical mobility in terms of frequent transatlantic crossings by steamship. Americans first played at Wimbledon—unsuccessfully—in 1884, and British visitors to American clubs and tournaments caused much excitement in the 1880s and 1890s. This informal Anglo-American rivalry became organized in 1900 when a young Harvard man, Dwight Davis, instructed a Boston silversmith to melt down almost fourteen pounds of silver for an International Lawn Tennis Challenge Trophy. An American team won the first tournament in 1900 amid howls of English protest against mushy balls and high grass at Longwood Cricket Club in Boston. The official but awkwardly long name of the event remained etched on the face of the trophy, but it quickly came to be known simply as the Davis Cup. In 1903 competition for the cup was thrown open to French, German, and other European representatives.

Taking to the Links

Although internationally popular, lawn tennis at the turn of the century was limited to the wealthy elite. Only people with spacious lawns and abundant capital could afford their own courts; only affluent, socially respectable citizens were invited and could pay the fees to belong to private clubs. In the United States, especially, tennis was the dominant sport sponsored by private social clubs that proliferated in large towns and cities during the last two decades of the nineteenth century. The first of these "country clubs" opened in Brookline, Massachusetts, in 1882. They could be identified from afar not only because they maintained tennis courts but also because they built golf courses and sponsored polo matches.

Originating in ancient Persia, modern polo was brought to England from India in the 1860s by British army officers. It came to the United States under the patronage of a wealthy eccentric, James Gordon Bennett, Jr., the owner of the New York *Herald*. A lover of aristocratic sports of all kinds, Bennett begrudged no time and spared no expense in pursuit of his sporting pleasures. In 1876 he purchased Texas ponies and English expertise to stage the first polo match in the United States, and he quickly established West-chester, New York, and Newport, Rhode Island, as the centers of polo activity. Memberships in polo clubs and country clubs were virtually inter-changeable. Many of the thirty-three American polo clubs existing by 1904 played their games on country-club property.

The game of golf was more integral to country-club life. Having originated centuries earlier in Scotland or Holland (or in both simultaneously), golf had long been primarily associated with provincial old Scotsmen who swung their wind-bent clubs made from small thorn trees, hitting little leather-cased balls stuffed with soaked feathers. A few early Victorian Englishmen played the game at Blackheath, near London, and at the newer Prestwick course, near Manchester, but St. Andrews was its mecca, and Scotland was its home.

Two technical innovations in the mid-nineteenth century revolutionized the game. The first was the introduction of the gutta-percha ball, made from a thick rubbery substance derived from Malayan trees. A St. Andrews clergyman, Dr. Robert Paterson, got the idea when he came across some gutta-percha packed around a valuable item shipped from India. He softened the substance by dipping it in hot water, molded it in the shape of a golf ball, then allowed it to harden. On the links, he found his "guttie" to be far more durable than the old "featherie." It resisted water and kept its shape; after a few rounds of clubbing and scratching, it also flew more accurately. The present indentations on golf balls originated with Scottish amateurs using nails to "rough up" their gutta-perchas. In 1850 Dr. Paterson took out a patent on his invention, and London and Edinburgh manufacturers immediately began mass-producing the "guttie."

The harder gutta-percha ball required more durable clubs. In cold weather especially, even the toughest woods often split on impact. Shrewd Scotsmen at first encased the heads of their clubs with leather strips, but they quickly innovated further by having ironmongers fix a small plate of iron on the face of the clubs. Thus did the new iron-headed club and gutta-percha ball derive from major facts of life in the nineteenth century: the Industrial Revolution and the world-wide expanse of the British Empire.

Like other British games, golf followed the flag and trade. Scottish military officers and merchants established golf clubs in Calcutta and Bombay (in 1829 and 1842, respectively), and in Pau, France (1856), before the game became popular in England. A handful of Scottish and English golfers began the British Open in 1860, to be played alternately at Prestwick and St. Andrews. Within the decade the famous North Devon Royal Club and several London clubs were founded, but golf was far more popular in distant Scottish immigrant colonies than in Victorian England. In the early 1870s golf clubs appeared in Australia and New Zealand, and in the mid-1870s prestigious Canadian clubs were established in Montreal, Quebec, and Toronto.

Within a decade a Scottish immigrant named John Reid laid out a golf course with three holes in a cow pasture in Yonkers, New York. Reid and his friends soon moved to an adjacent apple orchard, where they doubled the size of their course. From these crude beginnings they founded the St. Andrews Golf Club in 1888, the first permanent golf club in the United States. Two years later a new course was laid out in Newport, where the Carnegies, Astors, Vanderbilts, and Rockefellers led a large colony of wealthy summer enthusiasts in chasing the gutta-percha into bushes and streams. The craze was not limited to the Northeast. Golfers from San Francisco, Portland, and Tacoma participated in the first United States Open Tournament for men in 1894. Of the almost 900 golf clubs that existed in the United States by the end of the century, about 150 were west of the Mississippi.

Yet most Americans viewed golf not only as a rich person's game ("preeminently a game of good society," as *Harper's Weekly* put it in 1895), but also as a quaint foreign import unacceptable to rugged American tastes. Early American (and Canadian) golfers mimed the Scots, who wore scarlet coats and fore-and-aft caps on the links; worse still, they wore leg wrappings despite the fact that North American courses, unlike those in Scotland, had no prickly gorse requiring leg protection. For Americans accustomed to more physically competitive sports, the game itself seemed as eccentric as its costume. Nor did Sunday morning tee-times improve its image. One clergyman in the 1890s voiced a mass of unspoken opinion when he denounced golf as "a distasteful pastime, strictly for idlers, and no God-fearing citizen will be caught indulging himself in it."

For wealthy women, however, golf was a godsend. Like croquet, archery, badminton, and lawn tennis, golf allowed refined ladies to exercise and even to compete genteely. Golf, in fact, was perhaps the best of their sporting options. As one woman suggested, it was a good compromise between "the tediousness of croquet and the hurley-burley of lawn tennis." The beginning of an annual women's championship tournament, in 1895, at the Meadowbrook Club in Westbury, New York, bespoke the attraction of the game for refined women.

Eager to promote the commercial future of golf in the United States, A. G. Spalding and Co. sponsored a visit of Britain's best golfer, Harry Vardon, in 1900. Beginning in Florida, Vardon worked his way up the eastern seaboard, then west to the Rocky Mountains (Denver), exhibiting his techniques. Little could he or Spalding foresee that the future of golf belonged to Americans. Just a year before Vardon's tour, an unknown dentist in Cleveland, Coburn Haskell, invented a ball composed of elastic thread wound under tension around a rubber core. Covered with dimpled gutta-percha, Haskell's ball was both livelier and truer than the old solid "guttie."

The invention was an omen of America's emergence as a golfing power. In 1902 Sandy Herd, a Scottish professional, used Haskell's ball to win the British Open and thereby consigned the short-lived "guttie" to the museums. All the while, Scotsmen continued winning the U.S. Open. Not until 1913 did a native-born American, Francis Ouimet, win the nation's premier tournament. Within a decade American golfers, using an American-invented ball, charged to the forefront of the golfing community in the Western world.

PART FOUR

In Sunshine and Shadow: Sports in the Age of Conflict

The date is 4 June 1913. The place is Epsom Downs race track in England. The event is the Derby Stakes, Britain's premier horse race. As a horse owned by King George V leads the pack in front of the spectators' gallery, a young woman suddenly ducks under the rail and throws herself into the horse's path. The audience gasps as horse, jockey, and woman all crumple to the turf in a sickening heap. While doctors and trainers minister to the injured, the queen reportedly inquires of the woman's condition; the king wants to know if his horse and jockey have survived the fall. The king's interests are served: his horse and jockey escape serious injury. The woman dies without regaining consciousness.

She was Miss Emily Davison, a militant suffragette, a martyr for her cause. Frustrated by Parliament's refusal to grant them the vote, English women had begun slashing museum paintings, destroying mail, breaking windows, and bombing and burning property in order to call attention to their demands. Then, turning to the last bastion of male dominance, sports, they tore up the turf on bowling greens and golf courses and at cricket and football grounds. The suicidal act of Emily Davison represented a final, tragic form of militant protest.

This bizarre episode also appropriately represented the history of sports in the first half of the twentieth century, when politics intruded boldly and sometimes disastrously. The intrusion was not totally new, of course. Ancient Roman arenas, medieval tournaments, popular recreations in Stuart England, and nineteenth-century German gymnastics were all hedged about with political meaning. But premodern examples are mere momentary liaisons compared with the stolid union of sports and politics in this century. Politically charged from the outset, the modern Olympic Games were seldom free of chauvinistic conflicts. During the interwar period especially, sport became a barometer of national policies on race, economic systems, and international ambitions. Italian, German, and Soviet governments perfected the art of manipulating sports for political ends.

It was the best of times, the worst of times for athletes. As enterprising patrons set sport on an even keel of administrative efficiency and spectator appeal, it became firmly established in regions far removed from its earlier Anglo-American basis. Even during the "golden age" of American sports in the 1920s, the dominance of French cyclists, Finnish runners, South American soccer footballers, German and Italian auto drivers, and Canadian ice hockey teams bore eloquent witness to the emergence of new sporting nations. For much of the era, however, dark clouds of war and economic desperation hung heavy over fields of play. A male born in 1895 enjoyed youthful athletic options unknown to his grandfather, but by 1914 he was a ripe candidate for cannon fodder. If he survived World War I (and ten million men did not), he returned home to pick up the pieces of his life, only to see his society plunge into the devastating Great Depression in the early 1930s. Scarcely did he recover from that pit of despair before he had to pack his sons off to World War II. Sunshine and shadows mingled freely on whatever sports he played or watched.

Yet his sports were enriched by further technological progress. The invention of the internal-combustion engine provided two new competitive sports, auto and motorcycle races, which emerged alongside bicycle races as permanent features of the sports scene in the early years of the century. By the 1920s and 1930s, cheap, mass-produced family automobiles carried spectators to stadiums for sporting events. Radio and cinema also became mass commodities in the 1920s. For the first time ever, sports enthusiasts could hear first-hand accounts of distant boxing matches, baseball, and football games. In local cinema houses people viewed newsreel snippets of top-flight athletes about whom they had previously only read. Highly accessible and politically vulnerable, sports in the Western world took modern shape in the first half of this century.

Chapter **13**

THE SHAPING OF MODERN SPORTS

Despite all the news games, teams, and leagues available at the outset of the twentieth century, the future of organized sports was far from secure. The two most prominent American sports, professional baseball and college football, seemed bent on self-destruction. Major-league baseball clubs ruthlessly engaged in cutthroat competition for players and spectator support. College football entered the new century on an even more precarious course. A frightful record of injuries and deaths on the field prompted several major colleges to suspend play, and it provoked legislators to consider banning the game by law. Never did sports administrators have to resolve so many problems so quickly.

American sports were not the only ones in need of salvaging. The modern Olympic movement, begun with moderate success in 1896, fell on its face in Paris in 1900 and in St. Louis in 1904. In both cases the Olympic Games were held in conjunction with international world fairs, to the games' detriment. That awkward mixture of amateur sport and commercial enterprise accurately mirrored the unclear, often contradictory motives of the early patrons of the modern Olympics. From the beginning, the International Olympic Committee squabbled over sites, programs, and rules for the games. The infant modern Olympic movement struggled for stability.

Except in North America, soccer football expanded on the eve of World War I. All the while, competitive cycling and auto racing became permanent fixtures on the sports calendar, especially in Europe. Athletic expansion was apparent everywhere, but on the horizon brewed a storm. In Europe, the coming of World War I devastated athletics along with everything else. Although its effect was slower and less severe in North and South America, the war knocked all of Western civilization off its feet.

A Frenchman, Baron Pierre de Coubertin, combined athletic zeal with independent wealth to overcome numerous obstacles in the way of reviving the Olympic Games. This photograph of the Father of the Modern Olympics is taken from F. A. M. Webster, *The Evolution of the Olympic Games 1829 B.C.-1914 A.D.*, 1914.

Rekindling the Olympic Flame

As enthusiasm for sports boomed in the nineteenth century, interest in the ancient Olympic Games revived. From 1875 to 1881 a team of German archaeologists fired athletic hearts as well as scholarly minds with the excavation of the buried remains of Olympia. Prominent Greek citizens periodically raised funds for the restoration of the games, but the Greeks had only a golden distant past, no lively modern athletic tradition, to call upon. In England and the United States, where universities and private athletic clubs regularly sponsored competitive track-and-field events, several proposals for an "Anglo-Saxon Olympiad" surfaced late in the century. Fortunately those ill-conceived racist schemes never got off the drawing boards. The origins of the modern Olympics came not from the mightiest of the sporting nations, Britain and the United States, nor from Germany or Greece, but rather from France, a nation that had the least developed system of all the important European states. The task of rekindling the Olympic flame fell to the frail, small hands of Baron Pierre de Coubertin.

Born in 1863 to an aristocratic Parisian family, Coubertin was an ugly duckling. His nose was large and off center; his left eyelid drooped. He was a physical runt, five feet, three inches tall. Most of his photographs remind the viewer of a young Charlie Chaplin with a handlebar moustache. Yet Coubertin was highly intelligent, rebellious by nature, and inwardly driven to overcome his liabilities. As a youth he boxed, rowed, and fenced. To his parents' dismay, he adored English sports as described in Hippolyte Taine's

Notes sur Angleterre (1872) and Thomas Hughes's *Tom Brown's Schooldays* (1857), which was first translated into French in 1875. *Tom Brown* became Coubertin's bible. He read it again and again, soaking up the lively episodes of rowdy, independent life at Rugby School under the headmastership of the late Dr. Thomas Arnold. A pilgrimage to Rugby and Eton in 1883 merely confirmed Coubertin's admiration of the virile union of intellectual discipline and athletic prowess encouraged in the British public schools.

The youthful Coubertin loved English ways because he loved France the more. Like so many of his contemporaries, he was a patriot for whom the crushing French defeat at the hands of a Prussian army in 1870 rankled long after the event. The weakness of France, Coubertin believed, derived from an authoritarian, highly regimented educational system that left no place for individual initiative or physical activity. German and English systems seemed altogether different. Both balanced physical and intellectual pursuits; both bred supremacy, not decadence. Despising Germany, Coubertin turned to England for his model. In the mid-1880s he began making frequent public speeches and writing magazine articles extolling English-style education and sports as the means whereby France could be revitalized. In 1888 he convinced the French minister of public instruction to form a Committee for the Preservation of Physical Exercises in Education, and to appoint none other than Coubertin as its secretary.

His campaign met with little success. Whereas Coubertin's nationalism prompted him to welcome English sports and games in France, other nationalists resented the prospect of importations foreign to French traditions. Upper-class custodians of French culture especially feared that team sports would blur class lines. Coubertin's assurances to the contrary made little effect. Certainly Coubertin himself was no flaming radical. He approached sports, education, and social issues from the lofty aristocratic principle of noblesse oblige. Although he failed to become an effective patron of sports in France, his upper-class nationalist zeal combined with a romantic fascination for British sports to launch him on a crusade for renewal of the Olympic Games.

Coubertin's Olympic idea emerged slowly. He envisaged the Olympic games as international rather than national, summoning the youth of the world to compete on a playground rather than a battlefield. Most of all, the modern Olympics were the idealistic brainchild of a man who believed fervently in the nobility of athletics. To a small gathering of fellow French sports enthusiasts, Coubertin in 1892 first announced his intention to "reestablish a great and magnificent institution, the Olympic Games."

Coubertin corresponded with sports societies throughout the world. At his own expense he published pamphlets and articles propagating his views. In 1893 he made an extended visit to the United States to lecture and converse with sportsmen in distant points such as the University of California at Berkeley, Tulane University in New Orleans, and Princeton University in New Jersey. His aristocratic connections opened important doors, even to the home of a future president of the United States, Theodore Roosevelt, with whom Coubertin formed an enduring friendship.

In 1894 Coubertin organized a large international conference at the Sorbonne in Paris, to which he invited seventy-nine delegates from twelve countries to discuss the principles on which new Olympic Games should be governed. They agreed on five basic principles. First, the modern Olympics would be held every four years, like the ancient Games. Second, the contests would be modern, featuring sports of the nineteenth century rather than merely copying the ancient program. Third, competition would be limited to adults, without "boys' " events as in the original Olympics. Everyone assumed that the athletes would be adult *males*. Fourth, only amateurs could compete. Finally, the games would be "ambulatory," moving from city to city every fourth year. An International Olympic Committee (IOC) was formed to represent these principles to national sports societies represented at the conference. Most of the original members of the IOC were selected by Coubertin, whose title of "Secretary" made him the effective head of the organization.

Where, and when, would the first modern Olympic Games be held? Coubertin proposed attaching them to a Universal Exposition in Paris in 1900. Other members of the conference thought that date too far in the future. Fearing that enthusiasm might wane, they unanimously decided on 1896 as the target date. One delegate offered Stockholm as the site, but for obvious reasons most leaned to having the first games in Greece. Since little Olympia, recently excavated and impossibly remote, was unequipped to handle modern crowds, Athens was a logical choice. At a banquet on the final evening of the Sorbonne conference, Coubertin happily toasted "the Olympic idea, which like a ray of the all-powerful sun, has pierced the mists of the ages to illuminate the threshold of the twentieth century with joy and hope."

The euphoria quickly vanished in the face of practical problems. On the verge of bankruptcy, the Greek government informed Coubertin that it could not come up with the money to refurbish the decrepit Panathenaic Stadium, build other athletic facilities, and host foreign athletes. In November 1894 Coubertin spent three weeks in Greece estimating the expenses (unrealistically low, of course) and making contacts with key Greek officials. He found Crown Prince Constantine to be an avid supporter of the scheme. Shrewdly, he convinced him to direct the local organizing committee.

A change of governments in January 1895 worked to Coubertin's advantage. The new government raised money for the games by issuing commemorative stamps, then appealed to the nationalistic pride of rich Greek businessmen at home and abroad. Gifts of money flowed in, especially from the philanthropic hands of George Averoff, a Greek multimillionaire living in Alexandria. Averoff contributed almost a half-million dollars to rebuild the stadium that was originally constructed during the second century A.D. by another generous benefactor, Herodes Atticus. By the spring of 1896, a magnificent stadium of shining new marble, a newly built velodrome (bicycle race track), a shooting gallery, and tennis courts all were ready. Even city officials caught the spirit of improvement, paving the streets of Athens and lighting them with gas lamps.

Meanwhile, Coubertin was left with the task of gathering athletes from around the world. It was no easy task. As one contemporary observed, "Every nation except England and America is still in an absolutely prehistoric condition with regard to athletic sports." But even Britain sent only six athletes to Athens, two less than Hungary. The leading sports organization in the United States, the New York Athletic Club, ignored Coubertin's invitation. The head of the American Olympic Committee, William Milligan Sloane, a professor of history at Princeton, recruited four Princeton undergraduates. Filling out the American team were eight athletes from the Boston area; all except one were Harvard students or members of the Boston Athletic Association. In France and Germany controversy raged over the propriety of supporting international athletic contests. Finally, both sponsored teams slightly larger than the American contingency. Tsarist Russia sponsored not a single athlete. In the end, a mere hundred or so athletes from twelve different countries made their way to Athens, to be joined by more than two hundred Greek competitors.

Nor were the spectators at the Athens Games any more representative of international appeal. Some American visitors included Athens on their package tours of Italy, the Holy Land, and Egypt, and some sailors and officers from an American cruiser docked at a nearby port attended the games. But the vast majority of the 70,000 spectators who occasionally filled the Panathenaic Stadium were Greek citizens. As a forum for international athletic competition and spectator appeal, the modern Olympic Games began on a humble note.

The opening ceremonies were held on the afternoon of Easter Day, April 5, and on the following morning the games began. The first victor was an Irish-American from Boston, James Connolly, in the triple jump, the first of forty-three events held within a ten-day period. Contests such as broad jumps, sprints, discus throws, and wrestling matches were reminiscent of the ancient Olympics, although the styles had changed. Other events, such as fencing, high jumps and hurdles, pole vaulting, weight lifting, gymnastics, marksmanship, swimming, tennis matches, and cycling races were distinctly "modern" in accordance with Coubertin's aim to combine old and new sports.

Americans captured most of the track-and-field events. American tourists and sailors also distinguished themselves by their wild college-style cheers. Disappointed Greek partisans had little to cheer about—until the marathon. In a field of twenty-five, only four foreigners entered the marathon, which had been included on the program at Greek insistence. Three of the four foreigners collapsed before the end of the twenty-five-mile (later changed to twenty-six) ordeal. Spiridon Loues, an unknown peasant shepherd from the little Greek village of Marousi, finished first. As he entered the stadium seven minutes ahead of his nearest competitor, Prince Constantine and Prince George accompanied him to the finish line. The stadium crowd, packed to capacity, went into a frenzy. In that sterling moment, Loues won lifelong fame in the first race he had ever run. He never bothered to race again. He was amateurism personified.

Compared to more recent Olympics of course, the Athens Games were very amateurish. Few of the athletes had trained seriously. The tennis champion, I. P. Boland of England, merely happened to be in Greece at the time, and purchased a racket in order to compete. Certainly all the records for time, distance, and weights were vastly inferior to today's. Styles varied wildly. Americans taking a four-point stance to begin their sprints appeared odd beside the other starters, who assumed any number of tense, upright positions. Inexperienced Greek high-hurdlers hesitated in front of each barrier, then leaped across to land on both feet before proceeding to the next hurdle. Most telling of all was the simple explanation of a versatile Frenchman who was asked how he trained for events so different as the 100-meter dash and the marathon: "One day, I run a leetle way, vairy queek. Ze next day, I run a long way, vairy slow."

At a breakfast banquet on the last Sunday before the end of the games, the King of Greece proposed a toast to "Greece, the mother and nurse of the Olympic Games in antiquity." Observing that the renewal of the games in Athens had "surpassed all expectations," he urged Olympic officials to select Athens as "the stable and permanent seat of the Olympic Games." Coubertin cringed. Determined to keep the games "ambulatory," he also ignored a petition signed by American athletes to make Athens the permanent site of the games. Long before the King of Greece ended the 1896 games by awarding a silver (not gold) medal and olive branch to first-place winners, and a bronze medal and laurel bough to the runners-up, Coubertin had set his sight on the 1900 games in Paris.

Little did he reckon on opposition from his own countrymen. First, his proposal met with outright hostility from the officials of several French athletic clubs, who had simply never accepted Coubertin's assumption that international competition was in the best interest of French sports. Then, government officials, indifferent to athletics, balked at the plan to incorporate the games within the framework of the 1900 Exposition. Finally Coubertin got his way, but at great cost. The athletic events had to be held in poorly prepared parks, fields, and gyms scattered throughout Paris. Coordination of events and ceremonies was impossible. Although the number of contestants increased dramatically to 1,319 (including eleven women) athletes from twenty-two countries, the Paris Olympics of 1900 were an abysmal failure. "We have made a hash of our work," Coubertin sadly commented at the end of the games.

Even the numerical gain registered at Paris was erased at the third modern Olympiad in St. Louis in 1904. Time and expense required to travel from Europe to American shores by steamship, then by train or riverboat to St. Louis, were apparently not worth the bother to European athletes. Only fifty-one made the trip. At St. Louis, 617 athletes represented twelve nations, but 525 of them were Americans and another forty-one were Canadians. Worse still, despite the awful experience at Paris four years earlier, the St. Louis Olympics were held in conjunction with another world's fair. Competitors in track-and-field events enjoyed the serene beauty of the campus of Washington University, but a carnival atmosphere covered even the most serious of contests. "I was not only present at a sporting contest," reported a Hungarian sportsman to Coubertin, who himself did not go to St. Louis, "but also at a fair where there were sports, where there was cheating, where monsters were exhibited for a joke."

The Olympics ceased being a joke in 1906, ironically a non-Olympic year. Coubertin, having earlier resisted pressures to hold all Olympic Games in Greece, now compromised to allow "interim" or "extraordinary" games in Athens between the third and fourth modern Olympiads. After the difficulties in Paris and the farce in St. Louis, apparently the father of the modern Olympics was only too happy to return his troubled child to the scene of its birth. He was not disappointed. Once again the Athenians did a superb job of hosting the games. Huge crowds returned to the Panathenaic Stadium (named Averoff Stadium after 1896). About 900 athletes competed for laurels, and with verve. For the first time, most wore official team uniforms. Although the Athens games of 1906 cannot be found in the official record books, they were of crucial importance to the modern Olympic movement. Orderly but festive, they set the games on a firm foundation for growth.

Competition on Wheels

Bicycle racing, one of the new events in the modern Olympic Games, was a competitive sport born of a century-long evolution of leisurely activity and practical transportation. In the late eighteenth and early nineteenth centuries, eccentric upper-class Frenchmen, Germans, and Englishmen pushed themselves along on a wooden beam set on wheels, without a steering device. By 1860 an iron frame rested on a huge front wheel with a steering mechanism and pedals. Soon the wheels became equal in size, with a sprocket and chain attached to the rear. Yet tires of iron, then of solid rubber, made for extremely uncomfortable rides, until John Boyd Dunlop of Belfast, Ireland, patented a pneumatic tire around 1890. Shortly thereafter a Parisian, Edouard Michelin, developed detachable tires and inner tubes, completing the bicycle's evolution as an international invention.

It was a plaything of the rich. For a working man, a new vehicle would have cost half a year's salary in the 1880s. Throughout Europe and North America, bicycle clubs flourished as adjuncts to elite tennis and croquet clubs. The New Orleans Bicycle Club, for example, assumed that only "men of affairs and relatively high standing" would seek membership because the cost of a bike acted as "a sort of check against indiscriminate application for admission." Almost two decades before Thorstein Veblen blasted the conspicuous consumption of the leisured class, a contributor to *The Wheelman* observed that when a prosperous but ordinary-looking Englishman took to the bicycle he became "a personage of consequence and attractiveness." Like the characters who frequently adorned the cartoon pages of *Punch*, he instantly became "a notable feature in the landscape, drawing to himself the admiring gaze of all whose eyes are there to see."

Wealthy women especially took to the bicycle. Not only did it confer status, provide exercise, and serve as a means of easy transportation; it also broke the shackles of bulky Victorian garb. At first women cyclists wore baggy knickerbockers under their long frocks, but by the 1890s they sensibly introduced shortened "bloomers" with knee-length skirts. "A few years ago no women would dare venture on the streets with a skirt that stopped above her ankles, and leggings that reached obviously to her knees," noted an American journalist in 1896. But times had drastically changed. Now the bicycle was giving women "the liberty of dress for which the reformers have been sighing for generations."

For men, on the other hand, the bicycle provided yet another form of competitive sport—the first competition ever on wheels without the use of horses. As early as 1868 a reporter for the *New York Times* commented that the velocipede (a forerunner of the two-wheel bicycle) was "every man's horse and every man's gymnasium." In the following year transportation and mere exercise gave way to the competitive impulse as Europeans first began racing their mechanical "horses" in a long-distance route from Paris to Rouen. Yet not until the advent of pneumatic tires on wheels of identical size did competitive cycling boom. In 1891 the famous Bordeaux to Paris race began, and in the same year a Paris–Brest–Paris marathon beckoned hardy cyclists from all over Europe.

Competitive cycling had barely become established before it was overlapped by another rich boy's racing vehicle, the automobile, which appealed to an even wealthier, less athletic set. The first recorded auto race was held in 1894, on a stretch of seventy miles between Paris and Rouen. The winner, a Dion steam car, averaged 11.6 miles per hour. In the following year, a race of 732 miles from Paris to Bordeau and back attracted a large crowd of nouveaux riches competitors. With the establishment of the famous French Grand Prix in 1906, auto racing took on an international flavor. The first three winning cars were Renault of France, Fiat of Italy, and Mercedes of Germany, all expensive, high-performance cars; soon Peugot entered the victors' list. In 1911 the Monte Carlo Rally began.

Nor were British cars far behind. In 1900 about sixty-five sports car enthusiasts set out from London on a "trial" that was to take them over a thousand miles of English and Scottish public roads, more of an endurance test than a speed race. Parliament, concerned for the safety of horses, children, and unwary adults not nimble enough to clear a path, set a speed limit of twelve miles per hour. Soon the limit was raised to twenty miles an hour, but still the eager members of the new Automobile Club were not satisfied. Solely for sporting purposes, an aristocratic sponsor in 1906–7 built an enclosed oval-shaped course of cement, Brooklands Race Track, on his private estate near Weybridge, Surrey, just south of London.

Brooklands inspired American sportsmen to build the Indianapolis 500 in 1910–11, but with four corners of shallow bankings, and with brick rather than cement pavement. In the inaugural race in 1911, the victor was clocked at 74.59 miles per hour. For the first two years American automobiles captured the checkered flag, largely because few Europeans entered. But from 1913 to 1920, European cars dominated. Until 1923 a driver had to be accompanied by a "riding mechanic" who could help push a stalled vehicle off the track.

Around the turn of the century, French and British designers attached an internal-combustion engine to the bicycle to produce yet another racing vehicle, the motorcycle. Many of the earliest races, in fact, pitted motorcycles against automobiles. At first they raced from city to city on public roads and streets packed with spectators and ordinary traffic. In a 1903 race from Paris to Madrid, however, reckless motorcyclists caused several serious injuries and deaths to spectators, raising a public cry of outrage. In the end, racing motorcycles (but not automobiles) were banned from the roads of France. Since private racetracks were scarce on the Continent, the motorcycle fad momentarily subsided. In Britain, on the other hand, the sport became firmly established at Brooklands. In 1907 the first Tourist Trophy race was held on the Isle of Man, and four years later the course was expanded to include a notoriously stiff climb up a mountain. For almost two decades, British designs stood at the top of the small world of motorcycle racing.

Motorcycles and automobiles made expensive bicycles seem cheap by comparison. Indeed, in the early years of the twentieth century, the bicycle became a common mode of transportation for working people as well as office clerks and minor government officials. Finally mass-produced, relatively inexpensive to purchase (especially as the secondhand market expanded), and utterly simple to maintain, the bicycle became the people's vehicle throughout Britain and Europe. By way of contrast, North America's greater distances, poorer roads, and earlier production of cheap automobiles prevented the cycle from ever becoming a popular commodity in Canada and the United States.

Motor racing hardly diminished European enthusiasm for competitive cycling. Cycling, after all, was an altogether different sport, arguably requiring more athletic skill, fitness, and stamina. Yet cycling also flourished because it was lucrative business. No less than the motor industries, bicycle manufacturers advertised heavily in the specialized sports press and in turn received extensive coverage of their events. The two French sports papers enjoying wide circulation from 1900 to 1914, *Le Vélo* and *L'Auto*, both covered cycling as well as auto racing. Interesting events sold newspapers. Henri Desgranges, editor of *L'Auto*, founded the Tour de France in 1903 as a means of publicizing his newspaper. A six-stage bicycle race of 1,500 miles stretched out for several days, the Tour de France in 1905 was extended to include mountain routes over the Alps, and in 1910 over the Pyrenees. Imitators followed suit. The Giro d'Italia (Tour of Italy), begun in 1909, lasted three weeks over a route of 1,000 miles. In 1913 the Tour de Flandre was organized as an annual one-day race of 150 miles through the cities and towns of Belgium. In a manner unlike anything of its kind in the United States, competitive cycling began in the early years of this century in Europe, and it continues to the present.

American Crises

While European sports expanded, major-league baseball and intercollegiate football in the United States underwent severe crises. Either sport could have languished, yet both emerged from their difficulties stronger and better equipped for growth, spectator appeal, and media coverage.

Professional baseball entered the twentieth century in a state of disarray.

Since the early 1880s, clubs had engaged in ruthless competition, first between the old National League and the newer, upstart American Association, then (following the collapse of the American Association in 1891) with endless bickering and a fierce player-trade war within the National League itself. In the 1890s the Boston Beaneaters won five pennants, but at century's end there was little joy in Bean Town, Mudville, or anywhere else. Baseball seemed to be on the verge of tearing itself apart.

The situation worsened before it improved. In 1900 Byron Bancroft ("Ban") Johnson, a former newspaper magnate, formed yet another rival league, the American League of Professional Baseball Clubs. As in days of old, players' salaries escalated as they offered their services to the highest bidders in either league. Club ledgers once again went into the red. Finally, in 1903 the National League recognized Johnson's American League as a junior partner in an arrangement called "Organized Baseball," a kind of monopoly based on an elaborate set of rules concerning player-trades, minor-league affiliations, and playing schedules. Most of all, the heads of Organized Baseball were determined to squash any further rival teams or leagues. They would brand them as "outlaws," organize boycotts against their games, and raid their rosters. If all else failed, they would absorb them into Organized Baseball, an owners' cartel.

At the head of that agreement stood a three-man National Commission composed of the two league presidents and a third man selected by them. Club owners granted them permission to set and enforce rules, and to promote the game commercially. The commission immediately created a so-called World Series as a means of sustaining spectator interest to the end of each season. A playoff tournament between the champions of the National and American leagues, the first World Series was played in the early autumn of 1903. The Boston Americans beat the Pittsburgh Pirates five games to three.

The firm hand of the National Commission gave baseball owners the confidence to invest in the acquisition of players and improvement of facilities. Throughout both leagues, old wooden grandstands were replaced by concrete and steel structures. Between 1909 and 1913, four spacious new stadiums were built: Shibe Park in Philadelphia, Forbes Field in Pittsburgh, the Polo Grounds in New York, and Ebbets Field in Brooklyn. Attendance figures, and profits, soared. In 1903 the total major-league attendance was fewer than five million; by 1910 it was more than seven million. At least three times that number of fans made their way to minor-league parks throughout the nation.

Colorful managers and players provided the attraction. In that day of heavy-handed, strong-willed managers, John McGraw of the New York Giants was the toughest of all. At the drop of a hat, he fought with his own players, with opponents, and with league officials. In 1904 he prevented the second World Series from being played when he refused to allow his Giants to compete against the American League champions, whom he termed "a minor league aggregation" not worthy of his time.

One of his pitchers, the strong, durable, Christy Mathewson was undoubtedly one of the most idolized of all the players. Another Giant, Rube Marquard, won nineteen straight games in 1912. In that "dead ball" era, the outstanding offensive players were distinguished as much for their running as for their hitting. Between 1900 and 1911, Honus Wagner, shortstop for the Pittsburgh Pirates, won eight of twelve National League batting titles, but he also led the league five times in base stealing. The king of the American League was Ty Cobb, Detroit's "Georgia Peach," who claimed twelve of thirteen batting titles between 1907 and 1919, set a bevy of base-stealing records, and was best known for his fiery temper and untamed ways. For the most part, baseballers were still hard-drinking, heavy-gambling, loose-tongued individualists untempered by the civilities of a college education. Whatever their ethnic origins, they were people with whom urban immigrant masses could identify.

Despite its administrative conflicts and rough-hewn characters, professional baseball's problems paled beside the crisis confronting college football at the outset of the twentieth century. Football's reputation was notoriously bad. Variations on old mass formations such as the "flying wedge" and the "turtleback" continued to launch offensive backs surrounded by brawny linemen in pulverizing attacks on the opposition. In 1903–4 the rules were changed to specify the number of men required on the offensive line of scrimmage, but the savagery persisted. During the autumn of 1905, no less than eighteen fatalities (not to mention numerous serious injuries) resulted from intercollegiate games. In mid-season Teddy Roosevelt summoned representatives of Harvard, Yale, and Princeton to the White House. Himself a Harvard graduate and a keen advocate of "manly" sports, Roosevelt nevertheless demanded that brutality and foul play be removed from the game. His indictment of foul play suggests that the problem was not confined to mere roughness resulting from mass formations. Deliberate slugging, kicking, and "piling on" were common infractions. Determined to win at all costs, players recklessly bent and broke rules—and opponents' bodies.

Some leading universities, such as Columbia, Northwestern, California, and Stanford, called a momentary halt to football. As the president of the University of California put it in a telegram to football officials, "The game of football must be entirely made over or go." They made it over. In December 1905 about sixty-two representatives from the major football colleges and universities agreed to form an Intercollegiate Athletic Association to revise and enforce the rules of play and to oversee the general administration of the game. Five years later, the name of the new organization was changed to the National Collegiate Athletic Association (NCAA).

In January 1906 the Rules Committee met in New York to overhaul the tactics of the game. It reduced the length of games to sixty minutes, established a neutral zone ("the line of scrimmage") between the offensive and defensive teams, forbade ball carriers to hurdle tacklers, and restricted linemen from dropping back on offense. Most important, it opened up the game by legalizing the forward pass, and consequently it changed the rules to require ten yards rather than five for a first down. Yet the committee placed several restrictions on the forward pass. The ball had to cross the line

Scenes of injured football players, like this one from *Harper's Weekly*, 1891, were scandalously common in the era of mass mauls and led to the reforms of 1906.

of scrimmage five yards out to either side of the point where the play had begun. Old photographs of chalk lines running up and down the field, as well as across it, indicate the method by which referees detected infractions. From that visual grid effect came a new and lasting term for the field of play, the gridiron. Under the rules of 1906, when a pass was touched but not caught, it could be recovered by either side. Passing was a delicate and risky business, not to be engaged in lightly.

At first the forward pass hardly achieved the purpose for which it was intended. Designed to lessen the violent effect of mass offensive maneuvers, in fact it increased the brutality leveled against defensive tackles. In earlier times defensive backs all served as linebackers, bunched behind the tackles. With the new threat of the pass, however, tackles were left without support to ward off interlocked offensive rushes coming their way. In 1909 six tackles died of injuries, causing the Rules Committee in 1910 to ban blockers from interlocking their arms. Also, after 1910 pushing and shoving the ball carrier were forbidden; seven men were required on the line of scrimmage; and the forward pass could henceforth be thrown at any angle, but not more than twenty yards downfield.

Suddenly the momentum swung in favor of the defense, so much so that in 1912 a fourth down was added to make ten yards. Still, the Rules Committee stood firmly by its intention to open up the game, and to keep it open. Thus it created end zones ten yards deep, in which passes could be caught for touchdowns, and it removed the short-lived twenty-yard limit on the distance a pass could be thrown. By 1912 the transformation of American football was virtually complete, creating the game that is still played today. Even the kickoff, traditionally set on the receiving team's forty-five-yard line, was permanently moved back to the kicking team's forty-yard line. Moreover, after numerous alterations in the scoring system, officials finally settled on six points for a touchdown and three points for a field goal.

While all these technical changes were being made, a more colorful drama was taking place on the field. In 1902 the first Rose Bowl game was held in Pasadena on New Year's Day, with the University of Michigan romping over Stanford University, 49–0. The first decade of the century was a glorious era for Michigan football, coached by Fielding H. "Hurry Up" Yost. From 1901 to 1905 his teams won fifty-five games, lost one, and tied one, scoring 2,821 points to their opponents' 42. The only game they lost was to the University of Chicago in 1905. Chicago, too, was enjoying its finest hour on the gridiron. Coached by Amos Alonzo Stagg, the Chicago team of 1904–6 was a powerhouse. Its star was a diminutive quarterback, Walter Eckersall. Playing before the introduction of the forward pass, Eckersall relied on cunning, quickness afoot, tough durability, and an uncanny knack of stopping abruptly to place a well-aimed foot to the ball. Twice in his career he drop-kicked five goals in a single game.

The third strong team of the prewar era was Harvard, coached by Percy Haughton, a stern disciplinarian and master tactician. Long a doormat on which Yale men wiped their feet, Harvard annually enjoyed winning seasons from 1908 to 1915, including a stretch of thirty-three games without a loss. Nor was Harvard the only "Ivy League" team still successfully competing at the national level. Cornell went undefeated and untied in 1915, and at the end of that season Brown University was selected to represent the East in the Rose Bowl, resumed after fourteen years. Yet it was the last gasp of strength for the older, private universities of the Northeast. The emergence of Army in the East, Notre Dame, Nebraska, and Oklahoma in the Midwest, and several powerful squads on the West Coast (which formed the Pacific Coast Conference in 1915) all overwhelmed the elite eastern institutions, where American football had originated.

The single most dramatic contest occurred in 1913, between Notre Dame and Army. As Notre Dame won the game, 35–13, they catapulated from obscurity to national fame, firmly established the forward pass as an effective offensive weapon, and introduced Knute Rockne to the limelight. A Norwegian immigrant, Rockne was captain of the team. From his end position he teamed with quarterback Gus Dorais to reduce the Army defense to shambles. Dorais threw seventeen passes, an incredibly large number for that era. He completed thirteen for a total of 243 yards and five touchdowns, mostly to Rockne.

Their success was no fluke. All summer long they had worked together at a resort on Lake Erie, passing a football back and forth. Rockne mastered catching the ball with one hand, quite an innovation on the breadbasket technique commonly practiced. He also worked on running set patterns, making sharp cuts rather than simply running helter-skelter, hoping the ball would be thrown in his area. In a game prior to the Army contest, he and Dorais discovered the "buttonhook" pass by accident: Rockne fell down just as Dorais released the ball, but he bounced back to his feet, came back to meet the ball, and gained ten yards on the play. Thus was born one of the most effective of all maneuvers in offensive football.

By World War I, the forward pass had become an integral, though still minor, part of the game. More important, American college football had weathered a severe crisis of criticism and self-doubt to become firmly entrenched on the campuses of every major college and university in the United States. Open but deliberate, still violent though controlled, football reflected the variety, the contradictions, and the polarities of American life.

Stress and Storm

In sharp contrast to the sensible reform of intercollegiate football, pugilism on the eve of World War I reflected a dark side of American life. Long an underworld sport controlled by gambling interests, professional boxing had recently risen in public esteem on the broad shoulders of a popular American hero, John L. Sullivan. The use of padded gloves and the emergence of "Gentleman Jim" Corbett had further raised the image of the sport to such a degree that, by the turn of the century, bouts were legal in several states. But with public recognition came public pressures. While the Ku Klux Klan flourished, and while few Americans in 1906 thought twice about the dishonorable discharge of three companies of black soldiers on unproven accusations of rioting in the streets of Brownsville, Texas, the rise and fall of Jack Johnson, the black heavyweight champion from 1908 to 1915, was a case riddled with bigotry and injustice.

Jack Johnson would never have been given a shot at the title had not the heavyweight ranks been barren of attractive white challengers. Sullivan, Corbett, Bob Fitzsimmons, and James J. Jeffries all refused to fight blacks. When Jeffries retired in 1905, however, the supply of good heavyweights dried up. As the new champion, Tommy Burns, mauled his way through a string of inferior opponents, gate receipts plummeted. Promoters searched frantically for better drawing cards. Finally Burns, eager for a big-money bout, agreed to take on Johnson, the best of the segregated black fighters. It was a fateful decision. Fears of racial disturbance forced the removal of the bout from the United States to Sydney, Australia. No doubt the fears were justified. After toying with Burns for thirteen rounds, Johnson knocked him out with a vicious uppercut.

Having created a situation unacceptable to mainstream American opinion, fight organizers began looking for a "great white hope" who could regain the title. None could be found. Within the year, Johnson easily disposed of five white challengers. Then the retired Jeffries, still strong but now thirty-five years old and out of shape, accepted a lucrative offer to present himself as the savior of the white race. With the fight scheduled for July Fourth, 1910, in

San Francisco, George H. "Tex" Rickard, a wily promoter, played the issue of racial confrontation to the hilt. He shamelessly fabricated anecdotes and made racist slurs. Eager newspaper reporters cooperated, publicizing the bout in lurid terms. The heated controversy stirred such fears of racial riot that the governor of California forbade the bout in his state. Yet the prospect of profit outweighed the problems in the eyes of Nevada officials, who welcomed the fight to Reno. On the day of the fight crowds gathered outside newspaper and telegraph offices in small towns and cities throughout the United States, eagerly awaiting news of the outcome.

The fight was no contest. Johnson taunted, jeered, and jabbed, controlled the tempo from beginning to end, and finally knocked out his exhausted opponent in the fifteenth round. News of the black man's victory provoked ugly racial conflicts in no less than fifty American cities. Eight deaths were reported as proud blacks and humiliated, frustrated whites lashed into each other. A number of religious and political leaders quickly joined forces to prevent the films of the fight from being shown in movie theaters. Their crusade culminated in a congressional bill banning interstate transport of "any film or other pictorial representation of any prize-fight or encounter of pugilists." Ostensibly the brutality of the ring and the danger of further race riots inspired the bill, but in truth the fragile myth of white supremacy was at stake. A Boston minister veiled the point when he denounced the "disgraceful affair at Reno" as "a blot on our 20th century American civilization." More candidly, the editor of the *Chattanooga Times* observed that the spectacle of "a powerful negro knocking a white man about the ring" would maliciously "inspire the ignorant negro with false and pernicious ideas as to the physical prowess of his race."

Jack Johnson's physical superiority was only one aspect of the problem. Huge and handsome, black and proud, he dressed flashily, drove the finest cars, and violated the most rigid taboo of his society: he openly courted and married white women. His first white wife committed suicide in 1912, but within the year Johnson found another. Although he lived in Chicago, free of southern state laws banning interracial marriage, massive stacks of hate mail and threats of assassination greeted him daily. For some blacks, such as the aged, mild-mannered Booker T. Washington, he was an embarrassment to his race; for younger, more assertive blacks, he was a hero of epic proportions, a "bad nigger" who refused to bow and scrape to please white society.

The white man's law caught up with him. Under the Mann Act of 1910—which forbade the interstate transport of women for "immoral purposes," a measure to prevent big-city vice rings from forcing women into involuntary prostitution—Johnson in 1913 was charged with having taken Belle Schreiber, a prostitute daughter of a Milwaukee barber, across state lines on one of his famed rides. Predictably, he was found guilty, fined $1,000, and sentenced to prison for a year and a day. Yet again he refused to accept his fate. Freed under bond pending appeal of his sentence, he fled the country to Montreal, where he and his wife boarded a ship to Paris. "There are sad hearts in the country today among the colored people," commented the black editor of a small Richmond newspaper. "Their idol is shattered."

Jack Johnson was shattered more than anyone knew. Having lost his bond money, nightclub investments in Chicago, and easy access to the lucrative black theatrical circuit in the United States, he was pressed for money to live in the extravagant manner to which he was accustomed. In Paris he successfully defended his title against a couple of second-rate challengers, but the purses were pitifully small. Finally, he received a profitable offer to fight Frank Moran on 27 June 1914. He won the fight easily, but on the following day the news of the assassination of an Austrian archduke, Francis Ferdinand, reached Paris. Amid the turmoil of approaching war, Johnson never received his purse. He was a broken man, crushed between the stress of racial animosity and the storm of war.

Yet boxing was hardly the only sport filled with seemingly insoluble tensions on the eve of World War I. Even the Olympic Games, designed to foster understanding and peaceful competition among nations, reflected bitter divisions within the international community. At the London Olympics of 1908, old Anglo-American hostilities surged to the surface. As late as 1895 the two nations had almost been at war over a Venezuelan border dispute. Now British officials foolishly neglected to display the American flag among all the others on the opening day of the London Games, lamely explaining that they had been unable to find one. Infuriated American athletes carried small flags with them as they marched past the reviewing stand occupied by King Edward VII and Queen Alexandra. Traditionally, each team dipped its flag in tribute to the head of the host government, but the Americans refused to do so. "This flag dips to no earthly king," quipped one member of the team, thus establishing a tradition that persists to the present.

In the marathon, a frail little Italian runner, Dorando Pietri, approached the finish line reeling from exhaustion. To the horror of the spectators, he collapsed. British officials helped him to his feet, then ran alongside virtually carrying him across the finish line. Moments later an American, Johnny Hayes, charged into the stadium, but British officials raised the Italian flag in victory. Only after furious protest was Pietri disqualified and Hayes awarded the gold medal. More angry disagreement was to come. In the 400-meter race, British judges disqualified an American runner who had apparently won, provoking the leading American official to charge the Britons with unsportsmanlike conduct. As a result of these disputes, the International Olympic Committee wisely decided never again to allow the host country to choose their own judges and referees. But whatever the ultimate benefits, bickering and strife rather than friendly competition characterized the London Olympics of 1908.

More serious than old unresolved British-American conflicts were the hostilities of minor European nationalities against their imperial masters. Finland, for example, was then a part of the Russian empire. Tsarist officials informed the Finnish team that they must display the Russian flag, or no flag at all, in the Olympic ceremonies. In London the Finns marched without a flag. Again, at the Stockholm Olympics of 1912, their resentment against Russian rule found expression. When a Finnish runner, Hannes Kohlehmainen, won the 5,000-meter race, the Russian flag was hoisted. But as

Kohlehmainen took his gold medal, he turned, pointed to the Russian flag, and remarked loudly, "I would almost rather not have won, than see that flag up there." The fiery aspirations of suppressed peoples such as the Finns, Poles, Serbs, and Croats were a central ingredient in the making of World War I. While the major powers of Europe negotiated their secret treaties and armed themselves for imminent conflict, nationalistic tensions in the Stockholm Olympics of 1912 foreshadowed the catastrophe of 1914–18.

Yet Stockholm, like the prewar "proud tower" of elevated thought and culture which it represented, had its bright side. Colorful pageantry attracted huge crowds to a specially built stadium where almost 4,000 athletes represented twenty-eight nations (including China and Japan for the first time). Controversy was muted; disputes were few. Teams from thirteen European nations participated amicably for five days of gymnastic contests and displays. Finally it seemed that Baron Pierre de Coubertin's modern Olympic movement was set on a sound footing of festive, peaceful competition.

Little could anyone foresee that the brightest star of Stockholm was destined soon to fall from the firmament. Jim Thorpe, an American Indian already famous for his football, baseball, and track exploits at little Carlisle College in Pennsylvania, captured gold medals in the pentathlon and decathlon, the premier contests for versatility. The King of Sweden accurately acclaimed him "the most wonderful athlete in the world." Within six months of the Stockholm Olympics, however, an American sportswriter revealed that Thorpe had earlier played professional baseball (briefly, and for a pittance) with a minor-league club in Rocky Mount, North Carolina. "I did not play for the money," Thorpe lamely explained, "I played because I liked baseball." No excuse was acceptable. The Olympic guardians of gentlemanly sports stripped Thorpe of his medals. Perversely, the muses turned the brightest gold of Stockholm into dross.

The guns of August 1914 reduced everything to shambles. Athletic games gave way to a far more grim contest of strength and will. Fields of play became ugly zones of devastation marked by shell craters, barbed wire, and filthy trenches. The sixth modern Olympiad, envisaged by Coubertin as an event of "gladness and concord," had been scheduled for Berlin in the summer of 1916. Instead, the battle of Verdun claimed 700,000 lives. Distant from the European front, English professional soccer continued to be played until April 1915, when the "Khaki Final" brought a halt to organized sports. "You have played with one another and against one another for the Cup," announced Lord Derby as he presented the trophy to the winners, "play with one another for England now." Yet another official best voiced the sentiment of the nation when he urged that "every eligible young man will find in the service of the nation a higher call than in playing football."

For a time, sports in the Western Hemisphere continued as usual. Baseball especially reflected American isolationism. When the war began, a brash, strong nineteen-year-old pitcher named George Herman Ruth was leading Providence, a farm club of the Boston Red Sox, to an International League pennant. In 1915 Ruth catapulted to the majors, where his pitching ability was soon to be sacrificed for his awesome power at the plate. Even the sinking of the *Lusitania* could not detract from Ruth's publicity. College football, too, resisted European distractions. Scarcely had the smoke cleared from the barbarous battle of the Somme in 1916 when Yale footballers prepared to take the field against their most bitter rival, Harvard. "Never again in your whole life," Yale coach Tad Jones assured his players, "will you do anything so important." Obviously he had Harvard, not the Kaiser, in mind.

Two very different sports on opposite north-south extremities of the Americas took organizational form during the years of the Great War. In 1916 the first South American soccer championship was played in Montevideo, Uruguay. Far to the north, in November 1917 the National Hockey League was formed with three teams: the Montreal Canadians, the Ottawa Senators, and the Toronto Arenas. At the end of the season, Toronto emerged at the top of the small heap, winning the right to represent the fledgling NHL in the Stanley Cup playoffs against Vancouver, the winners of the western, more established Pacific Coast Hockey Association. An admonition of the Toronto coach indicated both the character of the game and the state of world affairs: "It does not require bravery to hit another man over the head with a stick. If you want to fight, go over to France." No doubt some hockey players continued wielding their sticks recklessly; certainly many athletes, Canadian as well as American, went "over to France" in 1917–18.

Of all the athletes caught in crisis, Jack Johnson was one of the most poignant. In April 1915 he defended his heavyweight title in Havana, Cuba, against yet another "white hope," the huge Jess Willard. In heat of 103 degrees under a blazing sun, the fight lasted twenty-six rounds before Johnson went down for the count. He later claimed that he had been offered a cash bribe to take a fall, and that American officials had promised he could return to the United States without legal prosecution for his earlier "crime." If there were promises, they were never kept. For five more years, Johnson lived in exile in England, Spain, and Mexico, finally returning to the United States in 1920 to serve a year and a day in prison. From beginning to end, the career of Jack Johnson epitomized the glory and tragedy of his era.

Chapter 14

DAYS DARK AND GOLDEN

While Johnny came marching home after the Armistice in November 1918, Europe lay devastated. Within the previous four years, more than ten million men had died in combat, and another ten million had been wounded and maimed. Survivors entered the "wasteland" of the 1920s suffering from a loss of confidence, trust, and hope. Economic chaos brought widespread political instability. The vindictive distrust that characterized the Versailles peace settlement of 1919 carried throughout much of the following decade. It was not a glorious decade for European sports. Yet as athletic events inevitably mirrored international hostilities and suspicions, shafts of light occasionally pierced dark shadows on European fields of play.

Remote from Europe's struggles, Americans enjoyed a decade of unprecedented affluence and glamor. The twenties roared with new, inexpensive automobiles, radios, and motion pictures. Sports stars such as Babe Ruth, Red Grange, and Jack Dempsey competed for public attention with Hollywood's Douglas Fairbanks, Rudolph Valentino, Mary Pickford, Lon Chaney, Tom Mix, and Charlie Chaplin. Filled to capacity, sports stadiums were enlarged to hold yet more spectators. Professional baseball, intercollegiate football, and boxing headed the list of spectacles. Golfers, tennis players, Olympic champions, billiards experts, and speedboat racers attracted less attention but still received more press coverage than ever before.

Fields Fit for Heroes

The first notable sporting fixture in postwar Europe was conceived, organized, and dominated by Americans. Shortly before the war ended, Elwood

Against a background of national flags, athletes competed in the Inter-Allied Games of 1919, as illustrated in this poster advertising the occasion.

S. Brown, a YMCA official serving as the director of athletics for the American Expeditionary Forces in France, proposed the Inter-Allied Games as a kind of "military olympics," which would illustrate the importance of athletics in the training of Allied armies and occupy the attention of "great numbers of troops during the somewhat restless period waiting their return home." In cooperation with the French government, Brown arranged competitive events in twenty-four sports involving 1,500 athletes from eighteen countries. In the spring of 1919 a stadium was constructed to hold 25,000 spectators on the outskirts of Paris. It was named in honor of the American General, John J. Pershing. For two weeks in the summer of 1919, about a half-million spectators turned out to see American athletes win the laurels in twelve of the twenty-five events.

In one sense the Inter-Allied Games were, as Brown suggested, a testimony to "the interest of the athletic world both in Europe and in America." From a larger perspective, however, they represented a divided Europe. They were victors' games, celebrations of Allied unity and victory. Most of the athletes and spectators were American servicemen, the largest group of able-bodied soldiers still stationed in France; others were primarily British, French, Italian, and Canadian. Athletes from the defeated nations of Germany, Austria, Hungary, and Bulgaria were not welcome; nor were the Russians, who had undergone a Bolshevik revolution in 1917. Basically the games were an athletic adjunct to the Treaty of Versailles, in which war-guilt and reparations clauses treated Germany and her allies as scapegoats, lepers to be excluded from the family of nations.

The official Olympics in the postwar era were little different. In Antwerp in 1920 and again in Paris in 1924, the International Olympic Committee excluded Germany and her allies from the games. In fact, the 1920 games were awarded to the Belgians partly as a gesture of sympathy for four years of German occupation. The gift was of dubious value. Physically and financially ravaged by war, Belgium needed new homes, shops, and factories rather than athletic facilities. The Antwerp Olympics were hastily and badly organized. Athletes lived in decrepit schoolhouses. The track, newly built for the games, was heavy and slow. Poorly publicized, the games attracted pitifully small crowds.

Yet athletes, and the nations they represented, turned eagerly "to happier, better things" than war. Several men who had competed at Stockholm eight years earlier symbolically linked the past with the present. Hannes Kohleh-mainen, the Finn who made such a fuss over the Russian flag in 1912, saw the flag of his independent Finland raised in celebration of his victory in the marathon. Many of the athletes at Antwerp, of course, were veterans of the war. Albert Hill, a thirty-six-year-old who had served for the duration of the war in the British army, won both the 800- and the 1,500-meter races. Bevill Rudd, a South African who had commanded the first British tank battalion ever to attack German lines, sprained an ankle at Antwerp, finished third in the 800 meters, but then returned to win the gold medal in the 400 meters. The crowd's favorite, however, was Jacques Guillemot, a Frenchman whose lungs had been seared by poison gas in the war; he struggled successfully to win first place in the 5,000 meters. As former victors and military veterans competed once again, the past loomed over Antwerp.

The future also beckoned. Paavo Nurmi, a Finnish runner whom Guille-mot beat in the 5,000 meters, returned three days later to take the 10,000 meters (beating Guillemot, incidentally), then the 8-kilometer cross-country race. One of the greatest runners in the history of the Olympic Games, Nurmi methodically trained himself to run by a stopwatch always strapped on his wrist. At Antwerp he led the Finnish team in tying the United States for the total number of gold medals, no small feat for such a tiny country. Antwerp inaugurated the decade of the Finns, with Nurmi at the head of the pack. In Paris in 1924 and in Amsterdam in 1928 he accumulated seven gold and three silver medals in the ten races he entered.

Several "firsts" occurred at the Olympics of 1920. For the first time, figure skating and ice hockey were introduced on the Olympic program. Canada's ice-hockey victory came as no surprise. In tennis, a French teenager, Suzanne Lenglen, made her debut as queen of the court. Also at Antwerp the official Olympic flag was first unfurled, with five interlocking circles on a white background. Each circle was of a different color, taken from one of the colors on every national flag in the world; the five circles represented the major land masses on the globe. Only one nasty incident violated that symbol of unity at Antwerp. A Czech soccer team walked off the field in protest against one of its players being ejected from the game after two questionable goals had been allowed a Belgian team.

Outside the Olympic format, soccer football became the handmaiden of nationalism in war-torn Europe. As feelings against "the Hun" still ran high in Britain, the Football Association refused to allow its teams to compete against German and Austrian teams. French, Belgian, Scandinavian, and Italian officials vigorously opposed such a policy, and in 1920 England's Football Association withdrew from the International Federation of Football Associations. Even when England returned to the European fold four years later, it still played only against teams representing former allied and neutral nations.

There was more to their withdrawal than mere political chauvinism. The English were losing their grip on the game they had given to the world. Innovative European teams came up with new styles of attack and defense; some began demanding slight alterations in the rules of the game. Proud of their heritage and happy with their own style and rules of play, the British refused to change. "We do not desire to interfere with the action of other Associations who do not agree with our rules," the secretary of Britain's Football Association wrote to the head of the International Federation in 1923, "nor do we desire that they should interfere with ours." Returning to European amateur soccer competition in 1924, England withdrew again in 1928, over yet another point of difference. European teams demanded a more liberal definition of amateur status, with players being paid for time lost from work. British officials remembered that such an arrangement led to full-blown professionalism in English soccer several decades earlier. They would not repeat that "mistake" at the international level.

At first it appeared that isolation from the larger European soccer community had little effect on the English game. At the end of the war, professional soccer boomed once again in Britain. Although the upper classes berated soccer as "the unpatriotic game" because it had continued well into the war, masses of spectators eagerly returned to the stadiums. Soccer matches reasserted an old pattern of life, traditional values in a world torn asunder. In truth, the loss or retirement of many of the better players had caused a decline in the quality of the game, but for most spectators such nuances did not matter. For three years the annual Cup Final at Stamford Bridge drew capacity crowds, and in 1922 a new stadium was begun at Wembley to hold 127,000 spectators. For the Cup Final in 1923, almost 200,000 fans crammed into the stadium, many scaling walls and fences to fill both the terraces and the field. Police had to shove people to the sidelines before the game could begin. Amid the bedlam, the presence of King George V lent symbolic official acceptance of the "people's game." With Wembley as its centerpiece, British soccer seemed to thrive.

But insularity proved its undoing. Divorced from European innovations in training techniques and team play, soccer in postwar Britain stagnated. The handwriting appeared on the wall in 1921, when an English international side lost to a French team, 2–1. But no one took much notice. At the Paris Olympics in 1924, the British team was soundly defeated—in sharp contrast to its four previous Olympic performances in which it had come away with three gold medals. Soccer matches in Britain continued to attract massive crowds, but the day of unquestioned British dominance on the field was past.

Part of the reason for Britain's relative decline was the expansion and dramatic improvement of soccer throughout postwar Europe. In France the Football Federation was founded in 1919 under the leadership of Henri Jooris, a rich businessman of Lille. Professionalism came on fast, raising standards of play and arousing public interest in the game. In 1919 there were only 659 French soccer clubs; by 1929 the number had leaped to 3,592, more than a 500-percent increase within a decade. As had happened earlier in England, soccer football swamped the rugby game in France in the 1920s. Although France remained the only continental nation that played much rugby, it was soccer, not rugby, that multiplied in its appeal to the masses.

Soccer was also the rage in interwar Italy, where Vittorio Pozzo managed a national team featuring an attacking center half; in Austria, promoted by a wealthy Viennese businessman, Hugo Meisl, and coached by Jimmy Hogan, an Englishman, who produced a *wunderteam* based on controlled patterns of short passes; and even in ravaged Germany, where a physical, disciplined style emerged in the early 1920s. All the while, new national football associations were being formed in most of the smaller countries, who breathed more freely after the Versailles settlement: Yugoslavia and Poland in 1919, Bulgaria and Turkey in 1923, and Greece in 1926 all formed national soccer organizations.

In the 1920s soccer also became the most popular summer sport in the Soviet Union. Government officials arranged for superior Moscow and Leningrad teams to tour small towns and villages giving exhibition matches and teaching the game to youngsters. In 1922 only four teams competed in the first soccer championship tournament ever held in Russia, but in the following year sixteen teams entered the tournament. Also in 1923, a soccer team represented the Soviet Union in a tour of Finland, Sweden, Norway, and Germany. Soccer was the only sport the Soviets yet promoted on an international basis.

Despite its dominance, soccer was by no means the only sport that thrived in postwar Europe. Rugby football in Britain and France, gymnastics in Scandinavia, Germany, and France, and boxing and tennis throughout Europe contributed to the physical and mental recovery of countries scarred by war. Car racing also revived and expanded. The year 1921 saw both the resumption of the French Grand Prix and the founding of the Italian Grand Prix, the latter at a new banked track built in a royal park on the outskirts of Milan. In 1923 French sportsmen established the Le Mans race, a twenty-four hour ordeal through towns and cities in the Sarthe district of France. Even more tricky was the Monaco Grand Prix, begun in 1929 as a torturous, exhausting race through the winding streets of Monte Carlo.

An American export, basketball, sank roots in European soil shortly after World War I. The founder of the game, James B. Naismith, later recalled touring American military bases in Europe and seeing basketball goals everywhere. Once he observed a crowd of Frenchmen watching American servicemen play. When the game ended, several spectators tried their hand at shooting baskets. "They were at first quite awkward in their attempts," Naismith commented, "but the rapidity with which they learned to pass and shoot was astonishing." No less astonishing was the spread of the game.

Largely ignored in France, England, and Germany, basketball caught on especially on the eastern fringes of Europe, where YMCA directors in Prague, Budapest, and Vienna promoted the game zealously. In 1924 several YMCA leaders in Istanbul translated the rules of the game into their own language. The following year, some American professors at Cairo University formed the Egyptian Basketball Union. Nor was the distant Soviet Union immune to basketball mania. Members of the Soviet State Military Academy translated the rules into Russian, and in 1923 a women's tournament attracted so much attention that a year later Russian men basketballers began holding similar tournaments.

By the end of the decade, western Europe had achieved some measure of economic and political stability. The Olympic Games in Paris (1924) and Amsterdam (1928) reflected that renewed health. Despite the controversial occupation of the Ruhr Valley by French troops (to extract reparations payments from Germany), the Paris Olympics produced few disputes. Amid 1,500 athletes representing forty-five nations, Paavo Nurmi remained the master of long-distance running, and Johnny Weissmuller emerged as the finest swimmer in the world. In Amsterdam the number of competitors doubled and for the first time since the war included athletes from Germany, Austria, Hungary, and Bulgaria. As a sign of the future, dominant American and Finnish athletes were challenged by members of previously inconsequential teams from Uruguay, Argentina, Chile, South Africa, Japan, Egypt, New Zealand, India, and Haiti.

Another indicator of European recovery was the beginning of the Winter Olympics. Ever since 1902, Nordic Games had been held in Scandinavia every fourth year, featuring cross-country skiing, ski jumping, and ice hockey. In 1920 the Norwegian Olympic Committee demanded Winter Games in the Olympics, but Coubertin resisted, fearing that such innovations would be detrimental to the Olympic program. Winter sports became popular in the Alps in the 1920s, however, apparently causing the International Olympic Committee to change its views. An international Winter Sports Week at Chamonix, France, in 1924 was two years later retroactively designated as the "first" Winter Olympics. At St. Moritz, Switzerland, in 1928 the Winter Games came of age. Almost 500 competitors from twenty-five nations entered the field. Alpine (downhill and slalom) skiing was introduced on an experimental basis. Most memorable was the figure-skating performance of a little blond, brown-eyed fifteen-year-old from Norway, Sonja Henie. At St. Moritz she won her first of three consecutive gold medals.

The most hopeful sign of the times occurred shortly after the Summer Olympics in 1928. Douglas Lowe, a British runner who won the 800 meters, had been beaten earlier in a London meet by a German, Otto Peltzer. An injury forced Peltzer to withdraw from the Amsterdam games, but a month later he challenged Lowe to a showdown in Berlin. Lowe accepted the challenge and narrowly won over a healthy Peltzer. The victory was less important than the gesture. Bitter enemies only ten years earlier, British and German athletes were now competing again in a sportsmanlike manner.

Little could anyone foresee that economic disaster and the rise of fascism would soon level yet another damaging blow to sportsmanship in the Western world.

Americana Golden

Free from Europe's struggle to recover from the effects of war, Americans enjoyed a golden age of sport in the 1920s. Baseball, generally considered the national pastime, stood in the limelight. In the early 1920s the introduction of a livelier ball and the banning of trick pitches such as the "spitter" transformed baseball from a defensive, punch-hitting, bunting, and base-stealing game into an offensive spectacle featuring the home run. Ty Cobb was the master of the old style; Babe Ruth represented the new. Spectators loved the change. During the decade fifteen of the sixteen major-league clubs made a profit; only the Boston Red Sox, who sold or traded away most of its stars, lost money. The New York Yankees led the list of moneymakers. Their prime attraction, of course, was "the Babe," whom they bought from the Red Sox in 1919.

In that same year, however, baseball suffered the most famous scandal in the history of sports. Entering the World Series of 1919, several members of the Chicago White Sox connived with gamblers to "throw" the series to the Cincinnati Reds. Teammates, the manager, and even the owner of the White Sox got wind of the fix, but lacking definite evidence they closed ranks to avoid controversy. Rumors of further gamblers' payoffs to players during the season of 1920 added fuel to the fire of inquiry. Finally, in September 1920, a grand jury received testimony of guilt from eight members of the White Sox. At the trial, records of those confessions were not to be found. A jury found the players not guilty, but the incident shook the baseball world so severely that all eight were banned from the game for life. An imaginative journalist created a poignant story of "Shoeless" Joe Jackson, the semiliterate but outstanding outfielder for the Sox, who supposedly came out of the courtroom to be met by a plaintive plea from a small boy: "Say it ain't so, Joe." A fictitious concoction, the episode nevertheless represented the sentiments of baseball fans everywhere, whose faith in the game was momentarily shaken. Shoeless Joe Jackson and his comrades lived out their lives as the infamous Black Sox of 1919.

Before the Black Sox trial, baseball owners convened to map out a plan to restore the image of purity to the game. They agreed to dispense with the old three-commissioner system that had governed major-league baseball since the turn of the century. In its place they put a single authoritative commissioner, a distinguished individual without any prior formal connection to baseball. Kenesaw Mountain Landis was their man. A thin, white-haired, scowling, blunt person, Landis was a federal judge in Chicago. An avid baseball fan, he was a man of limited education, with a strong authoritarian streak. He had defended management's interests in cases involving labor disputes, and during the war he had proved himself a superpatriot in cracking down on draft dodgers. He was rectitude personified , an individual ideally suited both in temperament and reputation to put baseball back on its pedestal.

He succeeded brilliantly, if ruthlessly. Even rich, powerful baseball barons bowed to his commands. Predictably, Landis came down hardest on players. He adamantly refused ever to reconsider the ban on the eight Black Sox, despite legal evidence and personal pleas to the contrary. In 1921 he banned three other players for life, one for associating with gamblers, another for negotiating a contract with an "outlaw" baseball club, and a third for being indicted for car theft. Nor were the superstars exempt. Landis once fined and suspended Babe Ruth for ignoring a league rule that forbade barnstorming at the close of the season without official approval. Ty Cobb and Tris Speaker retired under a cloud of suspicion that they had bet on a game years earlier, a cloud stirred up by investigators hired by Commissioner Landis.

By 1924 a total of fifty-four players were listed as ineligible to play in the major leagues, fifteen permanently. For Landis, law and order were at stake. He saw Ruth's case, for example, as "a question of who is the biggest man in baseball, the Commissioner or the player who makes the most home runs." Yet another motive was paramount. Baseball players who broke the laws of the land or the rules of organized baseball would, in Landis's words, "burden patrons of the game with grave apprehension as to its integrity." Although the commissioner became more lenient as he ruled major-league baseball until 1944, his first few years at the helm earned him the nickname "Czar" Landis.

A landmark Supreme Court decision in 1922 virtually gave baseball owners a blank check in protecting their investments. Speaking for an unanimous court in an antitrust suit against organized baseball, Justice Oliver Wendell Holmes ruled that professional baseball was not "trade or commerce in the commonly-accepted use of those words," and that it was not interstate commerce because the movement of ball clubs across state lines was "incidental" to the business. Thus owners' interests were given a legal stamp of approval.

Baseball in the 1920s also received a stamp of moral approval. In 1926 President Calvin Coolidge recognized it as "a real moral and physical benefit to the nation." Even Sunday baseball became respectable, breaking the prolonged Puritan stranglehold on American Sundays. By 1918 only half of the major-league teams played on Sunday; by 1928 all did except in Philadelphia and Pittsburgh, where Sunday professional sports finally became legal in 1934. New York and Boston were two of the last cities to win local options. A minister in Boston spent an entire sermon endorsing Sunday ball games: "I think Christ would be in favor of anything that would give the youth of the country honest recreation." Behind that moral endorsement of baseball stood not only the lobbying efforts of affluent owners but also the respectable, stern figure of Kenesaw Mountain Landis.

Yet sport does not thrive simply because it is respectable. On the contrary, too much respectability is a deadening weight in the public marketplace. The early limited appeal of lawn tennis, the cleanest and most gentlemanly sport, is a case in point. Popularity comes from glamor and excitement mixed with a bit of controversy, not decorum. For all his principled integrity and public authority, Czar Landis merely facilitated the golden age of baseball. He did not create it. In the players themselves lay the key to the popularity of the game.

The players were a colorful and talented lot. Many of the prewar stars, like Ty Cobb, Christy Mathewson, Walter Johnson, Grover Cleveland Alexander, Pie Traynor, Tris Speaker, and Rogers Hornsby, effectively ended their careers in the 1920s. Cobb finished with an armload of batting and base-stealing records, but he won no batting championship after 1919. Hornsby, on the other hand, concluded with a flourish, compiling a .402 batting average over five years, 1921–25, to crown his career with a lifetime average of .358. Youngsters such as Dizzy Dean, Charley Gehringer, and Lou Gehrig began their careers in the 1920s, destined for stardom. Yet the one colossus who towered over the era was Babe Ruth, a man in whom all the pleasure-seeking and power-loving tendencies of the age found expression.

The son of a Baltimore saloon keeper, Ruth was a man of gargantuan appetite. Food, drink, women, fame, fortune—he wanted them all. And he got it. Inordinate strength in the shoulders and arms amply compensated for spindly legs and a pigeon-toed gait. Until age caught up with him, he was fast afoot, sure with the glove, and strong of arm. Most of all, he hit a baseball like no one else, before or since. His home-run record is common knowledge: 60 in 1927, 714 for his career. Not so familiar is his all-around excellence. In 1921, his best-balanced year, he collected 59 homers, batted in 170 runs, scored 177, and collected 204 hits for an average of .378. When he retired in the mid-1930s, his lifetime batting average stood at .342, an extraordinary record for a man who was paid primarily to produce "the big bang."

But lifeless statistics hardly do him justice. Stories (some true, many fabricated) swirled about his name. He was a hero, larger than life. Brash and undisciplined, he could produce the right word or deed for each dramatic occasion. In the first game ever played in the new Yankee Stadium, "the House that Ruth built," he appropriately thrilled the packed house of 75,000 fans by clouting a home run. He was "the Babe," "the Bambino," "the Sultan of Swat." He was Baseball in its golden age.

While major-league baseball remained confined to the Northeast and industrial Midwest, college football became a national mania in the 1920s. The autumn game spread as a mode of mass entertainment for Americans east and west, north and south, rural and urban, rich and poor—for everyone near a college or university campus. Huge football stadiums, larger even than their baseball counterparts, sprang up across the nation. Football attendance doubled within the decade. Marching bands, majorettes, and cheerleaders took the field as supporting casts for the athletes. College football in the Roaring Twenties became an autumn ritual, a fiercely competitive game wrapped in tinsel and bathed in fervent partisanship. "It is at present a religion," *Harper's* observed toward the end of the decade; "sometimes it seems to be almost our national religion."

The foundations of big-time college football were laid in the 1920s. Officially designated as "amateurs," college players in fact received scholarships (tuition, room, and board) and whatever extra money they could negotiate from coaches and alumni. In the 1920s "athletic dorms" became the fashion on most college campuses, and professional trainers became part of the college athletic scene. Most important, full-time coaches and several assistants were paid to direct the entire show.

The passing of an older, more casual era was symbolized in the deaths of two outstanding coaches in 1924 and 1925. One was Percy Haughton. A winner at Harvard before the Great War, he served as a chemical-warfare officer in France, then returned home to take a position in finance, unrelated to college football. In 1923, however, he rose to the challenge of building a football program at Columbia University, which had seen many lean years. Shortly after Columbia won a hard-fought game in October 1924, Haughton suffered a fatal heart attack. He was only forty-eight years old. In the following March, the innovative "father of American football," Walter Camp, died while attending the annual meeting of the football rules committee in New York City. Having established himself at Yale as one of the game's greatest mentors, Camp had retired from coaching in 1910. He amassed a comfortable fortune by skillfully managing a clock company, yet he kept up his interest in the game by writing twenty books and numerous magazine articles, editing the annual rulebook for intercollegiate football, and selecting the annual All-American team. Both Camp and Haughton were intensely devoted to the college game, but both were gentlemanly enthusiasts who had interests other than football, and goals other than winning.

In sharp contrast to Camp and Haughton, the most prominent coach of the 1920s, Knute Rockne, was a *coach* first, foremost, and always. No side interest in finance or clock companies diverted his attention from the game. Always thinking football, Rockne in 1921 shifted his backs from the T-formation to a power formation right or left requiring a snap of the ball to the tailback, a formation that came to be known as the Notre Dame Shift or Box. He initiated the use of larger, slower players as "shock troops" to wear down opponents in the first few minutes of each half. More than any other coach, he believed in intersectional competition. His Notre Dame team traveled afar so often that they reportedly broke out in "Home, Sweet Home" every time they saw a Pullman coach. Yet they won, and they won big. From 1919 to Rockne's death in 1931, his teams compiled a 105–12–5 record, including five undefeated seasons.

Under Rockne, football at Notre Dame became something of a religion. "Outside the Church," in the gospel according to Rockne, "the best thing we've got is good, clean football." On the one hand, he preached the virtues of character, courage, determination, and good sportsmanship; on the other, winning was the essence of his game. Full of platitudes, he was master of the locker-room pep talk. His famous "Win one for the Gipper" speech stands at the forefront of American mythology. The speech was given in 1928, fully eight years after the talented George Gipp (a star Notre Dame back) died of pneumonia. With Notre Dame and Army tied 0–0 at halftime, Rockne emotionally recalled Gipp's dying words, which no one but Rockne himself

The old and new: Dapper, gentlemanly Walter Camp of Yale in 1924 (*left*), and an intense son of immigrants, Knute Rockne of Notre Dame (*right*). The football future belonged to the Rocknes of Notre Dame, not the Camps of Yale. (Courtesy of Yale University and the University of Notre Dame.)

seems to have heard. Notre Dame, of course, beat Army for the Gipper—and for Rockne.

The most famous of Rockne's players were "the Four Horsemen," Harry Stuhldreher, Don Miller, Jimmy Crowley, and Elmer Layden. Actually they were built like ponies, not horses. Their average weight was less than 160 pounds, hardly large enough for a good high-school team today. But they were gifted athletes all, masters of Rockne's complex offense. Most important, they tickled the fancy of the dean of American sportswriters, Grantland Rice. After Notre Dame beat Army in 1924, Rice began his report with the colorful, memorable words: "Outlined against a blue-gray October sky, the Four Horsemen rode again. In dramatic lore they were known as famine, pestilence, destruction, and death. These are only aliases. Their real names were Stuhldreher, Miller, Crowley, and Layden." The individual names soon faded from memories of most sports fans, but the legendary Four Horsemen and their forward wall, the "Seven Mules," stuck in the mind.

Their greatest moment came in the Rose Bowl on New Year's Day, 1925, when they beat Glenn "Pop" Warner's outstanding Stanford team, 27–10.

Stanford was led by Ernie Nevers, a bruising fullback whom Warner swore was a better athlete than even the great Jim Thorpe (whom Warner had coached at Carlisle College). During the regular season, both of Nevers's ankles had been fractured. He removed the casts only ten days before the Rose Bowl game and played the entire game heavily taped. Against Notre Dame he carried the ball thirty-four times for 114 yards, but he had two of his passes intercepted and returned by Layden for touchdowns; in the fourth quarter he was twice stopped within the one yard line. Fully recovered by the following season, Nevers in 1925 won unanimous All-American honors. One afternoon against the University of California he ran the ball on every play except three, leading Stanford to victory over their rivals for the first time in eight years.

Yet of all the outstanding football players in the 1920s, Harold "Red" Grange was undoubtedly the most spectacular. Less than six feet tall and weighing only 170 pounds, Grange was durable, quick, and swift. The line behind which he ran at the University of Illinois was never particularly strong, but "the Galloping Ghost" ran and passed with such skill that spectators filled the stadiums for virtually every game he played. Red Grange was to college football what Babe Ruth was to major-league baseball. Like Ruth on the opening day of Yankee Stadium in 1923, Grange stole the show when Illinois unveiled its new stadium in 1924. Against an undefeated University of Michigan team, he returned the opening kickoff ninety-five yards for a touchdown. Within the first twelve minutes he scored three more touchdowns on long, weaving runs and later scored a fifth and passed for another. Hardly could anyone have convinced the 66,609 fans who witnessed that performance that any footballer in Ameria equaled Red Grange.

Professional scouts certainly needed no convincing. They believed not only that Grange was the best but also that his crowd-appeal would bring success to the struggling National Football League. Founded in 1921, the NFL in its infancy was anything but successful. For the decade of the 1920s, the New York Giants and the Chicago Bears were the only franchises that made money. The Bears signed Grange to a lucrative contract shortly after the last game of his senior year. By modern standards, the agreement was preposterous: a barnstorming tour of thirty exhibition games, with Grange paid several thousand dollars for each game. At the beginning, the crowds turned out to see the spectacle. But interest soon waned, then plummeted once Grange was so bruised that he performed far below his normal level. The day of professional football lay still in the future. For the time being, college football reigned as the unrivaled king of autumn sports.

Maulers and Millionaires

Whereas baseball and football effectively built on prewar foundations to achieve unprecedented popularity in the 1920s, professional boxing had to overcome its prior reputation. It did so dramatically. A favorite means of preparing American servicemen for the rigors of hand-to-hand combat, boxing emerged from World War I cleansed of its seedy, back-alley image.

Two of the luminaries of the Roaring Twenties, Jack Dempsey and Babe Ruth, ham it up for the photographer. (From the Charley Miller Collection, University of Maine at Orono.)

Patriotic service made the sport respectable. Overnight it became a popular spectacle. For the first time, women unashamedly joined bankers, lawyers, and intellectuals at ringside. State after state legalized the ring, most setting a mandatory limit of ten rounds for each bout. Racial segregation played a part. After Jess Willard defeated Jack Johnson in 1915, white fighters, promoters, and the press unofficially closed the door on black challengers in order to make boxing more attractive to white spectators.

Two personalities dominated the 1920s. One was a promoter, George "Tex" Rickard, a former cowboy, gold prospector, and saloon owner. Rickard made and lost two fortunes by the time he was forty years old. He first promoted a prizefight in 1906, and in 1910 he arranged and adroitly publicized the notorious clash between Johnson and Jim Jeffries. With confidence written all over his face and a cigar dangling always from his mouth, Rickard was a man made for the swashbuckling, free-spending 1920s. He shrewdly offered large purses to book big bouts, which in turn reaped him huge dividends. He was a promoter without peer.

Much of Rickard's work was necessarily done behind the scenes. The most visible ring personality of the era was Jack Dempsey, a scrapping, smallish heavyweight from Manassa, Colorado, who had learned his fighting skills not in the army but in the hobo jungles of his rail-riding youth. If Rickard was the essence of entrepreneurial success, Dempsey was the stuff of which heroes were made in the 1920s. Born of poor Irish immigrant parents in a small town, he was a man with whom millions of Americans could identify. No intellectual, he exuded animal ferocity in the ring. He displayed little scientific finesse; he was a fighter of perpetual motion whose dramatic flamboyance was peculiarly suited to the new age of the automobile, jazz, and brash American confidence.

In Toledo, Ohio, on the Fourth of July 1919, Dempsey decisively seized the heavyweight crown from Jess Willard. Rickard of course promoted the fight. Willard, rich from previous ring earnings and investments in the oil fields of Oklahoma, was badly out of shape. He was a foot taller and sixty pounds heavier than Dempsey, but his puffy white skin stood out in sharp contrast to the tanned, hardened body of his young opponent. In the first round, Dempsey knocked him down seven times. At the bell Willard staggered to his corner, both eyes almost closed, his jaw broken, his cheekbone split, and one ear permanently damaged. For two more rounds he survived, only because Dempsey was arm weary. At the end of the third round, Willard's trainer threw in the towel.

For seven years Dempsey reigned as champion, taking on every challenger in sight—except blacks. One black fighter, Harry Wills, twice signed to fight him, but both times the controversial match was canceled over technicalities. Promoters and the public simply would not risk another Jack Johnson. The lack of worthy white American opponents sent Rickard looking overseas. Britain had little to offer, but a French light-heavyweight, Georges Carpentier, displayed quickness and intelligence. Rickard sold Carpentier to the American public as an intellectual and French war hero who had served valiantly in the aviation corps. Supposedly he was a man of virtues opposite to Dempsey, who had shirked military duty and made no pretense of being learned. The ruse worked. On 2 July 1921 almost 100,000 people paid about $1,800,000 to see the fight, which Dempsey won by a fouth-round knockout. Not only was it the first million-dollar fight gate in history, but it was the first prizefight ever broadcast over radio. Professional boxing had arrived as a major spectator sport.

While Dempsey's manager fretted for more than a year looking for another lucrative match, other fighters made the headlines. In January 1922 an inexperienced Gene Tunney beat "Battling" Levinsky, the former light-heavyweight champion. Later in the year Tunney lost a fifteen-round decision to Harry Greb, a much lighter but more experienced man. It was the only fight Tunney ever lost. Greb went on to become the world middleweight champion from 1923 to 1926. Two months after he lost the title, he underwent an eye operation and died of complications. Doctors then revealed that he had fought most of his championship bouts with only one good eye. Corruption still exploited courage in the squared circle. Of the courageous set was Benny Leonard, world lightweight champion from 1917 to 1924. Tough and wily, he retired with a crown untarnished by defeat.

But neither showmanship nor skill in the lighter divisions could obscure the importance of the heavyweights. Well aware of the need for attractive heavyweight bouts, Tex Rickard in 1923 asked Nat Fleischer, editor of *The Ring* magazine, to scout for talent in Germany while Fleischer was there on a writing assignment for the *New York Telegram*. Fleischer obliged. In his report, "Reconstruction in the Fatherland," he observed that Germany was "rapidly developing a nation of athletes, with boxing holding the attention of youth more so than any other sport. Germany is a nation to watch. Boxing is gaining a firm hold in the Fatherland." For the time being, however, Fleischer saw "not a professional worth discussing" with Rickard.

The United States remained the unrivaled center of the boxing world. In 1923 Dempsey decisioned a light-heavyweight, Tommy Gibbons, and later in the year attracted yet another million-dollar gate against Luis Firpo, a slow but huge, strong fighter from Argentina. As usual, sportswriters cooperated fully with Rickard's promotional scheme to nickname Firpo "the Wild Bull of the Pampas." The bull was bullish indeed. Within seconds of the opening bell, he floored Dempsey with a short right uppercut. Enraged, Dempsey unleashed a furious attack, dropping Firpo no less than six times within two minutes. Just before the end of the first round, however, Dempsey went sprawling through the ropes into the laps of ringside sportswriters. The referee delayed his count while Dempsey struggled to get back into the ring. No official timekeeper was present. Some observers swore that the champion was out of the ring at least twenty seconds. Whatever the truth of the matter, the single most exciting round in ring history ended with Dempsey once again charging Firpo and both men pounding away at the bell. In the second round Dempsey landed a smashing right to the jaw, sending Firpo crumpling to the canvas (as one witness recalled) "as if he had been one of his own pampas bulls hit by the axe of a butcher." He did not get up.

Once again Dempsey faced an horizon bare of challengers. In 1926 Nat Fleischer returned to Europe, and this time he spotted a promising German heavyweight champion, Maximillian Schmeling. Fleischer negotiated with

Schmeling and his manager to come to the United States to fight Dempsey, then reported to Rickard that German boxers were paid so poorly for their efforts that Schmeling would require advance payment of his passage and training expenses. Normally a shrewd gambler, Rickard for some reason refused the offer. Otherwise Max Schmeling would have fought for the crown while he was in his prime.

Instead, Gene Tunney was chosen by Rickard to contest Dempsey's crown. Since his loss to Greb, Tunney had twice won rematches and had then beaten the European champion, Emilio Spalla, knocked out Georges Carpentier, and handily defeated several lesser opponents. Tunney's career, like his boxing style, was steady, not flashy. He reached his goal on the evening of 14 September 1926 in a huge stadium built for Philadelphia's sesquicentennial celebration. About 120,000 people packed the stands, expecting to see the "Manassa Mauler" make quick work of this handsome, soft-spoken challenger, an ex-Marine who nevertheless seemed to lack a killer instinct.

They knew little of Dempsey's problems, or of Tunney's skills. Distracted by legal disputes arising from his ex-manager's suit for breach of contract, Dempsey was not sharp. Every time he crouched, charged, and flailed away, Tunney cagily stepped back, kept him at bay with a straight jab, and counterpunched with a right cross. The disparate styles reminded old-timers of champions of days past. Dempsey, coiled and aggressive, fought on the order of Jim Jeffries in his prime; Tunney, erect and "scientific," was reminiscent of "Gentleman Jim" Corbett. After the fifth round the issue was never in doubt. Tunney won the decision unanimously.

The sports world was astounded. Dempsey, Ruth, and Grange were names uttered in the same breath, champions all. Ruth was still going strong, and in the following season he hit his record sixty home runs. Grange had just turned professional after a dazzling college career. But now the great Dempsey had fallen. Having emerged in 1919 with the onus of "draft dodger" hanging over his head, he had won the grudging respect of boxing fans everywhere. Now, in defeat, he won their affection. Tunney, on the other hand, was too clean-cut and calm, too much the polished gentleman to be fit for mass adulation in the frenetic atmosphere of the Roaring Twenties. For their rematch, Dempsey was the overwhelming sentimental favorite.

Enterprising as ever, Tex Rickard milked the situation for all it was worth. For a warm-up, he matched Dempsey with Jack Sharkey in Yankee Stadium and happily reaped the first million-dollar gate for a nonchampionship fight. For the Tunney-Dempsey rematch, he selected Soldier's Field in Chicago, where he was assured of maximum press coverage and minimal rental fees. On 22 September 1927 twenty-four special trains rolled into Chicago. More than 100,000 spectators filled the stadium, some so far from the lighted ring that the boxers appeared as tiny flies under a distant light bulb. According to one reporter, 200 millionaires filled the first ten rows at ringside. Certainly Rickard was one of them: the gate receipt was $2,658,660, a record that still stands.

For six rounds the fight followed the pattern of the first encounter. Dempsey charged and stalked, but to little effect; Tunney, the superior boxer, piled up a decisive lead. About a minute into the seventh round, however,

Dempsey unloaded his entire arsenal. Tunney sprawled to the canvas on his back, jerkily grasping the lower rope with his left hand. As fighters in the past had always done, Dempsey stood over his fallen foe waiting for the count. But before the fight, both men had been reminded of a recent Illinois ruling that a fighter had to retire to the distant corner before the referee began his count. Excited, Dempsey either forgot or ignored the new rule. Finally, the referee took him by the arm and led him to the far corner, then returned to begin his count over the prostrate Tunney. At the count of six Tunney rose to one knee, struggling to clear his head. At the count of nine he came to his feet, and for the remainder of the round he backpedaled, sparred, and foiled Dempsey's savage charge. The famous "long count" was now history. Tunney recovered sufficiently to carry the final three rounds, retaining his crown by a unanimous decision.

Tunney's expert performance was overshadowed by the controversy that swirled around the long count. Old-timers berated the officials of the state of Illinois for their new rule; some criticized the referee for ignoring the timekeeper's count over the fallen Tunney. Estimates for the time Tunney was actually on the canvas ranged from fourteen to twenty seconds. Most writers agreed that Dempsey "wuz robbed." A few noted that Dempsey himself, not the rules or the referee, was at fault, the victim of his own mental lapse and lack of discipline.

Shortly thereafter, Dempsey retired. He was thirty-two years old, world-renowned, and rich. Tunney in 1928 defended his title one final time against Tom Heeney, an Australian. In the eleventh round the referee mercifully stopped the fight. Tunney collected his $525,000 purse, bringing his earnings for the last two years to about $2 million. Less than a month later he followed Dempsey into retirement as the first heavyweight champion ever to hang up his gloves before he was beaten. The golden age of boxing was at its end.

Prima Donnas

Boxers were by no means the only athletes in nonteam sports to come to public attention in the 1920s. In the United States, swimmers Gertrude Ederle and Johnny Weissmuller, sprinter Charles Paddock, jockey Earle Sande, speedboat racer Gar Wood, polo player Tommy Hitchcock, and billiards champion Willie Hoppe were all well known. Of all the famous individual athletes, however, golfers and tennis players received the most attention.

Golf remained the game of American businessmen and white-collar clerical workers, whose numbers expanded greatly in the 1920s. Whereas only 743 golf courses existed in the United States in 1916, by 1930 there were almost 6,000, one-fifth of them daily-fee courses. On the eve of the Great Depression, about two million Americans played golf regularly. More money was spent on golfing equipment than on baseball, football, basketball, boxing, and tennis equipment combined. In 1929 steel-shafted clubs were authorized, completing the evolution of golfing equipment from ancient bent limbs and "featherie" balls to the streamlined clubs and lively balls in use today.

Britain's long tradition and America's exceptional individual players made golf a predominantly Anglo-American affair in the 1920s. Two new team tournaments illustrated that dominance. The Walker Cup, created in 1922, pitted male British and American amateurs against each other; the Ryder Cup, inaugurated in 1927, set professional teams in transatlantic competition. They were held in alternate years.

America's rapid rise to the pinnacle of the golfing world first became apparent in 1922, when Walter Hagen became the first native American to win the British Open at St. Andrews. Hagen subsequently won three more British Opens, and sixty tournaments in all. More than his record, however, his colorful personality transformed the image of the golfer from staid respectability to heroic popularity. An outspoken advocate of professional golf, Hagen once remarked candidly: "I don't want to be a millionaire, I just want to live like one." In sheer ability he was merely equal if not sightly inferior to a contemporary professional, Gene Sarazen, a master of wood and wedge shots. But Hagen's showmanship made him the most famous professional golfer of his era.

In the amateur ranks, Glenna Collett surfaced in the 1920s as the first American woman golfer of note. She possessed phenomenal power for distance, and she won the U.S. Women's Amateur crown six times. Yet of all the golfers of the 1920s, professional or amateur, Robert Tyre "Bobby" Jones of Atlanta led the pack. As adamantly amateur as Walter Hagen was enthusiastically professional, Jones played competitively for only eight years, from 1923 to 1930. He entered twenty-seven major tournaments and won thirteen of them: four U.S. Opens, five U.S. Amateurs, three British Opens, and one British Amateur. In 1930 he captured all four championships, the first "grand slam" in the history of the game. Gentlemanly and efficiently businesslike, Bobby Jones personified the character of the golfing set in the 1920s. Despite the antics and unbridled opinions of professionals such as Hagen, golf remained primarily a weekend diversion for the affluent and socially aspiring, for whom the "nineteenth hole" (the "watering hole" at the club bar) provided both relaxation and useful business contacts.

Even more than golf, tennis also continued to cater to the upper classes. Most tennis courts in the 1920s were still privately owned or attached to socially exclusive clubs. All the major tournaments were strictly amateur, a sure sign that players possessed independent wealth. Tournament organizers constructed grand new facilities in the 1920s. In 1922 the All-England Club, sponsor of the Wimbledon tournament, moved from its old site to a new, larger one a mile or so away. The new grounds, requiring two years and £140,000 to prepare, were financed by the selling of shares. Investors received no cash dividends, but rather center-court seats to the annual Wimbledon playoffs. In 1923 a new stadium was built at the West Side Lawn Tennis Club in Forest Hills, New York, the home of the U.S. Lawn Tennis championships. Earlier the men's singles had moved from Newport and the women's singles from Philadelphia, making Forest Hills the centerpiece of American tennis. In 1927 France's national tournament also found a new, permanent home after years of alternating between several sites. The lush Stade Roland-Garros on the edge of the Bois de Boulogne at Auteuil was named after an aerial hero of World War I.

Like soccer football, lawn tennis had been created and dominated by the British until the Great War. During the 1920s Britons lost their grip on the game. Americans and Frenchmen not only reigned supreme in their respective national championships but also routed British opponents at Wimbledon. Between 1920 and 1930 only one Briton, Kathleen McKane, won Wimbledon singles (in 1923 and 1927, the latter as Mrs. L. A. Godfree). Otherwise, French and American competitors carried away the laurels.

In 1919 a stocky, fiery young Frenchwoman, Suzanne Lenglen, captured the first of five consecutive women's singles, and in 1925 she won yet another. Trained by her father to imitate the best male players, Lenglen possessed a scorching serve, charged the net frequently, and jumped around the court with abandon. Her style was revolutionary. Earlier, most women served underhand or sidearm, playing a defensive lob game. Her dress was also revolutionary. She discarded the tight corsets, baggy blouses, and petticoats traditionally worn by women competitors. Her one-piece dress, cut midway down the calves, shocked Wimbledon traditionalists. Had she been more attractive, she would have no doubt raised even more eyebrows. In fact, her body was made for action, not display. A long, heavy nose, large mouth, and prominent chin set on a short, squat frame scarcely qualified her as a beauty. Still, neither her daring attire nor her homely looks detracted from the quick, graceful moves that came from ballet lessons and hard training.

For her first Wimbledon crown, she narrowly defeated a seven-times champion, Mrs. Dorothea Lambert Chambers, 10–8, 4–6, 9–7. Subsequent opponents were delighted merely to win a set. Between 1919 and 1926 Lenglen lost only one singles match. In 1925 she won sixteen tournaments, including the women's singles, women's doubles, and mixed doubles at Wimbledon. But she was frail, constantly suffering from asthma and insomnia. Although her flashy style finally endeared her to Wimbledon audiences and inspired sportswriters to pronounce her "Queen of the Court," she was intolerably irritable and arrogant. In 1926 the prima donna side of her personality spelled her doom as a Wimbledon favorite. Queen Mary came specifically to watch her play a singles match, but Lenglen refused to play because she was peeved at not having an escort page her at the hotel. An hour late, she finally went to the locker rooms, and there she fumed, while the queen sat insulted in the stands. Jean Borotra, a fellow Frenchman, went into the dressing room (blindfolded for the sake of propriety) and implored Lenglen to play. By the time she finally took the court, the queen and her entourage had departed.

For conservative British tennis lovers, the deed was unforgivable. When Lenglen played in a mixed-doubles match with Borotra on the final day of the tournament, she received a few catcalls but was mostly greeted with stony silence. Furious, she decided never again to play at Wimbledon. Shortly thereafter, she turned professional for a $100,000 American tour, then returned home to found a lawn tennis and ballet school in Paris, where she largely disappeared from sight. The queen of tennis had a brilliant but short reign.

Her successor, Helen Wills, was an altogether different personality. A

Californian, Miss Wills lacked Lenglen's flair and emotion. Rather, she was cool and efficient to the point of being dubbed "Little Miss Poker Face." As a twenty-year-old, she lost to Lenglen in Cannes, but in 1927 she won the first of her record eight singles titles at Wimbledon (the last four under her married name, Helen Wills Moody). Although she also won seven American and four French championships, her last Wimbledon victory was undoubtedly her finest. After a long, arduous recovery from a slipped disc, she returned to Wimbledon in 1938 to claim the women's title in the same month that Suzanne Lenglen died of a blood disease.

The male counterpart to Lenglen and Wills, the "king" of the court in the 1920s, was William Tatem "Big Bill" Tilden, a rangy, graceful, intelligent fellow from the fashionable Main Line of Philadelphia. A Shakespearean actor as well as an athlete, Tilden combined theatrical showmanship with intense dedication to make himself the best and most popular of all male tennis stars in the 1920s. Early in his career a weak backhand left him vulnerable to the well-aimed shots of William M. Johnston, who destroyed him in the Forest Hills finals of 1919. Following that debacle, Tilden went into seclusion for the winter, corrected his flaw, and emerged with a backhand stroke that dependably complemented his cannonball service and powerful forehand.

He first became prominent in 1920 as a member of America's Davis Cup team. Teamed with the more experienced "Little Bill" Johnston in men's doubles, Tilden controlled the tempo of the game. In 1920, in fact, he lost not a single match, including Wimbledon and Forest Hills as well as the Davis Cup. He was the first American ever to win at Wimbledon. From 1920 to 1925 he captured six consecutive singles trophies at Forest Hills, and yet another in 1928. He also won at Wimbledon in 1921, in 1928, and in 1930, at the age of thirty-seven.

For eleven consecutive years, from 1920 to 1930, Tilden led the American team in the Davis Cup. In 1926, however, he was defeated by a Frenchman, René Lacoste, and in the following years lost yet again to Lacoste and three times to Henri Cochet. The French surge came as no surprise, for France's "Four Musketeers"—Lacoste, Cochet, Jean Borotra, and Jacque Brugnon—barged to the front of world tennis competition in the mid-1920s. From 1924 to 1929 Borotra, Lacoste, and Cochet even carried four Forest Hills trophies home to France. All the while, the Four Musketeers reigned like gods over the world of men's doubles.

As befitted their sport and social class, tennis stars in the 1920s were an individualistic, highly eccentric lot. While they dazzled the public, they harbored petty jealousies and quarreled endlessly among themselves. Tilden and Lenglen detested each other, probably because no room was big enough to contain both egos. Tilden later admitted to homosexuality. But for all their quirks, prima donnas in the 1920s made tennis a popular spectator sport for the first time in history. In arousing interest in the game beyond the confines of exclusive upper-class patrons, they made their mark alongside the Babe, the Galloping Ghost, and the Manassa Mauler on the golden age of sport.

Chapter 15

COPING WITH DEPRESSION

Indelibly etched in the memory of all American sports buffs is the wrong-way run of Roy Riegels. The date was New Year's Day, 1929; the occasion was the Rose Bowl game between Georgia Tech and the University of California. As 70,000 fans watched in mute amazement, Riegels, a California linebacker, scooped up a Georgia Tech fumble and ran seventy-four yards—in the wrong direction. He was finally caught and tackled by one of his own teammates, but not until he had rambled to his own one yard line. On the very next play, California attempted to punt, only to have the kick blocked for a Tech safety. At the end of the day, the scoreboard read 8–7 in favor of Georgia Tech, and ever afterward "Wrong-Way Riegels" had to live with the most famous goof in sports history.

Yet it was a fitting way to usher in the year 1929, for within that year the collapse of the Wall Street stock exchange sent the world economy on a wrong-way course. Banks and national currencies failed, causing the loss of massive fortunes, modest savings accounts, and home mortgages. Without buyers for their goods, industries closed down. As unemployment rose at a terrifying rate, governments struggled desperately to find remedies for disaster.

The sports bubble burst. Stadium turnstiles rusted from inactivity. Numerous private golf and tennis clubs folded. By 1933 the sale of sports equipment slumped to half of what it had been in 1929. In those economically hard times, competitive sports were a luxury that most people could ill afford to play, much less pay to watch. Yet several international sporting fixtures planned before 1929 came to fruition during the depths of the Great Depression. Inexpensive participant sports flourished, and with the recovery of

Western economies, professional spectator sports emerged stronger than ever. Sports not only shared the hardships of the depression; they also played a role in recovery.

The Crash Heard 'Round the Stadium

As spectator sports languished at the onset of the depression, professional baseball especially suffered. Major-league gate receipts dropped from an all-time high of $17 million in 1929 to less than $11 million in 1933. Similarly hard hit, minor-league clubs could not absorb the blow. Many folded; others survived by putting themselves under the ownership and control of "parent" major-league clubs. Thus the depression produced a "farm system" for which Cardinals' owner Branch Rickey had long petitioned the commissioner's office. Czar Landis yielded to economic necessity, not to owners' demands.

Withering crowds notwithstanding, major leaguers performed heroically. In 1930 a hard-hitting, hard-drinking outfielder for the Chicago Cubs, Hack Wilson, registered the best year of his outstanding career by batting .356, hitting 56 homeruns, and knocking in 190 runs (still a major-league record). In a World Series game against the Cubs in 1932, Babe Ruth gave his famous motion toward the pitcher, then deposited the next pitch over the center-field fence. Whether or not he "called his shot" matters little. The incident immediately took its place in the mythology surrounding the Babe. Such dramatic moments, however, could not conceal the decline of athletic prowess. Suffering the effects of too many years, too much booze, and too many nights on the roam, Ruth was traded in 1935 to the Boston Braves, where he ended his career on a sad, defeated note.

Even the mighty Babe felt the pinch of depression finances. When he held out for a salary of $80,000 in 1930, he was asked why he was demanding more money than President Hoover made. "What the hell has Hoover to do with it?" Ruth shot back. "Besides, I had a better year than he did." By 1934, however, Ruth's salary dipped to $35,000, quite a cut although still the highest in the majors. From an average of $7,000 in 1929, salaries dropped to $5,000 in 1932, bottoming out four years later at $4,500. Jimmy Foxx, the outstanding first-baseman for the Philadelphia Athletics, hit fifty-eight homers in 1932 and forty-eight the next year, but he still had to take a large salary cut because of his club's loss at the gate.

The depression virtually destroyed the Athletics, one of the finest teams in the history of baseball. Just before the Crash of '29, they ended the Yankees' stranglehold on the American League, then beat the Chicago Cubs in the World Series. Managed by Connie Mack, again in 1930 and 1931 they won the World Series. Their dynasty was short-lived. Despite the victories, management consistently lost money as people stayed home, sought jobs, and spent their meager means on essentials. Even after the Pennsylvania legislature in 1934 granted a local option for Sunday ball games, matters hardly improved. Desperate for operating capital, Athletic owners sold their stars to the highest bidders. It was a move from which the Philadelphia team never recovered.

The depression also jolted college football, major-league baseball's prime competitor for public attention in the 1920s. On the eve of the stock-market crash, the Carnegie Foundation released the results of a three-year study of American intercollegiate athletics. In fact, it was primarily a ringing indictment of major college football's thinly veiled professionalism in the form of ruthless recruiting, athletic scholarships, opulent living and training facilities, and the easing of athletes through their courses of study with the least possible effort. The report met with a storm of resistance from university administrators, whose entire athletic budgets depended on large gate receipts from winning football teams. What the Carnegie Report proposed, however, the depression momentarily accomplished. Even the best of the major college teams suffered declines of 30 to 40 percent in gate receipts, and athletic directors had to cut down on scholarships, equipment, and training procedures. According to an Associated Press survey in 1931, four of every five institutions were forced "either to economize sharply on athletic expenses or curtail activities."

Economic strictures put a premium on coaches who could discipline and inspire their teams. In the South, Wallace Wade took Alabama to the Rose Bowl following the 1930 season, then moved to an equally successful tenure at Duke. His capable successor at Alabama, Frank Thomas, competed on even terms with archrival neighbors Bob Neyland at Tennessee and Bill Alexander at Georgia Tech. In the East, Jock Sutherland at Pittsburgh and Fritz Crisler at Yale were overshadowed by no one except Lou Little of Columbia, who enjoyed outstanding depression seasons from 1931 to 1933 and on New Year's Day, 1934, defeated Stanford in the Rose Bowl. Nebraska's Dana X. Bible, Michigan's Harry Kipke, and Minnesota's Bernie Bierman were the class of the Midwest. On the West Coast, Howard Jones's fine Southern California teams dominated, winning the Rose Bowl in 1930, 1932, and 1933.

Another West Coast stalwart, Glenn "Pop" Warner, shocked the football world by leaving Stanford after a bad season in 1932, moving back East to Temple. No shock compared, however, to the tragedy that befell the coaching ranks the previous year. On 21 March 1931 the most famous coach in the United States, Notre Dame's Knute Rockne, was killed in a plane crash. Only forty-two years old, Rockne was, according to Grantland Rice's eulogy, "an artist as well as a football coach," whose loss was "a vital blow to millions." Certainly it was sad news for a nation suffering bad times.

Yet of all the sports that mirrored the nation's confusion and despair, professional boxing projected the most telling image. The fabulous gate receipts of the 1920s were a thing of the past, and not merely because of world economic difficulties. Following the retirements of Dempsey and Tunney, the heavyweight division was at a loss for quality champions. From 1930 to 1935 five different men momentarily held the crown: Max Schmeling, Jack Sharkey, Max Baer, Primo Carnera, and Jimmy Braddock. Carnera, a giant of a man from Italy, received the most press coverage, but he was as awkward and incompetent as he was huge.

To make matters worse, two great champions of the past failed miserably in comeback attempts. Dempsey, having tried his hand at refereeing, returned to the ring as a fighter in 1931, only to give an abysmal performance in winning a split decision. Although booed from the ring, he continued for three more years in a futile attempt to regain his lost prowess. More decisive was the failure of Benny Leonard, the former undefeated lightweight champion. After seven years' absence from the ring, he returned in 1932 as a welterweight. Against inferior opponents he won several bouts, but in October 1932, he was knocked out in the sixth round by a strong young Canadian, Jimmy McLarnin. Although McLarnin added some excitement to the ring by performing a forward somersault after knocking out his opponents, most people in 1932 had little to cheer about. Like boxing, the world economy was in the depths of disarray.

Sports in Europe suffered far less curtailment than did American sports during the depression years. Lacking the massive commercial expansion that Americans enjoyed in the 1920s, Europeans had little of the fancy equipment, the college scholarship system, and the inflated professional salaries that necessarily caused problems when the economy contracted. Activities such as German gymnastics, French cycling, and English rugby football were not only inexpensive forms of play, but also were traditionally indifferent to spectator appeal. Even professional soccer, the most commercial and international of all European team sports, was far more adaptable to hard times than were American spectator sports.

British soccer illustrates the point. In 1922 Football League officials set a ceiling on salaries at £8 per week, a limit that remained in effect until after World War II. Marginal players in the First Division and virtually all competitors at lower levels made considerably less than eight pounds. Team payrolls were therefore strikingly small in comparison to American baseball or college football budgets. Moreover, soccer required minimal capital outlay for training, equipment, and medical expenses. With low operating costs, owners could well afford to scale down the price of tickets to a level that soccer fans could afford, even in the most dire circumstance.

Despite economic distress, 130,000 people filled the stands of Hampden Park in Glasgow to watch an international match between England and Scotland in 1931. In the following year the British economy hit rock bottom. One in four of the work force went unemployed, and almost 7 million of a total population of 45 million lived "on the dole" (welfare). Yet in 1933 about 135,000 spectators again crammed into Hampden Park to watch another international match. In the following year 84,000 turned out to see Manchester City play Stoke City, a record attendance for a regular league game.

In cutting their pattern to fit the cloth of depression, owners and managers not only practiced good business but also performed a social service. Herbert Chapman, the manager of Arsenal (London) until his death in 1934, pioneered in making soccer more accessible and attractive to spectators. A tactical innovator in the 1920s, Chapman in the early 1930s first introduced floodlights for night games in order for workers to attend. With spectators in mind, he also proposed a large time clock, a white ball, and numerals on players' jerseys, innovations that conservative league officials rejected. But with imaginative managers such as Chapman and exciting players such as Stanley Matthews, a fleet winger who began his incredible thirty-three-year career with Stoke City in 1932, soccer provided inexpensive diversion for the unemployed, excitement for masses of people otherwise mired in the slough of despond.

Games as Scheduled

Despite the contraction of sports in the Western Hemisphere, several major athletic events conceived and planned during the expansive era preceding the Crash were successfully completed during the early 1930s. One was the World Cup, professional soccer's equivalent of the Olympic Games. The idea of an "open" tournament (in which the best players available, whether professional or amateur, would be eligible to represent their nations) was first introduced at the Antwerp Olympics in 1920, then discussed in more detail at the Paris Olympics in 1924. Finally, in 1926 the officials of the Federation Internationale de Football Association agreed with their secretary, Henri Delaunay, that international football could "no longer be held within the confines of the Olympics." Two years later the president of the organization, Jules Rimet, convened a meeting in Amsterdam in which members decided to begin the World Cup in 1930 and subsequently to hold an international tournament every four years squarely between the Olympic Games.

To host the first World Cup, five applicants submitted bids: Italy, Holland, Spain, Sweden, and Uruguay. Having won the last two soccer championships in the Olympics, tiny Uruguay held the upper hand. Although it boasted a population of only two million people, it offered to pay all the travel and lodging expenses of visiting teams and to build a new stadium in central Montevideo. To clinch its application, Uruguay sounded an emotional appeal: the stadium would be named Centenario Stadium in honor of the nation's one-hundredth anniversary of independence. At the FIFA congress in Barcelona in 1929, Uruguay was awarded the games.

Few European national football associations sent teams. The distance was prohibitive—several weeks by steamer—and by the summer of 1930 the depression was beginning to take a devastating toll on the national economies in industrial Europe. Peeved because their own applications had been rejected, Italy, Holland, Spain, and Sweden sent no teams; nor did Britain, who was not even a member of the FIFA. Leaders of Austrian, Hungarian, German, Swiss, and Czech football associations debated the matter, but all in the end decided not to sponsor representatives to Uruguay. After some political pressure was exerted, Belgium, France, Yugoslavia, and Romania agreed to participate. In addition to those four, eight Latin American countries (including Uruguay) fielded teams. Surprisingly, even the United States, no big soccer power by any means, sent a squad composed largely of immigrant Scottish and English professionals, sponsored by Bethlehem Steel.

From the time they received word that the World Cup would be held in their country, Uruguayans had only eight months to build the new stadium they had promised. Unfortunately, three of those months fell during the rainy season. For the preliminary round of World Cup play in July 1930, the stadium was not ready, so the games had to be played on local soccer fields scattered in and around Montevideo. Finally, midway through the playoffs, the Centenario Stadium, a three-tiered bowl designed to hold 100,000, was finished. Yet the stadium could not contain all the people clamoring to see the games. Ticket offices closed, all their tickets gone; black market scalping thrived. As gates to the stadium crumbled beneath the crush, local police were overwhelmed. Football fever ran rampant.

Competition was similarly intense on the field. In the semifinals Argentina beat the United States and Uruguay defeated Yugoslavia, both by the identical scores of 6–1. Apparently the gods had written the script for neighboring Argentina to confront the home team in the finals. Just across the River Plate from Montevideo lay Buenos Aires, and thousands of Argentine fans chartered ten packet boats on the morning of the game. As they arrived, each passenger was searched for guns and knives, a procedure that was repeated when they entered the stadium. The kickoff was scheduled for 2 P.M.; the stadium was packed to capacity by noon. Even the ominous sight of soldiers rimming the field with fixed bayonets did not dampen the festive, expectant atmosphere.

Behind 2–1 at halftime, Uruguay rallied to win, 4–2. Throughout the city bells rang and horns blared into the night. Ships in the port blew their sirens, and the next day was proclaimed a national holiday. Across the river the Uruguayan consulate in Buenos Aires was stoned by an angry mob, requiring police to disperse the crowd. The first World Cub contained all the fierce competitiveness, spectator appeal, and nationalistic partisanship that have characterized subsequent World Cups. For a brief moment, neither poor Uruguayan peasants nor a mounting world economic crisis seemed to matter.

Nor did economic woe deter a number of other internationally minded sportsmen. In 1930 the organizers of the America's Cup moved their premier yacht race from New York to Newport, Rhode Island, where it became a regular feature of the social calendar. In the same year the first British Empire Games were held in Hamilton, Ontario, attracting 400 athletes from eleven different countries. In 1932, when the world economy was at its worst, both the Maccabiah Games in Palestine and the Balkan Games (for Bulgarian, Romanian, Greek, and Yugoslavian athletes) were founded.

The Olympic Games of 1932 also obscured the grim facts of the depression. While soup lines lengthened daily as thirteen million Americans became jobless, officials in charge of the Winter Olympics at Lake Placid, New York, provided comfortable lodging for the athletes, constructed a new indoor ice-skating arena, and brought snow by the truckloads from Canada to help repair patchy ski slopes. Sonja Henie, the sensational Norwegian figure-skating star, won another gold medal. Even more noteworthy was the emergence of American athletes in winter events such as bobsledding, speed skating, and skiing, sports traditionally dominated by northern Europeans. The economic situation contributed heavily to that breakthrough. Of the 300 competitors at Lake Placid, about one-fifth were Americans. Many of the better European athletes simply could not afford the transatlantic passage.

Still a minor feature of the Olympic program, the Winter Olympics at Lake Placid paled beside the extravagance of the Summer Olympics in Los Angeles. Like Uruguay with the first World Cup, Los Angeles committed itself to the 1932 Olympics several years in advance. As early as 1920 a committee headed by William May Garland applied to the International Olympic Committee. European members of the IOC held out for Paris in 1924 and Amsterdam in 1928, but the IOC awarded the games to Los Angeles for 1932. For the young, fast-growing city, the Olympic Games promised international recognition. Well before 1929 the Community Development Association, headed by Garland and Zack J. Farmer, began making plans for the event. The Crash of '29 momentarily shook those plans.

Following spirited negotiations, Los Angeles city officials agreed to float bonds and subsidize the games to the tune of almost $1,500,000. The State of California appropriated yet another million dollars, and private contributions were solicited. On 321 acres high on the hills overlooking the Pacific, a comfortable Olympic Village featured two-room bungalows and dining quarters designed to provide cuisine uniquely attractive to the many different nationalities represented in the Olympics. The Los Angeles Coliseum was modernized and enlarged to accommodate more than 100,000 spectators. Civic pride was at stake; no expenses were spared.

Fearing that economic distress would discourage foreign athletes from making their way to distant California, the organizing committee issued assurances in 1930 that it would provide reduced steamship and railway fares, and that it would arrange housing, food, entertainment, and local transportation for only two dollars per day for each athlete. The scheme worked. For the tenth modern Olympiad, 1,500 athletes came from 34 nations to compete at Los Angeles. Yet even with all the concessions, some teams came at great sacrifice. Brazilians paid their way by traveling on a ship filled with coffee beans, selling the beans at each port of call on the way to California.

Their efforts were rewarded not only with smoothly run games, but also with a spectacle worthy of Hollywood's Cecil B. DeMille. Olympic flags covered the city as well as the stadium. In the opening ceremonies high-stepping majorettes led marching bands, a strange, eye-popping event for foreigners unaccustomed to American college football games. For the first time in Olympic pageantry, a runner carried a torch around the track and up the steps of the stadium to ignite the "eternal flame." Once the games began, an electric photo finish was introduced, and it proved to be invaluable in determining the winner of one of the sprints. Even the press enjoyed a technological innovation. Individual teletype printers allowed journalists to relay their reports with a speed and ease never before known. Finally, the Los Angeles Olympics began the ceremony in which gold medalists stood on the top step of a victory stand above the silver and bronze medalists while a band played the winner's national anthem.

Coincident to all these stylistic innovations, new athletic heroes emerged at Los Angeles. Gone were familiar victors such as Paavo Nurmi, who was declared ineligible because he padded his expense account in a European meet preparing for the Olympics, and Johnny Weissmuller, who was now

Mildred "Babe" Didrikson launches a javelin in the 1932 Los Angeles Olympics. She set world records in both the javelin throw and the 80-meter hurdles. (From *Report of the American Olympic Committee*, 1932.)

selling his physique and swimming talents in Tarzan movies in nearby Hollywood. The only gold medalist from the Amsterdam Olympics of 1928 to repeat at Los Angeles was a stocky Irishman, Patrick O'Callaghan, in the hammer throw. New athletes produced new records galore. Sixteen world records and thirty-three Olympic marks fell. For the first time, Japanese swimmers won most of the medals and established several new records. In track-and-field competition, in which nineteen of twenty-two events saw old marks shattered, a little black American speedster, Eddie Tolan, took gold medals in the 100-meter and 200-meter sprints, hotly pursued by his own teammates Ralph Metcalfe and George Simpson.

Most dramatic of all, however, were the exploits of Mildred ("Babe") Didrikson, an eighteen-year-old Texan, brash and slender. Perhaps the greatest female athlete of all time, she could run, leap, throw, ride, swim, and kick or hit any kind of ball with consummate ease and power. "Is there anything at all you don't play?" a sportswriter once asked her. "Yeah," she answered, "Dolls." Unfortunately, Olympic rules in 1932 limited female athletes to three competitive events. The Babe chose the javelin throw, the 80-meter hurdles, and the high jump. In both the javelin throw and hurdles race she won gold medals and broke world records. "I'd break 'em all if they'd let me," she was heard to say after her second feat. In the high jump, she and another American tied at a record height, but in the jump-off Didrikson was disqualified for diving over the bar, an infraction of a rule that then required a high jumper's feet to go over the bar first. Unhappy with the decision, she accepted the silver medal. From the Olympics of 1932 she launched a glittering career in women's basketball and softball, occasionally exhibited her skills in baseball and tennis, and finally settled on professional golf for her livelihood. Babe Didrikson was undoubtedly the biggest winner in the Los Angeles Olympics of 1932.

A New Deal for Recreation

The biggest loser in 1932 was not an athlete, but rather one-term President Herbert Hoover. In accordance with the custom of having the head of the host nation officially open the Olympic Games, the International Olympic Committee invited Hoover to lead the ceremonies at Los Angeles. Busy planning his campaign for reelection, he declined the offer but sent Vice President Charles Curtis to take his place. Hoover was as unwise as he was incompetent. An appearance at the Los Angeles Olympics would have identified him with an upbeat enterprise for a change; press coverage would have exposed him to more Americans in a single day than did dozens of his whistle-stop campaign speeches. His days in the Oval Office were numbered.

Immediately upon taking office early in 1933, President Franklin Roosevelt introduced his New Deal measures to tackle the problem of mass unemployment by setting people to work at government expense. Embedded in the New Deal was a richer sports and recreation life for Americans everywhere. Recovery programs such as the Civilian Conservation Corps, the National Youth Administration, the Public Works Administration, and the Works Progress Administration not only produced new highways, dams, bridges, and public buildings, but also new parks, playgrounds, athletic fields, gymnasiums, swimming pools, ice-skating rinks, ski trails, and public tennis courts and golf courses. Between 1935 and the beginning of World War II, the WPA alone spent more than a billion dollars on about 40,000 sport and recreation facilities.

Federal aid also supplemented the budgets of cities and towns in providing organized public-recreation programs. Within a single year, from 1934 to 1935, the number of cities employing recreation directors doubled. Gone from office, Herbert Hoover nevertheless voiced a dominant concern for those youths "who have to spend their outdoor lives upon the pavements in the congested areas of our big cities." Sport, he believed, was a way for them to "let off steam" in a constructive manner; sport was "that other great high school of morals" alongside the family and church. Yet health and morale as well as morals were at stake. Beginning in the mid-1930s, government agencies cooperated with the YMCA and YWCA, the Kiwanis, Lions, and Rotary clubs, the American Legion, Boy Scout and Girl Scout clubs, and churches and chambers of commerce in encouraging youths to swim, exercise at gymnastics, play ball, hike, and camp outdoors. The New Deal produced a kind of quiet revolution in the relation of American government to the sports and recreation of its citizenry.

Of all the traditional sports and games, tennis and golf were affected most.

While private clubs folded or made their facilities available to fee-paying individuals, new municipal tennis courts and golf courses opened both games to an entirely new sector of American society. For many people, of course, tennis and golf equipment was still prohibitively expensive. But free public courts and fee-paying municipal courses vastly diminished the age-old dominance of elite private clubs. Symbolic of the game's mass appeal, a simpler, quicker, inexpensive version of golf became popular in the 1930s. Especially in the South and Midwest, entire families enjoyed many a balmy summer evening playing "miniature" golf.

Like miniature golf, simple pleasures such as horseshoes, shuffleboard, and roller skating were inexpensive and open to both sexes and all age groups. Billiards remained mostly an all-male pursuit, but in YMCA "pool rooms" became a game divorced from smoke and liquor. Even more remarkable was the transformation of bowling. Not since the bowling fad prior to the Civil War had the game attracted respectable crowds. As the nation recovered from the depression, however, neatly polished and well-lit lanes appealed to women as well as men, church groups as well as industrial teams. Women especially turned to duckpin bowling with a lighter ball. Leagues quickly formed in virtually every small town and throughout the cities. Inexpensive and casual, bowling attracted about ten million participants annually in the late 1930s.

Softball, too, was ready-made for depression frugality, and it had the added advantage of being an outdoor game. In 1934 the Amateur Softball Association was formed, bringing some order to the various rules that had earlier governed the game. Also, the name of the game became standard: "softball" rather than "mush ball," "kitty ball," or "indoor baseball." No community picnic or summer family outing was complete without a softball game involving young and old, male and female. By 1935 about 1,000 lighted fields were catering to both fast-pitch and slow-pitch leagues, many sponsored by churches and industries. On the eve of World War II, the Amateur Softball Association claimed about 300,000 teams and more than three million players.

For more vigorous youths, new playgrounds and gymnasiums meant accessible basketball courts. Given a backboard and basket, the game met the basic requirement of depression popularity: equipment was both minimal and inexpensive. Sneakers were relatively cheap, and one ball sufficed for an entire community of disadvantaged city youths to drive, jump, and exhibit their shooting skills. On a more organized level, most YMCAs, settlement houses, armories, and school gyms had formal leagues. Like softball and bowling, basketball attracted church and industry sponsorship. It was a fast game, and clean. In the 1930s it became a favorite activity for physical education in schools. By 1940 about 95 percent of all American high schools had basketball teams. Adaptable to hard times, to outdoor or indoor play, for two or ten participants, Dr. Naismith's game first became widely popular during the depression.

So did an altogether different sport, amateur boxing. Founded by the

Chicago Tribune and the *New York Daily News* in 1928, the Golden Gloves tournament flourished during the depression decade. The Catholic Youth Organization, begun in 1930, encouraged boxing (and basketball) as an antidote to juvenile delinquency, prompting a Catholic cardinal to remark that "this is the first time I ever knew a soul could be saved by a punch in the nose." Lives, if not souls, of ethnic and racial minorities were saved by the discipline and commitment required to last three two-minute rounds in a Golden Gloves tournament. In 1932 the eighteen-year-old son of an Alabama sharecropper walked off the streets of Detroit into Brewster's East Side Gymnasium, borrowed an old pair of trunks and tattered tennis shoes, sparred a round with one of the local toughs, and immediately dreamed of becoming a Golden Gloves champion. Joe Louis was on his way, one of 8,000 or so Golden Glovers in the era of the depression. In 1937 a Golden Gloves national championship matched the local champions from cities scattered throughout the United States.

The popularity of amateur boxing extended beyond the United States. In 1937 an All-European championship began. More important, the larger pattern of sports and recreation in Europe during the depression was strikingly similar to the American scene. Faced with economic hardship, Europeans also turned to simple, inexpensive pleasures. Fortunately, the facilities were available and the equipment cheap for most of their physical activities. Gymnastics, cycling, bowling (in German, French, and British varieties), soccer football, hiking, boating, camping, and swimming all were popular in the 1930s. New American games as well as American music and movies appealed to Europeans. Basketball was widely played, and even "midget" (miniature) golf was a fad in Britain. For the most part, however, Europeans pursued their own distinctive games, such as the all-girls' sport of netball in Britain and a similar game in the Netherlands called korfball, in which boys and girls played together.

Even more than the Roosevelt administration, European governments took an active hand in promoting sports and recreation. Actually that trend had begun a decade or so before the depression. In the wake of World War I, liberal and authoritarian governments alike started sponsoring physical education in the schools. Not until 1933, however, did France and Britain take the lead in establishing colleges for the specific purpose of training teachers of physical education. In the same year Portugal began requiring two weekly periods of physical education in secondary schools; three years later the Portuguese government founded the Portuguese Youth Program, demanding that all boys seven to fourteen years of age should participate in games, gymnastics, and physical fitness programs. With war threatening once again, military more than athletic zeal lay behind that innovation.

Such pragmatism was scarcely the prime impetus for Britain's promotion of adult fitness. In 1935 a voluntary organization, the Central Council of Recreative Physical Training, was founded in London "to encourage the development of all forms of games, sports, outdoor activities, and dancing as part of post-school education." Two years later the Council began receiving government funds, as Parliament in 1937 debated a Physical Training and Recreation Bill, then voted two million pounds to set up a National Fitness Council.

Italian and German fascist governments, of course, heavily involved themselves in the promotion of sport as a part of national policy. With quite different motives the Soviet Union achieved similar results in the interwar period. Ever since the early 1920s the Soviet government had emphasized the role of "physical culture" in mass education and collectivism. Eager to improve the health and productivity of workers, it devised a program of "sport for the people" that was "national in form and socialist in content." The most important sports society in the Soviet Union, *Dynamo*, was founded in 1923 as an arm of the secret police. In 1930 the government set up an All-Union Physical Culture Council, a kind of department of sports, to coordinate and promote mass participation. First it organized intercity marathons, urging entire families to compete. In 1931 it began the annual May Day sports parade; within two years 105,000 citizen-athletes marched in Moscow and 96,000 in Leningrad.

Through sports, Soviet officials sought to emancipate Russian women from traditional peasant roles. Women as well as men participated in gymnastics, cycling, ice hockey, track and field, soccer, and skiing. Volleyball was the most popular of all team games. In 1932 the Trade Union Games began, to be held every fourth year as an all-Russian equivalent of the Olympics. Yet mass athletic involvement rather than elite prizewinners remained the goal of government-sponsored sports in the 1930s. Between 1935 and 1937 officials created sports societies in every province, connecting most of them to local industries. The authoritarian Soviet style was foreign to Western democratic nations, but it was highly productive for a nation that had long been backward in athletic as well as industrial development.

The Return of the Roaring Crowds

While taking an active hand in providing facilities and programs for mass participation in sports, governments in the 1930s also dispensed funds to build stadiums for spectator sports. In the Soviet Union several impressive multisport centers were constructed for swimming, tennis, basketball, gymnastic, and ice-hockey matches, all with huge seating capacities. Bakirov Stadium in Baku accommodated 80,000 spectators; Kirov Stadium in Leningrad held 150,000. Only the coming of World War II prevented the building of a stadium in Moscow designed to seat 250,000 spectators.

In the United States the federal government cooperated with local city officials and private investors to produce numerous municipal auditoriums and stadiums. Cleveland's Municipal Stadium, completed in the dark days of 1932, is a good example. Financed by government loans and local bonds, it was the largest playing field by far of all the major baseball teams: 435 feet (later shortened) along each foul line to the fence. Moreover, its seating capacity of almost 80,000 doubled most major-league parks.

With the recovery of the American economy in the mid-1930s, crowds flocked back to the stadiums. From a depression low of 300,000 in 1933, attendance at Detroit Tigers' games leaped to more than a million in 1935. The dramatic increase can be explained in part by the exciting performances of Hank Greenberg, Charlie Gehringer, and their teammates, who won the American League pennant and World Series for the first time in 1935. In larger measure, however, gate receipts rose as a result of a recovering economy.

Following the lead of some minor-league owners, who in 1930 began installing electric lights in order to attract day-shift workers to the ball park, the Cincinnati Reds erected 632 lamps to illuminate their diamond, and in late May of 1935 welcomed a crowd of more than 20,000 fans to witness major-league baseball's first night game. Players complained about the effects of night games on their arms and eyesight. Sportswriters warned that they could not finish their reports in time for early-morning editions. Many owners resisted launching baseball down the untraditional path of "night air and electric lights." But the paying public loved it. By World War II only five major league teams were still playing all their home games in the afternoon.

The "national game" thrived yet again, by night as well as by day. In the mid-1930s the St. Louis Cardinals' "Gas House Gang," led by Jerome "Dizzy" Dean, set the pace in the National League. Under manager Joe McCarthy the New York Yankees returned to dominance in the American League. In 1936 a lanky, graceful, bashful rookie center fielder by the name of Joe DiMaggio broke in with the Yankees, destined for stardom. At the time, a robust Lou Gehrig was on the way to his record 2,130 consecutive games, before an incurable form of sclerosis ended his career ("proud to be a Yankee") in 1938. As the depression receded, President Roosevelt rightly observed that "Major league baseball has done as much as any one thing in this country to keep up the spirit of the people."

Attendance at college football games also revived in the mid-1930s. The Minnesota Golden Gophers lost only one game over a span of three years, 1934–36, but the biggest news of the day was the creation of three major and several minor bowl games to compete with the Rose Bowl on New Year's Day. The Orange Bowl (1933), the Sugar Bowl (1936), and the Cotton Bowl (1937) catered to strong new southern and southwestern teams. Most exciting of all were teams from the Southwest, where Texas Christian University quarterbacks Sammy Baugh and Davey O'Brien led in opening up the game with numerous and accurate forward passes. Still, when the Heisman Trophy was first presented in 1936 to the college player of the year, a halfback who specialized in running for the University of Chicago, Jay Berwanger, won the award.

Even more dramatic than the recovery of college football was the emergence of college basketball as a popular spectator sport. Traditionally a slow, defensive game in which interminable stalls and center jumps after each basket made twenty-five points a high-scoring contest, basketball in the mid-1930s became more streamlined. In 1937 the center jump was discarded except to begin each half. The old two-handed stationary shot gave way to a running one-hander popularized by Hank Luisetti of Stanford University,

Young Sammy Baugh of Texas Christian University, whose strong arm established the forward pass as a potent offensive weapon, propelled the Southwest Conference into the national limelight. (Courtesy of Texas Christian University.)

and a newfangled fast break attracted fans who wanted to see action and high-scoring games. A New York promoter, Ned Irish, made college basketball a money-making proposition with his programs at Madison Square Garden. In 1938 the Garden hosted the first National Invitational Tournament; in the following year the NCAA tournament began. The final score of the first NCAA championship game—Oregon State 46, Ohio State 33—indicates that basketball still had a long way to go toward the game it now is, but by the end of the decade the hoop game was fast filling out the sports calendar between autumn football and spring baseball.

Similarly capitalizing on the recovery of the American economy, teams in the professional National Football League first became solvent and moderately popular in the 1930s. In 1933 they made radical changes in their style of play in order to increase spectator appeal. To encourage more field goals, they moved their goal posts from the rear of the end zone to the goal line; to assist offenses, they agreed that forward passes could be thrown from any point behind the line of scrimmage, and on out-of-bounds plays they brought the ball back onto the field ten yards from the sidelines. Most important, to avoid a decline in spectator interest toward the end of the season, when one team might be running away with the championship, the NFL in 1933 realigned itself into two divisions, creating a championship play-off between the division leaders. In the Eastern Division were teams from New York, Brooklyn, Philadelphia, and Pittsburgh; representing the Western Division were the Chicago Bears, the Chicago Cardinals, Green Bay, Cincinnati, and Portsmouth (Ohio).

Despite these improvements in style and administration, professional football before World War II was still inferior to the college game in both quality and appeal. In 1934 the College All-Stars began playing the professional champions annually in Chicago, and for the first five years the collegians won two, tied two, and lost one. At the top of the professional rosters were outstanding athletes such as Red Grange, Ernie Nevers, and Bronco Nagurski in the early 1930s, and Sammy Baugh, Don Hutson, and Cliff Battles later in the decade; their supporting casts, however, were largely mediocre. Compared to baseball players, footballers were poorly paid. The first collegian selected in the new player draft system devised in 1936 by Bert Bell, the owner of the Philadelphia Eagles, was Heisman Trophy winner Jay Berwanger. He refused to play.

Seldom did a Canadian youth similarly refuse to play professional ice hockey. Firmly established in new indoor arenas built in the affluent 1920s, the National Hockey League went from strength to strength despite the depression. Financial insolvency forced the Ottawa franchise to move from the Canadian capital to St. Louis and the Montreal Maroons to abandon the game altogether; but enthusiastic fans regularly filled most of the other arenas to witness the rough and flashy exploits of Eddie Shore, Charlie Connacher, King Clancy, and Howie Morenz. Although the Stanley Cup winners were evenly divided between Canadian and American teams in the 1930s, players continued to be predominantly Canadian.

In Canadian football the influence was reversed. The American style and organizational structure weighed heavily on the Canadian game in the 1930s. The Grey Cup, donated in 1909 by Earl Grey, the Governor-General of Canada, originally went to amateur champions of an English-style rugby football game. In the 1920s a center snap and forward pass transformed the game in the image of its popular American neighbor. As they refined those innovations, Canadians held out for several fine distinctions of their own (such as a larger field, a slightly different scoring system, three downs instead of four, limited downfield blocking, and backs moving toward the line of scrimmage before the snap of the ball), but they created a game far more akin to American football than to English rugby. By 1936 the Grey Cup was entirely professional as Canadian college teams dropped out of the competition.

The appeal of professional spectator sports was not limited to North America. Soccer was the biggest show (and the best business) in towns throughout South America and Europe. Even northern England's professional version of rugby football, Rugby League, thrived, producing one of that game's few superstars in the person of James Sullivan. A tough fullback for Wigan, Sullivan kicked a record 204 goals in the 1933–34 season. Growing apace, attendance records for Rugby League football reached their all-time high with 66,000 at Bradford and 69,000 at Manchester, topped by a capacity crowd of more than 100,000 for the Cup Final at Wembley in May 1939.

Parallel to the popularity of professional sports was a gambling craze in the 1930s. Governments legalized gambling because of the extra tax revenue it brought, and people eager to hit the jackpot regularly put down small bets in hopes of a large return. As in the past, horse racing was the favorite gambler's sport. Gallant Fox, War Admiral, and Whirlaway were the most famous of the Triple Crown winners between 1930 and 1941, but on races big and small, famous and obscure, pari-mutuel betting flourished in more than a dozen states in the United States as well as in France, where the system originated. In Dublin the Irish Sweepstakes originated in 1930, sanctioned by the Irish government because impoverished hospitals received a goodly portion of the profits. Nor was the turf the only professional sport on which legalized gambling thrived. The football pools in England conducted much of their business by mail, selling coupons for as little as a penny apiece for a long-shot chance of winning thousands of pounds by correctly predicting the winners of the week's soccer matches. Long a parasite on sports, gambling in some places proved to be an ally. In 1934 the Swedish government took over the national lotteries and used the profits to build new sports facilities.

In the end, the depression had a contradictory effect on people throughout the Western world. On the one hand, it made people more cautious and tight with their money. Yet it also set in motion the tendency to pay for excitement and physical activity. Out of work, people learned to play, and they took delight in watching others play. Sports and recreation were a new kind of investment, perhaps a better one than the stock market.

Chapter 16

TESTING THE SUPER RACE

While Western democratic governments intervened to repair the damages of war and economic disaster, fascist governments arose first in Italy, then in Germany, to provide different solutions to the same problems. The fascist remedy lay in totalitarian leadership, military strength, and nationalistic pride based on the premise of racial superiority. Sport suitably served these purposes. In schools and racially "pure" clubs, sport under the fascists became a means of training for military ends, a testing ground for the claims of a supposed super race.

For a brief time those claims withstood the test of international competition. In the mid 1930s, Italian and German athletes proudly carried the fascist flag to victory, culminating in the Berlin Olympics of 1936. A spectacle created by Hitler and his cohorts, the 1936 Olympics represented the triumph of Nazi will and efficiency. Even the dazzling performance of Jesse Owens scarcely diminished the luster of Hitler's achievement, not to mention the preponderance of gold, silver, and bronze medals won for the Fatherland by German athletes.

Then came the fascists' fall. As Hitler and Mussolini in the late 1930s began to set their plans of military conquest in motion, German and Italian athletes curiously faltered. The destruction of Max Schmeling at the hands of the American "Brown Bomber," Joe Louis, especially can be viewed as a kind of preview to the course of a far more important contest in which the super race went down for the count.

Sport under Fascism

The first of the two major fascist leaders, Benito Mussolini, seized the reins of Italian government in 1922. Through intimidation, mock elections, and terrorist tactics, he and his fascist followers consolidated their position, brought order to a most disorderly society, and restored a destitute economy to health. In the process, they ran roughshod over individual human rights such as freedom of speech, press, and assembly. "My objective is simple," Mussolini later wrote. "I want to make Italy great, respected, and feared." Stern laws, a strong army, and the totalitarian rule of Il Duce all worked toward those ends.

So did sport. Eager for Italian youths to be "trained through precise and delightful discipline in gymnastic exercise and in the general rules of a well-ordered national life," Mussolini created a new Department of Physical Education under the Ministry of Education. He required teachers and pupils to follow official government manuals on calisthenics, gymnastics, ball games, and track-and-field sports. Schools in Fascist Italy devoted four hours each week to compulsory physical education. The government also promoted sports programs outside the schools. Black-shirted youths played and paraded, competed and camped for health and fun, but ultimately for patriotic, military fitness. "Fascism avails itself of the various forms of sports," declared one of Mussolini's spokesmen in 1929, "especially those requiring large groups of participants, as a means of military preparation and spiritual development, that is, as a school for the training of Italian youth."

Mussolini wrote the Fascist script; Adolph Hitler initially followed it to the letter, then enlarged upon it. Coming to power in Germany in 1933, Hitler also employed the tactics of deception and terrorism to establish his position firmly at the head of the German state. Like Mussolini, he engineered a dramatic recovery of his nation's economy and a rebirth of national pride and military strength. Whereas Mussolini played on Italian fears of communists and socialists, Hitler made scapegoats of both and added a third: the Jews. His policy of Aryan "racial purity" determined the character of sport, like everything else, in Nazi Germany.

Fully a decade before his successful seizure of power, Hitler outlined his policies in *Mein Kampf,* a book crudely but candidly written while he was in prison for eight months (1923–24) following an unsuccessful coup. Woven into his views on patriotism, military strength, propaganda, education, and race was a clear estimate of the place of sport and physical education in a fascist society. Schools, he insisted, "should set aside more time for bodily exercise" rather than merely "pumping in mere knowledge." The "cultivation of the body" he saw not as a matter of individual or parental responsibility alone, but rather as a priority of the state: "There should be no day on which a boy should not have at least one hour's physical training, both in the morning and afternoon, in games and gymnastics."

For reasons of their own, the leaders of the unstable Weimar Republic took steps in the direction proposed by Hitler. American and English visitors to Germany in the mid-1920s invariably noted the rapid growth of sport and physical-education programs in the schools and universities. Athletic grounds, sports clubs, and gymnasiums proliferated, all sponsored by the government "not as a matter of diversion," according to one observer, "but as a means of building up a people, naturally vigorous, whose young people have been debilitated by the privations due to the war." Yet another foreign visitor saw sport in 1929 as a popular substitute for Germany's former mania for military training: "Since the abandonment of compulsory military service, Germany has devoted herself wholeheartedly to general track and field sports to which she is giving all that time and effort, training and practice, that used to be expended by the country's youth in the army."

Hitler, of course, viewed sport as a preparation, not a substitute, for military service. "Give the German nation six million bodies of flawless athletic training, all glowing with fanatical love of their country and inculcated with the highest aggressive spirit," he trumpeted in *Mein Kampf,* "and in less than two years if necessary a national state will have created an army." For his own tough Storm Troopers, he prescribed a program "set not on drill, but on training for sports," especially boxing and jujitsu. Relentless in his policy, he wrote a manifesto for the rising Nazi Party in 1930, urging a plan to build up the state by "increasing bodily efficiency by obligatory gymnastics and sports laid down by the law, and by extensive support of clubs engaged in the bodily development of the young."

Needless to say, once Hitler became Chancellor of the Third Reich early in 1933, he put his policies into practice. Classrooms became centers of Nazi propaganda; playgrounds became bustling arenas of sport and games designed to turn Hitler Youths into good German soldiers. By 1935 every German sport club and association came under the controlling hand of the Reich Federal Sports Association headed by Captain Hans von Tschammer und Osten, one of Hitler's earliest followers. Nazi propagandists easily rationalized these moves. "Athletics and sports are the preparatory school of political driving power in the service of the State," wrote Kurt Munch, the author of a textbook on which all German athletes were examined. "Nonpolitical, so-called neutral, sportsmen," he added, "are unthinkable in Hitler's State."

The most blatant propaganda was directed against Jewish athletes. In 1933 Storm Trooper Bruno Malitz wrote a treatise entitled *The Spirit of Sport in the Third Reich,* a book personally endorsed by the Propaganda Minister, Joseph Goebbels, and distributed to every local athletic organization in Germany. Playing on the anti-Semitism long present in German life, Malitz associated Jews with pacifists, who should have "absolutely no place in German sport." In a telling mixture of Nazi nationalism and racism, he assaulted all those "Frenchmen, Belgians, Pollacks, Jew-Niggers," and similar "alien elements" who had for too long "raced on German tracks, played on German football fields, and swum in German swimming pools."

Immediately upon taking office, the Nazis decreed a boycott of Jewish businesses and proceeded to purge Jews from the civil services, the army, universities and the professions. Exclusion of Jews from sporting organizations shortly followed. By the end of 1933 they were barred from every German boxing, rowing, gymnastic, skiing, and lawn tennis club. "We need waste no words here," declared the editor of a Nazi paper, *Der Sturmer,* "Jews are Jews and there is no place for them in German sports." Within two years all 40,000 or so Jewish athletes who had been affiliated with about 250 sporting clubs in Germany were expelled. Worse still, Jews were forbidden to swim in public pools and lakes, to ski at public resorts, or even to form their own athletic associations.

A few of the more outstanding Jewish athletes simply packed their bags and left the country. Rudi Ball, the nation's best ice-hockey player, defected to France, later to play on Swiss and Austrian teams. Alex Natan, a member of the national track team that in 1929 tied the world record for the 400-meter relay race, fled to England, as did Daniel Prenn, Germany's best tennis player and leader of its Davis Cup team. Yet these were the exceptional, fortunate few. Forced into premature retirement were numerous outstanding Jewish athletes such as Erich Seelig, the nation's middleweight and light heavyweight boxing champion; Lilly Henoch, a discus and shot-put champion; and Paula von Reznicek, the leading woman lawn tennis player.

Not until a Nuremberg rally on 15 September 1935 did Hitler announce to the world his plan to protect "the purity of Aryan blood" by depriving German Jews of their citizenship and protection under the law. Jewish citizens already knew the truth. Certainly in German athletic and recreational circles, the racist underside of the Nazi use of sport for political ends bore accurate witness to the totalitarian character of the Nazi regime.

Fascist Sport Triumphant

Briefly during the mid-1930s, athletes representing Fascist Germany and Italy registered an impressive string of victories in international contests. Their incentive was great. They competed under the banners of proud, newly formed governments whose leaders took personal interest in their performances. Moreover, they brought the enthusiasm of newcomers to the international sporting arena. Except for German gymnastics in the nineteenth century and Italian aristocratic sports in the distant era of the Renaissance, the world had little cause to take seriously the sporting endeavors of either country. Now both barged to the forefront of world attention, especially in soccer matches, motorcar races, and boxing bouts.

In 1932 the International Football Association decided that Italy would host the second World Cup in 1934. Mussolini's government seemed orderly, and it offered to pay the balance of expenses for the games. A strong, agressive Italian team set its sights on victory and to that end recruited the best members of Argentina's national team—men of dual Argentine-Italian citizenship. "If they can die [that is, be recruited for military service] for Italy," reasoned the Italian coach, Vittorio Pozzo, "they can play for Italy."

Strengthened by their imports, especially the outstanding Luisito Monti, the Italian team easily disposed of a weak American side in the first round of the 1934 World Cup. Then it mauled Spain in a physically brutal manner worthy of fascist thugs. The team roughed up the Spanish goalkeeper, Ricardo Zamora, so badly that when the game ended in a tie requiring a playoff the next day, Zamora was unable to return. Against Austria in the semifinals, Italy squeaked to a 1–0 victory despite the spectacular play of Austria's nimble, lanky center forward, Mathias Sindelar. A tragic symbol of the age, Sindelar was half Jewish. He was destined to die in a Nazi concentration camp after being betrayed by one of his own teammates.

The preliminary matches were variously played in Naples, Turin, and Florence, with the final scheduled for Rome. Press attention and colorful pageantry gave the event a carnival atmosphere. In a script apparently written for the occasion, Italy won the World Cup by defeating Czechoslovakia 2–1 in overtime. Mussolini, wearing a yachtsman's cap, excitedly watched and joined in the partisan screams, applause, and whistles when an Italian player scored the winning goal. The Fascist press predictably lauded the victory as a triumph for Il Duce, an affirmation of "the masculine energies of a bursting vitality in this our Mussolini's Italy."

Italy's victory was made easier because Uruguay, World Cup hosts and winners in 1930, refused to send a team. Uruguayan officials were still miffed over the absence of the leading European teams in Montevideo four years earlier. Also absent from the World Cup of 1934 was the English team, but for different reasons. The English Football Association was still at odds with the international football community over questions of rules and the definition of amateur status.

British athletic insularity reflected its political isolationism: a reluctance to admit the ominous implications of the growth of Italian and German fascism. When British soccer teams visited Nazi Germany for matches, the Foreign Office advised them to go ahead and courteously give the Nazi salute. For a return visit of a German team to London in 1935, however, controversy arose. Labor organizations in Britain opposed the visit; the Trades Union Congress warned that British sympathizers of the Nazi regime would use the occasion to win recruits to the Fascist movement in England. The Home Office turned a deaf ear, insisting that the match had "no political significance whatever." Although the English team won the game, 3–0, the Germans scored a propaganda point. The Swastika flew alongside the Union Jack from the stadium roof, a tacit recognition of Hitler's regime; both before and after the game the German team boldly greeted fans with the Nazi salute.

More measurable were the achievements of German and Italian auto racers in the mid-1930s. Until 1932 French and British cars continued, as in the past, to carry away most of the prizes in the twenty or so major races on the European Grand Prix circuit. In 1933, however, virtually every national Grand Prix was won by Maserati, an Italian firm that had begun producing high-powered racing cars only seven years earlier. For the duration of the decade, even the previously dominant French entry, Bugatti, ate the dust of Maserati and Ferrari, the latter a new racing car produced by one of Italy's oldest firms, Alfa Romeo. Their only serious competitors were Auto Union and Mercedes-Benz, products of German corporate fascism.

Not surprisingly, the great drivers of the era were Italians (Nuvolari, Fagioli, and Caracciola) and Germans (Von Stuck, Rosemeyer, and Von Brauchitsch). At the wheel of a Maserati, Nuvolari won the Italian Grand Prix in 1934, and the following year he drove a Ferrari to first place in the German Grand Prix at Nurburgring. Then, in a move signifying Fascist sport solidarity, he switched to a German Auto Union car, in which he continued successfully to chase the checkered flag. All the while his fellow Italians, Fagioli and Caracciola, made their marks as Mercedes drivers.

Behind this rapid rise of Italian and German racing cars lay a ruling of 1932 (set to go into effect two years later) by the International Automobile Racing Club, limiting weights of machines to 750 kilograms. Designed as a measure to decrease power and danger, it instead inspired German and Italian manufacturers to innovate with weight-saving rigid tubular frames and independent suspension systems. Lighter bodies allowed for heavier, supercharged engines, which of course increased speed. Fascist political interests and capital investment supported racing-car technology, and not merely for reasons of prestige that might be gained from winning international auto races. Mercedes-Benz and Alfa Romeo, especially, provided Hitler and Mussolini with laboratories for technical improvement of engines essential for military prowess. Mussolini pumped so much money into Alfa Romeo that by the late 1930s the government owned controlling interest in the company. When the Italian army invaded Ethiopia in October 1935, its planes, tanks, and trucks were powered by engines strong and finely tuned.

The year 1935 was a momentous one in world affairs. Seven months before Mussolini attacked Ethiopia, Hitler publicly denounced the disarmament clauses of the Treaty of Versailles and proceeded to introduce military conscription and a program of German rearmament. Unopposed by Western Allies who were divided in strategy and timid in resolve, Hitler a year later announced to the Reichstag that Germany would no longer honor the neutral buffer zone along the borders of Holland, Belgium, Luxemburg, and France. As he spoke to the Reichstag, 35,000 German soldiers marched into the Rhineland. All the while, German citizens were hard at work rebuilding their economy from the ruins of World War I and the depression. Renewed strength brought confidence, and with confidence came patriotic pride and zeal. Victories in international sporting contests fed the flame of nationalism, for Mussolini's Italy as well as Hitler's Germany.

Yet there was a fundamental difference between the two fascist states. Barely detectable in the mid-1930s, Italy was a paper tiger. Germany, on the other hand, was a lion with heart and claws suitably equipped for jungle combat. Two heavyweight boxing matches in 1935–36 symbolically represented the differences.

One involved Primo Carnera, an Italian behemoth. Standing nearly six feet six inches tall and weighing about 260 pounds, Carnera held the heavyweight crown briefly after knocking out Jack Sharkey in 1933. But he was incompetence personified, a victim of manipulative managers and promoters hungry for a heavyweight with crowd appeal. Several of his bouts stank of "fix" before Max Baer took the title by knocking him down eleven times in eleven rounds in the summer of 1934. On the downside of a career that was going nowhere, Carnera signed to fight a twenty-year-old American black, Joe Louis, in Yankee Stadium on 25 June 1935. The match had all the makings of a media event. The American press identified Carnera with Fascist Italy and especially with Mussolini, who had been airing threats to invade

Ethiopia since early in the year. American blacks, of course, felt kinship with the Ethiopians. They detested Carnera as a Mussolini man and turned out in droves to cheer on their black representative.

Having boxed professionally for only a year, the young Joe Louis had already disposed of twenty-two opponents, eighteen by knockouts. In sharp contrast to the previous black champion, Jack Johnson, Louis was modest, respectable, and tight-lipped, "a credit to his race." Yet he was able to break the color barrier only because there were so few good white heavyweights available. He made quick work of Carnera, knocking him out in the sixth round.

In the following year, however, he met a far more formidable foe in the person of Maximillian Schmeling, a German. Once again the press touted the bout in political terms. According to one New York columnist, Schmeling wanted to beat Louis "to show the world that the German people are a superior race." In truth, Schmeling was thirty years old and desperately needed to make a good showing in order to get another crack at the title that he had held momentarily in 1930. Scarcely a rabid Nazi, he was a tough, aggressive fighter. His left eye closed in a toe-to-toe exchange in the third round, he floored Louis in the fourth, kept pressing the attack, and finally stunned the partisan Yankee Stadium crowd by knocking out his American opponent in the twelfth round.

Because of the time difference, Germans listened to the fight over radio in the early hours of the morning. They responded ecstatically to Schmeling's victory. Nazi officials gloated. "Most cordial congratulation for your splendid victory," read a message over the wire service to Schmeling from Hitler, who simultaneously sent flowers to the hero's wife. The more effusive Propaganda Minister, Goebbels, concealed none of his delight in the political importance of the event. "I know you fought for Germany; that it was a German victory," he wired immediately to Schmeling. "We are proud of you. Heil Hitler!"

Proud indeed were the Nazis. For Schmeling they arranged a special berth aboard a zeppelin, the *Hindenburg,* and upon his arrival in Berlin gave him a hero's welcome. Hitler personally received him and his wife for lunch in the Reich Chancellery. Politically indifferent as Schmeling apparently was, he and his achievement were grist for the Nazi mill.

So were the Olympic Games of 1936.

The Nazi Olympics

Born of a nationalistic age, from their beginnings in 1896 the modern Olympic Games had been played amid a martial display of flags, military marches, patriotic anthems, and nationalistic rivalries. The Nazis did not create this atmosphere; they merely carried it to its absurd limits. They cloaked the Olympics of 1936 in political and military garb, using them as a showpiece of German engineering skill, cultural taste, and athletic prowess.

Of all the Olympic host countries deserving a boycott of the games on humanitarian principles, Nazi Germany heads the list. American, British, and French leaders of the International Olympic Committee well knew of Nazi discrimination against non-Aryans, and certainly of their policies against Jewish athletes. In 1933–34 controversy raged in the United States over the case of Helene Meyer, a German born of a Christian mother and Jewish father. A gold medallist in fencing at the Amsterdam Olympics of 1928, Meyer competed unsuccessfully in Los Angeles in 1932, then stayed on to study international law and languages at the University of Southern California. When the Nazis began purging Jews from their sporting clubs in 1933, she was informed by her fencing club at Offenbach that her name was being removed from its membership. Although the German Fencing Association simultaneously assured her that she could continue competing in national and international matches, the American press took up her cause as an example of Nazi anti-Semitism.

An enraged American Amateur Athletic Union, led by its president, Jeremiah Mahoney, voted to boycott the Berlin Olympics if Germany did not allow non-Aryans to compete for places on its national team. A more conservative body, the American Olympic Committee (AOC), believed that the games should go on as scheduled, regardless of politics. Its president, Avery Brundage, went to Germany in 1934 to see for himself whether or not the Nazis were as bad as the American press was reporting. In the following year, Charles E. Sherrill, a member of the International Olympic Committee as well as the AOC, undertook a similar mission to Germany and Italy. Neither man, in fact, was disposed to find much wrong with fascism. Brundage, a self-made millionaire, and Sherrill, a retired army officer, both came away favorably impressed with German stability and prosperity. Guided carefully by their Nazi hosts, they saw no evidence of discrimination against the Jews. The games would go on.

The opposition of American church leaders, labor organizations, and several major newspapers did not cease. It was simply drowned out in a chorus of voices urging that sport and politics be kept separate. Minority views in Canada, Britain, Sweden, the Netherlands, and Czechoslovakia were similarly squelched. Only the socialist government of Spain supported their national Olympic committee in its decision not to participate at Berlin, and in the end it scheduled alternate summer games ("the People's Olympics") to be held July 19–26 in Barcelona, a week before the opening of the Berlin Games. Small ragtag teams from all over the Western world set out for Barcelona, only to have the Spanish Civil War break out on the morning of the opening ceremonies. Athletes ended up running for cover rather than medals.

Six months earlier (in early February), the Winter Olympics at Garmisch-Partenkirchen set the tone for the forthcoming summer games in Berlin. Through lightly falling snow, Swastika armbands, banners, and flags were everywhere visible. Five Mercedes-Benz limousines regularly came and went from nearby Munich, transporting Hitler and his entourage surrounded by tough SS guards. Several thousand armed troops daily readied themselves in camouflaged military trucks to intervene in case of any disorderliness among the huge crowd of spectators. At times the crowd swelled to 75,000, and for the final event, the popular ski jump, about 150,000 people crowded the

Hitler and the Nazi salute relegate the Olympic flag
to the background at the opening of the Berlin Olympics in 1936, from *Die Olympischen Spiele 1936*.

slopes to watch. In the evenings Nazi officials hosted festive banquets, beer
parties, musical concerts, and ballet performances in Munich for visiting
journalists and dignitaries.

Although the spectacles tended to dwarf the sports, three Norwegians
stole the athletic show. The one now curiously least remembered, Ivar
Ballangrud, won the most medals: golds in the 500-, 5,000-, and 10,000-meter
speed-skating events, and a silver in the 1,500 meters. Birger Ruud, winner

of the ski jump at Lake Placid in 1932, repeated at Garmisch-Partenkirchen. The real star of the 1936 Winter Games, though, was Norwegian figure-skater Sonja Henie, whose narrow victory over an English upstart, Cecelia Colledge, capped a decade of championship amateur competition. Cutely dressed in white, the petite Henie was the darling not only of the fans and press but also of Hitler.

For all their glamor and efficiency, however, the Winter Games were outdone by the spectacular summer Olympics in Berlin. Twelve days before the opening of the games on August 1, a torch was lit from the sacred altar at Olympia, to be carried by more than 3,000 runners (each covering about one kilometer) through Greece, Bulgaria, Yugoslavia, Hungary, Austria, and Czechoslovakia, timed to arrive at the Olympic Stadium in Berlin at just the right moment in the opening ceremonies. More than 110,000 spectators filled the stadium. Thirty trumpets sounded over amplifiers as Hitler appeared, dressed in the drab brown uniform and high leather boots of a Storm Trooper. He was flanked by Air Marshall Hermann Göring, impressively garbed in the sky-blue uniform of a Luftwaffe officer, and Minister of Propaganda Goebbels, nattily attired in a white business suit.

Never short on *kultur*, the Nazis had Richard Strauss, the aged composer, lead a huge orchestra and chorus in "Deutschland uber alles" and "Horst Wessellied," followed by a new "Olympic Hymn," which Strauss had written specially for the occasion. Then came the athletic teams marching in review before Hitler. Those that dipped their colors and gave the Nazi salute evoked cheers from the massive crowd; the others were met with stony silence. Just before Hitler officially opened the games, a recorded message from the aged father of the modern Olympics, Baron Pierre de Coubertin, was relayed to the audience. Sick and dying in Lausanne, Coubertin spoke in a frail voice, with an idealism untarnished by the years: "The important thing at the Olympic Games is not to win, but to take part, just as the important thing about life is not to conquer, but to struggle well." The words fell on deaf ears.

Outside the stadium, red, white, and black Nazi flags flew from virtually every public building and home, except in Berlin's Jewish quarters. The Nuremberg Laws of 1935 forbade Jews from flying the German flag. Jewish homes and shops were easily recognizable because they were covered with the official Olympic flag of five different colored rings set on a white background. For German Jews, however, the Berlin Olympics provided momentary respite from anti-Semitic slogans on walls and references in newspapers. To appease Western critics, Hitler commanded the slurs to cease for the duration of the games.

In the games German athletes dominated gymnastic, rowing, and equestrian events, and in the final tabulation they won more gold, silver, and bronze medals than any other team. In total points the United States team came in second, and Italy a distant third. America's strong showing, sandwiched between the two Fascist powers, came largely as a result of its winning twelve of its twenty-four gold medals in track-and-field events. Most of those victors were blacks, a dramatic refutation of Nazi racial supremacy matched only by the sterling performance of yet another non-

Mental concentration, superb conditioning, and athletic gracefulness characterize the efforts of the young Jesse Owens as he trains for the Berlin Olympics of 1936, in which he won four gold medals. (Courtesy of Ohio State University.)

Aryan, Korea's Kitei Sun, who won the marathon wearing the insignia of the Rising Sun on his shirt because Japan occupied his country at the time.

Of all the stars, Jesse Owens shone brightest. Born of poor black parents in Alabama, he well knew the practical effects of the ideological racism being spouted by the Nazis. When he was seven years old, his family moved to Cleveland, where he emerged in the early 1930s as an outstanding sprinter and long jumper. Married and the father of a baby daughter by the time he was twenty, he nevertheless worked his way through Ohio State University, for whose track team he set five world records in a single day in 1935. At Berlin he won gold medals and set new Olympic records in the broad jump, the 200-meter sprint, and the 400-meter relay (a team record), and tied the record while winning his gold in the 100-meter sprint.

His narrowest victory, in the broad jump, provided one of the dramatic highlights of the Berlin Olympics. Not until his last leap did he qualify for the finals. Then, tied with a German, Luz Long, he uncoiled on his last leap for the magnificent distance of twenty-six feet, five and five-sixteenths inches. During the course of their competition, Long and Owens became friends. In a gesture of sportsmanship that transcended Nazi prejudice, the blond Long walked arm in arm with his black conqueror around the stadium track, waving to an astounded mass of spectators.

Hitler supposedly snubbed Owens. American journalists made much of the fact that whereas Hitler had personally congratulated victorious German athletes on the first day of competition, he turned abruptly and left the stadium when Owens won. The truth is less dramatic. Having been informed by the president of the International Olympic Committee that he should congratulate all or none of the winners, Hitler henceforth refrained from any further public gestures, for German as well as foreign athletes.

In fact, Owens's subsequent treatment exposed a dark side of American life more tellingly than it reflected Nazi racism. "I wasn't invited to shake hands with Hitler," he later noted, "but I wasn't invited to the White House to shake hands with the President either." Following his Berlin triumph, Owens returned home to find his native brand of discrimination unchanged. Several commercial "offers" failed to materialize, requiring Owens to engage in degrading races against dogs, horses, and cars. Despite his gold medals, he was still a member of a minority race in a society where racism was effectively practiced if not blatantly announced. For all their ruthlessness, the Nazis had no corner on prejudice.

Falling Stars

Exuberant over Germany's victory in the 1936 Olympics, Hitler hailed his athletes as "the forerunners of new types of Germans, . . . tough, well-informed men and graceful women." Aryan athletes were to be admired "not as sportsmen, but rather as political troops who treat the sporting contests only as their particular branch of the great struggle as a whole." To ensure their fame and his own, Hitler commissioned Leni Riefenstahl, a filmmaker who had earlier proved her worth by producing *Triumph of the Will* and several other Nazi propaganda films, to record the Berlin Olympics for posterity. Under Riefenstahl's direction, about eighty cameramen and their assistants shot more than a million feet of film, which took Riefenstahl two years to edit. The finished product was a vivid dramatization of the athletes, spectators, and officials at Berlin. Hitler appears in several frames, intently watching and occasionally expressing his delight with the performance of victorious German athletes. Yet the film is largely neuter politically. Certainly no German athlete dominates the camera's attention as fully as do Jesse Owens and Kitei Sun. The artist in Riefenstahl won out over the propagandist.

By the time the film was first shown publicly in the late summer of 1938, the German juggernaut was being unleashed. Early in the year Hitler annexed Austria and began laying groundwork for the takeover of the Sudentenland of Czechoslovakia. While *Olympiad* made its rounds of German cinema houses, Hitler was duping Western leaders (notably England's Prime Minister, Neville Chamberlain) at Munich in September. Yet German athletic dominance failed to keep pace with the early military and diplomatic triumphs of the Nazis. At the very moment that Hitler's star peaked, German athletes began to falter on the field of international competition.

The case of Baron Gottfried von Cramm, Germany's premier tennis player, is a good example. Born of aristocratic lineage, Von Cramm was suitably blond and handsome, a good Nordic type potentially useful for Nazi propaganda purposes. But Von Cramm adamantly resisted ever joining the Nazi party, even when German officials refused to allow him to leave the country to compete in the French championships early in 1937. He knew that the forthcoming Davis Cup was of far greater propaganda value to the Nazis, and that they could ill afford to keep him off the national team.

He was right, of course. Having won the French championships in 1934 and 1935, he had narrowly lost to the Englishman Fred Perry at Wimbledon in 1935 and 1936. When Perry then turned professional, knowledgeable tennis enthusiasts assumed that the amateur crown would pass to the head of Von Cramm. No one counted on the emergence of a skinny, red-headed American, Don Budge. In the fifth and deciding match of the Davis Cup interzone contest between the United States and Germany, Budge and Von Cramm confronted each other at Wimbledon in the summer of 1937.

By now, no international sporting event pitting German or Italian athletes against representatives of Western democratic nations could fail to be tinged with political overtones. "War talk was everywhere," Budge later recalled; "Hitler was doing everything he could to stir up Germany. The atmosphere was filled with tension although Von Cramm was a known anti-Nazi and remained one of the finest gentlemen and the most popular player on the circuit." Just as Von Cramm was about to take the court, someone tapped him on the shoulder, informing him of an urgent long-distance telephone call. He returned to the clubhouse and talked—or listened, mostly—for ten minutes or so. Once he was heard to say, "Ja, mein Fuhrer." Finally, he laid down the receiver and joined Budge for their walk to center court for the decisive match. Visibly shaken, Von Cramm muttered in broken English, "It was Hitler. He wanted to wish me good luck."

Von Cramm needed it. He won the first two sets, lost the next two, and then went up 4-1 in the final set. He played, as Budge later observed, "as if his life depended on every point." Budge matched competitive fire with fire. Desperately charging the net after each serve, he ran the score to 4-4, 5-5, 6-6, and finally won 8-6 just before darkness descended over the court. Big Bill Tilden, who had sold his services to coach the German team, noted that this was "the most beautiful match of tennis ever played." Certainly it was a match that deprived Hitler of further vindication for his supposed super race.

Even Fascist athletic victories in the late 1930s were clouded over by dark and ugly scenes. In France, during the summer of 1938, Italy repeated as World Cup soccer champions, but the feat was overshadowed by the nearby Spanish Civil War, in which Franco was using Italian and German military aid to crush his opposition with a frightful toll in civilian lives. Moreover, the makeup of the German soccer team further reminded Westerners of Fascist designs: four Austrians played on the German squad, all recruited after the recent *anschluss*. A first-round match in Marseilles, between Italy and Norway, accurately reflected the bitter atmosphere. Expatriates from Mussolini's Italy screamed obscenities and threats as the Italiam team presented their Fascist salute prior to the game. Their coach, Vittorio Pozzo, kept his arm stiffly extended until the noise subsided, then dropped it and cried, "Team, attention! Salute!" Again they clicked their heels, shot up their arms, and kept them aloft until the catcalls ceased. The Italians easily won the match, and later the Cup, but no friends.

Another international sporting event that fell under the gathering clouds of war was the return bout between Joe Louis and Max Schmeling, scheduled for 22 June 1938 in Yankee Stadium. Since Schmeling's knockout victory in 1936, James J. Braddock had briefly held the heavyweight title, refusing to fight Schmeling for fear of an anti-Nazi boycott. Braddock instead fought Louis in 1937. It was an unwise move; Louis seized the crown with a smashing right to the jaw in the eighth round. Thus the stage was set for a rematch between Louis, the champion "Brown Bomber," and Schmeling, the supposed representative of Nazi Germany.

American journalists had a field day playing up the political angle. They painted Schmeling as "another fulcrum in Hitler's propaganda machine," a "product of Reich training and an example of Hitlerism." They shamelessly put racist remarks in Schmeling's mouth and eagerly gave the worst possible interpretation to the Swastikas displayed in the German's training camp. Schmeling was upset and baffled. Supposedly Louis himself rose to the bait. "I'm backing up America against Germany," the mild-mannered, inarticulate young champion was quoted as saying, "so you know I'm going to town."

Whatever his patriotic motives, Louis burned with revenge for his earlier humiliation at Schmeling's hands. Revenge he quickly got. From the opening bell he landed three quick jabs to the head, then a left hook. Schmeling responded with a grazing right to the chin, whereupon both fighters dug blows to the body. A left, right, and another right to the head sent Schmeling to the canvas. He bounced to his feet without a count, only to fall again under another right. His lights were going out. On his third time down, he struggled on all fours as the referee, Arthur Donovan, stopped the fight with only two minutes and four seconds having elapsed.

About 70,000 hysterical fans watched the slaughter. Included in that mass of happy Americans who streamed out of Yankee Stadium were J. Edgar Hoover, director of the Federal Bureau of Investigation; James Farley, Postmaster General of the United States; and Homer Cummings, U.S. Attorney General. Surely no sensible person believed that Schmeling's fall bespoke German weakness, but one can be equally sure that American patriots everywhere rejoiced over this dint in the armor of Nazi arrogance. Hitler, meanwhile, barely noticed. He was busy elsewhere, setting in motion his more consequential schemes.

Except for Italy's tarnished World Cup in 1938, the only significant international sporting victories chalked up by fascist powers after the Berlin Olympics were in power-driven racing vehicles. Both German and Italian automobiles continued to dominate the sports-car circuit. Beginning in 1936 with the German lightweight motorcycle, the DKW, complex new engines and improved frame and suspension designs kept German and Italian motorcycles in the forefront of international competition. British and French manufacturers remained wedded to the idea that a racing motorcycle was simply a refined version of an everyday transport vehicle. The German DKW and BMW, and the Italian Guzzi and Gilera, on the other hand, were scientifically streamlined and supercharged specifically for competition. They adapted easily to the military sidecar vehicles that appear so prominently in the early photographs and films of World War II.

Perhaps sport is, like Cherokee lacrosse, the "little brother of war." Yet it is also, like property and civilian life, a victim of war as we know it in the twentieth century. Total war from 1940 to 1945 brought a halt to international sport competition. The Olympic Games of 1940, scheduled four years earlier by the International Olympic Committee to be held for the first time in a non-Western nation, Japan, had to be canceled because of the Indo-China War. The IOC switched the games to Helsinki, only to have Finland fall under Russian military rule in the spring of 1940. The Games of 1944 were even more impossible. Their scheduled site, London, lay in rubble, devastated by German planes and buzz bombs.

The war disrupted many athletic careers, but it ended many more. The experiences of three German athletes tell the story. Luz Long, Jesse Owens's opponent and friend at the Berlin Games, died in Sicily while fighting in the German army. Max Schmeling, within a year of his defeat by Joe Louis, was sent to the eastern front with a paratrooper unit. He was wounded but survived the war. Whatever their respective commitments to the Nazi cause, both Schmeling and Long presumably served their country no less honorably than did innumerable French, British, and American athletes.

So did Baron Gottfried von Cramm, whose road to honor was far more torturous. Following his defeat at Wimbledon in 1937, he was arrested on a charge of homosexuality. Finally released in 1939 (after agitation led by his old American nemesis, Don Budge), he returned to England to play in the Queen's Club Tournament, a traditional prelude to Wimbledon. He demolished a brash young Californian, Bobby Riggs, 6–1, 6–0 in the finals, but then Wimbledon officials barred him from their elite tournament because of his prior arrest. In a cruel touch of irony, two weeks later Riggs won the Wimbledon crown. Shortly thereafter, Von Cramm was recruited into the

German army. Sent to the Russian front, he was wounded and received the Iron Cross for bravery.

Brave or not, German athletes and soldiers alike failed, finally, to prove Fascist superiority. In his definitive study, *The Nazi Olympics* (1971), Richard D. Mandell concludes with Hitler on the eve of World War II planning a massive new stadium for future Olympic Games. Designed by Albert Speer, the stadium would seat 400,000 spectators, the largest facility ever imagined for a public spectacle. The games, confined to racially pure Germans, would supposedly "take place in Germany for all time to come." Ironically, the completion date for the stadium was set for 1945, the year the Nazi nightmare ended in a Berlin bunker.

PART FIVE

Yesterday's Sports Page: Dominant Themes since 1945

Shortly after World War II, people weary of sacrifices and deprivation gave themselves over to a mentality of mass consumption. As economies recovered throughout the industrialized West, citizens sought material comforts such as better housing, more automobiles, and automated home appliances. They worked hard for economic security, but they also turned eagerly to new leisure opportunities. The sports boom that is still in progress is an integral part of a kind of second leisure revolution, in which Americans now spend more than one-fifth of their total consumer's budget for play, travel, and spectator sports.

Already highly politicized in the prewar era, sports after the war continued to reflect the politics of international conflict. As Germany lay defeated and British and French leadership appeared bankrupt, the United States and the Soviet Union emerged from the war against fascism locked in fierce competition for dominance. The alternatives seemed stark: American democratic capitalism or Russian Communism. Each side believed the other to be fanatically commited to triumph by any propaganda and military means available. Each gathered blocs (coalitions) of nations within its sphere of influence. Featuring all the intensity of war without actual combat, this struggle came to be known as the Cold War. From 1945 to the present, it has colored every aspect of international relations, including sports. No less than the Berlin Blockade, the Korean War, and the Cuban Missile Crisis, East-West athletic contests represented tests of will as well as strength and skill.

Also important for the course of sports since 1945 was the rise of discontented nationalities and minority groups. Native peoples long subjected to European rule in Africa, Asia, and the Near East won independence in the 1950s. In many of these emerging Third World nations, sports became a means of fostering national unity, identity, and visibility. Simultaneous social upheavals occurred within nations of the West, especially in the United States, where pent-up resentments of black citizens burst forth in demands for civil rights. As doors to churches, schools, and economic opportunity were pried open, the doors to locker rooms, gymnasiums, and playing fields also opened for American blacks—and for women, too, in the 1960s and 1970s. A militant feminist movement has won for women an enlarged, more equal participation not only in business and professional fields, but also in sports.

Several technological innovations, begun on a limited basis prior to World War II and expanded in the postwar era, facilitated the development of modern sports. Passenger airlines, for example, have transformed the map of competitive athletics. In the United States the expansion of professional baseball, football, basketball, and ice-hockey leagues westward in the 1950s would have simply been impossible had not the airplane superseded the train as a means of mass transport. International, even intercontinental, competition is now common because of rapid and comfortable jet passage that the steamship could not provide. Another technological experiment in the 1930s, the use of electric lights for outdoor ball games, was improved shortly after World War II. By 1950 only one American major-league baseball park provided no night games; in the 1950s summer amateur softball leagues and autumn high-school football games became nocturnal rituals. Within two decades, several huge domed stadiums employed sophisticated lighting systems and yet another commercial product for sports use, synthetic turf.

Of all the commercial, technological influences on modern sports, television has undoubtedly been the most decisive. On the eve of World War II, a few British soccer and rugby games, a handful of American baseball and football games, and several boxing matches were beamed on snowy screens to tiny, select audiences. Still, by 1950 less than 10 percent of American families gathered around television sets, but for consumer societies throughout the West television became a most coveted commodity. By 1970 the electronic box informed and entertained more than three-fourths of all homes in Great Britain and Sweden, two-thirds of West German households, and about half of the population in East Germany, Belgium, Italy, and Switzerland. Today, no less than 98 percent of all American homes possess at least one television set. For sports, television is the great popularizer, benefactor, and dictator. It encourages the growth of organized sports at all levels; it ensures huge profits for professional owners, promoters, and athletes; it has subtly changed the character of both amateur and professional sports.

Chapter **17**

EAST-WEST GAMES

To the idealist who insists that sports and politics should be kept separate, the realist replies that they seldom ever have been. Recent history especially is on the side of the realist. Various social upheavals, nationalistic rivalries of major powers, and the ambitions of newly emerging nations have all impinged heavily upon international sport since World War II. The intrusion of politics in the nine Olympics from 1948 to 1980 make even the Berlin Olympics of 1936 seem politically tame by comparison.

The United States and the Soviet Union figure prominently in the story of Cold War politics and sport. Emerging from the devastation of World War II as the world's two superpowers, they stood ideologically and militarily opposed to each other. By 1949 both possessed the atomic bomb and by 1953 the hydrogen capability to destroy the world. Each established its own sphere of influence and control in a world roughly divided into Western democratic and Eastern communist blocs, with both competing for the allegiance of new Third World nations in Asia, Africa, and Latin America. No less than debates on the floor of the United Nations, international sporting contests regularly reflected the Soviet-American conflict. As George Orwell prophetically observed in 1945, "At the international level sport is frankly mimic warfare. . . . In other words it is war minus the shooting."

Cold War Gamesmanship

Long excluded from the international community of sport, the Soviet Union was invited to send a team to the London summer Olympics of 1948. Russian coaches and officials were of the opinion, however, that their athletes were not yet ready for Olympic competition. Instead of athletes, they sent trainers and coaches, who took copious notes, snapped numerous photographs, and planned their strategy for future Soviet participation.

In London they witnessed an improvised event similar to the Antwerp Olympics following World War I. The scars of war were visible everywhere. Despite feverish British efforts at reconstruction, buildings destroyed by German bombs still lay in rubble. Postwar austerity measures touched everything. Athletes stayed in bleak school buildings and military camps on the outskirts of the city. A slow, hastily constructed track at Wembley Stadium cut down the times of all the competitors. Constant rain and fog cast a dreary pall over the entire event.

Still, of the 4,500 or so athletes who represented fifty-eight nations in the London Olympics, several stood out. Fanny Blankers-Koen of the Netherlands carried away four gold medals in track, surpassing even the spectacular accomplishments of Babe Didrikson in 1932. Emil Zatopek, a gritty long-distance runner from Czechoslovakia, charged dramatically onto the Olympic stage with a gold in the 10,000 meters. A fellow East European, Laszlo Papp of Hungary, seized the first of his three successive boxing championships. Most impressive of all was the decathlon victory of a seventeen-year old Californian, Bob Mathias, who led the American team in reclaiming its Olympic supremacy, which had been interrupted by the Germans in 1936. As Russian coaches observed the feats of Mathias and his compatriots Mel Patton, Harrison Dillard, and Mal Whitfield in track and the seven-foot giant Bob Kurland in basketball, they looked ahead to the Helsinki Olympics of 1952 as a supreme test of Soviet-American athletic prowess.

Americans relished the prospect. "The United States has to have its strongest possible representation just to teach the Red brothers a lesson that can't be excused or concealed," wrote Arthur Daley in the *New York Times* on 10 June 1952.

> There will be 71 nations in the Olympics at Helsinki. The United States would like to beat all of them, but the only one that counts is Soviet Russia. The Communist propaganda machine must be silenced so that there can't be even one distorted bleat out of it in regard to the Olympics. In sports the Red brothers have reached the put-up-or-shut-up stage. Let's shut them up.

Things did not work out that way.

At Helsinki the Russians did remarkably well. They entered contestants for every event except field hockey and finished with seventy-one medals, compared to seventy-six for the United States. Despite repeat victories by Mathias, Whitfield, and Dillard (as well as Zatopek and Papp), and the championship emergence of Bob Richards in pole-vaulting, Clyde Lovellette in basketball, and Floyd Patterson in boxing, until late in the games the Soviet squad led in the unofficial point totals. Only a late surge by American boxers, who won five gold medals in the waning moments, tied the United States with the U.S.S.R. in the scoring system espoused by the *Olympic Bulletin*. Western sportsmen were astonished. Given the fact that very few of the Soviet athletes had previously competed against world-class opposition

Although the politics of the Cold War weighed heavily on the Helsinki Olympics of 1952, athletes performed gracefully under pressure. Here Mal Whitfield of the United States leads the field, in classic form, into the final stretch of the 800 meters. (Courtesy of John Lucas.)

outside the U.S.S.R., their performances at Helsinki seemed little short of miraculous.

Had Westerners known more about the highly organized system of sport and "physical culture" in the Soviet Union, they would not have been taken by surprise. Helsinki was no fluke. From their distant tsarist past the Russians inherited a strong tradition of weight lifting, wrestling, speed skating, and gymnastics. After the Bolshevik Revolution in 1917, Communist officials socialized those traditions by taking sport out of the hands of private clubs and making it available to all Russian citizens. They instigated a new program of sport and physical exercise to overcome old class prejudices, to improve the health of the Russian people, to integrate diverse geographical sections of the country, and to build up the Red Army. In 1931 they devised a system of awards for all-around physical development, offering a coveted "GTO badge" to each adult citizen who passed a series of stiff practical and theoretical tests on physical fitness; soon a BGTO badge was similarly created for schoolchildren. Also in the 1930s Soviet officials distinguished between a program of physical activity for all and a more specialized program to produce elite competitive athletes. The postwar system of sport in the Soviet Union built on these prewar foundations.

It was a system created and controlled by government. The All-Union Physical Culture Council, founded in 1930, was replaced early in the postwar era by the Committee of Physical Culture and Sport, an arm of the Central Committee of the Communist Party (CCCP). Facilities, equipment, coaches, and material incentives ultimately derived from party headquarters. So did programs of physical exercise for preschoolers, elementary and secondary school children, university students, police and military personnel, trade unions, and even farm collectives. Each group formed a link in the organized chain of Soviet life, a life in which high premium was placed on health, physical strength and agility, and athletic excellence.

With the onset of the Cold War, Soviet officials looked on their athletes as both warriors and ambassadors. In an international arena symbolically charged with prestige, Russians athletes could "defeat" their country's ideological enemies. Sport, no less than economic development and military strength, was a key element in the Soviet drive for "world supremacy." In December 1948, within months of the Soviet blockade of Berlin, the CCCP called on all schools, universities, and sports societies "to spread physical culture and sport to every corner of the land, and to raise the level of skill, so that Soviet sportsmen might win world supremacy in the major sports in the immediate future." Behind the combative rhetoric lay political motive. Sport was an excellent means of advertising the excellence of the socialist way of life. "Each new victory is a victory for the Soviet form of society and the socialist sport system," declared one party spokesman; "it provides irrefutable proof of the superiority of socialist culture over the decaying culture of the capitalist states."

Great were the incentives for Soviet athletes. Not only did sport provide the social acclaim that customarily accompanied winning performances (whether in the East or West); athletic prowess in the Soviet Union also meant political recognition and material benefits. Beginning in October 1945, party officials offered cash prizes for athletes who broke world or national records. The amounts were set on a graduated scale according to the relative importance given to each sport, as were similar cash bonuses offered to first-, second-, and third-place winners in the U.S.S.R. championships. Deadly serious in its intention to produce record-breaking performers, the government put its better athletes on salaries and set up eighty sports schools to train top-flight athletes.

This system of undisguised professionalism lasted only two years. For Soviet athletes to be eligible to compete in prestigious international sporting events, they had to be amateurs. Therefore, in July 1947, the Soviet sports committee reversed its earlier arrangement: it withdrew cash salaries and bonuses in favor of giving only gold, silver, and bronze medals to champions. In truth, however, the professionalism simply took on an amateur facade. Athletes continued to train and compete full time, but "salaries" came indirectly from university student stipends, security police and armed-forces appointments, and jobs as physical-education instructors in sporting clubs attached to trade unions.

At best a kind of semiprofessionalism in Western terms, this system has over the years undergone minor alterations, remaining essentially intact to the present. Within the Soviet bureaucratic scheme of things, the sports system works efficiently to produce world-class athletes; to its credit it provides job security in the form of coaching and managerial positions for retired athletes. Transparently "shamateur" as it seems, it also satisfies the criteria for membership in the major international amateur sports organizations. Between 1946 and 1958 no less than thirty U.S.S.R. national sports associations became affiliated with international federations.

In the "Iron Curtain" phase of the Cold War, Russian sport became a modern window to the West. Reversing a prior reluctance of the Soviet government to allow its athletes to compete abroad, a prominent Moscow soccer team visited Sweden, Norway, and Britain only two months after the war. It fared surprisingly well, winning two and tying two matches against Britain's leading professional clubs. In 1946 Soviet weight lifters competed in the world championships, coming in second to an American team. In the following year Soviet wrestlers won three titles in the European championships, and in 1949 the men's volleyball team became world champions while the women's team claimed the European crown. The debut of the U.S.S.R. in international athletic competition was an auspicious one.

Despite their ambition to excel in the international arena, Soviet officials remained true to a traditional pattern of Russian fear and suspicion of all things foreign. During the last years of Joseph Stalin's repressive rule, athletes and high-ranking sports leaders suffered periodic purges—arrests, mock trials, and Siberian labor camps—little different from deviant diplomats and party members. In 1948 the chairman of the sports committee was purged, followed by the fall of several outstanding athletes who had traveled abroad and brought back foreign ideas and tastes. In that same year only twenty-three Soviet sports groups were allowed to compete abroad, and only twelve foreign teams were granted visas to enter the U.S.S.R. The sporting window to the West was momentarily closed, if not sealed.

The Helsinki Olympics were held during the last year of the Stalinist era. Whereas Westerners were amazed at the abilities of Soviet athletes, they were appalled at the Iron Curtain mentality that intruded upon the Olympic Village. Soviet officials adamantly refused to let their athletes live alongside Westerners. Originally they had planned to shuttle competitors daily from Leningrad, then out again as soon as they finished their contests. Instead, they decided to set up a separate "Eastern camp" to house not only the Soviets but also athletes from the satellite nations of Hungry, Poland, Bulgaria, Romania, and Czechoslovakia. Huge banners adorned with portraits of Stalin flew from the buildings. In classic Russian posture with a Cold War face, the Soviets kept their own athletes under close supervision and allowed no visitors into their compound.

While a grim form of Stalinism hung over the Soviet Olympic Village, the larger shadow of the Korean War darkened Soviet-American relations. Yet Russia's support of North Korea and the participation of the United States in defense of South Korea occasionally receded into the background as Russian and American athletes mingled in competition. In a few cases, at least, athletic respect leaped the barriers of language and ideological differences. A kind of mutual admiration society momentarily flourished between Bob Richards and his three Russian rivals in the pole vault. Richards knew only one word of Russian, *"khorosho,"* meaning "good," and his opponents knew only one English word, "beautiful." "So when I finished a jump," Richards later recalled, "they all cheered 'Beautiful,' and when they finished, I said 'Khorosho.' " Humor also came to the fore. A Soviet rower, playfully pinning a hammer and sickle emblem on the shirt of an American rower, joked in broken English, "If you should wear this in the United States, they would put you in the electric chair." Apparently he had read *Pravda's* lurid accounts of the Communist witch-hunt being staged in the United States by Senator Joseph McCarthy. Even in their most jovial exchanges, athletes could not escape the realities of Cold War gamesmanship.

Competitive Coexistence

Within a year of the Helsinki Olympics, the political climate began to change in both the United States and the Soviet Union. By 1953 the demagoguery of the McCarthy era had lost its steam, partly because of an armistice ending the Korean War and partly because of the conservative but pragmatic presidency of Dwight D. Eisenhower. Also in 1953, the death of Joseph Stalin brought on a new generation of less belligerent Soviet leaders. In 1955 Soviet, American, British, and French heads of state convened at Geneva in a guarded but conciliatory mood. Certainly the Cold War was not over. The world would continue to oscillate between tension, conciliation, and renewed tension. But since both the United States and the Soviet Union now held the hydrogen bomb, their struggle for supremacy took on a new form:

"peaceful coexistence." Of all the acceptable alternatives to war, competitive sport loomed large.

Having refused to participate in the Oslo Winter Games of 1952, at Cortina (Italy) in 1956 the Soviets made a dazzling entry into the Winter Olympics. Toni Sailer of Austria stood tallest of all the individual performers with his three gold medals in skiing, but his Austrian team finished a distant second to the Russians in the overall unofficial point totals. As expected, the Soviets scored heavily in speed skating, taking three of the four gold medals. Their showing in ice hockey, however, came as a shock to Westerners, who assumed that the Canadians, winners of six of the previous seven Olympic titles, would repeat as champions. Only ten years earlier (1946) had the first Soviet ice-hockey team been formed. In the final round at Cortina they blanked the United States, 4–0, then stunned Canada, 2–0.

Between the Winter and Summer Olympics of 1956, the Soviets held their first Spartakiad of the Peoples of the U.S.S.R., a sports spectacular of the first order. Every town and province held qualifying events, in which about 23 million people participated. For the finals, on August 6–16, the new Lenin Stadium on the banks of the Moscow River bulged daily with 104,000 spectators. All the prominent party officials attended, as did a number of foreign dignitaries, including the president of the International Olympic Committee, Avery Brundage. Mass gymnastics and formation displays added to the festive, patriotic mood as 9,000 athletes competed for medals. A grand celebration of Russian sporting achievement, the First Spartakiad was a culturally unifying event. Most important, it prepared Soviet athletes for the Melbourne Summer Olympics scheduled for November (summer in Australia).

Within the month prior to the opening of the Melbourne games, two political events shook the fragile foundations of the Olympic community. One was the Suez crisis. Egypt, receiving arms from Russia, attempted to seize control of the Suez Canal which had long been freely used as a passage for oil to industrial nations in western Europe. On October 29 Israel attacked Egypt across the Sinai Peninsula; two days later, Britain and France intervened militarily to keep the canal open. Then a strange thing happened. In a move indicative of the new pragmatic character of Soviet-American relations, the United States joined with the Soviet Union in a U.N. General Assembly order to cease fire. In an act prophetic of the course of future Olympics, Egypt unsuccessfully demanded that the nations "guilty of cowardly aggression" should be expelled from the Melbourne games. Its plea rejected, Egypt joined with fellow Arab nations Lebanon and Iraq to boycott the games, thus establishing the boycott as a political weapon.

For the Melbourne games, however, a crisis in Hungary was far more disruptive. Beginning on October 23, students and workers in Budapest took to the streets in protest against their Communist government, which was run from Moscow. Russian tanks and armed troops ruthlessly crushed the rebellion. Ironically, several members of the Hungarian Olympic team were already on their way to Australia aboard a Soviet steamship. The remainder of the team was in Czechoslovakia, waiting to board a plane for Melbourne. They considered returning to Hungary as freedom fighters but found the border firmly sealed by Russian troops. Reluctantly they flew on to Melbourne, where they were met at the airport by hundreds of Hungarian expatriates who had earlier fled Communist rule.

In protest against the Soviets' savage treatment of Hungarian dissidents, Switzerland, Spain, and the Netherlands withdrew from the Melbourne Olympics. The Spanish Sport Federation curtly explained that its athletes would not compete at games "while the liberty of peoples is being trampled on." Dutch officials went one better, donating a substantial sum of money to Hungarian sufferers and unanimously voting to withdraw from the Melbourne Olympics because the Hungarian tragedy "had spoiled the festive Olympic atmosphere."

Following the predictable response of Avery Brundage—"We are dead against any country using the Games for political purposes, whether right or wrong"—the games went on. A sports-loving people, the Australians served as efficient, gracious hosts. One Australian athlete, Betty Cuthbert, an eighteen-year-old from Sydney, proved to be the outstanding woman athlete at the 1956 games. She easily won gold medals in the 100- and 200-meter races, then produced a powerful sprint on the last leg of the 400-meter relay barely to beat a British team. Her three gold medals were equaled in identical men's track events by a tall Texan, Bobby Morrow. The biggest surprise, however, came from a stocky, blond Ukrainian, Vladimir Kuts, who emerged as the first Soviet track man ever to win a gold medal. In fact, he won two (the 5,000 and 10,000 meters), and both in record Olympic times.

In a reversal of the pattern of the 1952 Olympics, the U.S. team opened up an early large lead over its Soviet rivals only to see it dwindle and finally disappear. As usual, the Russians could not come close to challenging American track-and-field men. In addition to Morrow's feats, Bob Richards repeated his gold performance in the pole vault, and Harold Connolly, a schoolteacher from New England, beat Mikhail Krivonosov, a schoolteacher from Minsk, in the hammer throw. But then the competitors went indoors, where Russian wrestlers and gymnasts were utterly dominant. Triumphs of Paul Anderson in weight lifting, Pete Rademacher in heavyweight boxing, and the American basketball team, led by Bill Russell and K. C. Jones, could not stem the tide of Russian versatility. In the end the U.S.S.R. claimed ninety-eight medals, with thirty-seven golds; the United States won seventy-two in all, thirty-two golds. If the Olympic Games are a fair indication of athletic prowess, at Melbourne the Soviet Union emerged as the premier athletic nation on earth.

Needless to say, the Soviets received no applause from Hungarian competitors or spectators. Upset over the recent Budapest disaster, Hungarian athletes performed poorly at Melbourne. Except for Laszlo Papp's unprecedented third straight boxing title, they had little to cheer about. In the Olympic Village they angrily ripped the Communist insignia off their flag and replaced it with the flag of free Hungary. When Jozsef Kovács came in second to Vladimir Kuts in the 10,000 meters, he made a point of refusing to shake hands with his Russian conqueror. Gestures and taunts turned to violence in a semifinal water polo match between the Soviet Union and Hungary. Despite an apparent concern to wield elbows more than to play the ball, the Hungarians were ahead 4–0 in the closing minutes. Finally, a Russian retaliated to a push by butting his Hungarian nemesis in the face, drawing a massive stream of blood into the water. It was the battle of Budapest anew.

Amid all the tensions and friction, however, symbols and visible evidence of international amity surfaced at Melbourne. No longer kept separate from the Olympic Village, Russian athletes lived beside Americans and fraternized as much as the language barrier would allow. In the closing ceremonies, for the first time in Olympic history, the athletes marched not as separate nations but informally as a single group, East mingling with West, blacks and whites, men with women. The Melbourne Olympics even set in motion a literal marriage between East and West. Following a whirlwind romance in the Olympic Village, the American hammer thrower, Harold Connolly, and a Czechoslovakian discus thrower, Olga Fikotova, tied the nuptial knot in Prague the following spring. It was a marriage made in Olympic heaven: Emil Zatopek, the double-gold Czech marathoner, acted as best man.

Soviet-American relations remained peaceful but highly competitive in the late 1950s. The "space race," begun with Russia's successful launching of Sputnik in October 1957, tellingly cloaked rival technologies and political ambitions under a sports metaphor. In January 1958 both nations signed the first of a series of agreements to exchange cultural, technical, and educational expertise. Three months later a team of Soviet wrestlers visited the United States, and in the summer an American track team competed in Moscow for the first time. From 1958 to 1966 annual track-and-field meets were hosted alternately by each side. They attracted wide press and television coverage, subtly breaking down stereotypes of "the enemy." A convivial summer track meet in Philadelphia helped pave the way for a visit of Soviet Premier Nikita Khrushchev to the United States in the autumn of 1959.

Good will persisted in the 1960 Winter Olympics at Squaw Valley, California, where the Soviets yet again padded their team score early in the speed-skating events, then hung on to claim victory in the unofficial totals. Patriotic Americans had something to cheer about, however, when the American ice-hockey team won its first-ever Olympic gold. Two sets of brothers, Roger and William Christian from Minnesota, and Robert and William Cleary from Massachusetts, led upsets over Canada, 2–1, and the U.S.S.R., 3–2, then a decisive 9–4 win over Czechoslovakia in the finals.

The American Summer Olympics team anticipated similar success at Rome in 1960. Their track-and-field squad especially was heralded as the best team ever. But they failed miserably. In events traditionally won by Americans, they lost eight of the first eleven events they entered. John Thomas of Boston, touted as the best high jumper in history, finished third behind two Russians. The champion hammer thrower of 1956, Harold Connolly, failed even to qualify for the final round. The 400-meter relay team set a new Olympic record but was disqualified for a faulty baton exchange. On the positive side, Rafer Johnson captured the decathlon gold medal. Ralph Boston's broad jump of twenty-six feet, seven and three-quarter inches broke the last of Jesse Owens's records. A slim young Tennesseean, Wilma Rudolph, became the first American woman to win three gold medals: the 100- and 200-meter dashes, and the 400-meter women's team relay. But generally at Rome the American track-and-field team came unglued, relinquishing the field to New Zealander Peter Snell, Australian Herb Elliott, and a host of eager, strong Russians.

Neither the brash mouth of light-heavyweight boxing titlist Cassius Marcellus Clay nor the basketball skills of Oscar Robertson, Jerry Lucas, and Jerry West could prevent the inevitable clean sweep by the Russians in gymnastics. Larisa Latynina's three gold medals, two silvers, and one bronze outdid her Melbourne performance. In the frequency of her trips to the victory stand she was second only to Boris Shakhlin, who collected four golds, two silvers, and one bronze. To these predictable feats the Russians surprisingly added medals in cycling, fencing, rowing, yachting, and even show jumping, events long the exclusive territory of Western athletes. By the time the Olympic flame was extinguished at Rome, the U.S.S.R. team had swamped the United States, its nearest rival, by a total of 103 medals to 71.

America's lost athletic superiority rankled all the more because the Communist Revolution in Cuba, the building of the Berlin Wall, the Bay of Pigs disaster in 1961, and the Cuban missile crisis in 1962 all suggested that the tide of international affairs was turning Red. Unlikely partners joined hands in the call for American athletic recovery. In 1962 John J. Kurch, a spokesman for the American Legion, outlined in fifteen steps a remedy, including a cooperative effort of government and private agencies "to obviate the necessity of door-to-door begging for transportation and living expenses." The suggestion was not new. Ever since the Helsinki Olympics, tentative proposals of governmental assistance of Olympic athletes had regularly made their way into the *Congressional Record*. Nor was there anything new in Kurch's emphasis on winning. "We should stress victory, not merely participation," he insisted. "In the Olympics and international meets, only the winners are honored."

Hubert Humphrey, a liberal Democratic Senator from Minnesota, agreed. For the widely read *Parade Magazine,* Humphrey wrote an article in January 1963 entitled "Why We Must Win the Olympics." In fashionable Cold War terms, he portrayed a "relentless struggle between freedom and Communism [embracing] almost every level of life from spacemen to sprinters." He accused the Russians of converting "the once-idealistic Olympic games into an ideological battlefield." Like Kurch, Humphrey specified a point-by-point plan for America's athletic resurgence. Included in his program were an increase in the physical fitness of American youths, a national junior Olympics with emphasis on games not popular with native Americans, and a campaign to involve females in competitive sports. Humphrey agreed with Kurch in supporting a more active governmental role, including financial aid, in the promotion of Olympic sports.

The mixed motives of national physical fitness and Olympic respectability lay behind President John F. Kennedy's appointment of Charles "Bud" Wilkinson as director of the President's Council on Physical Fitness. Wilkinson, an outstanding former football coach at the University of Oklahoma, decided to steer clear of direct government subsidy. Instead, he proposed a foundation privately financed by a group of affluent citizens. His scheme came to a crashing halt with the assassination of Kennedy in November 1963. Wilkinson resigned shortly thereafter to run for political office. As the Olympic year of 1964 approached, several American congressmen presented pieces of legislation that would have provided government funding for both the winter and summer Olympic teams, but all failed.

The Winter Olympics of 1964, in Innsbruck, Austria, proved to be an unmitigated disaster for the United States. Out of thirty-four events, the U.S.S.R. took first place in eleven. The runner-up team, Norway, won a mere four gold medals and the United States only one. The championship American ice-hocky team of 1960 came away empty-handed. "It may be time," announced one U.S. congressman who had earlier led the fight against federal involvement in sport, "to reconsider our traditional reluctance to provide Government support to U.S. Olympic teams. The present situation is humiliating for the athletes involved and destructive of team performance and morale." More to the point, the situation was humiliating to the American nation in its propaganda struggle against Russian supremacy.

Although federal assistance was not forthcoming, the political attention focused on the Olympic Games apparently stirred American amateur organizations and individual athletes to extraordinary efforts in the summer Olympics of 1964. The site was Tokyo, where 5,565 athletes represented ninety-four countries. Track stars Bob Hayes, Fred Carr, Billy Mills, and Bob Schul led in a miraculous recovery of American superiority in track-and-field competition. Al Oerter overcame a bad back and bruised ribs to win his third straight gold medal in the discus throw. Fred Hansen used a new figerglass pole to perfection in the pole vault. Peter Snell of New Zealand achieved the first middle-distance double gold (the 800-meter and 1500-meter races) in forty-four years, but in twenty-four track-and-field events, the United States men's team won twelve gold, five silver, and three bronze medals. Even more successful were the swimmers, who heard an abbreviated version of the "Star Spangled Banner" played at the presentation of no less than sixteen gold medals in twenty-two events. Don Schollander broke two world records and anchored two relay teams to become the first Olympic swimmer ever to win four golds.

Except for Joe Frazier, who won the heavyweight boxing title, American boxers fared poorly. Soviet pugilists came on strong, and as usual the Soviets swept the boards in weight lifting, wrestling, and gymnastics. Two medals each of gold, silver, and bronze gave the beautiful and durable Larisa Latynina a fabulous retirement record of nine gold, five silver, and three bronze medals for a career stretching over three Olympics. In basketball, too, the Russians anticipated victory, but Bill Bradley and company handled a seven-foot, three-inch giant Russian center, Yan Kruminsh, with remarkable ease.

In the final tabulations, the U.S.S.R. claimed ninety-six medals compared to ninety for the United States, and it narrowly scored highest in the unofficial point totals. The minimal difference erased some of the embarrassment suffered by American athletes at Rome in 1960. The Americans also enjoyed a few jokes at the Russians' expense. When Nikita Khrushchev was ousted from his position as head of the Soviet Union within the first week of the Tokyo games in 1964, the president of the AOC commented, "I knew we were doing pretty well against the Russians, but I didn't know it would cause Khrushchev to resign."

The Emergence of New Sporting Nations

While Soviet and American athletes continued to hog the headlines, the Tokyo Olympics of 1964 signaled a new era in which sport became important to the "emerging nations" of Asia, Africa, the Near East, and Latin America. Numerous nations newly independent after World War II adopted sport as a unifying, stabilizing force to overcome tribal insularity, language differences, and social barriers. At the international level, sport provided instant recognition and prestige. In a pattern little different from the practice of older, Western nations, emerging nations used sporting contests to cement ties of friendship with their political allies and to exclude or bludgeon their diplomatic foes.

Surfacing at Tokyo, these nationalistic functions of sport were rooted in the early postwar era. At the London Olympics of 1948, eight Asian nations (Afghanistan, Burma, Ceylon, India, Indonesia, Pakistan, the Philippines, and Thailand) drafted a constitution for an Asian Amateur Athletic Federation. In the following year the AAAF changed its name to the Asian Games Federation and in 1951 organized the first Asian Games, in New Delhi. A kind of Asian Olympics set squarely between the quadrennial Olympic Games, these games were held at Manila in 1954 and at Tokyo in 1958.

Material difficulties and political controversy surrounding the Asian Games of 1962 reflected many of the problems of organized sport in emerging nations. The projected site was Jakarta, Indonesia, a politically unstable country run by the dictatorial hand of President Sukarno. Despite an appalling level of poverty, illiteracy, and poor health among the Indonesian citizenry, Sukarno enthusiastically welcomed the games. But economically backward Indonesia possessed few good roads, fewer respectable hotels, no stadium, and hardly any tracks or gymnasiums. Sukarno turned to the world's two superpowers for assistance. From the U.S.S.R. he received a huge credit loan, and from the United States a new highway linking the harbor of Jakarta with the sports complex. In truth, the Sukarno regime was more aligned with Communist China than with either the Soviet Union or the United States. Like China, Indonesia was large in population and rich in natural resources, but it was economically undeveloped and politically suspicious of both Soviet and American motives. A large Arab element in Indonesia also encouraged Sukarno to be on good terms with emerging Arab nations.

In accordance with his diplomatic connections, Sukarno refused to grant visas for athletes from Taiwan and Israel to participate in the Asian Games of 1962. The IOC in turn suspended Indonesia indefinitely, pending guarantees that no further political discrimination would be practiced. Viewing that measure as simply another attempt of Western imperialistic powers to dominate underdeveloped nations, Sukarno reacted swiftly by calling for a new format for international sports in the Third World: the Games of the New Emerging Forces of the World (GANEFO), which would be limited to Asian, African, Latin American, and socialist countries. To the First GANEFO at Jakarta in 1963, teams from sixty-eight nations were invited to participate. Once again the IOC intervened, threatening to ban all GANEFO participants from the forthcoming Tokyo Olympics. The bluff was hollow. Of the teams representing forty-eight nations at the First GANEFO, one was from the largest Olympic nation, the U.S.S.R., and another was from the Olympic host for 1964, Japan. In the end the IOC backed down, but in the simmering GANEFO controversy emergent Asian nations made their mark on the Tokyo Olympics.

African athletes also first became visible at Tokyo. The lone African medalist at Rome in 1960, Abeke Bikila of Ethiopia, repeated as the winner of the marathon, this time with shoes on (having run barefooted four years earlier), and with energy to spare for doing callisthenics at the end of his twenty-six-mile ordeal. At Tokyo he was joined on the awards podium by several other Africans, such as Mohammed Gammoudi of Tunisia, who captured a silver medal in the 10,000-meter race, and Wilson Kipragut, Kenya's first Olympic medalist, who finished third in the 800 meters. However modest their success at Tokyo, the Africans represented yet another emerging force in international sport.

Before World War II only four independent states existed on the African continent; by 1960 no less than thirty-nine nations had broken the bonds of European colonialism. New African governments, eager to accelerate economic growth for their impoverished populations, evolved quickly from British, French, German, or Dutch foundations to distinctive systems that would best serve native needs. Another European legacy, organized sport, was also adapted to suit African tradition and taste. As in Asia, sport provided internal cohesion and international recognition for new African nations.

Governments promoted games and physical education in the schools. Tribal customs of dance and play blended with more organized Western forms of physical exercise. The first All-African Conference on Health and Physical Education convened in Liberia in 1962, but a lack of facilities and trained personnel made Africa, like Asia, susceptible to Western influence. Soviet and American governments eagerly sent money and sports advisers in an attempt to win the allegiance of African governments. Noting "a widespread passiveness towards athletics" in Asia, the U.S. State Department in 1965 earmarked Africa as a prime target of American aid.

At the competitive level, national sports federations arranged trans-African gatherings. In 1957 the African Cup of Nations, modeled on the

World Cup for soccer football, began in Khartoum. Three years later Nigeria hosted the first West African Games in Lagos, with a program akin to the Asian Games. The "Games of Friendship," begun in 1961 as a combined French- and English-speaking athletic tournament, brought athletes from twenty-four African countries together at Dakar, Senegal, in 1963. Finally, in 1965 these regional contests gave birth to the All-African Games, first held in the Congo Republic with 3,000 male and female athletes representing twenty-eight independent states. Native African dances opened the ceremonies, followed by spirited contests in track and field, soccer, boxing, basketball, volleyball, tennis, swimming, cycling, table tennis, handball, and judo. At the conclusion of the games, the Supreme Council of Sport in Africa was founded, with permanent headquarters in Yaounde, Cameroon.

All this activity went largely unnoticed in two of the most sports-loving of all the African states, South Africa and Rhodesia. Both remained bastions of white supremacy, isolated from the course of black African life. Racial segregation, long practiced informally by sports clubs in South Africa, became a cornerstone of official government policy in 1948. White rugby, soccer, and cricket teams, not to mention individual boxers, golfers, and tennis players, confined their games to all-white opposition. Black teams and organized matches were pitifully few, since most South African blacks were economically destitute. Those who could afford to pay were allowed to attend most games as spectators (especially games involving visiting teams), but by law they were required to sit in strictly segregated stands. For black African sportsmen as well as statesmen, this apartheid system made South Africa and Rhodesia the lepers of the African community of nations.

In 1962 the Soviet Union, courting the favor of black African states, successfully launched a movement to have South Africa banned from the Olympic Games. Their efforts bore quick fruit. The exclusion of the South African Olympic team from the Tokyo Olympics was the first of a long series of measures that have made white South Africans the most isolated of all athletes in the world. Yet the road to the present has been uneven. In February 1968 a special three-man committee of the IOC decided that South Africa's apartheid policy had been revised sufficiently to allow the South Africans to participate in the Mexico City Summer Olympics. African nations—thirty-two in all—reacted furiously. They threatened to boycott en masse if South Africa competed. Finally, just six months before the 1968 Summer Games, the IOC reversed its decision.

While the South Africans stayed home and played their racially segregated games, black Africans shone brightly in the thin air of Mexico City. Mohammed Gammoudi of Tunisia bettered his 1964 effort by winning the gold medal in the 5,000 meters, as did Kenya's Wilson Kipragut, who took the silver in the 800 meters. Mamo Wolde of Ethiopia captured first place in the marathon and second in the 10,000 meters. Benjamin Kogo of Kenya took the silver in the steeplechase. Most impressive, however, were Kenya's three gold medalists in long-distance races: Kipchogo Keino, Naftali Temu, and Amos Biwott. All admittedly enjoyed the advantage of having trained at a high altitude similar to the Mexico City elevation. But whatever the circumstance, African performances at Mexico City fulfilled the promises held out at

Tokyo four years earlier, reminding the world that competitive sport was flourishing on the "dark continent."

In Latin America, too, sport expanded dramatically after World War II. Building on its prewar popularity, soccer football became a Latin obsession. Of the six World Cups held between 1950 and 1970, the first host was Brazil, another was Chile (1962), and the last was Mexico. More to the point, of those six Cup winners, one was Uruguay (1950) and three were Brazil (1958, 1962, and 1970). In the 1958 World Cup, in Sweden, a seventeen-year-old Brazilian displayed energy, skill, and power never before seen on the soccer field. He scored six of his team's eleven goals during the final three rounds of play. According to baptismal records at Saō Paulo, his name was Edson Arantes do Nascimento. The world knew him as Pelé. Latin Americans idolized him as the godlike master of their most important game.

The attraction of soccer football for backward, impoverished Latin Americans is not difficult to explain. A simple, inexpensive game, it could be enjoyed by peasants and street urchins as well as by highly trained professionals. For numerous villagers and townspeople, for whom athletic facilities and equipment were woefully inadequate, soccer was the only game available. Without gymnasiums and coaches for Olympic-style sports in Latin America, for years the Pan-American Games, first held in Buenos Aires in 1951 (by design a year before the Olympic Games), were dominated by American and Caribbean athletes.

Athletics became an open door for American influence in Latin America. "All over Latin America and Asia, Soviet coaches and teams are having a field day with the athletes and crowds of emerging countries," warned one United States congressman in 1962. "Red sports stars," he added, "give a decidedly different image to people throughout the world than Red Soldiers who patrol the Wall of Shame in Berlin." Predictably, he urged "a massive increase in the U.S. athletic exchange program." His colleagues leaped to the task. Whereas from 1952 to 1962 the American government annually budgeted about $100,000 for the promotion of athletics in emerging nations, the sum grew steadily to $300,000 by 1967. Through the People-to-People Committee founded during the Eisenhower years, and then through the Peace Corps founded in 1961 by President Kennedy, individual athletes, coaches, and teams became unofficial but effective American ambassadors to underdeveloped nations. Between 1964 and 1969 about forty-eight coaches and physical-education specialists received government grants to visit twenty countries in Central and South America.

Developments in Cuba lent urgency to the American mission in Latin America. Following Fidel Castro's overthrow of the dictatorial Batista regime in 1959, Cuba leaned toward economic and diplomatic amity with the U.S.S.R., and it was finally pushed into the Russian lap by an American economic blockade and the Bay of Pigs invasion of 1961. Soviet athletic coaches, advisers, and equipment accompanied Russian grain and missiles to Cuba. Beginning with fourteen Soviet coaches in 1962, the number rose gradually to a high of twenty-eight in 1971, then trailed off as the Cubans began producing their own coaches.

In Castro's Cuba, sport was made available to all citizens through schools and local clubs, with rewards based on merit rather than social status. Old private sports clubs, catering to a privileged minority, were banned. Professional sports, deemed expressions of "capitalistic decadence," were also abolished. Meritorious "amateur" athletes received living allowances and financial perquisites from government funds thinly disguised as university scholarships or police, army, or trade-union appointments. This miniature copy of the Soviet system produced quick and impressive results in the international arena. Beginning in 1971, Cuban teams consistently came in second only to the United States in the Pan-American Games.

Except for a handful of fencing medalists in the Olympics of 1900 and 1904, Cuban Olympians had never mounted the victory stand until the Tokyo Games of 1964, when a silver medalist emerged. Ten Cubans, mostly boxers and sprinters, won silver medals at Mexico City in 1968. At Munich four years later, three golds were numbered among a total of twenty-two Cuban medals. Teófilo Stevenson, a powerful heavyweight boxer, led the charge, which was to rank tiny Cuba eighth from the top of the unofficial point totals of all the nations competing at Montreal in 1976. A victorious sprinter, Albert Juantoreña, was asked by a Montreal journalist how radically the Castro revolution had changed sport in Cuba. He answered simply, "Well, let's see, do you recall any medals we won before the revolution?"

Stars and Strife Forever

The optimist who wishes to see international sports competition as a means of fostering good will among nations must look beyond the Olympic Games to exchanges such as the "ping-pong diplomacy" of 1971. Peking's invitation for an American table tennis team to visit Communist China both reflected and accelerated the improvement of Sino-American relations. A series of friendly exhibitions ended in a cordial reception by Premier Chou En-lai, who in turn accepted an invitation for Chinese players to tour the United States. Barriers dissolved in the warm interaction of hosts and guests. At the official level, "detente" was the word. In 1972 President Richard Nixon made his historic visit to the People's Republic of China.

In the same year, tragedy struck the Munich Olympics. In the early hours of September 5, the day after Mark Spitz won his record seventh gold medal in swimming, eight armed members of a Palestinian (Arab) terrorist group scaled the fence surrounding the Olympic Village and made their way to the quarters of the Israeli team. In cold blood they murdered two Israelis and took nine survivors hostage. Demands, negotiations, and delays ensued. Finally, after fifteen hours, the captors and their hostages were taken by helicopter to a nearby airfield, supposedly to be given safe passage to an Arab nation. As they stepped from the helicopter, however, German sharpshooters opened fire. The Palestinians retaliated, and within minutes all nine hostages, five of the terrorists, and three Germans lay dead or dying.

Yet the games went on. "I am sure the public will agree," declared Avery Brundage, "that we cannot allow a handful of terrorists to destroy this nucleus of international cooperation and goodwill we have in the Olympic movement." Others saw the matter differently. Red Smith, veteran sports columnist for the *New York Times,* derisively referred to Brundage as the "high priest of the playground" and blasted the myopia of IOC officials: "Walled off in their dream world, appallingly unaware of the realities of life and death, the aging playground directors who conduct this quadrennial muscle dance ruled that a little blood must not be allowed to interrupt play." The Olympic Games of 1972 inevitably left bad memories all around, convincing many that the idealistic brainchild of Pierre de Coubertin had turned out to be a monster—too big, too commercial, and too susceptible to political manipulation.

The Montreal Games of 1976 did little to allay those fears. Expenses for the 1976 Summer Olympics, originally estimated at $250 million, ran in the end to about $1.5 billion, sending the Canadian government scrambling for new taxes to liquidate the debt. But Canada's financial liability was a manageable problem compared to the intractable political conflicts that surfaced at Montreal. Having officially recognized the People's Republic of (Communist) China, Canada now refused to allow Taiwan athletes to appear under the flag and name of the Republic of China. The American Olympic Committee threatened to withdraw its entire team if Taiwan was excluded from the games. Finally, Taiwan withdrew of its own accord, but Secretary of State Henry Kissinger turned down an invitation to the games because of Canada's position on Taiwan.

Taking a cue from the world's leading powers, twenty-nine Third World nations withdrew in protest against New Zealand's sporting ties with the white supremacist nation of South Africa. The visit of a New Zealand rugby team to South Africa in the early summer of 1976 sparked the controversy. On July 16, the day before the opening of the Montreal games, Tanzania led thirty-one black nations in requesting that the IOC expel New Zealand from the games. Their request denied, all withdrew except the small teams of the Ivory Coast and Senegal.

The biggest boycott of all occurred at the Moscow Summer Olympics of 1980. Late in the previous year, the Red Army invaded Afghanistan, provoking President Jimmy Carter to announce in early January that the United States would not appear in the forthcoming Moscow Games unless the Russians withdrew their troops. American officials put pressure on friends and dependents to join in the boycott. Governments throughout the Western world found themselves in tension with their national Olympic committees. Britain's Conservative government, headed by Margaret Thatcher, decided to support the American position, but the British Olympic Committee chose otherwise. Under similar political pressures, the Australian Olympic Committee voted 6–5 to send a team to Moscow, but it allowed each sports federation to make its own choice; four chose to stay home. Canada, Japan, and West Germany headed the list of sixty-two nations that followed the American lead.

Of the eighty-one teams appearing at Moscow, sixteen refused to carry their national flags in the opening ceremonial march. The entire British team refrained from marching and instead sent a single individual to carry the

Olympic flag in place of the Union Jack. For New Zealand, five athletes followed a raised black flag on which were superimposed a white olive branch of peace and the five interlocking rings of the Olympic emblem. From beginning to end the Moscow Olympics were bathed in political gestures and rhetoric, thus raising again an international chorus of voices demanding that the Olympics be held regularly at a single neutral site—possible the Winter Games in Switzerland or Norway, and the Summer Games in Greece—and that chauvinistic symbols such as national anthems and flags be abolished.

Some would-be reformers of the Olympic rules also insist on dispensing with the distinction between amateur and professional athletes. Such critics are of the opinion that Soviet-style systems of sport are in fact professionalism in thin disguise. They hold that the Olympics should simply be thrown "open" to the best athletes in each country, professionals and amateurs alike. This issue of athletes' eligibility, no less than the questions of site and nationalistic displays, will no doubt continue to plague the international Olympic community.

Communist Bloc athletes now dominate the Olympics. Between Helsinki 1952 and Moscow in 1980, only at the Mexico City Summer Games of 1968 was the Russian stranglehold momentarily broken. Bob Beamon's record-setting long jump, Al Oerter's amazing fourth consecutive discus title, Bill Toomey's decathlon gold, and Dick Fosbury's innovative "flop" technique in the high jump led the American team to a decisive victory in the unofficial point totals. But Mexico City represented a mere detour, not a new route. At Munich four years later, the U.S.S.R. returned to business as usual: winning. And with a vengeance. In a disputed last-second effort, its basketball team even beat the American squad at its own game.

Certainly Russian and satellite athletes shone brightest among the Olympic stars of the 1970s. Outstanding were Mark Spitz's seven golds in swimming at Munich, Finland's Lasse Viren's long-distance marks in 1972 and 1976, Bruce Jenner's decathlon victory at Montreal, Eric Heiden's five gold medals in speed skating at Lake Placid in 1980, and the dramatic long-distance victories of Britain's Steve Ovett and Sebastian Coe at Moscow. The darlings of the decade, however, were gymnasts Olga Korbut of the U.S.S.R, who stole the world's heart at Munich, and Nadia Comaneci of Romania, whose seven perfect scores at Montreal prompted a *Newsweek* reporter to comment that "amid the political feuds, cheating scandals and impromptu squabbles that have become semiofficial Olympic events, Nadia in flight was Montreal's doll-like symbol of what's right with the Games."

Two Communist musclemen, Vasili Alexeyev of the Soviet Union and Teófilo Stevenson of Cuba, towered over all opposition. Beginning in 1972 with a quick knockout victory over an American white hope, Duane Bobick, Stevenson demolished all heavyweight boxing challengers in three consecutive Olympics. Weight lifter Alexeyev, with heavy jowls, massive belly, and spindly legs, proved himself unquestionably the strongest man in the world in 1972 and 1976. For eight years he went unbeaten in international meets, accumulating eighty-two records. In 1978 he retired momentarily. When he failed at a comeback in 1980, his crown was taken by yet another Russian giant, Sultan Rakhmanov.

Even more impressive than individual stars is the team versatility of the Russians. Unlike the American team, which is traditionally strong in track-and-field, swimming, and boxing contests but weak in other events, Soviet medalists are spread throughout all the various events. So are East German (Geman Democratic Republic) athletes, whose sports system is modeled after the U.S.S.R.'s. East Germany is the modern Olympic miracle story. A nation with a total population of only seventeen million people, it won forty gold medals, and ninety medals in all, at Montreal in 1976—more than the United States, Great Britain, and Japan combined. At both Montreal and Moscow, East Germany finished second to the much larger U.S.S.R. in the unofficial team totals.

The East German system is awesomely efficient. Athletes are screened and tested at a youthful age, placed in special sports schools, and provided with the finest equipment and coaching available and some of the best sports medicine in the world. American critics look on such a program as a form of totalitarian coercion, but in fact it is based on the incentives of social recognition and material benefits. At Montreal, when Kornelia Ender's four golds led East German women swimmers to win eleven of their thirteen events, one Western journalist suggested to the coach that his athletes seemed to be methodically efficient but lacking fun in their competition. "The American men are as successful as our women. Aren't they having fun?" came the quick reply. "Of course, the argument is invalid. It isn't possible to do this well and not have fun." For Communist athletes, as for Americans, fun is winning.

Swamped consistently by the Soviets and their satellite athletes, American competitors have not had much fun lately in the Olympic Games. In February 1980 at Lake Placid, American pride rose on the strong legs of Eric Heiden in speed skating, only to sink with an injury to Linda Fratianne, which ensured the Russians of yet another figure-skating medal. Then a remarkable thing happened. While millions of Americans sat glued to their television sets, holding their breath, a gang of amateur ice-hockey players—mostly college kids—defeated a heavily favored Soviet team, 4—3, in the semi-finals, then finished off Finland, 4–2. Never did gold glitter so brightly. For one shining moment, Americans forgot their economic woes, their countrymen captive in Iran, Russian troops in Afghanistan, and the impending boycott of the Moscow Summer Games.

Victory over the Russians meant most of course. It was an improbable feat. For four consecutive Olympics, the Soviet Big Red Machine had won gold medals; in both 1972 and 1976 they lost not a single game. Nor did they confine their quick skating, precision passing, and disciplined teamwork to the Olympic format. Beginning with an eight-game series in 1972, they regularly challenged professional Canadian and American veterans of the National Hockey League. Every series was close; several times the Russians won more games than they lost. Just prior to the Lake Placid Games, they waltzed to a 10–3 demolition of the youthful American Olympic team in an exhibition game in New York City. "You defense them one way, they come at you another way," complained Herb Brooks, the American coach. Realistically, Brooks feared embarrassment in the Olympics. "You know what our chances are? Slim to none."

A 2–2 tie with Sweden in the opening round barely improved those prospects. Then goalie Jim Craig, captain Mike Eruzione, talented foward Mark Johnson, and a scrappy supporting cast ignited, blowing away the European champions, Czechoslovakia, 7–3, and Norway, 5–1. "Who knows?" Eruzione wondered aloud. "We may do something nobody dreamed of us doing." Americans everywhere began similarly to wonder, and to dream. Suddenly ice hockey, never a favorite American sport outside the Northeast and upper Midwest, became a hot media item. For the contest against the Russians, scheduled for a Friday night, living rooms, drinking parlors, and university television rooms all over the United States were crammed with viewers. Two Soviet first-period goals dimmed American hopes momentarily, but the Whiz Kids were not to be denied. By the end of the first period they had tied the score, and finally, with just over six minutes left in the game, they went ahead to stay. At the game's end, American players hugged, pounded, and sprawled on top of each other, dramatizing the excitement felt throughout the nation: "We beat the Russians."

Surely in a best of seven series, and probably even in a miniseries of three contests, the Soviets' experience and discipline would have overwhelmed their gutsy competitors. But it did not matter. In this single war on ice, American youths momentarily retrieved some honor and pride in the Cold War confrontation between East and West.

Chapter 18

BREAKING BARRIERS THROUGH SPORTS

Until recently the four-minute mile seemed beyond the reach of mortal man. Paavo Nurmi, the "Finnish Flash" of the 1920s, prided himself on running against a watch strapped to his wrist, ignoring his opponents, but the best time he ever recorded in the mile was a mere 4:10. Subsequent runners whittled away seconds from the record. In 1945 a Swede, Gunder Hägg, lowered the time to within a second of the magic mark. Yet the four-minute mile remained unbroken, a barrier psychological as well as physical. Finally, on a raw and blustery day, 6 May 1954, at the Iffley Road Track in Oxford a young English medical student, Roger Bannister, registered 3.59.4. Officials excitedly recorded the event, and an eager press publicized it around the world. The barrier had fallen. Today the four-minute mile is commonplace. In all sports, in fact, statistical records now regularly fall as modern athletes take advantage of better equipment and training.

More important than statistical records are the social barriers broken through sports. During the past century, for example, class barriers have fallen. Gymnasiums, tennis courts, golf courses, and even fields for organized games were once reserved for affluent, socially respectable athletes. Now humble origins and meager resources no longer bar participation. Obviously some sports, such as tennis and golf, continue to attract high-income participants, but since social status is irrelevant in the competitive arena where strength, quickness, and wit determine winners, sport is a great social leveler in modern capitalist and communist countries alike.

Since 1945, barriers of racial and sexual discrimination have begun to fall. In the United States especially, sport has partly led, partly followed, a wave of vast social change that has opened the door of opportunity for blacks and females. The door has yet to be wedged wide open; old racist and sexist attitudes die slowly, and with agonizing results. But athletic facilities and rewards that were once separate and definitely unequal are now increasingly available to all, regardless of racial or sexual distinctions. The breaking of these barriers is perhaps the most remarkable achievement of contemporary America. It is an achievement in which sport has played an important and controversial role.

Crossing the Color Line

In 1945 a black youth scanned the sports page in vain for heroes of his own kind. Long had Jesse Owens, the black star of the 1936 Olympics, retired from athletics. Except for Joe Louis, still the holder of the heavyweight crown, and Ike Williams, a new black lightweight champion, even boxing featured Caucasian champions such as light heavyweight Gus Lesnevich, middleweight Tony Zale, and featherweight Willie Pep. Yet boxing, the traditional avenue of black fame in white America, seemed liberally integrated compared to major-league baseball, football, and basketball, where a color line firmly barred black athletes.

Baseball practiced the oldest and most rigid segregation pattern. Ever since the late 1880s, when "Cap" Anson led a crusade for an unofficial "gentleman's agreement" against the employment of black players, organized baseball had refused to allow blacks on the same teams with whites. In the early years of the twentieth century, black baseball clubs proliferated, first forming a separate professional major league in 1920. Black National and American leagues annually competed in their own World Series in the 1930s, but financial instability constantly plagued even the better teams, such as the Kansas City Monarchs, the Birmingham Black Barons, the Cuban Giants, and the Homestead Grays. At the height of their popularity in the early 1940s, black major-league teams still averaged only 1,600 spectators per game; the best players pocketed a mere $500 each month.

Largely ignored by the media, black baseballers toiled in obscurity. Theirs was a struggling sideshow, not the spectacular main event. Years later, Larry Doby, the first black to play in the American League, remembered that as a high school student growing up in the late 1930s, "there was nobody for me to identify with" except white New York Yankee stars. Black youths fantasized disguising themselves as whites, displaying their abilities for all the world to see, but realistically assumed that black people would never play baseball in the major leagues.

College football seemed a more promising alternative. "Blacks were playing, and that's what I wanted to get involved in," Doby later recalled. In truth, except for southern Negro colleges, pitifully few blacks played on university squads, even in those regions beyond the segregated South. A few prominent backfield stars such as Ozzie Simmons at Northwestern, Kenny Washington and Jackie Robinson at UCLA, Homer Harris at Iowa, Wilmeth Sidat-Singh at Syracuse, Buddy Young at Illinois, and Marion Motley at Nevada concealed the fact that black college football players were few and far between. Certainly the professional ranks were reserved "for whites only," just as surely as were public drinking fountains and toilet facilities in the Deep South.

Because of its slower development and closer connection to the college scene, professional football became racially segregated much later than did organized baseball. Black collegiate All-Americans Paul Robeson of Rutgers, Fritz Pollard of Brown, Jay Mayo "Inky" Williams of Brown, and "Duke" Slater of Iowa all played in the fledgling National Football League in the 1920s. Yet they were token representatives of their race. Only six blacks dotted the rosters of eighteen NFL clubs in 1926, and annually from 1928 to 1933 only one black player could be found. At the end of the 1933 season, NFL owners informally agreed to ban black players from their teams. When Kenny Washington, a triple-threat All-American, graduated from UCLA in 1939, he was totally ignored by NFL scouts.

The case of another college graduate, William "Dolly" King, best reflects the color barrier that limited even the exceptionally gifted black athlete before 1945. A three-year All-Scholastic choice in three sports at Brooklyn's Alexander Hamilton High School, King matriculated at Long Island University to star as an end on the football team, a catcher in baseball, and a basketball center-forward. When he graduated in the early 1940s, he received the cold shoulder from the New York Yankees, Giants, and Knickerbockers, which left him to drift into the hinterland of segregated black teams. Most devoted to basketball, he played for several inferior clubs before finally crossing the color line to play with the Rochester Royals in 1946. By then he was thirty years old.

In his earlier athletic youth, King's professional options were painfully few. One possibility was the New York Renaissance Big Five, the "Rens," an all-black touring team that had originated in Harlem in 1923. They were the rage in the late 1920s and 1930s. In their best season ever, 1932–33, they won 120 games and lost only eight. Often they beat the outstanding white team of the day, the Original Celtics. Their only serious competitors for black talent were another touring squad, the Harlem Globetrotters, a club founded by Abe Saperstein in 1927. Based in Chicago (the Harlem tag was a public-relations ploy), the original Globetrotters were disciplined, highly talented players, who regularly challenged the Rens for the unofficial professional black basketball championship.

Unlike the Rens, the Globetrotters survived the gas-rationing austerity of World War II. But they paid a high price for survival. Years earlier they had begun to enliven lopsided games against inferior local teams by introducing comic routines. Athletic pride succumbed to the necessity of commercial showmanship. With the arrival of an incomparable dribbler, Marques Haynes, and a gangly mimic, Reece "Goose" Tatum, the Globetrotters became the clown princes of the court. They warmed up to the music of "Sweet Georgia Brown," then proceeded to pass, fake, dribble, and shoot hilariously, turning basketball into more of a vaudeville act than a competitive sport. White and black spectators alike turned out in massive numbers to witness the outrageous performance. Unfortunately, the Globetrotters' antics merely confirmed white stereotypes of black men as physically talented but undisciplined, mischievous boys. Black youths no doubt laughed along with everyone else, but the Globetrotters hardly satisfied the youthful need for authentic athletic heroes.

During World War II the color barrier began to waver. In 1941 President Franklin D. Roosevelt issued an Executive Order forbidding racial discrimination in the hiring of workers in national defense industries, and in the course of the war, army units that had previously been segregated slowly broke with the Jim Crow tradition. Black soldiers fought and died alongside white Americans, prompting a congressman to introduce a resolution in the House of Representatives on 26 April 1945 calling for an end to "racial discrimination in our national game," baseball. The proposal died in committee. In the end, legislation and moral principles rode on the strong back of baseball owners' economic self-interest in breaking the racial barrier. Since many of their white stars were away at war, club directors saw their teams flounder, and they began to entertain the notion of stocking their rosters with some of the abundant black talent available in the two black major leagues.

Several tentative schemes surfaced in 1943. A rumor circulated to the effect that the lowly Pittsburgh Pirates were giving tryouts to three blacks, one of whom was a stocky, power-hitting catcher for the Baltimore Elite Giants, Roy Campanella. Nothing came of the rumors, but in the same year the owner of the Los Angeles Angels of the Pacific Coast League publicly announced tryouts for a trio of black players. The plan was smothered under a deluge of opposition from other owners. All the while the unorthodox owner of the Milwaukee Brewers in the American Association, Bill Veeck, planned to buy a shaky major-league franchise, the Philadelphia Phillies, subsequently to introduce proven black talent. Another entrepreneur beat him to the franchise and kept the Phillies white.

Where others failed, Branch Rickey, president of the Brooklyn Dodgers, succeeded. "We're gonna beat the bushes and take whatever comes out," Rickey told a business acquaintance in 1943, "and that might include a Negro player or two." Long hidden in the bushes of black baseball, several outstanding players commanded Rickey's attention. At the head of the Homestead Grays' charge to nine straight Negro World Series crowns (1937–45) were Buck Leonard, a smooth-fielding, powerful first baseman; Josh Gibson, a barrel-chested catcher of notorious strength who hit 800 or so home runs in a career that stretched over sixteen years; and James "Cool Papa" Bell, a swift outfielder who once stole 175 bases in a single season and hit .480 in another. Scattered among the other black professional clubs were the likes of Satchel Paige, a lanky, durable pitcher who was unquestionably the strongest drawing attraction of all the black stars, catcher Roy Campanella, and outfielders Monte Irvin and Sam Jethroe.

Rickey considered all these prospects. He sought intelligence as well as skill, courageous character no less than physical strength, youthful promise more than a proven record. On the last point alone he was forced to ignore many of the established black stars. In 1945, veterans Paige, Bell, Gibson, and Leonard averaged about forty years in age. "They say I was born too soon," Cool Papa Bell later remarked. "I say the doors were opened up too late."

As every sports fan knows, the door to professional baseball was opened when Branch Rickey selected Jackie Robinson as the first black in modern times to play in the major leagues. Born in 1919, in Cairo, Georgia, Robinson grew up in Pasadena, California, where his mother moved with her five children after being deserted by the father. The mother worked as a domestic maid in rich white homes in order to feed and clothe her children. Gang rumbles in the melting-pot neighborhood of poor Mexicans, Japanese, and blacks brought predictable brushes with the law. Only a local sports program kept Jack and his older brother, Mack, off the social rubbish heap. While Mack finished second to Jesse Owens in the 200 meters at the 1936 Olympics at Berlin, Jack starred in four sports (baseball, football, basketball and track) at Pasadena Junior College, then went on to do the same at UCLA. Shortly after Pearl Harbor he entered the army, and in late November 1944 he was discharged as a first lieutenant. In the spring of 1945 he signed to play with a professional black baseball club, the Kansas City Monarchs, for $400 a month.

Branch Rickey knew all this. Robinson's athletic versatility, college education, military experience, and relative youth (twenty-six in 1945) all weighed in his favor. Most important, he was still a proud determined man, scarred but unbroken by the racist attitudes and laws under which he had lived. Once at Camp Hood, Texas, he was ordered to the back of an army bus. He refused to comply, citing the law that banned racial discrimination on military bases. Brought to court-martial for "trying to start a race riot," he stood his ground and saw the charges dismissed. Jackie Robinson was no Uncle Tom.

Branch Rickey capitalized on that strength. In their first meeting, in August 1945, he played the devil's advocate as he grilled Robinson for three hours. "He knew every taunt, dig, threat and underhand device of the bigots," Robinson later recalled. "What will you do when they call you a dirty nigger bastard?" Rickey asked. "You have the wrong nigger," shot back Robinson. Backing down was not his style. Then Rickey made his point: "I want you to be strong enough *not* to fight back. You've got to do this job with base hits and stolen bases and by fielding ground balls, Jackie, nothing else." Out of that bizarre conversation, Robinson obtained a contract and a year's seasoning with the minor-league Montreal Royals, where he hit .349. In 1947 his scrappy style and pigeon-toed gait became permanent fixtures with the Brooklyn Dodgers. During a ten-year career, he played at five different positions, led the Dodgers to six National League pennants and one World Series crown, and compiled a lifetime major league batting average of .311.

Contrary to popular opinion, however, Robinson was not the first black athlete to cross the color line in professional sports after World War II. Two of his old teammates at UCLA, Kenny Washington and Woody Strode, broke into the National Football League in the autumn of 1945, shortly after Robinson first signed with the Dodgers. For a new NFL franchise, the Los Angeles Rams, Washington and Strode probably were signed as much for their local appeal as for their abilities. Strode lasted only one year; Washington played several seasons, but injuries prevented him from ever reaching his earlier All-American peak. In 1946, the year Robinson played in Montreal,

Characteristic of Jackie Robinson's scrappy style of play was this steal of home in the 1955 World Series. Yankee catcher Yogi Berra had a slight disagreement with the umpire. (Courtesy of the Los Angeles Dodgers.)

a new team in a new professional football league played two blacks, fullback Marion Motley and guard Bill Willis, who were signed by coach Paul Brown of the Cleveland Browns in the All-America Conference. Even a couple of black basketballers beat Robinson to the big leagues. For the season of 1946–47, William "Pop" Gates played with the Buffalo Bisons and Tri-City Blackhawks, and William "Dolly" King toiled for the Rochester Royals in the National Basketball League.

Yet Robinson's breakthrough, while not the first, was unquestionably the most important. In terms of spectator appeal and media coverage, baseball was still America's national game, rivaled only by college football in the postwar era; professional football and basketball were still struggling. More-over, Robinson's difficulties and accomplishments combined to create an epic drama unequaled by any of the other athletes breaking the color barrier. Southern hostility in spring training and exhibition swings northward, opposition from several bigoted teammates, and constant taunts from opponents all made Robinson's Rookie of the Year honors in 1947 a massive achievement. He kept his proud, fiery temper under wraps until 1949, when Branch Rickey finally released him from his vow of compliance. In that year he began to talk back to umpires, opponents, and hostile fans; he also enjoyed his greatest year ever at the plate, batting .342, and was voted the Most Valuable Player in the National League.

By then Robinson was no longer a lone black man in a white baseball world. Roy Campanella and Don Newcombe had joined the Dodgers. Larry Doby had broken the color line in the American League by starting in center field for the Cleveland Indians in 1947, and at mid-season of the next year the Indians hired a forty-two-year-old rookie, Satchel Paige, who came through with a 6–1 record. By 1950 five major-league clubs fielded blacks. Nor was the new National Basketball Association far behind. In 1950 Earl Lloyd joined the Syracuse Nationals, Chuck Cooper the Boston Celtics, and Nathaniel "Sweetwater" Clifton the New York Knickerbockers, trailblazers on the path that was to lead to black dominance of the hoop game. In the same year Althea Gibson became the first black ever to compete for the United States tennis championship at Forest Hills.

In the Deep South of course, college athletics, minor-league baseball, and even public tennis and golf facilities remained racially segregated throughout the 1950s. A landmark Supreme Court decision of 1954, *Brown v. Board of Education of Topeka*, prohibited enforced segregation of schools, thereby setting in motion a long-term change in southern athletic activities. Bitter resistance to that change came as no surprise to outside observers. Not so predictable was an outburst of black resentment in the 1960s against subtle discriminatory practices in supposedly integrated sports.

The Revolt of the Black Athlete

In the wake of the initial breakthrough of black athletes, several emerged in the mid-1950s with the ability to overshadow all their white competitors. Willie Mays, for example, in his first full season with the New York Giants (1954) hit 41 home runs, drove in 110 runs, and finished with a batting average of .345. More than statistics, Mays electrified crowds with his timely hits, circus catches, and dashing style on the bases. His sensational catch of a 450-foot shot off the bat of Vic Wertz in a 1954 World Series game at the Polo Grounds still stands as one of baseball's all-time gems. In the same year, and with much less fanfare, a modest young black, Henry "Hank" Aaron, made his debut in the National League, destined to achieve the unimaginable feat of breaking Babe Ruth's career home-run record.

While Mays and Aaron set their sails, a gangly six-foot, ten-inch center at the University of San Francisco led his basketball team to a phenomenal two-year record of fifty-seven wins and one loss. A masterful defensive rebounder and blocker of shots, Bill Russell joined the Boston Celtics in 1956 to anchor eleven of the next thirteen NBA championships. His only individual challenger of note was another black giant, seven-foot, one-inch Wilt ("Wilt the Stilt") Chamberlain, who entered the NBA in 1959, and in 1961–62 set league records for average points per game (50) and most points in a single game (100). Never in the history of the NBA has a match-up equaled the intensity and skill of the Russell-Chamberlain rivalry.

All the while, fullback Jimmy Brown was undoubtedly the dominant player in the National Football League for the entirety of his career with the Cleveland Browns from 1957–1966. Big, fast, and strong, Brown set numerous records, including an average of 5.2 yards each time he carried the ball. Until he retired to pursue an acting career, he played in every Pro Bowl for which he was eligible. He stood as a colossus astride the professional football world, and he remains the standard by which the best running backs are evaluated.

Yet exceptional performers did not a general pattern of integration and equality make. Only in 1959 did the last major-league baseball team, the Boston Red Sox, sign a black player. By 1963 native-born blacks still represented a mere 10 percent of all players in organized baseball; colored Latin Americans, always marginally acceptable, constituted another 5 percent. Professional football and basketball rosters were somewhat more representative of black talent, but barely. At any rate, beyond the formal criteria of numbers lay more serious problems of discrimination. By 1960 black athletes still often found themselves socially and physically segregated from their white teammates on road trips. Their professional salaries were noticeably smaller. They were stereotyped for a limited number of positions (for example, running backs and receivers, not quarterbacks and centers in football). On college campuses, they were customarily banned from most fraternities. Originally in the vanguard of the postwar movement for civil rights, the sporting establishment in the 1960s was weighed and found wanting in its treatment of black athletes.

The revolt of the black athlete was part of a larger surge of militant action for justice and self-respect. First were sit-ins and pray-ins, freedom rides, and freedom marches for equal opportunity in housing, employment, education, and public facilities. Martin Luther King's message of passive resistance was met with ugly incidents of violence in southern towns such as Montgomery, Little Rock, Greensboro, Nashville, and Selma. In the mid-1960s blacks responded in kind in the northern ghettos of Newark, Detroit, and Milwaukee, and in the Watts section of Los Angeles. "Burn, baby, burn," declared Malcolm X, Stokely Carmichael, and H. Rap Brown, articulate spokesmen of Black Power. "Black is beautiful" became the rallying cry for black pride, uniqueness, and strength.

In 1963 Dick Gregory, a black activist and comedian, attempted to organize a boycott of an American-Russian track meet, protesting the inferior housing and social activities provided for black athletes. In the following year he led a small band of blacks in picketing the Tokyo Olympics. Quickly that trickle of protest turned into a flood. In 1965, when black players arrived in New Orleans to compete in the American Football League's East-West All-Star game, they found the doors of the city's leading social clubs closed in their faces. They quickly agreed to boycott the event, requiring the commissioner of the league to move the game to another city. For the first time, the solidarity of black athletes forced a change in business as usual.

Movements require leaders. Three emerged to the forefront of the black athletic revolt. One was Bill Russell, the perennial championship center of the Boston Celtics, whose autobiography, *Go Up For Glory* (as told to William

In his usual dominant fashion, Bill Russell blocks a drive to the basket by Happy Hairston of the Cincinnati Royals, while two NBA youthfuls, John Havlicek and Oscar Robertson, look on. (Courtesy of the National Basketball Association.)

McSweeny), appeared in 1966 as an entirely new kind of athlete's journal. Amid all his notes on locker-room gossip and basketball strategies, Russell was primarily concerned with issues of human rights and dignity. He refused to align himself with the Black Muslims but nevertheless defended the Black Power movement as "a focal point for the torments of men who needed a far-out proposal to shock them from their depravity." Most of all, he identified himself as a strong-willed black man who happened to be an athlete: "For the record, I am a proud, reasonably happy man, who was blessed by God in being born a Negro. I am happy to be a Negro. I am happy to share in the problems of the Negro here in America." No social activist, Russell fed black pride by word and athletic presence.

Similar pride led another outstanding athlete to cast his lot with the Black Muslims. Cassius Clay, the "Louisville Lip" of 1960 Olympics fame, reacted to the racist attitudes in his hometown by throwing his gold medal in the Ohio River. In 1964 he defeated Sonny Liston for the heavyweight crown and promptly shocked the sporting world by changing his name to Muhammad Ali. To identify openly with the Black Muslims was one thing; to appear unpatriotic in the midst of the Vietnam War was another matter altogether. "I ain't got nothin' against them Viet Congs," Ali announced publicly early in 1966. His Louisville Draft Board, under pressure from the Justice Department, revoked an earlier deferment and reclassified him 1-A. As racist slurs and patriotic rhetoric pelted down from all quarters, on 28 April 1967 Ali refused induction into the army. In an unprecedented move, the New York Athletic Commission stripped him of his title before his case came to trial. Subsequently, Ali was convicted of draft evasion, fined $10,000, and sentenced to five years in prison. Finally, in 1971 the Supreme Court reversed the decision on the grounds that the Justice Department had tampered with Ali's local draft board. Out of the ring for more than three years, Muhammad Ali became, in the words of Harry Edwards, "the warrior saint in the revolt of the black athlete in America."

While Ali and Russell provided inspirational models of courage, Harry Edwards emerged in 1967 as an organizing force in the movement for black dignity. Verbally gifted and physically large like Ali and Russell, the six-foot, eight-inch Edwards had hung up his athletic togs for an academic position as a junior professor of sociology at his alma mater, San José State College, California. Unlike Ali and Russell, he was most concerned with racial discrimination at the intercollegiate level. Examples of the problem were easy to find. In 1966 Texas Western (now the University of Texas at El Paso) defeated Kentucky, 72–65, in the finals of the NCAA basketball championships. Five black starters, all recruited from the New York City area, magnificently represented the predominantly white Texas college. Shortly after the season, however, they began dropping out of school. Academically deprived and socially frustrated, not a single one graduated. Jack Olsen later publicized the case in a series of five articles entitled "The Black Athlete—A Shameful Story" in *Sports Illustrated* (July 1968). "All the standard methods of dealing with black athletes are used at UTEP," concluded Olsen, "and in the sum they add up to the same old story: the black athlete is there to perform, not to get an education, and when he has used up his eligibility, he is out."

For the opening game of the 1967 football season, San José State was scheduled to host the University of Texas at El Paso. Edwards, supported by a number of black graduate students and athletes, planned a boycott of the game to call attention to the racism at both schools. His group, the United Black Students for Action, distributed circulars and held rallies, declaring that they would resort to any means necessary to prevent the game from being played. The governor of California, Ronald Reagan, threatened to call out the state militia to ensure the safety of players and spectators, but the president of San José State intervened to cancel the game at a loss of thousands of dollars of gate receipts. Edwards's organization then submitted nine specific demands for action against athletic and academic discrimination at San José State.

The forthcoming Olympic Games provided a larger, more visible forum for protest. In October 1967 Edwards formed the Olympic Committee for Human Rights to organize a boycott of the 1968 Olympics. Jesse Owens, Ralph Metcalfe, Rafer Johnson, and several other black Olympic medalists opposed the plan. In a classic example of the generation gap, Owens vigorously argued that sports were the great social equalizer, but he was dismissed as an Uncle Tom out of touch with the new, angry mood of American blacks. In February 1968 the Olympic Committee for Human Rights picketed a track meet sponsored by the New York Athletic Club. Next they "white-listed" the athletic programs at the University of Washington and the University of California at Berkeley, exerting so much pressure at Berkeley that the athletic director and head basketball coach finally resigned. In all, demonstrative gestures of discontent shook thirty-seven major colleges and universities in 1967–68.

Complaints varied from place to place, but most common were demands for fair housing, open fraternity policies, and equal perquisites such as summer jobs and part-time work; for more black coaches and athletic administrators; for better academic tutoring programs, and for courses in black history and literature. Some bold souls even called for the dismissal of tenured faculty and coaches who appeared to be blatantly racist. "But the real motive behind the demonstrations," insisted Edwards, "was the regaining of black dignity, pride, and some degree of self-determination."

The revolt peaked in 1968 at the Mexico City Olympics. A few black athletes, such as All-American basketballer Lew Alcindor (Kareem Abdul-Jabbar) of UCLA, boycotted the games altogether. Others, such as sprinters Tommy Smith and John Carlos of San José State, reluctantly decided to compete rather than fragment black representation on the Olympic team. In the 200-meter race, Smith finished first and Carlos third. They mounted the victory stand shoeless, wearing black socks; Smith wore a black scarf around his neck. As the "Star-Spangled Banner" played, both men lowered their heads and raised a clenched, black fist. Silently they stood, defying American prestige and Olympic protocol. They were immediately expelled from the team and ejected from the Olympic Village. Yet their protest was seen, and felt, around the world. No longer could Americans ignore what Pete Axthelm of *Newsweek* called "the angry black athletes."

Not all blacks acted out their anger, of course. Ten days after Smith and Carlos gave their black-power salutes, George Foreman finished off a Russian opponent in the finals of the heavyweight boxing division, then danced around the ring waving a small American flag. "I'm just proud to be an American," he later explained. "That wasn't intended as any kind of demonstration." Intended or not, it was interpreted as a patriotic gesture. Significantly, Foreman was praised, not reprimanded, for his political act. Americans beleaguered by two recent assassinations (of Martin Luther King and Robert Kennedy) and student demonstrations against the Vietnam War grasped at straws of warm-hearted patriotism. That the demonstration came from a black Olympic champion was all the more consoling.

Yet racial tensions persisted. In October 1969 fourteen black football players for the University of Wyoming Cowboys decided to wear black armbands in a game against Brigham Young University, to protest the

Articulate as well as strong, fast, and durable, tailback Herschel Walker of the University of Georgia began the decade of the 1980s as one of the many black athletes dominating the campus scene in the previously segregated South. (Courtesy of the University of Georgia.)

Mormons' refusal to ordain blacks. The Wyoming coach reacted by dropping the entire black contingency from his squad. Faculty, athletic department, and local Laramie citizens fought bitterly over the issue. Finally, in 1972 a Circuit Court of Appeals ruled that the university, as represented by its football coach, had acted within its rights. By then the issue of the black athlete had risen to the surface of the Big Ten, one of the earliest integrated and most racially tolerant of all the intercollegiate conferences. Originating at Michigan State University, a report to the Big Ten Commissioner detailed the grievances of black athletes. The report concluded on a candid note: "The patterns of racial discrimination both overt and covert, institutional and individual, found in the larger society are reflected in and perpetuated in athletics in the United States." This point of view seemed obvious by 1972, but only because it was brought to the fore in the 1960s.

Born in the era of civil rights, Black Power, and the antiwar movement, the revolt of the black athlete subsided in the early 1970s. While black Americans everywhere abandoned confrontation tactics in favor of orderly political, economic, and educational gains, black athletes similarly turned to more moderate measures. During the 1970s even southern athletic teams became fully integrated. By 1980 a freshman black quarterback called the signals at the University of Alabama. Another freshman, Herschel Walker, led the University of Georgia to a national championship, and a black at the University of South Carolina, George Rogers, won the Heisman Trophy. Various covert forms of discrimination still exist, but black athletes no longer sit passively at the back of the bus.

Women on the Move

Women athletes are now also a force to be reckoned with. In 1977 an all-male International Olympic Committee decreed that women in the 1980 Olympics should not be allowed to compete in a 3,000-meter race (about two miles) because it was too grueling for "the fairer sex." Within the week of that decision, however, a young Texan named Peggy Kokernot ran sixteen miles through the state of Alabama as part of a women's relay team conveying a torch from Seneca Falls, New York (the site of the first women's rights gathering in 1848), to the opening of the National Women's Conference in Houston. More than two thousand women participated in the relay, all wearing T-shirts stamped with the motto "Women on the Move." Once the flame went out. Unable to find a new wick, a woman produced a Kotex, stuffed it in the brass tube, lit it, and continued the relay. As the torch arrived in Houston, Bella Abzug, an outspoken New York politician who was fifty-seven years old and overweight, ran alongside the T-shirted trackster into the packed convention hall. Three First Ladies, Rosalynn Carter, Betty Ford, and Lady Bird Johnson, joined in the celebration of women's rights. "We've had to run pretty hard to get some doors open," one participant observed. The mixture of athletics and feminism was symbolically appropriate.

So was the presence of women politicians, for the new visibility of women athletes is largely a spin-off from the feminist movement of the 1960s, when Betty Friedan, Kate Millett, and Gloria Steinem led women out of the kitchen and into the political arena. Within the past decade women have become competitive, and in sports especially, they are discarding an age-old image of passivity and weakness.

Even the best of the female athletes before World War II performed as oddities in an athletic world defined by men. The postwar situation was hardly any different. Florence Chadwick, who achieved widespread publicity by swimming the English Channel in 1951, and Maureen "Little Mo" Connolly, who won the Grand Slam of tennis (Wimbledon, Forest Hills, and the French and Australian titles) in 1953, both typified the loneliness of the female athlete. A famous one-liner in the mid-1950s immortalized the difference between the athletic male and the proper ladylike image. "Hey, Mr. President, how's Mamie's golf?" Babe Didrikson Zaharias teasingly asked President Eisenhower each time they met. Mamie, of course, did not play golf, Ike's favorite game. When Babe Zaharias won her last Woman Athlete of the Year award in 1954, she was considered no less unusual than when she took the 1932 Los Angeles Olympics by storm. Althea Gibson, the first black ever to win a Wimbledon championship (1957), and Wilma Rudolph, the Tennessee track star who dazzled the audience at the 1960 Olympics, similarly challenged but hardly destroyed the assumption of female athletic incompetence. Like Dr. Samuel Johnson's woman preacher in the eighteenth century, a female athlete in the 1950s and early 1960s seemed comparable to a dog walking upright on its hind legs: it could not walk well, but people were surprised to see it walk at all.

Women athletes in the Soviet Union and Iron Curtain countries fared somewhat better. The Soviets promoted women's as well as men's sports to publicize the virtues of the Communist system in the Olympic Games. More important, Communist ideology called for the social emancipation of women, and sport was encouraged to that end. In truth, older Soviet sportswomen merely added athletic programs to their traditional chores as mothers and housewives, but gifted schoolgirls were encouraged to put sports uppermost in their minds. Gymnastics, long popular in Eastern Europe, were made to order for supple females, as were the shot put and discus throw for brawny peasant women. Soviet teams dominated the Olympics in the 1950s and early 1960s largely because their women athletes piled up such huge scores.

In the less regimented West, women athletes struggled individually against sex sterotypes before women's sports became a part of the female liberation movement in the mid-1960s. Billie Jean King is a representative transition figure. Born Billie Jean Moffitt in 1943, she was a tomboyish softball enthusiast in her California youth, but she took to tennis because it seemed a more ladylike game. Yet the lady was not for bridling. Humble origins fired her competitive impulse, producing a forceful, aggressive style of play. In 1961, at seventeen, she won her first doubles title at Wimbledon, and in 1966 she captured her first of five Wimbledon singles championships. Four singles titles in the United States Open and one each in the Australian (1968), Italian (1970), and French (1972) championships combined with her Wimbledon feats to make her the most widely known female athlete of her era.

In sheer athletic achievement, King trailed Margaret (Smith) Court, a tall, strong Australian whose twelve-year tennis career sparkled with singles, doubles, and mixed-doubles titles in every major championship. In 1970 Court repeated "Little Mo" Connolly's Grand Slam. When she retired from competitive tennis in 1974, her tournament trophies numbered eighty-five, a record without parallel in the history of the game.

Yet it was Billie Jean King, not Margaret Court, who hitched the female athlete's wagon to the feminist star. In the late 1960s, King twice led boycotts against tournaments in which cash prizes for women amounted to only 10 percent of the money offered male competitors. In 1970 she convinced Phillip-Morris Tobacco Company to invest in a new venture for women, the Virginia Slims Tournament, and in the following year she became the first female athlete ever to earn $100,000 for a year's effort. "Money is what people respect," she remarked, "and when you are a professional athlete, they want to know how much you have made. They judge you on that."

Commerical sponsors similarly judged women athletes and in the early 1970s found them profitable investments. Colgate-Palmolive, featuring the Colgate Dinah Shore golf tournament, did for women golfers what Virginia Slims did for the tennis circuit. In 1970 the twenty-one tournaments sponsored by the Ladies Professional Golf Association offered only $435,000 in prize money; by 1980 their purses bulged to about $5 million, a tenfold increase within the decade. Women's professional tennis made even greater gains, from $200,000 in 1970 to more than $9 million in 1980.

One of the more dramatic sporting events of the decade occurred in the Houston Astrodome on the evening of 30 September 1973, when Billie Jean King carried the women's banner against Bobby Riggs. Wimbledon champion of 1939, the fifty-five-year-old Riggs was far past his athletic prime. But he was a hustling showman, a self-proclaimed "male chauvinist pig." Earlier in the year, purposely on Mother's Day, he had challenged and soundly defeated Margaret Court. Prior to his match with King, he mercilessly taunted feminists with the promise that he would trounce King and thereby "set women's lib back twenty years, to get women back into the home, where they belong." His antics stirred up massive interest in the match. More than 30,000 fans, the largest live audience ever assembled for a tennis match, showed up at the Astrodome, and some 48 million watched on television. After the first set, the outcome was never in doubt. Riggs puffed and duffed; King dashed and slashed to a 6–4, 6–3, 6–3 victory. In one sense, the match proved merely that a female tennis player in her prime could easily defeat an aged male opponent. But the event, a media extravaganza as much as an athletic contest, focused attention on female athletes in a way never before imagined.

For all her bold strokes and outspoken ways, however, Billie Jean King won her fame in a game traditionally open to females. Chris Evert, Tracy Austin, and Martina Navratilova followed suit in tennis, as did Debbie Austin and Nancy Lopez in golf, the other sport long infiltrated by women. More unorthodox were women such as Diane Crump, Barbara Jo Rubin, Robyn Smith, and Mary Bacon, the first female jockeys. All began racing in 1969. The jockey profession, requiring lightweights with stamina rather than brute strength, was ideally suited to the female frame; only social convention had kept women out of the stables and off the tracks. But on 2 May 1970 Diane Crump became the first woman jockey ever to ride in the Kentucky Derby, and in the following year Mary Bacon became the first to ride 100 winners in a single season.

Women also invaded the male-dominated world of auto racing during the 1970s. Until 1973 no women—including racers' wives—were allowed even in the pits of the Indianapolis 500. In 1977, however, the barrier came crashing down as the traditional starting signal, "Gentlemen, start your engines," had to be revised in recognition of Janet Guthrie. "In company with the first lady ever to qualify at Indianapolis," blared a careful announcer, "gentlemen, start your engines." Mechanical difficulty forced Guthrie to drop out in 1977,

As Title IX focuses attention on women's sports in schools and universities, young women annually improve their skills in vigorous competition. This scene at a high school basketball tournament is regularly
enacted throughout the United States. (Courtesy of the *Bangor Daily
News*.)

but in the following year she finished ninth, ahead of Indy stalwarts such as
Mario Andretti and Johnny Rutherford. Yet even Janet Guthrie's competitive
profile is low compared to the fierce determination of Shirley Muldowney, a
petite professional drag racer who earns about $200,000 a year. "It's incredi-
bly exciting—and cutthroat," says Muldowney of her profession. Her eyes
agleam as she talks of winning, Muldowney captures the essence of athletic
women on the move: "I found I just have the knack for this sport, and a lot of
the fellas hate to race me 'cause they know they're gonna get whipped."

Male auto drivers getting beaten by concealed, goggled women drivers
was one thing; thinly clad long-distance runners trailing female competitors
was another matter altogether. In 1967 Katherine Switzer registered for the
Boston Marathon as K. Switzer and was not detected until she began
shedding her baggy sweatsuit. Horrified males attempted to remove her
bodily from the race. Until 1971 the rules of the Boston Marathon expressly
forbade the participation of women. In the following year Nina Kuscsik, a
thirty-three-year-old mother of three, finished ahead of 400 men marathon-

ers. Long-distance women runners became common in the course of the decade. Whereas only one woman entered (and failed to finish) the New York Marathon in 1970, no less than 2,465 ran in 1980.

Female participation in top-flight marathons stemmed largely from the burgeoning of cross-country and track-and-field programs for girls in American high schools and colleges. The number of high school girls on cross-country teams, for example, rose from a mere 1,719 in 1970 to 59,005 in 1979; schoolgirl track-and-field competitors in the same period leaped from 62,211 to 430,266. The women's movement had percolated down to the schools, allowing girls to shed old stereotypes of physical inactivity. More important, a legislative bombshell, Title IX of the Education Amendment Act of 1972, had a revolutionary effect on girl's sports programs in the schools. In the words of Title IX, "No person in the United States shall, on the basis of sex, be excluded from participation in, be denied the benefits of, or be subjected to discrimination under any educational program or activity receiving federal financial assistance." Here was a mandate for administrators of about 17,000 public school systems to begin correcting the imbalance in male and female athletic facilities, equipment, coaches, and travel funds.

Greater still were the benefits of Title IX for women athletes in the 3,000 or so colleges and universities in the United States. A new governing body for women's competitive sports, the Association for Intercollegiate Athletics for Women (AIAW), founded only a year prior to the passage of Title IX, served as a pressure group for enforcement of the legislation. Its opposition was predictably strong. The ruling body of men's intercollegiate athletics, the National Collegiate Athletic Association (NCAA), spent more than $200,000 lobbying against the bill. Once Title IX became law, however, athletic directors were forced to walk the thin line between compliance with the law and protection of big money-making sports such as men's football and basketball. No doubt almost every college campus in the United States had its own unique cases of conflict arising from the implementation of Title IX. Some involved grossly unequal facilities, equipment, uniforms, and coaching staffs; others had to do with the time allotted for training and practice sessions; still others were concerned with travel budgets and arrangements. But all are local variations on a national theme of traditional male prerogatives being challenged by female athletic interests.

Women's swimming, track, field hockey, and gymnastic teams especially gained from the equal-opportunity emphasis of Title IX. Most of all, women's intercollegiate basketball programs flourished. By 1980 about 900 schools sponsored varsity women's teams, compared to 215 in 1970. Like Third World nations struggling for recognition through sports, small colleges turned to women's basketball as a fast avenue to recognition. Old Dominion University in Norfolk, Virginia, is a good example. According to its athletic director, Old Dominion saw "the potential for visibility and the potential for revenue" in a championship squad. It got both. Led by Nancy Lieberman, a quick, aggressive floor general, and Inge Nissen, a six-foot, seven-inch center imported from Sweden, the team regularly played before packed houses on their way to the national championship in 1978.

Highly competitive basketball tournaments are of an altogether different order from sexually integrated physical-education classes, women bowling and playing softball for fun, or turning out for daily jogs alongside male companions. Yet all these activities signify the arrival of the new sporting woman. All are extensions as well as products of the women's movement for equality of opportunity, freedom of choice, and (most important) self-respect.

Miles to Go

For women, as for blacks, the struggle is far from over. Billie Jean King made the point succinctly in an interview shortly after she devastated Bobby Riggs in 1973: "Tennis has always been reserved for the rich, the white, the males—and I've always been pledged to change all that. There's still a lot to be done." Now almost a decade later, many questions remain unanswered; directions seem unclear.

Title IX heads the list of imponderables. How can it be applied equitably for women without destroying the men's spectator sports, which produce revenue for the support of entire athletic programs? Originally the Department of Health, Education and Welfare (HEW) interpreted the antidiscriminatory core of Title IX literally. Confronted with a flurry of opposition from college presidents, athletic directors, and NCAA lobbyists, HEW officials backed down. Each year they dispensed progressively weaker guidelines of implementation. In 1979 they came up with a formula based on the "participation rate" of women and men athletes, but the trend is toward a hands-off policy on revenue-producing men's teams. In the United States in the 1980s under President Ronald Reagan, who campaigned for less governmental intervention in local affairs, the future of Title IX is bleak.

Also bleak is the dilemma facing women athletes when they consider the implications of total integration of the sexes in competitive events. Women jockeys and auto drivers can compete against men because smaller physiques work to advantage as horses and machines provide raw strength. Football, baseball, and basketball require quite a different set of physical attributes. One of the best basketballers in the college class of '79, Ann Meyers of UCLA, lasted less than a week in the training camp of the professional Indiana Pacers. Even in tennis and golf, a total disregard of sexual differences would probably work to women's disadvantage. "If they had to tee up from the same place as the men, play the same golf course under the same conditions, they wouldn't qualify," says Arnold Palmer. "And I think all the women would agree with me." All *might* not agree; most would. Certainly the AIAW recognizes that sexual integration of all athletic teams would merely allow males to dominate rosters as well as the administrative control of sports. Thus the AIAW has charted a separate-but-equal course for women's intercollegiate athletics. The problem is that such a policy easily degenerates into a separate-and-inferior status on the order of black Americans before 1954. The need to balance female athletes' rights against the uniqueness of women's sports is an item high on the agenda for the future.

While adults acknowledge physical differences in male and female athletes, some schoolgirls have proved themselves on a par with boys their own age. Several court cases in the 1970s enabled pigtailed girls to compete on Little League baseball teams. In 1978 a Texas federal judge ruled that a girl, Linda Williams, should be allowed to play on a boy's high school baseball team. In the same year an Ohio judge decreed that no girl could be banned from rough team sports such as football and ice hockey simply because of her sex. These breakthroughs brought latent biases to the surface. Even the liberal-minded James Michener suggests (in *Sports in America*) that the customary separation of male and female athletes between the ages of twelve and twenty-two "conforms to some permanent psychological need of the human race." If the urbane Michener can argue "that to reverse the custom might produce more harm than good," then one can only conclude that though slim Virginias have "come a long way, baby," they still have a long way to go in dispelling myths about female participation in sports.

At the professional level, women athletes have miles to go before they can claim equality with men. A woman jockey has yet to win a Kentucky Derby; no female auto driver has even come close to taking the checkered flag at the Indianapolis 500. Despite the rapid improvement in cash prizes available for women golfers and tennis players, their purses are still considerably less than the men's. One of the latest ventures in sports, women's professional basketball, struggled for its life. Founded in 1978, the Women's Basketball League (WBL) barely survived its first season. The New Orleans franchise, for example, drew 7,000 curious spectators to its first game, but then saw its crowd drop to a mere 1,545 the next night. Attendance at one game dipped to a disastrous low of 425. The pattern was common throughout the league as the novelty of the new game wore off. During the second season of play, attendance averaged only 3,000. At season's end, just three of the original eight clubs remained intact.

Entering the 1980–81 season, the WBL for the first time featured several players who had won fame in intercollegiate competition—names such as Ann Meyers, Nancy Lieberman, and Carol Blazejowski. In her last season at Montclair State (New Jersey), Blazejowski averaged about forty points a game, ending her collegiate career with a record total of 3,199 points (second only to "Pistol Pete" Maravich). Her scoring potential was the kind of tonic needed to complement the teamwork, tight defense, and hustle that might have brought popularity to women's professional basketball. Unfortunately, the WBL folded in the middle of the 1981–82 season.

Inexperience similarly plagues women sportswriters and sportscasters. Female sportswriters are still pitifully few and (in most cases) professionally weak. Questions of modesty and jock conservatism aside, women will overcome the reluctance of male athletes to open locker room doors only when they prove themselves analytically respectable as reporters. Most women television sportscasters have even farther to go. Except for the occasional female tennis or Olympic commentator, women on camera at televised sporting events are ornaments at best. As of 1982, women in the various studios producing professional football games on Sunday afternoons are as commercially packaged and mindless as are the gaudy, scantily clad cheerleaders on the sidelines. Someday an athletic equivalent of Barbara Walters will shed light upon Monday night football or the World Series. Women in the broadcaster's booth, the coaching box, and the administrator's office will signify a culmination of the emergence of women in sports.

Historically related to the female quest for equality, black athletes also have some unfinished tasks to accomplish. Despite the protests of the 1960s, blacks in team sports are still "stacked" at certain positions. In football they continue to fill running back, wide receiver, and cornerback slots rather than quarterback, center, pulling guard, or inside linebacker. Only 4 or 5 percent of all major-league pitchers and catchers are black. No doubt some choice is involved. Early in their athletic life, young blacks apparently decide to play at positions in which they might best succeed. They usually imitate black collegiate and professional stars, therefore choosing positions customarily assigned to blacks. Whatever the reasons for the stacking, with not a single black pitcher or catcher in the 1980 World Series between the Phillies and the Royals, and with only two starting quarterbacks out of twenty-eight teams in the National Football League, one can only conclude that blacks still have a way to go in claiming the glamor positions in American sports.

Several sports remain foreign to blacks. At the moment few golfers can be seen following the tortured path of Charlie Sifford, who first played in the Greensboro Open in 1960, or Lee Elder, the first black participant in the Masters Tornament in Augusta, Georgia, in 1974. Major tennis tournaments are similarly lily-white. If a Black Tennis Hall of Fame were created tomorrow, Wimbledon champions Althea Gibson and Arthur Ashe would be lonely comrades in an otherwise empty room. Ice hockey is another sport from which blacks are virtually absent. Prohibitive cost is too easy an explanation of the problem, especially with all the public courts, links, and rinks now available. Customary patterns of preference dissolve slowly, and blacks have customarily turned to boxing and the team sports of baseball, football, and basketball. Black as well as white racial attitudes, pressures, and practices persist in subtle forms.

Not so subtle is the discrimination against blacks at the management level in sports. America has few black doctors, lawyers, and congressmen, but it has even fewer black coaches and athletic administrators. By 1982 the National Football League had yet to hire a black head coach, although more than half the players in the NFL are black. At the college level, no black coach led any of the top twenty teams ranked by the Associated Press. For teams in the National Basketball Association, three-quarters of whose rosters were composed of black players, only three black coaches—Lenny Wilkens, Al Attles, and Paul Silas—called the shots. College basketball ranks, similarly dominated by black athletes, were no better in terms of black coaches. Of the 249 top-division college basketball programs (including twelve predominantly black universities) in the United States in 1980, a mere thirteen were run by black coaches.

Nor has organized baseball fulfilled the promise of the Jackie Robinson saga. Only three blacks have ever managed major-league clubs. When managerial posts become open, with dull consistency the bright, veteran black candidates are ignored in favor of unknown whites. Front-office positions seem similarly closed to blacks. Henry Aaron, the director of player personnel for the Atlanta Braves, is the only black occupying an important front-office job for any big-league club. Now that black professional athletes are enjoying the high salaries, commercial endorsements, and media acclaim once reserved for whites only, surely management is the next frontier on which the black struggle for equality will be waged.

On their way to the promised land, however, a few black athletes have stopped to sound a warning to ghetto youths who unwisely set their sights on the milk and honey of professional sports. All play and no study makes Jack, black as well as white, a dumb boy, useless for anything except the risky jock world. As a career option, sports is a risky choice indeed. Of the innumerable high school players, relatively few receive athletic scholarships to college. Of the thousands of college athletes, only a handful receive professional contracts, to embark upon a most uncertain and brief career. Georgetown University's outstanding black basketball coach, John Thompson, wisely keeps a deflated basketball in his office, reminding him that when his athletes no longer have basketball they had better have a college degree.

The road from Ebbets Field, where Jackie Robinson first crossed the color line in 1947, can easily become a dead end filled with the wreckage of black youths, who waste their educational and career opportunities in pursuit of sports. "We have been on the same roads—sports and entertainment—too long," declared Arthur Ashe in an interview for the *New York Times* in 1977. "We need to pull over, fill up at the library, and speed away to Congress and the Supreme Court, the unions and the business world." For too many whites as well as blacks, for females as well as males, sport easily becomes a barrier—rather than a breaker of barriers—to the good life.

Chapter 19

SPORTS BIZ

There is no business like show business—except sports business. Produced, packaged, and sold as entertainment in a manner reminiscent of vaudeville and the Hollywood film industry, sports since World War II have taken on all the characteristics of show biz. Commercial interests reign. As eager investors supply the capital, a star system provides the glitter that attracts an audience for the show. Agents take their cut of the profits, as do stagehands, equipment companies, and promotional advertisers. Allied especially with television, sports biz thrives throughout the Western world.

In the wake of World War II, soccer football in Europe and South America exemplified the tendency of modern sport to expand its commercial base, for professional athletes to demand higher salaries and better contractual terms, and for spectator appeal and television revenue to make it all possible. Yet American entrepreneurs wrote the script on how to succeed in sports biz by really trying. Professional baseball, football, basketball, and ice-hockey leagues expanded geographically to saturate the nation with live as well as televised sports events. College and university athletic programs similarly plunged headlong into the business maze. Athletes at all levels performed heroically, but often as pawns for commercial purposes. The best athletes prospered.

Within the past two decades, traditional amateur athletes such as tennis players, golfers, Olympic competitors, and even cricketers have forsaken their amateur heritage in favor of money. As never before, the character of sports and games is undergoing fundamental changes in response to the demands of the marketplace.

Cups of Gold

Outside North America, soccer football is the most popular and commercially prosperous of all sports in the Western world. In South America especially, it

Whether in the World Cup, club matches, or school competition, soccer is the one game that is universally popular. (Courtesy of the University of Maine at Orono.)

is played, promoted, and watched with an intensity that borders on the fanatical. For the final match in the 1950 World Cup, more that 200,000 spectators filled monstrous Maracaña Stadium in Rio de Janeiro to watch their home team, Brazil, lose narrowly to archrival Uruguay, 2–1. The Brazilian coach, Flavio Costa, reportedly earned the equivalent of nearly $3,000 a month for his efforts. Virtually all the players were of humble origins, requiring that they and their families be paid for time spent in training. Compared to common laborers' salaries, they were paid sumptuously. For four months prior to the World Cup, Costa cloistered them in a house just outside Rio, drilled them daily on the field, and demanded total dedication of mind and energy. They were professionals in every sense of the word.

Of the five subsequent World Cups, Brazil won three. In 1954, however, the laurels went to the Federal Republic of Germany (West Germany). Only nine years after Germany's destruction in World War II, the World Cup of 1954 heralded the emergence of a talented, professionally trained German team. It was also the first World Cup ever to be televised all over Europe. Moreover, it bore eloquent witness to spectator interest in the game. For the final match against an apparently superior Hungarian club, 30,000 Germans traveled to Berne, Switzerland, to cheer their team to victory. They were drenched with rain throughout the match, but their team's 3–2 squeaker set off beer party celebrations that lasted for a week throughout the country.

In *The New Germany* (1955), Alex Natan identified soccer football as Germany's most popular sport. Amateurs far surpassed the number of professionals in the German Sports Federation, founded in 1950, and even the German national team was still composed of both amateurs and professionals. That situation changed quickly, however, as a Federal League *(Bundesliga)* was formed in 1963 to administer five regional professional leagues. The winner of the *Bundesliga* became the official West German championship team—professionals all. By 1974 eighteen first-division clubs competed for the title. Another eighty-two professional teams comprised five lower-division leagues organized on a regional basis. Professionalism enhanced the amateur game, which in turn fed its best players into the professional ranks. By the mid-1970s more than three million West Germans belonged to soccer clubs in the German Sports Federation, the most players per capita of any country in Western Europe. The rampant popularity of soccer was best indicated by the fact that gymnastics, Germany's oldest native sport, stood a distant second, with only two-thirds as many club members.

Spain's ancient and supposed "national" sport of bullfighting was also overshadowed by soccer football shortly after World War II. Once a ritualistic spectacle attracting all segments of Spanish society, bullfighting became mere entertainment for tourists and peasants come to town from the rural hinterlands during summer fiestas. An American journalist, Robert Daley, observed in 1963 that modern bullfighting was the social equivalent of prizefighting in the nineteenth century, since few Spaniards above the rank of hotel clerk would admit to having anything to do with it. "But soccer," Daley added, "draws men, women and children to the stadium in enormous numbers." He could have said the same for soccer in Portugal, Italy, Austria, and every other European nation except in Scandinavia, where professional football was still frowned upon, and in France, where individual rather than team sports were held in highest esteem.

The growing importance of professional soccer was reflected in the founding of four major new European tournaments between 1955 and 1961. Most important was the European Champion Cup (popularly known as the European Cup), begun in 1955 as a commercial endeavor to attract spectators to annual home- and away-games against the best foreign clubs. As Eurovision beamed the games into homes all over Europe, Real Madrid won the first five trophies. Victory brought prosperity. Alfredo Di Stefano, star center-forward for Real Madrid, made more than $200,000 for the season of 1961. Yet Spain's dominance was short-lived. Offering huge salaries to attract the best players from England and Scandinavia, Portuguese and Italian teams in the 1960s and Dutch clubs in the early 1970s wrested the European Cup from all competitors.

England, where the game of soccer football originated, fared poorly in international competition after World War II. England's rise from mediocrity in 1950 to the world championship in 1966 provides a study in miniature of the changing nature of the game of soccer. The change was monumental. In postwar Europe, only professional standards could win games and thus attract spectators. The incompetence of English soccer was in no small measure the result of its earlier refusal, between the wars, to compete with and to learn from European clubs. Moreover, although professional soccer began first in Britain, players and managers still took the game much too casually. They trained little, and with amateurish techniques. Their refusal even to use a ball in practice was a standing joke in European circles. Club owners still looked upon their players simply as working men who happened to be talented enough to win moderate wages on the soccer field. In 1947 the maximum wage per week was raised from £8 to £12 and by 1959 it had gradually risen to £20, but that still amounted to an income roughly the same as a skilled laborer. Little wonder that several of the outstanding English footballers—John Charles, Jimmy Greaves, Gerry Hitchens, and Denis Law—abandoned Britain in the 1950s for lucrative salaries offered by ambitious professional clubs in Spain and Italy.

Little wonder, too, that soccer crowds in Britain dropped off sharply in the 1950s. From an all-time high of forty-one million total spectators in the season of 1948–49, attendance plummeted to twenty-eight million in 1960–61. The reasons for the decline, of course, were complex. Numerous counterattractions beckoned. Television made the comforts of home entertainment more appealing than an afternoon spent standing in cold wind and rain to watch soccer matches. Cheap new automobiles allowed working-class families to take Saturday afternoon drives at the time customarily given to soccer games. Most important, old die-hard local supporters were being replaced by new fans who could travel afar by automobile to first-class matches. Larger clubs such as Leeds, Manchester United, Liverpool, Arsenal, and West Ham prospered at the expense of smaller, more provincial clubs. No longer were English spectators satisfied with second-rate local teams. They wanted quality football; they wanted winners.

Their appetite for winning could presumably be satisfied in FA Cup matches, but in international competition they met only with frustration. In 1950 England competed for the World Cup for the first time. A kind of all-star squad composed of the nation's best professionals, they performed pitifully. With an ill-coordinated attack and an undisciplined defense, they beat a poor Chilean team, but were then thrashed by American and Spanish clubs. The pill was hard to swallow: England was a second-rate soccer power. The truth came crashing home on 25 November 1953, when an English international squad hosted Hungary at Wembley Stadium. Within the first minute of play, Hungary scored a goal. They never let up, winning handily, 6–3. Insult piled on injured pride as an English team went to Budapest in the spring of 1954. On the way, they lost to Yugoslavia in Belgrade, then were demolished by the Hungarians, 7–1. Later in the year, in the World Cup, they tied Belgium and lost to Uruguay.

Disappointed British soccer enthusiasts turned their attention from the international team to the leading individual club in Britain, Manchester United. Winner or runnerup in virtually every FA Cup competition for the past decade, United entered the European Cup in 1956–57. In the semifinals the team lost to Real Madrid, but by such a close margin as to raise expectations that in 1957–58 they would unseat the perennial European champions. Early in 1958 Manchester United defeated Czechoslovakian and Yugoslavian teams, and by playing to a draw with Yugoslavia in Belgrade they won their way into the semifinals against Milan. Then tragedy struck. On the way home from Belgrade, the team plane crashed on an icy Munich airfield, instantly killing seven players, three staff members, eight journalists, and three other passengers. Nine players and the manager, Matt Busby, were injured, some seriously. Two weeks later Duncan Edwards, perhaps the most brilliant player in all of England, died from injuries sustained in the crash. In a memorial eulogy, the Bishop of Chester reflected on the role of professional athletes in English society. They were men "trained to a high standard of technical efficiency," but they were also "inspired with a loyalty to the club and to the game which has been a pattern for the best that men can achieve. . . . They are admired, idolized, glamorized, imitated." Having shouldered the responsibility "not only to play efficiently but to play well," the deceased had made Manchester United "a by-word for those who play a good game wherever football is played."

Yet professional British soccer players wanted more than moral praise. They wanted higher salaries and more flexible laws governing their terms of employment. A players' union, the Professional Footballers' Association, pressed its case and in 1960 threatened to strike unless the wage ceiling was removed. Within three days of the deadline, the owners relented. In the same year, football officials also decided to allow regular League (professional) games to be televised, at least in a token fashion: the first five minutes and the entire second half of twenty games. For rights to televise, the British Broadcasting Corporation (BBC) paid the Football Association £150,000 (about $420,000). So by 1960 British football featured escalating salaries and a profitable television contract, two common ingredients of modern professional sports.

Another new tendency was for professional athletes to win the right to choose where and for whom they would play. In a court case of 1963, British soccer players were freed from a "transfer system" that had bound them to their owners in a manner similar to the reserve clause in American baseball. After 1963 footballers could refuse to be traded, and upon accepting a trade they received half of the "transfer fee" that put their services at the disposal of a new owner.

For all its internal reforms, however, British soccer still suffered the stigma of defeat at the international level. Since 1946 Walter Winterbottom had coached the English team, but with little success. At Stockholm in 1958 England won not a single game in the opening rounds of the World Cup; in the 1962 World Cup, the team barely reached the quarter-finals, only to fall to Brazil. Winterbottom, a former officer in the Royal Air Force, remained unruffled. His aloof calmness was part of the problem: he was an amateur at heart. Of upper-class origins, he was not a man who could effectively instruct, much less inspire, working-class footballers. In 1962 he resigned.

His successor, Alf Ramsey, was cut from an altogether different piece of cloth. Of plebeian birth, Ramsey spoke with a Cockney accent. Himself a former outstanding international footballer, he identified easily with his players but drove them relentlessly in pursuit of excellence. Like his American contemporary, Vince Lombardi, Ramsey coached to win. "We shall win the World Cup," he announced the moment he took office.

He made good his promise. In England's first outing under Ramsey, they were swamped by an undistinguished French squad, 5–2. Ramsey quickly rebuilt his team around new players handpicked by himself rather than through the customary channels of a selection committee. Then he introduced a more defensive, tightly coordinated style of play, which worked well on a European tour in the summer of 1963. During the following summer, however, a trip to Brazil ended disastrously. After falling to Brazil and the brilliant Pelé, 5–1, England lost every subsequent game to South American sides. Worse still, the 1964 tour brought Ramsey into conflict with several of his best players, who chafed under his curfews, hard training sessions, and single-minded zeal to win. Yet Ramsey stood firm. In preparation for the World Cup, he secluded his team at a recreation center, Lilleshall, and drove them so mercilessly that they nicknamed the place "Stalag Lilleshall."

The dedication produced huge dividends. Hosting the World Cup in 1966, England easily disposed of France and Mexico in the early rounds, narrowly squeaked by Argentina in the quarter-finals and Portugal in the semifinals, then lined up against West Germany for the showdown at Wembley. West Germany, led by Franz Beckenbauer, Uwe Seeler, and Helmut Haller, scored first. Six minutes later, England evened the score. Rain began to fall at the start of the second half, but England's Nobby Stiles, Jackie and Bobby Charlton, Alan Ball, and Geoff Hurst complemented the work of captain Bobby Moore and goalkeeper Gordon Banks to go ahead 2–1 just twelve minutes before the final whistle. But West Germany refused to quit. With less than a minute left to play, they scored to send the game into overtime. Finally, a controversial goal by Geoff Hurst put England ahead, and in the game's dying moments Hurst scored again on a clean left-footed shot. For the first and only time ever, the Cup designed by Jules Rimet in 1930 was won by the country where football began.

The World Cup of 1966 represented the culmination of England's recovery as a football power, a recovery that was achieved by disciplined training at the hands of a strong-willed coach. Of no small importance was an intense determination to win rather than merely to play the game for the game's sake. The 1966 World Cup revealed, in fact, just how far professional soccer players were willing to go in quest of victory. After one particularly rough game against Argentina, Alf Ramsey complained that England was interested only in playing against a team "which comes out to play football, not to act as animals," but in truth most of the teams played like animals. Numerous fouls, fights, and arguments spoiled game after game. More than a dozen players were ejected for illegal roughness. The great Pelé was so physically abused in Brazil's opening match against Bulgaria that he was unable to play in the second round. Returning against Portugal, he was again shoved, tripped, and kicked so severely that he had to be carried off, swearing that he would never again play in a World Cup. The glare of publicity and the deafening roar of the stadium prompted professional athletes to revert to tactics akin to jungle warfare.

Another staple of modern professional sports, the enthusiastic, boisterous fan, came to the fore in the World Cup of 1966. Spectators filled Wembley not merely to watch the games, but also to participate in the drama by cheering, chanting, jeering, taunting, and even invading the field. "We want goals! We want goals!" screamed thousands of English partisans during a boring defensive match in the early rounds. An Argentinian player ejected for foul play had to run a gauntlet of thrown objects and insults on his way to the dressing room. Yet ugly emotional outbursts were hardly reserved for one's opponents. After the Italian team was beaten in the first round by an upstart squad from North Korea, the Italians attempted to slip home to the Genoa airport in the dead of night. Their plan failed as hundreds of their angry supporters pelted them with rotten tomatoes. Everywhere evident in 1966 were the fiercely partisan spectators who made hooliganism a problem for the soccer establishment.

Also evident was the importance of television. Approximately 400 million people watched the 1966 World Cup Final between England and West Germany. That estimate was doubled four years later for the final in Mexico City. The lengths to which the World Cup Committee went in 1970 to reap the financial rewards of an international television contract bespoke yet another fact of life for professional sports. In order for European television audiences to watch the game in the early evening, organizers agreed to begin all their Sunday matches at twelve noon—in the intense heat of a Mexican summer, 7,000 feet above sea level. Northern European athletes paid the price. For an early-round match at Guadalajara between England and Brazil, the thermometer registered ninety-eight degrees. As Brazil barely prevailed, 1–0, English players staggered about dehydrated and dazed at the end.

For the soccer world, however, the televised World Cup Final in 1970 provided a spectacle of unsurpassed drama, beauty, and skill. Brazil beat Italy, 4–1, but the score was not the important thing. At the head of Brazil's dazzling display of aggressive, imaginative football reigned the king of the world game, Pelé. Having reneged on his threat in 1966 to retire from international competition, he made a spectacular leap to head in the first goal, then set up two others with skillful assists. At the end of the game, delirious Brazilian fans invaded the field to strip their heroes of their bright yellow shirts, hoist them on their shoulders, and parade them around the field. While the world looked on, fans, patrons, coaches and players drank deeply from the biggest golden cup of all.

All-American Hustlers

For all its international appeal and entertainment value, soccer football paled beside the tinsel world of American sports. In postwar Europe and South America, soccer was the only notable spectator sport in town; in the United

States, on the other hand, boxing, baseball, football, and basketball competed for the spectator's dollar. High stakes elicited the shrewdness of Wall Street investors, Chicago gangsters, and Hollywood showmen in the production and selling of American sports.

Much earlier than in Europe, television regularly beamed sports events into American living rooms. As boxing's intense action in a limited space made it a sport peculiarly suited to the screen, professional prizefights were the first prominent televised spectacles in the postwar era. For several years Gillette Blue Blades sponsored weekly "Friday Night Fights." Although less than 10 percent of all American homes had television sets by 1950, the Gillette telecasts became a kind of neighborhood ritual. Regularly on Friday nights, sons and fathers visited with friends who happened to own television sets. "Look sharp, feel sharp, be sharp" was the first of many catchy slogans from advertisements associated with televised sporting events. The "Friday Night Fights" served as a precursor to baseball's "Game of the Day" in the 1950s, "The Wide World of Sports" in the 1960s, and "Monday Night Football" in the 1970s.

The effects of the Friday night fights on boxing also provided an omen to other sports. In taking television's golden egg, boxing almost cooked its own goose. Boxing suffered from overexposure. Numerous neighborhood gyms and small-town arenas quickly went out of business, unable to compete with the quality of bouts on the box. The ring's lackluster condition in the 1950s resulted in large measure from the death of those local clubs that had traditionally brought raw talent along slowly. Nor was boxing the only sport to suffer a damaging blow at hands of television. Minor-league baseball, whose function was roughly equivalent to local fight clubs, fell off disastrously with the televising of big-league games. At an all-time high of 42 million spectators in 1949, minor league attendance fell to 15 million in 1959, then to a mere 10 million in 1969.

In the first telecast World Series, viewers in 1947 intently peered at the snowy screen when the New York Yankees' Floyd "Bill" Bevens came within a single pitch of a no-hitter against the Brooklyn Dodgers. The Yankees won the series, four games to three, and the clubs split their television fee of $65,000, which thirty years later would not even pay for a portion of a one-minute commercial. Yet baseball, the oldest organized American sport, was on its way to a new era of public appeal and profit. Several elderly gentlemen owners retired in the 1940s, to be replaced by aggressive entrepreneurs such as Larry MacPhail of the Yankees and Walter O'Malley of the Dodgers. These new owners had no fear of turning sport into a business; they assumed that it already was.

Bill Veeck, Jr. ("Veeck as in wreck"), out-hustled them all. Before World War II Veeck served an apprenticeship under the staid regime of Philip K. Wrigley, the chewing-gum heir and owner of the Chicago Cubs. A gentle, retiring, conservative man, Wrigley refused ever to allow lights to be installed for night baseball. For Wrigley, the traditional way was the best way. It was not Veeck's style. After sustaining a severe leg injury in combat, Veeck returned home to purchase a minor-league club, the Milwaukee Brewers, then in 1946 gained controlling interest in a sagging major-league franchise, the Cleveland Indians. He believed that fans wanted primarily to have a good time at the ball park rather than simply to savor the niceties of the game. He gave them a good time in the form of fireworks, gate prizes, comfortable seats, and plenty of beer at reduced prices. He catered to families, even to the extent of providing free baby-sitting service. Later with the inept St. Louis Browns, he sent in a midget to bat and laughed along with everyone else when he drew a walk on four high pitches. "Hustler" Bill Veeck was too much for his day, and perhaps for any day, but his imaginative showman-ship was the essence, in exaggerated form, of American sports biz.

If Veeck brought a new managerial style, Dan Reeves set a new direction in administrative savvy. Owner of a money-losing franchise, the Cleveland Rams in the National Football League, Reeves in 1946 sought a fresh start in an altogether different city, Los Angeles, where entertainment was king. Competing for spectators with the Los Angeles Dons of the rival All-American Conference, Reeves first of all needed to produce a winning team. Under coach Clark Shaughnessy, who had perfected the T-formation at Stanford University, the Rams won big. Local favorites such as former UCLA stalwarts Kenny Washington and Bob Waterfield attracted crowds, driving the Los Angeles Dons out of business in 1949. In that same year the Rams won the first of three consecutive division championships. Visiting oppo-nents were amazed, and delighted, to find the Los Angeles Coliseum virtually filled with crowds approaching 100,000.

In 1950 Reeves experimented with telecasts of the Rams' home games. Fans stayed home to watch in the comfort of living rooms, prompting Reeves to impose a blackout of screens within a seventy-five-mile radius of Los Angeles. The innovation was of major importance for all American sports. Baseball clubs and college football teams quickly copied the practice. The National Collegiate Athletic Association endorsed one network football game a week, but with local stations blacked out. The legality of the practice was tested in a federal court, in a suit brought by the Justice Department charging the NFL with restraint of trade under the Sherman Antitrust Act. Club owners, seeing clearly the long-term importance of the decision, contributed $200,000 for preparation of the defense. On 12 November 1953 a federal judge denied the government's case, upheld the blackout, and thereby launched American sports into an era of unparalleled glamor and growth.

Untapped radio and television audiences as well as fresh spectator poten-tial led major-league baseball to expand geographically in the 1950s. In 1953 the Boston Braves, long the National League counterpart to the Red Sox, moved to Milwaukee, where attendance figures and media income immedi-ately soared. The following year saw the comatose St. Louis Browns shipped out to Baltimore, to take the nickname "Orioles." In 1955 the Philadelphia Athletics, losers since the early 1930s, packed off to Kansas City. But in 1958 came the two most shocking moves of all. Despite rabid fan support at decrepit Ebbets Field, the Brooklyn Dodgers under Walter O'Malley left for greener pastures in Los Angeles, and the New York Giants similarly departed the Polo Grounds for San Francisco. All except one of these moves were made westward, from older cities that had previously supported at least two major-league clubs to newer cities that had none. Western city officials eager for a major-league franchise offered tax breaks, municipal loans, and stadiums built at city or county expense.

Yet the 1950s belonged to the fast-growing adolescent giant of sport, pro football, whose average game attendance leaped from 25,000 in 1950 to 40,000 in 1960. After the collapse of the rival All-American Football Conference in 1950, the darlings of the National Football League were the Cleveland Browns, led by quarterback Otto Graham and placekicker Lou Groza, and the Detroit Lions, starring flashy Doak Walker, gutsy Bobby Layne, massive Les Bingaman, and bullish Leon Hart. For the purposes of sports biz, however, a quiet administrative innovation was as important as the athletes' public feats. In 1952 the Lions' front office offered season tickets to their avid fans, thus guaranteeing the same seats in the stadium for all home games, and in turn guaranteeing a predictable base for gate receipts. More than 17,000 people bought season tickets the first year they were offered. Three years later the number exceeded 36,000, and by 1958 the Lions assured themselves of regular sell-out crowds by booking 42,154 season tickets in a stadium that held 45,555.

Pro football came of age as an American spectacle on 28 December 1958, in a play-off championship game between the Baltimore Colts and the New York Giants. More than 64,000 spectators crammed into Yankee Stadium to see the game, and 45 million or so watched it on national television. Evenly matched in size, speed, and talent, the Colts and Giants surged up and down the field in a wide-open manner foreign to the college game, which at the time was mired in one-platoon rules requiring a deliberate ground-control style of play. Players previously unknown instantly became household names: Gifford, Conerly, Webster, Rote, Robustelli, Summerall, Katcavage, and Tunnell for the Giants; Unitas, Ameche, Moore, Berry, Mutscheller, Marchetti, and Lipscomb for the Colts. Unitas, a thin twenty-five-year-old quarterback, only two years earlier had been relegated to the semiprofessional leagues and had won a starting position only because his predecessor at quarterback had suffered a broken leg. Behind 17–14 within the last two minutes of the game, Unitas won superstar status by driving the Colts seventy-three yards to set up a short field goal in the final seven seconds. For the first time in the history of the NFL championships, the game went into sudden-death overtime.

Drama intensified as the Giants failed by the length of the ball to gain a first down in their first possession during overtime. They punted, the Colts took over on their own twenty-yard line, and Unitas mixed running plays with pinpoint passing to march them down to the Giants' one-yard line. In perhaps the most famous scene in the picture history of the NFL, Alan Ameche bulled through a gaping hole on the right side of his line for a 23–17 victory. Fans drained of emotion filed slowly out of Yankee Stadium, while millions of Americans sat stunned but ecstatic in front of their television sets. They had seen pro football at its dramatic best. They liked what they saw, and they hungered for more.

More they got. Far be it from American enterprise to turn its back on hunger—if the hungry can pay to have their appetites satisfied. So reasoned Alvin "Pete" Rozelle, who became commissioner of the NFL early in 1960. Differences between Rozelle and his predecessor, Bennville "Bert" Bell, signified a new direction for pro football. Bell played college football at the University of Pennsylvania, then coached for a few years at the same school, and in the 1930s became both the owner and coach of the Philadelphia Eagles. He served at the helm of the NFL from 1946 until his death in the midst of a capacity crowd at an Eagles-Steelers game in the autumn of 1959. As player, coach, owner, and commissioner, Bert Bell lived and literally died football. Rozelle, on the other hand, never played the game, and he certainly never coached it. As a student at Compton Junior College and the University of San Francisco, he worked as athletic news director. He was barely twenty-six years old when he became head of the publicity office of the Los Angeles Rams. After three years he left briefly to join a public-relations firm, but in 1957 he returned as the Rams' general manager. Trained to package and market a product, Rozelle was a management-media man all the way.

His move into the NFL commissioner's office would alone make 1960 a pivotal year in the saga of American sports biz. But 1960 was important for another reason: within months of Rozelle's taking office, television whiz Roone P. Arledge left the highly successful National Broadcasting Company (NBC) for the struggling American Broadcasting Company (ABC), convinced that the best way to raise the ratings of ABC was to give extensive, imaginative coverage of sports. "The Wide World of Sports," begun by Arledge in 1961, became an immediate success with an American public looking for variety as well as excitement. More than any other person, Roone Arledge was responsible for exposing American viewers to the delights of the Olympics, winter sports of all kinds, foreign feats and games, and the wacky exploits of a new group called the American Football League.

Conceived in the bulging pocket of a Texas multimillionaire, Lamar Hunt, the American Football League (AFL) was born in 1960 as a rival to the NFL. Franchises in Dallas, Houston, Denver, Los Angeles, Oakland, Buffalo, Boston, and New York began their first season assured of a total income of two million dollars from a five-year television contract with ABC. They needed it. In their entire first season of play, the AFL drew only 926,156 customers, an average of 16,539 each game, compared to the NFL's total of more than three million and average per game of 40,106.

Crucial to the success of the AFL was its franchise in New York City, still the center of American finance and communications. Unfortunately, the original New York entry, the Titans, were a bust—in the front office, on the field, and in the stands. In eight home games in 1962, the Titans drew a total of 36,161 spectators, less than any single-game average in the NFL. In 1963 a businesslike savior, David A. "Sonny" Werblin, gathered a syndicate of big-money men to buy the Titans. They changed their nickname to the Jets, hired Weeb Ewbank (the coach of the championship 1958 Colts), and appropriately changed the colors of the team to money-green and white. They dispensed the greenbacks freely, especially to a gimpy-kneed, strong-armed quarter-

Vince Lombardi rode the crest of success at the helm of the Green Bay Packers for much of the decade of the 1960s. For all his tough demeanor, he was admired by his players and fans alike. (Courtesy of the Green Bay Packers.)

back from the University of Alabama, Joe Willie Namath. Capitalizing on a fierce bidding war between the NFL and the AFL, Namath signed a four-year contract for $427,000, an astronomical figure at the time. Included in the package deal was a green Lincoln Continental. In his first season with the Jets (1965), Namath brought class and excitement to the AFL. He was not a bad quarterback either.

His salary opened a floodgate that even the dictator of the most conservative regime in the NFL could not close. Rough on the field, coach and general manager Vince Lombardi was notoriously tight-fisted in salary negotiations with his Green Bay Packers. Annually at the first team meeting, he announced: "We do not have losers. If you're a loser, mister, you're going to get your ass out of here and you're going to get your ass out of here right now. Gentlemen, we are paid to win. Gentlemen, we *will* win." Win they did: five NFL titles and the first two Super Bowls in the 1960s. Well-paid they were not—not even stars Bart Starr, Paul Hornung, and Jim Taylor. In 1966, however, as both Hornung and Taylor talked of retirement, Lombardi dug deep into the Green Bay corporate coffers to sign two of the best backs available in the college draft. To the astonishment of veteran Packers, Donny Anderson and Jim Grabowski signed for a combined figure exceeding a million dollars.

Packed stadiums and fat television packets made the higher salaries possible. Inflationary contracts seemed limitless until the warring leagues devised a plan to stabilize their payrolls. In 1966 they agreed to merge. On the way to realigning the two leagues in 1970, they created the Super Bowl, a bonanza that would further increase their income. Supposedly championship play-offs between the NFL and AFL league winners, the first two engagements turned out to be blooper bowls. In 1967 the mighty Packers destroyed the AFL titlists, the Kansas City Chiefs, 35–10, and as though to emphasize NFL consistency romped over the Oakland Raiders a year later by an almost identical score, 33–14.

The Raiders' game, in fact, was something of an anticlimax after the NFL championship "ice bowl" drama between the Packers and the Dallas Cowboys on 31 December 1967, two weeks prior to Super Bowl II. While Dallas quarterback Don Meredith and his mates shivered on the sidelines wondering why good ole' Texas boys would ever come to Wisconsin to play in the dead of winter, the thermometer registered fourteen degrees below zero at kick-off time. The weather warmed up two degrees by the game's end as Bart Starr sneaked over from the one yard line to win, 21–17, with only thirteen seconds left to play. No doubt the "ice bowl" confirmed millions of American television viewers in their preference for living-room comfort over live-action agony, but it certainly made the second Super Bowl seem pallid by comparison.

In Super Bowl III, on 12 January 1969, a startling upset occurred. In a spectacle that can only be compared to the Colts-Giants play-off in 1958, Joe Namath led the AFL New York Jets to a solid victory over the Baltimore Colts, 16–7. Ruggedly handsome, nonconformist, and outspoken, Namath was a young man made for, and by, the media of the late 1960s. Reporters hounded his every move, in bars and bedrooms as well as on the gridiron. Occasionally they quoted his words. "We're going to win, I guarantee it!" Namath predicted publicly before the game. No one took him seriously until a tenacious Jets' defense and Namath's patient play-calling and accurate passes redressed a nine-year dismissal of the AFL as "that other league." After the game, Weeb Ewbank crowed: "We are a great team and this is the start of a new era." He was half right. The Jets quickly proved themselves to be no great team at all, but in 1969 professional football did stand poised on the eve of a new era in which the merger of rival leagues and expansion to new cities were to tighten even further the game's grip on the nation's purse strings.

At the end of the 1960s the future of college football also appeared rosy. An unwritten agreement for all professional games to be played on Sunday, and all college games on Saturday, meant that each complemented rather than detracted from the other. By the mid-1950s the colleges offered full football scholarships as a matter of course, and by the mid-1960s they were playing two-platoon football in a fashion popularized by the professionals. No less than pro football, the college game became a huge commercial spectacle, and with the added advantages of alumni loyalties, cheerleaders, marching bands, and traditional bowl games. During the 1960s, total attendance figures leaped from twenty million to almost thirty million; from 1964 to 1969, television revenue doubled from three to six million dollars. With perennial

Broadway Joe Namath combined athletic talent, personal charm and controversy, and clutch performances to rise to the top of the sports biz scene in the 1960s. (Courtesy of the New York Jets.)

powers such as Oklahoma, Notre Dame, Ohio State, Alabama, and Michigan leading the way, college football entered the 1970s as one of the cornerstones of American sports biz.

So did professional and college basketball. The National Basketball Association (NBA), formed in 1950 as a merger of two struggling circuits, enjoyed a phenomenal growth of popularity in the 1950s and 1960s. The twenty-four-second rule, introduced in 1954, required a team to shoot the ball within twenty-four seconds or turn it over to the opponents, thereby speeding up the game. Confrontations between the game's two biggest and best men, Bill Russell and Wilt Chamberlain, increased fan interest, as did the ball-handling wizardry of Bob Cousy, who led the famed fast break of the Boston Celtics. Beginning in 1957, the Celtics won eleven of the next thirteen NBA championships.

Supposedly such dominance by one team would have diminished spectator interest, but league attendance totals almost tripled in the 1960s. A long-term contract with ABC, signed in 1964, provided substantial income. A sure sign of appeal, a rival league, appeared in 1967. Similar in style as well as name to the earlier American Football League, the American Basketball Association (ABA) introduced various show-biz wrinkles such as a red, white, and blue ball and a three-point goal for shots made from beyond a distant perimeter. Most important, the ABA forced up professional basket-ballers' salaries by raiding NBA rosters and offering exorbitant contracts to the best college players.

The supply was abundant. Despite "point-shaving" scandals in 1951 and 1961, college basketball flourished as a popular spectacle. In fact, the scandal of 1951, in which thirty-two players from seven colleges succumbed to the wiles of New York City gamblers, set college basketball on a new course. The NCAA, formerly a mere rules-making body, intervened and began empha-sizing its own tournament at the expense of the National Invitational Tourna-ment (NIT), whose prior strength (its location in New York City) suddenly became a weakness. The NCAA tournament quickly emerged as the prime showpiece of college basketball champions. Asphalt playgrounds in inner-city ghettos and backyard goals throughout the rural Midwest provided the best talent. Compared to football, basketball teams were smaller in size and therefore less expensive to recruit and maintain. One or two key players could transform a team, allowing smaller colleges such as LaSalle, San Francisco, Cincinnati, Loyola of Chicago, and Texas Western University to win places in the limelight as NCAA champions.

In 1964, however, the University of California at Los Angeles launched a decade-long dynasty of nine of ten NCAA titles under the tutelage of John Wooden. On their way to the crown in 1968, the undefeated Bruins took on the University of Houston Cougars, another team with an unblemished record. Both the setting and the dramatic action of the game indicated how far college basketball had come as an American spectacle. A record crowd of 52,693 fans nearly filled the cavernous Houston Astrodome (built in 1965 primarily for football and baseball), and a television audience of millions looked on. Houston's Elvin Hayes scored twenty-nine points in the first half, thirty-nine in all, to lead the Cougers to a narrow 71–69 victory over the Bruins, whose giant, talented center, Lew Alcindor, suffered with double vision from an eye bruised in an earlier game. Later in the NCAA semifinals, UCLA with a healthy Alcindor demolished Houston 101–69, but their Astro-dome match-up stood as the most memorable college game of the decade. A huge live audience, hyped-up national television coverage, and a thrilling, evenly matched display of basketball at its best all combined to establish the college game as an important part of American sports biz.

Agents of Change

While both college and professional promoters of basketball and football entered the 1970s with swashbuckling confidence born of recent success, major-league baseball seemed to be losing its grip on the American public. Admittedly, baseball's total attendance figures had gradually increased, and since 1961 the major leagues had enjoyed packaged contracts with the television networks. But baseball's crowds, television ratings, and profits had hardly kept pace with basketball, much less with football. America's oldest game was also its slowest, seemingly out of touch with the frenetic bustle and conflict of the 1960s and early 1970s. Even baseball's recent expansion apparently worked to its detriment. Franchise shifts from Washington to Dallas, from Milwaukee to Atlanta, and from Kansas City to Oakland further severed the ties of local loyalty, a traditional strength of the game. The creation of weak new clubs such as the Los Angeles Angels, the New York Mets, the Houston Colt .45s, the Montreal Expos, the San Diego Padres, the Kansas City Royals, and the Seattle Pilots spread out talent that was already thinned by the shrinkage of the minor leagues.

The most pressing problem of all, however, was player discontent with the business management of baseball. "Now that sports are becoming bigger business," remarked Marvin Miller, "they are adopting the problems of big business." Miller made it his business to turn those problems to players' advantage. A graduate in economics, he served as chief counsel for the United Steelworkers of America before being hired in 1966 as a highly paid executive director of the Major League Baseball Players' Association. From a high-rise office on Park Avenue in Manhattan, he fought for players' rights in an articulate, forceful manner never before encountered by the owners of baseball. The players' pension plan was the first point of contention. By the spring of 1969, Miller rallied the support of all 600 major-league players to threaten a players' strike if their pensions were not improved. Rising television revenue made the demand reasonable; the prospect of lost revenue prompted owners to avert a strike by agreeing to a new graduated pension scheme tied to the growth of television income.

The pension question was merely a prelude to a larger, more fundamental issue of player-management relations: the reserve-clause system. Born in a prior age of powerful big business (1879), the reserve clause essentially bound a player to a club for life. Owners could sell, trade, or fire players, but no player was free to sell his talents to the highest bidder. Supreme Court decisions in 1922 and 1953 upheld the reserve clause by exempting professional baseball from federal antitrust legislation. Yet once again, in December 1969, the issue rose to the surface when a St. Louis Cardinals' star outfielder, Curt Flood, was traded to the Philadelphia Phillies. Business interests in St. Louis made Flood loathe to leave, despite an offer of an extra $10,000 added to his $90,000 salary. Under the reserve clause, he was required either to accept the Phillies' offer or to retire from baseball. Declaring that owners treated players "like slaves and pieces of property instead of as human beings," Flood took his case to court.

He lost the battle, but other athletes won the war. Between 1970 and 1976, legal suits brought by Oscar Robertson of the NBA, John Mackey, Kermit Alexander, Joe Kapp, and Yazoo Smith of the NFL, and Gerry Cheevers and Bernie Parent of the National Hockey League (NHL) won free-agency rights for players in the three major professional sports that had copied baseball's reserve clause. Details varied from sport to sport. Pete Rozelle's office shrewdly negotiated a restrictive "compensation clause" for NFL owners, making any team signing a free agent liable to the player's former club for a draft choice and a sum of money determined by the commissioner. Moreover, NFL clubs could automatically retain a free agent by matching the offer he received from another team. Within the first three years of that agreement, only four of the 295 free agents in the NFL signed with new teams.

The abolition of major league baseball's reserve clause came as something of a fluke. Apparently the failure of Curt Flood's suit, in a Supreme Court decision of 1972, gave owners a false sense of security. When Andy Messersmith of the Los Angeles Dodgers and Dave McNally of the Montreal Expos refused in 1975 to accept the terms of the contracts offered them, their owners confidently agreed to take the cases to neutral arbitration. Owners were astounded to receive the ruling that a team could renew a contract for only one year, but no more, making the players free agents thereafter. Courts upheld the arbitrator's right to rule, and the ruling itself. The reserve clause came crashing down.

Players' salaries shot up. The average major-league baseballer's salary in 1975 was $44,000; by 1979 it was $110,000 and rising fast. Millionaire athletes suddenly became a dime a dozen. Some were veteran stars such as Nolan Ryan, Pete Rose, and Rod Carew; others were men whose talents would have been only moderately marketable ten years earlier. Dave Winfield led the latter pack. In 1979 he batted .308, hit 34 home runs, and drove in a league-leading 118 runs for the San Diego Padres. In 1980, however, he hit only .276 with 20 homers and 87 runs batted in. Yet his free-agent status set him bargaining on the open market. Early in 1981 he signed a ten-year contract with the New York Yankees for a package reputedly worth $15 million, possibly $22 million with inflation adjustments.

Even higher than baseball salaries, the average annual income in the National Basketball Association rose 700 percent between 1969 and 1979, largely because of the bidding war with the rival ABA. By 1981 the average NBA salary approached $200,000. Although inordinately generous sums paid to superstars such as Kareem Abdul-Jabbar and Julius "Doctor J" Erving misleadingly warped the picture, NBA players fared considerably better—more than twice as good, on the average—than National Football Leaguers for whom the "Rozelle rule" stood as the best hedge yet devised against inflation. Escalating baseball and basketball salaries made the contract signed by the National Hockey League's first free agent, Marcel Dionne, seem like an owner's bargain by comparison: Dionne in 1975 moved from Detroit to Los Angeles for an increase from $80,000 to $350,000 a season.

Free-agency established player agents as financial representatives of the stars of sports biz akin to the agents long common in Hollywood show biz. "I put agents in business," commented Marvin Miller in 1978. "We created the framework within which they can function. . . . We raised the minimum salaries, we structured the pension fund, we provide exhaustive information and services free to any agent who calls. We changed the rules of the reserve clause. In a very real sense, we freed the players." True, but only half true. Miller and the Players' Association gave agents the tools with which to work and made their work easier; they did not create agents. In the expansive 1960s players began turning for expert advice and negotiating skills to lawyers, certified public accountants, and the like.

Before agents became commonly accepted by sports management, however, the results of their efforts were not always satisfactory. In 1964 Jim Ringo, an annual All-Pro center for the Green Bay Packers, took an agent with him to negotiate a new contract with Vince Lombardi. Following the introductions, the atmosphere cooled. "Excuse me," snapped Lombardi, as he went into another room and slammed the door behind him. Five minutes later he reappeared. Ignoring Ringo, he informed the agent that he was "negotiating with the wrong person. Mr. Ringo has just been traded to Philadelphia." Lombardi's position was both clear and definite: "I will flatly refuse to deal with any representative of any player on this team."

Vince Lombardi was a man of the 1950s who happened to succeed most in the 1960s. Unfortuntely, he died of cancer in 1970, shortly after moving from the Packers to the Washington Redskins. Had he lived through the decade, and had he refused to change, his life would have been miserable. Few professional athletes would now consider entering into contract negotiations without representation. Long-term agreements, deferred payments, insurance schemes, incentive clauses, and all the other numerous options now available to professional athletes require an expertise that most athletes do not possess. Thus they rely on agents, whose ethics run the gamut from the legitimate to the larcenous. Some agents take as much as 10 percent of the massive financial packages they devise. Some coldly insist that their client-athletes hold out for better contracts, even at the risk of irreparable damage to athletic careers. One of the better agents, apparently, is Bob Woolf, a Boston attorney who began handling athletes' contractual affairs in the late 1960s. Concerned with the lack of laws requiring agents to be licensed or bonded, Woolf recalled when owners once shamelessly exploited athletes, then added: "But I'm afraid that today, many agents are exploiting players, too."

Whether accomplices or parasites, agents are the result, not the cause, of the vast changes that have transformed the financial structure of sports in the 1970s. Nor is free-agency the culprit. Owners pay the salaries demanded and recklessly outbid each other in order to produce winning teams of commercial appeal. The greatest agent of change is television. Professional clubs would go broke tomorrow if their television contracts fell through. New ventures regularly succeed or fail according to their ability to land network coverage. The unstable American Basketball Association, for example, survived for ten years only because of its television revenue. As players' salaries escalated wildly, eleven teams changed ownership 27 times before the four best franchises were absorbed into the NBA in 1976. With minimal local and no network telecasts, the new World Hockey Association lasted only six years, from 1972 to 1978. Unable to land any television income whatsoever, the fledging World Football League folded after two disastrous seasons (1974–75). Like the awesome God of old Calvinist theology, television possesses the sovereign power to save or to damn new leagues, franchises, and athletic careers.

The verdict is still out on the North American Soccer League, founded in the robust late 1960s. For a game so foreign to American traditions, the NASL recruited mostly English and European players to fill its early rosters, and in 1975 it paid $7 million for the attractive but aged Pelé to perform for three years with the league's showpiece team, the New York Cosmos. Despite its foreign roots, the active, inexpensive, nonviolent game of soccer exerted strong appeal at the popular level of school sports. Yet the NASL still struggles to survive. Some critics say that it is too foreign, nonviolent, and low-scoring for American tastes, but its fundamental problem is its inability to satisfy the commercial demands of television. Soccer is a game of continuous action interrupted only by injuries and a halftime break. Where can television commercials be inserted? Not between inning or rounds, as in baseball and boxing; not after touchdowns or at natural breaks in the action, as in football; not at timeouts, as in basketball as well as football, whose promoters even grant the networks extra stoppages for advertisement purposes. The athletic beauty and universal appeal of soccer, its graceful ebb and flow, render it a game not made for Michelob weekends. To succeed as a televised event, soccer will have to change its ways.

Other professional sports already have. For general spectator appeal and especially for the television audience, football, baseball, and basketball rules were revised in the 1970s to favor exciting offensive displays. "We need points on the scoreboard to get ratings," Howard Cosell once said of Monday Night Football. "We need a high-scoring, competitive game." NFL officials agreed to the extent of setting goal posts at the back of the end zone to discourage field goals in favor of more touchdowns, setting hash marks nearer the center of the field to give the offense more maneuvering room, and changing the rules to favor passers and pass receivers. Similarly intent on beefing up a crowd-pleasing offensive style of play, baseball officials lowered the pitching mound and reduced the strike zone. Although the National League refused to cooperate, the American League allowed designated hitters to replace pitchers in the batting order. Nor did the National Basketball Association sit on its hands. Early in the 1970s it widened its three-second lane to prevent large inside men from clogging up offensive drives to the basket. From its former rival, the ABA, the NBA borrowed the popular three-point play primarily to allow losing teams to catch up late in the game. Not incidentally, close games hold television audiences to the end.

The one major sport in North America that has changed little to accommodate television is ice hockey. Not surprisingly, it trails all the others in network coverage, despite much local programming. Like soccer, ice-hockey scores are low. Worse still, the puck is small and black, extremely hard to follow on a television screen. Founders of the short-lived World Hockey Association debated using a colored puck but dropped the idea. Network executives have the answers, of course. "We could do a big job with hockey," says one, "if they agreed to make the goal much wider to hype the scoring; and they'd have to make the puck much larger, too, to improve its visibility on the screen. Hey, a 45–44 hockey score would be a great show for the fans, right?"

Wrong, probably. But for the sake of "a great show for the fans," sports other than ice hockey have been all too susceptible to innovations. In numerous stadiums throughout the United States, for example, synthetic turf has replaced natural grass to provide faster, mud-free games, regardless of the danger to athletes' knees, elbows, and heads. Similarly indifferent to tradition, many baseball teams have packed away their customary white home uniforms and gray road garb for brightly colored uniforms that grip the attention of color television audiences. The creator of that novelty, Charles Finley, also proposed using orange baseballs and scheduling World Series and All-Star games at night for prime-time television audiences. The owners of baseball scoffed at both ideas, until NBC offered a fat contract for important evening games. By the mid-1970s the World Series was being played at night in near-freezing October weather. Professional football and basketball establishments were no less responsive to network commands. The Super Bowl is now regularly begun at five or six o'clock (Eastern time) on a Sunday afternoon—a most unusual, awkward time for athletes—in order to capture early evening prime-time viewers. Jerry Colangelo, the general manager of the NBA Phoenix Suns, admits only half facetiously that "If TV wants us to play at 4 A.M., we'll just have to leave early wake-up calls." The Suns reap almost a million dollars each year from television.

Of all the innovations brought on by television, Monday Night Football is undoubtedly the most successful. Conceived by Roone Arledge at ABC, Monday night games began in 1970 as a public marriage between sports and the media, and instantly they became the hottest item in regular-season viewing. In the second year, play-by-play announcer Frank Gifford took over as master of ceremonies, riding herd on a string of former athletes—notably Don Meredith, Alex Karras, and Fran Tarkenton—who supposedly provided technical comment on the action. The dominant figure in the booth, however, was Howard Cosell, whose intelligence and extensive vocabulary, combined with an arrogance and brash determination to "tell it like it is," made him simultaneously the most adored and most despised of all television sports announcers. A poll taken by *TV Guide* in 1978 confirmed the dominance of Monday Night Football: Cosell, Gifford, and Meredith, in that order, ranked at the top of the best-liked television sports personalities. Yet the same poll also underscored the ambivalent reputation of Cosell, who ranked thirty-six percentage points above his nearest rival, Curt Gowdy, for the least-liked commentator. A man loved or loathed, Cosell is certainly never ignored. He is a household name. His face and voice are widely recognized. He is sports biz.

Gentlemen Prefer Money

Long before Monday Night Football extended to occasional Thursday Night Football and Sunday Night Football, ABC's success set NBC and CBS to bidding outrageously high sums for sports events. Network profits in turn inspired the beginning of a new all-sports cable television system, the Entertainment and Sports Programming Network (ESPN). "We believe that the appetite for sports in this country is insatiable," said William Rasmussen, the founder of ESPN. Begun unabashedly in 1979 as "a network for sports junkies," ESPN operates around the clock, twenty-four hours a day. To fill its programming schedule, it televises events such as fencing, water polo, and slow-pitch softball, sports never before noticed by the electronic media. The staple of ESPN, however, is regional college sports. A contract with the NCAA allows coverage of hundreds of basketball and football games, the latter on a tape-delayed basis in order not to interfere with ABC's exclusive rights of live coverage. ESPN is a reminder, as though one needs to be reminded, that college sports head the list of numerous "amateur" sports fully entangled in the money game.

Even golf and tennis, originally the two most socially exclusive and therefore the most amateur of all sports, joined the sports-biz crowd in the 1960s and 1970s. As early as the decade of the golden 1920s, both became popular spectacles, but in that era amateurs Bobby Jones, Suzanne Lenglen, and Big Bill Tilden were satisfied with mere competition and media attention. Times have vastly changed. Modern gentlemen and ladies prefer money to honor, records, or trophies. "It wasn't much fun being an amateur," said Patty Sheehan recently upon joining the Ladies Professional Golf Association tour. "I got tired of polishing the silverware."

Walter Hagen, the first professional golfer who enthusiastically sought greenbacks rather than silverware, was so successful in spawning imitators that no amateur golfer won the United States Open after 1933. Hagen's leading successors in the late 1930s and 1940s, Ben Hogan, Sammy Snead, and Byron Nelson, certainly earned comfortable livings at the game, but the new age of golf burst upon the world, and upon television screens, in the person of young Arnold Palmer. National Amateur Champion in 1954, Palmer turned pro to win the Canadian Open in 1955, the Masters four times beginning in 1958, the British Open twice, and the United States Open and Australian Open once each. Yet Palmer, like all authentic superstars, was something more than a string of records. His boyish grin at a good shot, or pained grimace at a slice or bad putt, won him a following ("Arnie's Army") that was probably larger than any golfer's in history. They followed him because he won consistently, and often in grand style. Palmer's "charge" from an apparently hopeless situation to cop victory on the final round became a stock feature of the professional tour, an event to be anticipated and savored. "He reminds me of a fighter," remarked Gene Sarazen, winner of the 1935 Masters. "He's most dangerous when he's on the rope, ready to be counted out." Palmer's feats made him a millionaire of international renown and won him the Associated Press selection as the "Athlete of the Decade" for the 1960s.

In 1962 a youthful challenger, Jack Nicklaus, confronted Palmer in the Oakmont Open. Ten years Palmer's junior, the twenty-three-year-old Nicklaus was powerfully built—overweight, in fact—and drove for astounding distance. He and Palmer finished in a tie after seventy-two rounds, as Palmer's patented charge failed. Ignoring the impolite cheers of "Arnie's Army" and jeers to "Miss it, Fat Boy!" Nicklaus won the playoff by three strokes. "That big, strong dude," Palmer observed years later. "If I had beaten him in that playoff, I might have held him off for several years. But in losing, I presented him with a big load of confidence which he never lost."

Nicklaus never looked back. He went on to win more major golf championships than any man ever, including Bobby Jones. He won more prize money

Soon to be overshadowed by Jack Nicklaus, the young Arnold Palmer was the darling of the fairways when golf first became a televised spectacle in the 1950s. Here Arnie's Army follows one of his shots with awe and delight. (Courtesy of Arnold Palmer.)

than did Palmer. But although he spruced up his image by losing forty pounds and letting his blond mane grow modishly long in the late 1960s, he never replaced Palmer in the public's affection. Nicklaus was incredibly strong and efficient, but he was too calmly patterned ever to be a sports-biz idol. In any case, such comparisons with Palmer are unfair, for Palmer made his mark at the very moment that television arrived on the major courses. Television made him, and he made televised golf.

Television certainly made professional golf a most profitable enterprise for the few hundred leading golfers in the world. By 1980 forty or so, including several women, earned more than $100,000 annually in more than a hundred tournaments effectively subsidized by network and regional television revenue. Americans such as Nicklaus, Lee "Tex Mex" Trevino, Johnny Miller, Tom Watson, and Nancy Lopez led the list of moneymakers, with Briton Tony Jacklin and South African Gary Player not far behind.

More internationally popular, tennis is now even more commercial than golf. It was not always so. The first professional tennis tour, in the United States in 1926 starring Suzanne Lenglen, was a flop. When Bill Tilden turned professional in the 1930s, he had difficulty finding adequate competition, much less financial support, for his barnstorming tours. Jack Kramer, winner at Forest Hills in 1946 and 1947 and at Wimbledon in 1947, turned professional shortly thereafter and for years crusaded for tournaments "open" to professionals and amateurs alike, but with no success. British and American officials especially resisted mixing professionals and amateurs, although they knew that "shamateurish" thrived in the form of fake expense accounts, under-the-table payoffs, and secret bonuses from sponsors. "Tennis has not been a genuinely amateur sport for at least twenty-five years," wrote one of Britain's leading sports journalists, Brian Glanville, in the *Sunday Times* of London in 1963. "The tennis world is neither fish nor fowl, neither truly amateur nor honestly professional."

At the top of that world stood not British or American players, but rather Australians such as Lew Hoad, Ken Rosewall, Ashley Cooper, Neale Fraser, Roy Emerson, John Newcombe, and Rod Laver. From 1950 to 1967 Australians won fifteen of eighteen Davis Cups and waltzed away with most of the Wimbledon and Forest Hills laurels. In 1962 Rod Laver, a compact, fiery left-hander, won the Grand Slam—British, American, French, and Australian championships—and within the year joined Hoad and Rosewall on the professional tour. Five years later another Australian, John Newcombe, won both at Wimbledon and Forest Hills and immediately announced his professional intentions. It was the final straw for Wimbledon officials, who had witnessed champion after champion step down from the amateur ranks and thus declare themselves ineligible for Wimbledon, supposedly the arena for the best tennis in the world. In December 1967 the British Lawn Tennis Association voted 295–5 to transform Wimbledon into an open tournament, beginning in 1968. Within the year every major tennis tournament in the world followed suit. In 1969 Rod Laver became the first, and undoubtedly the last, professional ever to repeat a Grand Slam that he had earlier achieved as an amateur.

The birth of open tournaments coincided with two major developments in international tennis. One was the new popularity of women stars such as Americans Billie Jean King and Chris Evert, Australians Margaret Smith Court and Evonne Goolagong, and Briton Virginia Wade. The other was greatly increased television coverage of the tournaments. Between 1970 and 1973 the three major American networks tripled the total amount of time devoted to tennis, including telecasts of new events such as the Grand Prix and World Championship Tennis tours, and various local extravaganzas as well as the traditional tournaments. Media exposure quickly made tennis the fastest-growing sport at the popular level. In the early 1970s hundreds of indoor centers mushroomed, especially in the United States, where the number of players and the sale of tennis equipment quadrupled within five years.

Commercial tennis severely damaged the Davis Cup. Although Davis Cup nations began to pay their players, the salaries were minuscule compared to the sums professionals made on tour. Top players snubbed the Davis Cup because of lucrative commitments elsewhere, leaving the oldest of the international tournaments in the hands of youthful tennis nations. Previous unknowns, South Africa and Sweden, won the Davis Cup in 1974 and 1975, respectively. The Swedish victory meant more than a mere Davis Cup, for the leader in that effort was a craggy-faced, long-haired teenager, Bjorn Borg, who emerged in 1975 as the dominant tennis player in the world.

From 1976 to 1980 Borg won five consecutive men's singles at Wimbledon. Calm, powerful, and efficient, he regularly beat two exciting but excitable Americans, Jimmy Connors and John McEnroe. Another superstar created by and for sports biz, Borg was a walking commercial advertisement. In 1977 he wore a headband touting Tuborg beer and a shoulder patch advertising Scandinavian airlines. Tretorn supplied his tennis shoes, Fila his shirts, shorts, socks, and warm-up suits, and Bancroft his rackets. These companies, plus endorsements for cars, cereals, games, jeans, and towels, netted Borg nearly $2 million a year.

Yet just as Borg hit the scene, both tennis and golf began to wane as television attractions. Advertisers had happily paid huge sums to reach tennis's and golf's supposedly wealthy viewers. More than team sports, tennis and golf allowed viewers to identify with players and to improve their own games by emulation. But between 1975 and 1980, television ratings of tennis and golf dropped sharply, causing sponsors to withdraw their support. Television coverage had overextended to numerous inconsequential tournaments involving unknown competitors. Possibly more to the point, both tennis and golf were games limited in variety, pace, and drama, except for the very best matches.

Another traditional amateur program, the Olympic Games, has proved to be filled with the variety and fast-paced action that tennis and golf apparently lack. Certainly Olympic sports and athletes have, in the 1970s, become entangled in a commercial maze. Beginning in the 1960s, ABC made the Olympics into a media extravaganza. When the United States boycotted the Moscow Summer Olympics in 1980, American television and advertisers lost millions of dollars. If one can judge from past procedures, the best athletes also lost bundles. Mark Spitz, winner of seven gold medals in swimming at Munich in 1972, and Bruce Jenner, victor in the decathlon at Montreal in 1976, translated gold medals into gold-studded contracts to endorse everything imaginable. Spitz and Jenner were not the first to capitalize on Olympic fame, of course. Johnny Weissmuller did it in 1928, Babe Didrikson in 1932, and Sonja Henie in 1936, to name just a few. But now the practice has become such a fine art, such an expected ritual, that Eric Heiden was thought somewhat strange when he refused to lend his name to profitable endorsements after winning several gold medals in ice-skating at Lake Placid in 1980.

His ice-hockey comrades had no such qualms. The shouting had barely subsided after America's victory over the Russians and Finns before a half-dozen of the American gold medalists signed multiyear contracts with teams in the National Hockey League for salaries averaging almost $100,000 a season. Star goalie Jim Craig especially received royal treatment. On the day after the final game, Craig and his mates went to the White House to meet President and Mrs. Jimmy Carter. On the very next morning, Craig appeared on the nationally televised "Good Morning America" before flying on to Boston, where a fleet of limousines and motorcycle policemen escorted him from Logan Airport to his home in nearby North Easton. Amid the hoopla, Craig signed a three-year contract with the Atlanta Flames, a young NHL franchise that had drafted him two years earlier following his sophomore season at Boston University. Craig received a $45,000 bonus for signing, a salary of about $85,000 a year, and a guarantee of endorsements. From Coca-Cola alone he pocketed $35,000 for a one-minute television commercial. As he lined up in goal against the Colorado Rockies less than a month after his Olympic conquest, a packed house of more than 15,000 shook the rafters with cheers. No longer an amateur even in name, Jim Craig was now a legitimate member of the sports-biz team.

Lest anyone conclude, however, that Americans have a monopoly on commercial sports, recent developments even in the old English game of cricket exemplify the direction of modern sports. Professionals had long played alongside amateurs in first-class cricket, but "players and gentlemen" distinctions traditionally kept the differences clear. Amateur gentlemen held the upper hand. At the administrative level, cricket was governed by some of the most conservative elder sportsmen imaginable, men spiritually akin to the rich founders and defenders of Olympic amateurism. Concerned with protecting the "purity" of the game, they labored voluntarily and apparently expected players to do the same. Cricketers were the worst-paid professionals of any major sport in the world.

All that changed in 1977 when Kerry Packer, an Australian television and publishing magnate, sought to televise the popular England versus Australia series over one of his Sydney channels. Conservative governors of the game rejected the proposal outright, prompting the aggressive Packer to create a World Series Cricket organization on his own terms. He offered huge salaries to the best professionals, who were threatened with expulsion for life from parent cricket organizations. Undeterred, players flocked to Packer's payroll, casting international cricket into a state of civil war. The classiest players in England, Australia, and the West Indies formed pirate teams. They also violated all the unwritten laws of style and ethical norms long practiced in cricket. For the sake of television appeal, they dressed in red, yellow, and blue uniforms instead of traditional all-white garb. They played games at night, using a white rather than a customary red ball. Offered bonuses for winning, they competed fiercely even to the point of "bowlers" (pitchers) purposely intimidating batsmen.

It was "not cricket," it was sports biz. After two years of outlawry, Packer agreed to a truce with the Old Guard of cricket. In 1979 he handed the game back to them in return for television rights and with the understanding that none of the rebel players would be penalized. But the game could never be the same again. Today, a dozen or so of the top players make $250,000 a year, and they compete in a fashion that makes older enthusiasts mourn the death of "a game that was once played by gentlemen." Like most amateur and professional sports, cricket was thrown into a blender with commercial enterprise, television revenue, and rabid spectator interest. The resultant concoction was sports biz.

Chapter **20**

SPORTS IN PERSPECTIVE

As the economic dog wags the tail of sports, much of modern sport seems twisted and bent out of shape. Effectively silenced is the voice of Grantland Rice, who several decades ago championed the amateur ideal of sportsmanship. His famous doggerel merely irritates the minds of modern sportsmen. "Grantland Rice, the great sportswriter, once said, 'It's not whether you win or lose, but how you play the game,' " observes Gene Autry, the former Hollywood cowboy who now owns the California Angels baseball club. "Well," Autry candidly concludes, "Grantland Rice can go to hell as far as I am concerned."

Primarily concerned with the ledger sheet of his business enterprise, Gene Autry's heart is with Vince Lombardi, not with Grantland Rice. "The teams that win the most make the most money," Lombardi once reasonably remarked. Given his premise, Lombardi's conclusion was perfectly logical: "Winning isn't everything; it's the only thing." Yet that logic is fundamentally flawed, for even professional sport cannot live by it and long endure. Certainly at levels beneath the professional ranks, the attitude popularly associated with Vince Lombardi but more crudely practiced by others has become a blight on sports. When winning becomes the sole criterion of athletic achievement, college recruiters callously break rules and lie to prospective athletes, coaches treat young men and women as mere "meat on the hoof," violent tactics become the acceptable norm, and even children's games are marred by adult ambitions.

The spirit of Grantland Rice roams restlessly, unable to find a home. Long has it struggled for a place in the modern Olympic Games, where idealistic sportsmanship tends to be sacrificed to fame and fortune under the name of patriotism. Not even Wimbledon, the most staid and prestigious of all the tennis championships, is exempt from the win-at-all-costs mentality. "I won. That's the important thing," crowed John McEnroe after he defeated Bjorn Borg for the crown in 1981. Unfortunately, McEnroe's "winning attitude" produced the most vulgar display of abusive language and petty behavior ever witnessed on center court. Such outbursts lend credence to the harsh judgments of pundits like Leonard Shecter, author of *The Jocks* (1969), who lambasts "the greedy professionals and posturing amateurs, the crooks, thieves, the knaves and fools" associated with modern sport. Having little good to say about athletes, "the spoiled brats" of modern society, Shecter admits to being "a man who hates sports." His tirades are tiresome, although mercifully without the Marxist jargon of critics such as Paul Hoch, whose *Rip Off the Big Game: The Exploitation of Sports by the Power Elite* (1972) insists that the system of modern sport is foul at the core as sport replaces religion as the demonic "opiate of the people."

Far more noteworthy is a new breed of critic that has emerged within the past decade. For the first time in history, athletes themselves have stepped out of the locker room to admit that all is not wonderful in the wonderland of sports. An American major-league baseball pitcher, Jim Bouton, led the parade in 1970 with a controversial best seller, *Ball Four*. No doubt compelled by economic interests as well as candor, Bouton audaciously revealed that certain players (whom he called by name) idolized by the public were in fact philanderers, drunkards, and simpletons of mind and tongue. According to baseball commissioner Bowie Kuhn, Bouton did the game "a grave disservice."

Yet *Ball Four* was only a firecracker compared to the bombshells dropped by several football players in the early 1970s. Dave Meggyesy's *Out of Their League* (1970), Bernie Parrish's *They Call It a Game* (1971), Ralph "Chip" Oliver's *High for the Game* (1971), and Gary Shaw's *Meat on the Hoof* (1972) were born of a decade of consciousness awakened to the evils of war, racial prejudice, and exploitation. All these authors were experienced athletes who had become soured on the brutal, dehumanizing process to which coaches and players alike succumb for the sake of the bitch goddess, gridiron glory. Several contemporary novelists wrote from a similar point of view. Don DeLillo's provocative *End Zone* (1972), Dan Jenkins's zany *Semi-Tough* (1972), and Peter Gent's bizarre *North Dallas Forty* (1974) depict American footballers as a bunch of juveniles inhabiting brawny adult bodies, bent on sex, booze, drugs, violence, and crudity. Through all this prose, fiction and nonfiction alike, runs a stream of revulsion against a complex system of pressure from parents, fans, coaches, and teammates to win, whatever the cost to human relationships, civilized behavior, or physical safety.

Products of a critical, self-doubting era in American life, these wholesale indictments of football hardly represent the whole truth. Perhaps American football is the most violent of all sports, rivaled only by professional boxing and ice hockey. But certainly not all, or even most, football players and coaches fit the profile of a psychotic personality. Still, the raw revelations of Dave Meggyesy and his kind cannot be easily dismissed—not as long as a young man named Darryl Stingley sits crippled in a wheelchair from a legal, lethal blow from the forearm of an opponent who prides himself on being an "assassin"; not as long as one of the biggest winning coaches in the United States, Woody Hayes, declares that football is "just damn near everything" to him, but within the next month is fired for angrily assaulting an opposing player on the sidelines; not as long as a writer for *Sports Illustrated*, John Underwood, continues to document the debacle, as in *The Death of an American Game: The Crisis in Football* (1979).

One would be remiss, however, to point the accusing finger solely at American football. Violent excess for the sake of victory is endemic to most sports today. National Hockey League warriors scandalously wield their sticks like machetes and fight at the drop of a puck. "If you can't beat them in the alley, you can't beat them on the ice," says one crusty old NHL owner in all seriousness. Even the supposedly nonviolent game of NBA basketball is not immune to alley fighting. Huge inside men ruthlessly muscle for position under the boards; a savage blow by Kermit Washington to the face of Rudy Tomjanovich was merely one of several violent brawls in the bloodletting season of 1977.

Nor do North Americans have an inside track on violence. Unnecessary roughness frequently rouses the emotions of Latin American soccer players and fans to a fighting pitch. In English Rugby Union football, presumably "a game for hooligans played by gentlemen," injuries to legs, heads, and spines have risen at an alarming rate. The gentlemen now play like hooligans. Investigations sponsored by the British Medical Association indicate that one-third of the mounting list of injuries are caused by "foul play." Rugby football in distant Australia and New Zealand is characterized by an even more gloomy record of abuse. Of the hundreds of major injuries suffered in 1978, six produced quadriplegics and twelve resulted in death.

Even the most gentlemanly team sport of all, cricket, now seethes with danger at the international level. Fast West Indian bowlers especially delight in making mincemeat of English batsmen. They send the ball careening off the ground at a hundred miles an hour, evening old scores or simply trying to intimidate the batter. "It's frightening," admits England's most famous cricketer, Geoffrey Boycott, "and anyone who says anything else is stupid. Imagine standing on the central divider of a freeway and every few minutes stepping into the fast lane. If the first three missiles don't get you, the fourth one will." Shades of the death of gentlemanly sport: Boycott now wears a plastic helmet and face visor.

Some perspective is in order. Within the past two decades, violence at all levels of Western society has become more visible, largely because of the all-probing television camera. Visibility apparently leads to imitation. Ugly confrontations between police and citizens, outrageous hooligan riots, numerous acts of terrorism and crime, vicious outbreaks of "limited war" between nations—these constitute the daily diet of Western television audiences. As usual, the character of sport is in tune with the temper of the times.

Sport in fact has never lacked violence. From the earliest contests of strength in primeval forest clearings to the latest stretcher case on a Saturday afternoon, severe injuries and occasional deaths constantly recur in the history of sports. The ancient Greek pancration, medieval jousts, peasant football matches, bare-knuckle pugilism, and the American college football crisis in the early years of this century are simply the most glaring occasions of bygone athletic brutality. Yet the present scene is altogether different. In *Seasons of Shame: The New Violence in Sports* (1979), Robert C. Yeager considers today's problem as one of larger, stronger players than ever before; of equipment such as the hard-shell football helmet designed to inflict harm as much as to protect players; and most important, of a pervasive attitude of intimidation encouraged by coaches and other officials. In the final analysis, the "new violence" in sports stems from the assumption that winning *is* everything.

Youths have to be taught not only to fight wars, but also to strive single-mindedly for athletic victory. In American sports especially, the indoctrination begins early. Before parents allow their children to compete in Little League baseball, Pop Warner football, YMCA basketball, or Peewee ice-hockey programs, they would do well to read Martin Ralbovsky's *Lords of the Locker Room* (1974). In Ralbovsky's estimation, "the American way" of coaching young athletes represents a clear and present danger to every sensible democratic principle on which the Republic was founded. Ambitious, noisy parents as well as coaches are called to task by Thomas Tutko and William Burns in *Winning Is Everything and Other American Myths* (1976). A more balanced assessment of youth programs by Rainer Martens, editor of *Joy and Sadness in Children's Sports* (1978), still offers little hope that the legacy of Vince Lombardi is anything but alive and well in the American sporting cradle.

All hope abandon, ye who enter the American high school and college scenes. Most high school athletes—especially the "successful" ones—are now professionals in the ancient Greek sense: training full time year-round for their competitive games. The versatile, all-around athlete is an endangered species. In order to excel in one's best sport, a potential passport to a college scholarship, one must now specialize, lift weights regularly, train and play off-season practice games, and in some cases stay in high school an extra year for growth and athletic experience. Appropriately tacked to the walls of many high school locker rooms is the cliché "Winners never quit, and quitters never win." Winners certainly never quit; they hardly ever rest from their athletic labors.

The best high school athletes graduate to a college job market that has been candidly surveyed by Kenneth Denlinger and Leonard Shapiro in *Athletes for Sale* (1975) and by Joseph Durso in *The Sport Factory: An Investigation into College Sports* (1975). For "blue chip" candidates, many college recruiters eagerly bend and break every rule possible; programs rise or fall primarily on the basis of effective recruitment. "The need to win—it's such nonsense!" declared Joe Paterno, the highly successful head football coach at Penn State University. "There's enough glory on the field for both sides," he added. "Why is it necessary, if a team wins by a point, to make them heroes and the other guys bums?" But Paterno was referring to children's sports programs, not to his own world of intercollegiate athletics. In "big-time" college sports the expectations of university officials and alumni create a pressure to win that is as intense as any present at the professional level. Gentlemanly Joe Paterno, for all his reflective, professorial image, keeps his job because of his excellent win-loss record. Winning programs make money, and more money produces stronger programs and thus more victories. As success builds on itself, ruthless recruiting tactics, illegal subsidies, and loose eligibility standards for academically weak athletes all tend to obliterate the traditional concept of the student athlete.

Indictments of the college "win-at-any-cost" ethic appear in the most unexpected places. In 1979 Norm Ellenberger, the head basketball coach at the University of New Mexico, was dismissed for having violated NCAA recruitment policies. Subsequently, he was charged on twenty-two counts of fraudulently taking money from the athletic budget. At his trial in the early summer of 1981, the jury found him guilty on all but one of the charges, making him liable for an extended prison term. At the sentencing, however, Judge Phillip Baiamonte astounded the courtroom by imposing a mere one-year unsupervised probation. As Baiamonte explained, he was simply unwilling to imprison a coach for "basically doing what almost everybody in this community wanted him to do—win basketball games at any cost and by whatever means might be necessary to do that." It appeared that "just about everybody looked the other way as the rules or law were either being bent or broken—until the defendant got caught." Having attended only one New Mexico Lobos basketball game, Judge Baiamonte admitted frankly to being "appalled at the crowd screaming its disapproval at every call the referee made against the Lobos." Whether the referee was right or wrong mattered little: "There again, it seemed that it didn't matter how the game was being played but whether the Lobos won or lost that counted." The judge concluded: "Naturally the rules and laws were bent. Is anyone surprised?"

Certainly not. Nor can lovers of sport afford to close their eyes to such warped, unhealthy tendencies. Love is blind at its own peril. Long ago the founder of the modern Olympic Games, Baron Pierre de Coubertin, warned that "Athleticism can occasion the most noble passions or the most vile; it can develop impartiality and the feeling of honor as can love of winning; it can be chivalrous or corrupt, vile, bestial; one can use it to consolidate peace or to prepare for war." Only a fool would insist that sports today are free of vile passions, corrupt attitudes, and bestial behavior. But only a confirmed cynic will let the case rest there.

Despite all its abuses, sport deserves two cheers on the order of the "Two Cheers for Democracy" proposed by the English novelist E. M. Forster on the eve of World War II. As the democratic West entered into a life-and-death struggle with fascism, Forster saw democracy as an imperfect but nonetheless admirable form of government. Flawed as it was, it was the best system available. It deserved not three cheers, but it surely deserved two. Modern sport is similarly worthy of two cheers.

Two cheers for sports today because they are open to all. Within the past century, numerous economic, racial, and sexual barriers to athletic participation have fallen. Blacks in South Africa are still excluded from white men's games, and subtle forms of social discrimination still exist throughout the Western world. But most people in most places—whether poor or rich, female or male, black or white, handicapped or physically hardy—can find appropriate sports and reasonable levels of competition. Although there is only one NCAA championship team each year, the intercollegiate, intramural, YMCA, and industrial basketball teams number in the hundreds of thousands. Jack Nicklaus and Bjorn Borg are in a class to themselves, but the worst duffer imaginable can now compete on the golf course or tennis court, and at minimal cost. Rare indeed are the superstars on the order of Pelé, Pete Rose, O. J. Simpson, and Muhammed Ali; common as grains of sand are handballers, bowlers, softballers, and volleyball players of all sizes, ages, and shapes.

In communist and capitalist countries alike, mass participation in sports is at an all-time high. In East Germany more than 8,000 sports and recreational clubs are attached to factories, collective farms, craft cooperatives, universities and colleges, technical schools, and army and police units, attracting several million active members. In the more democratic nations of western Europe, "trim" movements everywhere feature cycling, swimming, and running programs. Some are sponsored by governments, others by private clubs. Ski slopes and ice-skating rinks are jammed with winter participants, as are public swimming pools and neighborhood playgrounds in the summer. Organized "fun runs" are common. The "Sports for All" movement is an international event. Sport is a universal language.

In the United States sport is a national obsession. According to a U.S. Department of Health, Education, and Welfare report in 1978, about 42 percent of the American population twenty-two years of age and over participate in at least one sport. For both sexes, bowling, tennis, softball, golf, basketball, and volleyball headed the list of competitive games. Even more popular is jogging—for health, trim physiques, and the supposed "inner joy" that comes with exercise and fitness. In 1979 pollster Louis Harris estimated that American joggers numbered about 17 million. Many joggers, not content with the daily grind of casual, individual effort, compete in the hundreds of annual marathons that have sprung up in cities and towns throughout the United States. The recent growth of the Boston Marathon illustrates the trend. More than 8,000 entrants in 1979 prompted Boston officials to enact stringent qualifying requirements in order to reduce the number of runners. Greater still has been the dramatic expansion of the New York Marathon. Begun in 1970 with only 126 entrants, it was jammed with 14,000 competitors in 1980, and it had to turn away another 20,000 applicants.

Only the most hostile critics withhold applause for healthy mass-participant sports. Commercial spectator sports are another matter altogether. The "big game" and its huge crowds are often compared to ancient Roman "bread and circuses." Modern gladiators, prone to exploitation, violence, and win-at-all-costs attitudes, are easy targets of criticism. So are modern spectators. On the one hand they are condemned by association

The modern athlete's skill, artistry, and competitive verve provide some of the beauty and excitement formerly reserved for theatrical performances, as illustrated here at a University of Maine ice hockey match played under the lights to a packed house. (Courtesy of the University of Maine at Orono.)

with the few hoodlums and drunken rowdies who inevitably show up at sporting contests; on the other hand, they are supposedly lulled into insensible, politically inactive dummies little different from their ancient Roman forebears. Often on the receiving end of "cheap shots," spectator sports constitute one of the few subjects on which Neo-Marxists, liberal intellectuals, and effete conservatives can agree.

Two cheers for sports because they provide drama and excitement for spectators. Sports arenas are the theaters for modern man. Like wandering medieval actors who attracted the entire village to the front steps of the parish church, today's athletes inspire city folks from widely divergent ethnic and economic backgrounds to gather around a common spectacle. As did ancient Greek drama, modern sporting events invite vicarious participation in conflict, tension, and resolution. A skilled, disciplined, physically exciting performance delights sports fans no less than it does viewers of classical ballet.

Amid all the commercial trappings, drama and beauty remain the essential, wholesome attractions of modern spectator sports. On the edge of their seats, spectators become enraptured in a close, hard-fought game, then spontaneously erupt in demonstrative appreciation for a decisive play. Perhaps it is their only opportunity for emotional release for the entire week. Better one than none. A courageous goal-line stand, a twisting drive to the basket, a leaping catch against the outfield wall, a spectacular breakaway and release of the puck or soccer ball into the net—such feats represent moments of excellence communally shared. Christopher Lasch, author of the highly acclaimed *Culture of Narcissism* (1979), says it well: "Games and athletic contests offer a dramatic commentary on reality rather than an escape from it—a heightened reenactment of communal traditions, not a repudiation of them."

Hardly are most sports spectators passive, mindless gawkers at a spectacle far removed from their experience. Likely as not, spectators are themselves active or former athletes, knowledgeable connoisseurs of good play. According to researchers in both Europe and the United States, the majority of spectators simply do not fit the stereotype of sedentary, inactive individuals. Nor are they predominantly one-dimensional people interested in little else but sports and beer swilling. Several recent studies suggest that people who attend athletic events also read more books, attend more concerts and plays, visit more museums, and participate more regularly in politics than do nonspectators. No doubt the aggregate profile of armchair viewers of televised sport is somewhat different. But two cheers for spectators as well as for the sports they enjoy.

Yet sports are primarily about, and for, athletes. Two cheers for sports because they provide unique opportunities for the testing and honing of one's physical skills. Bill Russell's personal experience represents a universal pattern. As a teenage basketballer, the painfully awkward Russell first imitated his more polished peers, then imagined himself making certain moves with and without the ball, and finally invented his own distinctive style of play. "Every day turned into an adventure," Russell remembered years later. A way with words, a love of music, and a growth in social grace all contributed to Bill Russell's youthful adventure. Two cheers for all those discoveries, and for the expansive, adventurous possibilities he found in sports.

Two more cheers for the pleasures that come with mature athletic achievement. Like creative artists whose moments of splendor occur after months and years of work to perfect their craft, athletes savor those rare, scintillating moments when mind, body, and soul function in triumphant unison. Few athletes can run the four-minute mile, but many know the authenticity of Roger Bannister's "moment of mixed joy and anguish" when there was "no pain, only a great unity of movement and aim." For Bannister in 1954, "the world seemed to stand still, or did not exist" as he sprinted down the stretch knowing that it was his chance "to do one thing supremely well."

The essence of athletics is in doing something supremely well. Not for the fans in the stadium. Not for the sportwriters and commentators. Not for the coach on the sidelines. But rather for oneself, for the satisfaction and pride that come with performing at one's peak. Yuri Vlasov, the great Soviet weight lifter, hails the "precious, white moment" of athletic prowess: "At the peak of tremendous and victorious effort, while the blood is pounding in your head, all suddenly becomes quiet within you. Everything seems clearer and whiter than ever before, as if great spotlights had been turned on. At that moment you have the conviction that you contain all the power in the world, that you are capable of everything, that you have wings."

If this language sounds similar to the language of religious mysticism, sexual delight, or even a drug trip, so be it. But what about the supposed character-building value of sports? According to the claims of Muscular Christians in the nineteenth century and their modern (usually secular) successors, sports instill discipline, courage, and the ability to cope with pressure. Paul "Bear" Bryant, head football coach at the University of Alabama, reasons that when his players learn to fight doggedly on the gridiron, they develop those qualities of character necessary for future success: "When you're 35 and you got the ranch mortgaged and your children need clothes and the banker turns you down, and you drive home and your wife's run off with a drummer . . ., by God, you better know how to fight by then!" True, and perhaps the demands of intense athletic competition will have fostered such determination. But so do the less spectacular pressures of school debates, elections, and examinations; ballet and piano recitals, job interviews, and preparations for a professional career. Sports tend to whet competitive impulses to an addictive level that is useful for career building but potentially damaging in the more personal realms of friendship, marriage, and family. Like all other competitive endeavors, sport builds mature character in some participants and makes egocentric, infantile characters of others.

Given its ambivalent possibilities as a moral agent, if sport is not fun then it is not worth the bother except for professional purposes. "We should stop preaching about sport's moral values," says Bruce Kidd, the Canadian Olympic distance runner. "Sports, after all, isn't Lent. It's a pleasure of the flesh." Ironically, professional athletes best articulate this point. In *Life on the Run* (1976), Bill Bradley tells about one particularly satisfying game with the New York Knicks, when an excellent performance momentarily pushed aside the tedium and fatigue of a long NBA season. "There are not many aspects of life," observes Bradley, "where contentment follows so quickly the exhilaration of a total coordinated effort."

Coordinated team efforts are especially liable to produce memorable moments of delight. In one of the finest passages of the best book ever written by a former athlete, Bill Russell in *Second Wind: The Memoirs of an Opinionated Man* (1979) remembers "that special feeling" when Celtic games rose to new levels of instinctive excellence—when both teams were competitively even and playing their best. Such "magical spells" usually began when three or four star players suddenly "heated up," serving as catalysts for the rest. "The feeling would spread to the other guys, and we'd all levitate," writes Russell. "Then the game would just take off, and there'd be a natural ebb and flow that reminded you of how rhythmic and musical basketball is supposed to be." As opponents became engulfed in "a white heat of competition," Russell somehow did not feel competitive; the score became irrelevant. He found himself rooting for the other team to keep up the spine-tingling spell of expert faking, cutting, passing, shooting, and blocking shots. Then an injury, a bad play, or a bad call by the referee broke the spell, which could seldom be retrieved. Yet those spells, adds Russell, "were sweet when they came, and the hope that one would come was one of my strongest motivations for walking out there."

A natural ebb and flow, rhythmic and musical, magically sweet to the soul—that is sport at its best. When all the critics have leveled their worst indictments against the commercial, inhumane tendencies of modern sports, we are still left with a ritual that is no less magical to us than to our primitive ancestors. Sports today, as always, are about life and liveliness. According to social scientist Ernest Becker, they are still a ritualistic affirmation of life over death. An ardent baseball fan, Yale University President A. Bartlett Giamatti says it best:

> Of course, there are those . . . who grow out of sports. And there are others who were born with the wisdom to know that nothing lasts. These are the truly tough among us, the ones who can live without illusion. I am not grown-up or up-to-date. I am a simpler creature, tied to more primitive patterns and cycles. I need to think something lasts forever, and it might as well be that state of being that is a game; it might as well be that, in a green field, in the sun.

Or in a gymnasium, under the lights. Or perhaps even in a domed stadium. Two cheers for sports.

Sources and Suggested Readings

For the first edition of his *Sports and Pastimes of the People of England*, Joseph Strutt in 1801 admitted to "many omissions, as well as many errors" because he had often been forced "to proceed without any guide, and explore, as it were, the recesses of a trackless wilderness." Although that wilderness is now much better charted, the quality of the guides varies greatly. The purpose of this essay is to acquaint general readers and students with the most reliable sources now available on sports history.

Some of the best sources are in German and other non-English languages, but for the sake of brevity only titles in English will be mentioned. This list is also restricted to books. Serious scholars interested in the history of sports know that articles are to be found regularly, and increasingly, in the various historical journals. Of the many scholarly journals that concentrate specifically on sports, the *Journal of Sport History*, *Stadion*, the *Journal of Sport and Social Issues*, the *Canadian Journal of History of Sport and Physical Education*, *Research Quarterly*, *Quest*, the *Journal of Sport Behavior*, and the *International Review of Sport Sociology* head the list. Each issue of the *Journal of Sport History* devotes a section to surveys of periodical literature.

Reference and General Histories

For a critical survey of the sources available for sports studies with emphasis on the United States, see Robert J. Higgs, *Sports: A Reference Guide* (Westport, Conn.: Greenwood, 1982). Most of the individual sports have specialized encyclopedias, but for more general reference, see Frank G. Menke, *The Encyclopedia of Sports* (New York: A. S. Barnes, 1978, 6th revised ed.), and J. A. Cuddon, *The International Dictionary of Sports and Games* (New York: Schocken, 1980). Best of all is John Arlott, ed., *The Oxford Companion to Sports and Games* (London: Oxford University Press, 1975), which gives brief, fairly accurate histories of most all the sports and games known in the West.

A concise survey of sports history, Peter C. McIntosh, *Sport in Society* (London: C. A. Watts, 1963), centers primarily on British sports. Walter

Umminger, *Supermen, Heroes and Gods: The Story of Sports through the Ages*, trans. James Clark (London: Thames and Hudson, 1963) is more international in focus but thematically rather than chronologically organized. Much information on sports as well as physical education can be found in Deobold B. Van Dalen and Bruce L. Bennett, *A World History of Physical Education: Cultural, Philosophical, Comparative* (Englewood Cliffs, N.J.: Prentice-Hall, 1953, 1971). Useful but uneven in quality are two compilations of essays by Earle F. Zeigler, ed., *A History of Sport and Physical Education to 1900* (Champaign, Ill.: Stipes, 1973) and *History of Physical Education and Sport* (Englewood Cliffs, N.J.: Prentice-Hall, 1979).

Numerous surveys of sport and recreation are available for England, Canada, and the United States. In order of reliability, for England see H. A. Harris, *Sport in Britain: Its Origins and Development* (London: Stanley Paul, 1975); Norman Wymer, *Sport in England: A History of Two Thousand Years of Games and Pastimes* (London: Harrap, 1949); Christina Hole, *English Sports and Pastimes* (London: Batsford, 1949); and John Armitage, *Man at Play: Nine Centuries of Pleasure Making* (London: Frederick Warne, 1977). For Canada, Nancy Howell and Max L. Howell, *Sports and Games in Canadian Life: 1700 to the Present* (Toronto: Macmillan of Canada, 1969), is strong on documentation, weak on analysis. *Sport Canadiana*, edited by Barbara Schrodt, Gerald Redmond, and Richard Baka (Edmonton: Executive Sport Publications, 1980), provides useful chronological data and fine illustrations.

The physically active character of sport naturally lends itself to pictures. The first important history of American sports, John Allen Krout, *Annals of American Sport* (New Haven: Yale University Press, 1929), weaves a light narrative around pictures, as does Wells Twombly, *Two Hundred Years of Sport in America: A Pageant of a Nation at Play* (New York: McGraw-Hill, 1976). Even lighter are the texts of John Durant, *Pictorial History of American Sports* (New York: A. S. Barnes, 1952), and Herbert Manchester, *Four Centuries of Sport in America, 1490–1890* (New York: Derrydale, 1931).

For more solid narratives, see Foster Rhea Dulles, *America Learns to Play* (New York: Appleton-Century, 1940, reprinted in 1965 as *A History of Recreation: America Learns to Play*); Betty Spears and Richard A. Swanson, *History of Sport and Physical Activity in the United States* (Dubuque, Iowa: William C. Brown, 1978); and John A. Lucas and Ronald A. Smith, *Saga of American Sports* (Philadelphia: Lea & Febiger, 1978). Another narrative, John Rickards Betts, *America's Sporting Heritage: 1850–1950* (Reading, Mass.: Addison-Wesley, 1974), is filled to the point of congestion with rich documentation. By far the most analytical, sophisticated survey of American sports is Benjamin G. Rader, *American Sports: From the Age of Folk Games to the Age of the Spectator* (Englewood Cliffs, N.J.: Prentice-Hall, 1982).

Except for James Riordan, *Sport in Soviet Society: Development of Sport and Physical Education in Russia and the USSR* (Cambridge: Cambridge University Press, 1977), and Richard Holt, *Sport and Society in Modern France* (London: Macmillan, 1981), no surveys of the history of sports in Europe are available in English. The German, Italian, and Scandinavian stories especially need to be made accessible to English readers, as do the altogether different histories of sport in Africa and South America.

Part I (to c. 1500)

For the relation of play to competitive impulses, one must turn to anthropologists such as Elliott M. Avedon and Brian Sutton-Smith, *The Study of Games* (New York: Wiley, 1971), and Margaret Mead, ed., *Cooperation and Competition among Primitive Peoples* (New York: McGraw-Hill, 1937); to historians such as Johan Huizinga, *Homo Ludens: A Study of the Play Element in Culture* (Boston: Beacon, 1955), and Allen Guttmann, *From Ritual to Record: The Nature of Modern Sports* (New York: Columbia University Press, 1978); to philosophers such as Roger Caillois, *Man, Play and Games*, trans. Meyer Barash (New York: Schocken, 1979), and Paul Weiss, *Sport: A Philosophic Inquiry* (Carbondale, Ill.: Southern Illinois University Press, 1969); and to psychologists such as Arnold R. Beisser, *The Madness in Sports: Psycho-Social Observations on Sports* (New York: Appleton-Century-Crofts, 1967), and Susanna Millar, *The Psychology of Play* (Baltimore: Penguin, 1968).

A popular treatment of the ancient ritualistic origins of sports can be found in R. Brasch, *How Did Sports Begin? A Look at the Origins of Man at Play* (New York: McKay, 1970). More stolid is the anthropological research of Theodore Stern, *The Rubber Ball-Games of the Americas* (Seattle: University of Washington Press, 1949), and Stewart Culin, *Games of the North American Indians* (New York: Dover, 1975, originally published in 1907). Fine pictures accompany the judicious text of A. D. Touney and Steffan Wenig, *Sport in Ancient Egypt*, trans. Joan Becker (Amsterdam: Grüner, 1971).

The classic treatment of the earliest organized athletic contests is E. Norman Gardiner, *Athletics of the Ancient World* (Oxford: Clarendon, 1930). The Greeks stand tall in the story, of course, as outlined in Gardiner's *Greek Athletic Sports and Festivals* (London: Macmillan, 1910), and H. A. Harris, *Greek Athletes and Athletics* (London: Hutchinson, 1964). John Murrell, *Athletics, Sports and Games* (London: George Allen & Unwin, 1975), is brief and simple but reliable enough to be useful for readers on the run. For the more serious-minded, Rachel S. Robinson, ed., *Sources for the History of Greek Athletics* (Chicago: Ares, 1980, originally published privately in Cincinnati, 1955), is invaluable.

At the pinnacle of the Greek athletic circuit, remote little Olympia comes alive in E. Norman Gardiner, *Olympia: Its History and Remains* (Oxford: Clarendon, 1925), and even more so in Ludwig Drees, *Olympia: Gods, Artists and Athletes*, trans. Gerald Onn (New York: Praeger, 1968). Nicolas Yalouris, ed., *The Eternal Olympics* (New Rochelle, N.Y.: Caratzas, 1979), combines a popular narrative with dazzling pictures of Greek athletes taken from vases, statues, and the like. For the best of current critical scholarship on the Olympics, see M. I. Finley and H. W. Pleket, *The Olympic Games: The First Thousand Years* (London: Chatto and Windus, 1976).

The transition from Greek to Roman games is admirably sketched in H. A. Harris, *Sport in Greece and Rome* (London: Thames and Hudson, 1972), and the Roman spectacles are critically surveyed in Auguet Roland, *Cruelty and Civilization: The Roman Games* (New York: Humanities, 1972). The organization, excitement, and social function of chariot races are detailed in Alan Cameron, *Circus Factions: Blues and Greens at Rome and Byzantium* (Oxford: Clarendon, 1976). Michael Grant, *Gladiators* (London: Weidenfeld and Nicolson, 1967) describes the gaudy gore of the Colosseum.

The best source on the introduction and adaptation of ancient ritualistic ball play in medieval Europe is Robert W. Henderson, *Ball, Bat and Bishop: The Origin of Ball Games* (New York: Rockport, 1947). For one of the earliest ball games recognizable to modern readers, see Albert de Luze, *A History of the Royal Game of Tennis*, trans. Sir Richard Hamilton (Kineton: Roundwood, 1979). Various forms of football also emerged in the Middle Ages, according to Francis Peabody Magoun, Jr., *History of Football from the Beginnings to 1871* (Bochum-Langendreer: Poppinghaus, 1938; Johnson Reprint, 1979), and the early chapters in Morris Marples, *A History of Football* (London: Secker and Warburg, 1954), and Percy M. Young, *A History of British Football* (London: Stanley Paul, 1968).

For archery, a favorite medieval sport as well as military necessity, Edmund Burke, *The History of Archery* (New York: Morrow, 1957), and Robert Hardy, *Longbow: A Social and Military History* (Cambridge: Patrick Stephens, 1976), are useful. On upper-class tournaments, no recent book can replace two older volumes, Francis Henry Cripps-Day, *The History of the Tournament in England and France* (London: Bernard Quaritch, 1918; AMS Reprint, 1980), and R. Coltman Clepham, *The Tournament: Its Periods and Phases* (London: Methuen, 1919). Brief summaries of medieval aristocratic pleasures can be found in Charles Homer Hoskins, "The Latin Literature of Sport," in *Studies in Medieval Culture* (New York: Frederick Ungar, 1958), and Austin Lane Pole, "Recreations," in *Medieval England*, vol. II (Oxford: Clarendon, 1958). Unfortunately, no comprehensive history of medieval sports is available.

Part II (c. 1500 to c. 1850)

Renaissance sports also await an author who can deal with the pastimes of both the masses and the upper classes, French, German, and Italian courtiers as well as English gentlemen. On races and mimic combat in the Italian states, William Heywood, *Palio and Ponte: An Account of the Sports of Central Italy from the Age of Dante to the XXth Century* (New York: Hacker, 1969, originally published in 1904), is good. Far more fully documented are the sports and pastimes of Renaissance Englishmen: Marcia Vale, *The Gentleman's Recreations: Accomplishments and Pastimes of the English Gentlemen 1580–1630* (Totowa, N.J.: Rowman and Littlefield, 1977), and Roger Longrigg, *The English Squire and His Sport* (London: Michael Joseph, 1977). Reginald Lennard, ed., *Englishmen at Rest and Play* (Oxford: Clarendon, 1931), considers various aspects of leisure from 1558 to 1714. Covering precisely the same period but much more fully and critically is Dennis Brailsford, *Sport and Society: Elizabeth to Anne* (London: Routledge and Kegan Paul, 1969), which effectively explains the reasons for Puritan opposition to popular sports.

The best treatments of sport in Colonial America are still tucked away in scholarly journals. Robert W. Henderson, *Early American Sport* (Rutherford, N.J.: Fairleigh Dickinson, 1976, 3rd ed.), is analytically thin. The judgments of John Hervey, *Racing in America, 1665–1865*, 2 vols. (New York: Jockey Club, 1944), need revision. More useful is the survey by Jane Carson, *Colonial Virginians at Play* (Charlottesville: University Press of Virginia, 1965).

For the history of yachting and horse racing, two upper-class sports that first began to thrive in Stuart England, see Douglas Phillips-Brit, *The History of Yachting* (New York: Stein and Day, 1974), and Wray Vamplew, *The Turf: A Social and Economic History of Horse Racing* (London: Allen Lane, 1976). An activity that was even more uniquely aristocratic is described in Raymond Carr, *English Fox Hunting: A History* (London: Weidenfeld and Nicolson, 1976), and David C. Itzkowita, *Peculiar Privilege: A Social History of English Fox-Hunting, 1753–1885* (New York: Humanities, 1972); see also Carl B. Cone, ed., *Hounds in the Morning: Sundry Sports and Merry England* (Lexington: University of Kentucky Press, 1981).

Of all the old British sports and games, cricket is best represented in historical literature. The standard account is H. S. Altham and E. W. Swanton, *A History of Cricket* (London: Allen and Unwin, 1948, 4th ed.). Two newer, more lively treatments of the subject are Rowland Bowen, *Cricket: A History of Its Growth and Development throughout the World* (London: Eyre and Spottiswoode, 1970), and Christopher Brookes, *English Cricket: The Game and Its Players through the Ages* (London: Weidenfeld and Nicolson, 1978). Readers looking for a glossy format and simple story will like Trevor Bailey, *A History of Cricket* (Boston: Allen and Unwin, 1978), but will find two-thirds of the narrative devoted to cricket since 1945.

The beginnings of modern boxing are poorly documented. Trevor Wignall, *The Story of Boxing* (New York: Brentano's, 1924), and Nat Fleischer, *The Heavyweight Championship: An Informal History of Boxing from 1719 to the Present Day* (New York: Putnam's, 1949, 1961), are both written much better than they are researched. Somewhat better is Alexander Johnston, *Ten—and Out! The Complete Story of the Prize Ring in America* (New York: Ives Washburn, 1947, 3rd. ed.). J. C. Reid, *Bucks and Bruisers: Pierce Egan and Regency England* (London: Routledge and Kegan Paul, 1971), is a much more solid piece of work, as is Alan Lloyd, *The Great Prize Fight* (New York: Coward, McCann, and Geoghegan, 1977), on the Heenan-Sayers fight of 1860.

A little pamphlet by John Plumb, *The Commercialisation of Leisure in Eighteenth Century England* (Reading: University of Reading Press, 1973), charts the early growth of organized spectator sports in English towns and cities. In a more comprehensive fashion, Robert W. Malcolmson, *Popular Recreations in English Society, 1700–1850* (London: Cambridge University Press, 1973), attends to informal rural, plebeian traditions of recreation, then traces their decline as a result of the vast changes that accompanied the Industrial Revolution. The best of the several historians who have flocked to the subject of the origins of English mass leisure are Hugh Cunningham, *Leisure in the Industrial Revolution c.1780-c.1880* (London: Croom Helm, 1980), and Peter Bailey, *Leisure and Class in Victorian England: Rational Recreation and the Contest for Control, 1830–1885* (London: Routledge and Kegan Paul, 1978). For the larger European picture, see the brief account by Michael R. Marrus, *The Rise of Leisure in Industrial Society* (St. Louis: Forum, 1974).

Information on the beginnings of mass leisure in the United States, prior to the Civil War, is harder to find in a single volume. Jennie Holliman, *American Sports (1785–1835)* (Durham, N.C.: Seeman, 1931), is weak. Books on specific topics must suffice. For the racing craze, see John Cumming, *Runners and Walkers: A Nineteenth Century Sports Chronicle* (Chicago: Regnery, 1981), and Dwight Akers, *Drivers Up: The Story of American Harness Racing* (New York: Putnam's, 1938, 1947). Competitive rowing and yachting, the two aquatic sports in vogue in early nineteenth-century America, are popularly presented in Thomas C. Mendenhall, *A Short History of American Rowing* (Boston: Charles River, 1981), and Ian Dear, *The America's Cup: An Informal History* (New York: Dodd, Mead, 1980), but both are skimpy on the origins.

On the major sporting traditions transported to North America by immigrants, Scottish games are documented far better than are German and Swedish gymnastics. Both the continental origins and the transatlantic passage of gymnastics still need their histories told in English. For the Scottish games, on the other hand, one can turn to David Webster, *Scottish Highland Games* (Edinburgh: Reprographia, 1973). For their popularity and pervasive influence in North America, see Gerald Redmond, *The Caledonian Games in Nineteenth-Century America* and *The Sporting Scots of Nineteenth-Century Canada* (Rutherford, N.J.: Fairleigh Dickinson, 1971 and 1981 respectively).

Part III (c. 1850–1900)

James Walvin, *Leisure and Society, 1830–1950* (London: Longman, 1978), and John Lowerson and John Myerscough, *Time to Spare in Victorian England* (Brighton: Harvester, 1977), tell the broad story of the expansion of leisure activities in Victorian Britain. Concentrating on the city of Bristol, H. E. Meller, *Leisure and the Changing City, 1870–1914* (London: Routledge and Kegan Paul, 1976), does for England what Dale A. Somers, *The Rise of Sports in New Orleans, 1850–1900* (Baton Rouge: Louisiana State University Press, 1972), does for the United States. Both provide intensive studies of specific urban settings, thus inviting comparisons with leisure and sports in other places.

For the Victorian frame of mind that fostered physical activity, see Bruce Haley, *The Healthy Body and Victorian Culture* (Cambridge, Mass.: Harvard University Press, 1977). In the "public" schools, especially, games flourished as J. A. Mangan, *Athleticism in the Victorian and Edwardian Public Schools: The Emergence and Consolidation of an Educational Ideology* (Cambridge: Cambridge University Press, 1981), explains fully and well. The favorite schoolboy game was football, whose division into soccer and rugby can be studied in James Walvin, *The People's Game: A Social History of English Football* (London: Allen Lane, 1975), and Eric Dunning and Kenneth Sheard, *Barbarians, Gentlemen and Players: A Sociological Study of the Development of Rugby Football* (New York: New York University Press, 1979). On the mania for professional soccer football that swept over Victorian society, see Tony Mason, *Association Football and English Society 1863–1915* (Brighton, Sussex: Harvester, 1980), and Steven Tischler, *Footballers and Businessmen: The Origins of Professional Soccer in England* (New York: Holmes and Meier, 1981).

Unlike English soccer and rugby, American football has yet to inspire a reliable history. Early chroniclers of the game, such as Parke H. Davis, *Football: The American Intercollegiate Game* (New York: Scribner's, 1912), and Alexander M. Weyland, *American Football: Its History and Development* (New York: Appleton, 1926, reprinted as *The Saga of American Football*, 1955), are easy reading but simplistic. More recent books such as Allison Danzig, *The History of American Football: Its Great Teams, Players, and Coaches* (Englewood Cliffs, N.J.: Prentice-Hall, 1956), and John McCallum and Charles H. Pearson, *College Football U.S.A., 1869–1971* (New York: National Football Foundation, 1971), indiscriminately mix anecdote, hero-worship, and facts in a most unsatisfactory manner.

Historical accounts of American football appear all the more inferior when compared to the history of baseball. Harold Seymour, *Baseball: The Early Years* (New York: Oxford University Press, 1960) is graceful and informed; David Quentin Voight, *American Baseball: From Gentleman's Sport to the Commissioner System* (Norman: University of Oklahoma Press, 1966), is a vigorous, incisive treatment of baseball's beginnings. Robert W. Henderson, a scholar who did much to demolish the Doubleday myth, provides the more serious student with *Baseball: Notes and Materials on Its Origins* (New York: New York Public Library, 1940), and Harold Peterson, *The Man Who Invented Baseball* (New York: Scribner's, 1973), examines the life and times of the real father of baseball, Alexander Cartwright.

For the history of outdoor winter sports, see Raymond Flowers, *The History of Skiing and Other Winter Sports* (New York: Methuen, 1977); Charles M. Dudley, *60 Centuries of Skiing* (Brattleboro, Vt.: Stephen Daye, 1935); Nigel Brown, *Ice-Skating: A History* (New York: A. S. Barnes, 1959); W. A. Creelman, *Curling, Past and Present* (Toronto: McClelland Stewart, 1950); and John A. Stevenson, *Curling in Ontario 1846–1946* (Toronto: Ontario Curling Association, 1950). Unfortunately, no first-rate history of ice hockey is available. Frank Orr, *The Story of Hockey* (New York: Random House, 1971), devotes little attention to the origins of the game. For a synthesis of the beginnings of all these outdoor sports in nineteenth-century Canada, see H. Roxborough, *One Hundred—Not Out: The Story of Nineteenth-Century Canadian Sport* (Toronto: Ryerson, 1966).

For track and field athletics, Roberto L. Quercetani, *A World History of Track and Field, 1864–1964* (London: Oxford University Press, 1964), is dull but reliable. Both outdoor and indoor activities flourished in new sports clubs such as the New York Athletic Club, whose story is told in Bob Considine and Fred B. Jarvis, *The First Hundred Years: A Portrait of NYAC* (London: Macmillan, 1969). The story of the most famous of all the indoor arenas, Madison Square Garden, is attractively told by Joseph Durso, *Madison Square Garden: 100 Years of History* (New York: Simon & Schuster, 1979), and Zander Hollander, ed., *Madison Square Garden: A Century of Sport and Spectacle on the*

World's Most Versatile Stage (New York: Hawthorne, 1975). For the star of one of those spectacles, see Ben Weider, *The Strongest Man in History—Louis Cyr* (Toronto: Mitchell, 1976). A good, critical biography is badly needed for the best-known sports performer of the age, John L. Sullivan, although Donald Barr Chidsey, *John the Great: The Times and Life of a Remarkable American, John L. Sullivan* (Garden City, N.Y.: Doubleday, 1942), is a notable attempt to pierce through the yarns and anecdotes surrounding the Sullivan legend.

For the origins of basketball, one can do no better than go directly to the founder's own story: James B. Naismith, *Basketball: Its Origins and Development* (New York: Association, 1941). Bernice Larson Webb, *The Basketball Man: James Naismith* (Lawrence: University Press of Kansas, 1973), is a useful but uncritical biography. Popular histories of basketball, such as Alexander M. Weyland, *Cavalcade of Basketball* (New York: Macmillan, 1960), Neil Isaacs, *All the Moves: A History of College Basketball* (Philadelphia: Lippincott, 1975), and John D. McCallum, *College Basketball U.S.A. since 1892* (New York: Stein & Day, 1978), add little to the Naismith story.

The history of lawn tennis is to be found mostly in glossy picture-books of the coffee-table variety, such as Will Grimsley, *Tennis: Its History, People, and Events* (Englewood Cliffs, N.J.: Prentice-Hall, 1971), and Lance Tingay, *History of Lawn Tennis in Pictures* (London: Stacey, 1973). The best of this kind is Gianni Clerici, *Tennis* (London: Octopus, 1976). More specifically on American tennis is Parke Cummings, *American Tennis: The Story of a Game and Its People* (Boston: Little, Brown, 1957).

For pictures and a light narrative on the golfing boom in the late nineteenth century, see Will Grimsley, *Golf: Its History, People, and Events* (Englewood Cliffs, N.J.: Prentice-Hall, 1966). Attentive to the beginnings of golf in the United States are Harry B. Martin, *Fifty Years of American Golf* (New York: Dodd, Mead, 1936), and Herbert Wind Warren, *The Story of American Golf* (New York: Knopf, 1975, 3rd ed.). For Canadian links, see L. V. Kavanagh, *History of Golf in Canada* (Toronto: Fitzhenry and Whiteside, 1973).

Part IV (c. 1900–1945)

Brian Dobbs, *Edwardians at Play: Sports 1890–1914* (London: Pelham, 1973), surveys the British sporting scene at the turn of the century. It was a scene featuring new racing vehicles, illustrated in A. B. Demaus, *Victorian and Edwardian Cycling and Motoring from Old Photographs* (London: Batsford, 1977), and popularly described in John Woodforde, *The Story of the Bicycle* (London: Routledge and Kegan Paul, 1970). On the bicycle in the United States, see Robert A. Smith, *A Social History of the Bicycle: Its Early Life and Times in America* (New York: American Heritage, 1972).

For background to the beginnings of the modern Olympic Games in 1896, see John J. MacAloon, *This Great Symbol: Pierre de Coubertin and the Origins of the Modern Olympic Games* (Chicago: Universty of Chicago Press, 1981), and Richard D. Mandell, *The First Modern Olympics* (Berkeley: University of California Press, 1976). The subsequent history of the Olympics is documented in William O. Johnson, Jr., *All That Glitters Is Not Gold: The Olympic*

Games (New York: Putnam's, 1972); John Lucas, *The Modern Olympic Games* (New York: A. S. Barnes, 1980); Peter J. Graham and Horst Ueberhorst, eds., *The Modern Olympics* (Cornwall, N.Y.: Leisure, 1976); Michael Morris Killanin and John Rodda, eds., *The Olympic Games: 80 Years of People, Events and Records* (London: Barrie and Jenkins, 1976); and Dick Schaap, *An Illustrated History of the Olympics* (New York: Knopf, 1975, 3rd ed.).

A biography of *Paavo Nurmi: The Flying Finn*, by Sulo Kolkka and Helga Nygren, trans. John O. Virtanen (Helsinki: Otava, 1974), helps to fill out the Olympic story in the 1920s, as do the early sections of *"Whatta-Gal": The Babe Didrickson Story*, by William O. Johnson, Jr., and Nancy P. Williamson (Boston: Little, Brown, 1977), for the 1932 Olympics. Curiously, no good biography has yet been written on the greatest of all the Olympic champions in 1936, Jesse Owens, although he shines brightly in the solid work of Richard D. Mandell, *The Nazi Olympics* (New York: Macmillan, 1971).

A New York sportswriter, Nat Fleischer, covered boxing for the first half of this century and wrote about it in *50 Years at Ringside* (New York: Fleet, 1958). All the talk before World War I was about the proud black American Jack Johnson. The best of several biographies of Johnson, Finis Farr, *Black Champion: The Life and Times of Jack Johnson* (New York: Scribner's, 1964), suggests that Johnson was a better fighter than the memoirist, shown in *Jack Johnson Is a Dandy: An Autobiography* (New York: Chelsea House, 1969). Al-Tony Gilmore, *Bad Nigger! The National Impact of Jack Johnson* (Port Washington, N.Y.: Kennikat, 1975), is filled with raw, undigested material, but still conveys Johnson's controversial importance.

Fortunately, we have good biographies of both the best fighter and the best promoter in the 1920s: Randy Roberts, *Jack Dempsey: The Manassa Mauler* (Baton Rouge: Louisiana State University Press, 1979), and Charles Samuels, *The Magnificent Rube: The Life and Times of Tex Rickard* (New York: McGraw-Hill, 1957). For the dominant ring personality of the 1930s, see Barney Nagler, *Brown Bomber* (New York: World, 1972); Anthony O. Edmonds, *Joe Louis* (Grand Rapids, Mich.: Erdmans, 1973); and Gerald Aston, *"And a Credit to His Race": The Hard Life and Times of Joseph Louis Barrow* (New York: Saturday Review, 1974).

Baseball continues to attract the best historians. Harold Seymour, *Baseball: The Golden Age* (New York: Oxford University Press, 1971), and David Quentin Voigt, *American Baseball: From the Commissioners to Continental Expansion* (Norman: University of Oklahoma Press, 1970), both sustain the high standards established in earlier volumes. For baseball on the eve of World War I, lively first-hand accounts can be found in Lawrence S. Ritter, *The Glory of Their Times: The Story of the Early Days of Baseball Told by the Men Who Played It* (New York: Macmillan, 1966), which can profitably be read in conjunction with a thematic analysis, Steven A. Riess, *Touching Base: Professional Baseball and American Culture in the Progressive Era* (Westport, Conn.: Greenwood, 1980). A similar balance of the anecdotal and analytical is also available for the interwar period: Donald Honig, *When the Grass Was Real: Baseball from the Twenties to the Forties Told by the Men Who Played it* (New York: Coward, McCann, and Geoghegan, 1975), and Richard C. Crepeau, *Baseball: America's Diamond Mind, 1919–1941* (Orlando: University Presses of Florida, 1980).

On baseball's most famous scandal, see Eliot Asinof, *Eight Men Out: The Black Sox and the 1919 World Series* (New York: Holt, Rinehart & Winston, 1963, 1979). For a sympathetic biography of the central figure in that tragedy, see Donald Gropman, *Say It Ain't So Joe! The Story of Shoeless Joe Jackson* (Boston: Little, Brown, 1979). From the Black Sox scandal came the first powerful commissioner of baseball, who is the subject of J. G. Taylor Spink, *Judge Landis and Twenty-Five Years of Baseball* (New York: Crowell, 1947).

For the broader canvas of the 1920s, see Allison Danzig and Peter Brandwein, eds., *Sport's Golden Age: A Close-up of the Fabulous Twenties* (New York: Harper, 1948), whose variety is represented in biographies of diverse figures: Frank Deford, *Big Bill Tilden: The Triumphs and the Tragedy* (New York: Simon & Schuster, 1975); and Dick Miller, *Triumphant Journey: The Saga of Bobby Jones and the Grand Slam of Golf* (New York: Holt, Rinehart & Winston, 1980). The giant of the day, of course, was Babe Ruth, about whom at least ten biographies have been written. The most recent and best are Marshall Smelser, *The Life That Ruth Built* (New York: Quadrangle/New York Times, 1975); Robert W. Creamer, *Babe: The Legend Comes to Life* (New York: Simon & Schuster, 1974); Ken Sobel, *Babe Ruth and the American Dream* (New York: Ballantine, 1974); and Kal Wagenheim, *Babe Ruth: His Life and Legend* (New York: Praeger, 1974).

At the back side of the so-called "golden age" was an ugly reality of racial discrimination, the subject of Robert Peterson, *Only the Ball Was White* (Englewood Cliffs, N.J.: Prentice-Hall, 1970); A. S. Young, *Negro Firsts in Sports* (Chicago: Johnson, 1963); Ocania Chalk, *Pioneers of Black Sport: The Early Days of the Black Professional Athlete in Baseball, Basketball, Boxing, and Football* (New York: Dodd, Mead, 1975); Edwin B. Henderson, *The Negro in Sports* (Washington, D.C.: Associated, 1949); and William Brashler, *Josh Gibson: A Life in the Negro Leagues* (New York: Harper & Row, 1978).

For ice hockey, the major professional sport that barged to the fore between the wars, see Brian McFarlane, *60 Years of Hockey: A Complete History of the National Hockey League with All the Records and Statistics* (Toronto: McGraw-Hill–Ryerson, 1977), and Neil Isaacs, *Checking Back: A History of the National Hockey League* (New York: W. W. Norton, 1977). Another professional sport, American football, was still struggling for stability and spectator appeal, according to Harold Claasen, *The History of Professional Football* (Englewood Cliffs, N.J.: Prentice-Hall, 1963), and Tom Bennett, et. al., *The NFL Official Encyclopedic History of Professional Football* (New York: Macmillan, 1977). For one of the early leaders of the game, see George Vass, *George Halas and the Chicago Bears* (Chicago: Regnery, 1971).

On European sports during the interwar period, books in English are few but substantial. What Richard Mandell did on sports in Nazi Germany as background to the 1936 Berlin Olympics, Victoria de Grazia does even more fully for fascist Italy: *The Culture of Consent: Mass Organization of Leisure in Fascist Italy* (Cambridge: Cambridge University Press, 1981). For interwar France and Russia, see Richard Holt, *Sport and Society in Modern France* (London: Macmillan, 1981), and James Riordan, *Sport and Soviet Society: Development of Sport and Physical Education in Russia and the USSR* (Cambridge: Cambridge University Press, 1977).

Surprisingly, the contours of sport in Britain between the wars are poorly documented, except for Robert Graves and Alan Hodge, *The Long Weekend: A Social History of Great Britain, 1918–1939* (London: Faber and Faber, 1940), and Stephen Studd, *Herbert Chapman, Football Emperor: A Study in the Origins of Modern Soccer* (London: Peter Owens, 1982). Even more glaring is the absence of any source in English for the dramatic expansion of organized soccer football competition in Latin America, a subject lightly covered by Brian Glanville, *The Sunday Times History of the World Cup* (London: Times Newspapers, 1973).

Part V (1945–present)

The universal meshing of competitive sports and politics is the theme of Benjamin Lowe, David B. Kanin, and Andrew Strenk, eds., *Sport and International Relations* (Champaign, Ill.: Stipes, 1978); Richard Espy, *The Politics of the Olympic Games* (Berkeley: University of California Press, 1979); and Richard Edward Lapchick, *The Politics of Race and International Sport: The Case of South Africa* (Westport, Conn.: Greenwood, 1975). Reflecting the importance of sports in this era of the Cold War is the war metaphor in Philip Goodhart and Christopher Chataway, *War Without Weapons* (London: W. H. Allen, 1968); Scott Young, *War on Ice: Canada in International Hockey* (Toronto: McClelland and Stewart, 1976); and Howard Senzel, *Baseball and the Cold War: Being a Soliloquy on the Necessity of Baseball* (New York: Harcourt Brace Jovanovich, 1977).

James Riordan, ed., *Sport Under Communism* (Montreal: McGill-Queen's, 1978), surveys the history, organizational structure, and function of sport in the Soviet Union, Czechoslovakia, East Germany, China, and Cuba. For more on Soviet sports, see Riordan's previously cited *Sport and Soviet Society;* Henry W. Morton, *Soviet Sport: Mirror of Soviet Society* (New York: Collier, 1963); N. Norman Schneiderman, *The Soviet Road to Olympus: Theory and Practice of Soviet Physical Culture and Sport* (Ontario: Ontario Institute for Studies in Education, 1978); and Yuri Brokhin, *The Big Red Machine: The Rise and Fall of Soviet Olympic Champions*, trans. Glenn Ganelik and Yuri Brokhin (New York: Random House, 1977). Brokhin is as hostile toward the Russian Soviet system as Doug Gilbert, *The Miracle Machine* (New York: Coward, McCann and Geoghegan, 1980), is sympathetic to the East German system of sports. For yet another Soviet satellite, see Józcef Vetö, ed., *Sports in Hungary* (Budapest: Corvina, 1965).

Highly critical of recent mixtures of ideology and sports are Jean-Marie Brohm, *Sport—A Prison of Measured Time*, trans. Ian Fraser (London: Ink Links, 1978); Groussard Serge, *The Blood of Israel: The Massacre of the Israeli Athletes*, trans. Harold J. Salemson (New York: Morrow, 1975); and Baruch A. Hazan, *Olympic Sports and Propaganda Games* (New Brunswick, N.J.: Transaction, 1982).

Information on modern sports, leisure, and physical education in Scandinavia can be found in Emanuel Hansen, *Sports in Denmark* (Copenhagen: Det Danske Selskab, 1955); *Sport and Recreation in Sweden* (Stockholm: Swedish Tourist Traffic Association, 1967); *Sport in Denmark: The Development of*

Danish Physical Education and Training (Copenhagen: Det Danske Selskab, 1978); and *Physical Education and Sports in Finland* (Helsinki: Finnish Society for Research in Sports and Physical Education, 1979).

For Western European sports in the 1950s, contributors to Alex Natan, ed., *Sport and Society: A Symposium* (London: Bowes and Bowes, 1958), are especially helpful on French, German, and Italian themes. For all his idiosyncratic judgments, American journalist Robert Daley presents a lively picture of *The Bizarre World of European Sports* (New York: Morrow, 1963). English journalist Brian Glanville considers European as well as English and American athletes in *People in Sport* (London: Secker and Warburg, 1967).

For the place of leisure activities in modern Britain, see S. R. Parker and M. A. Smith, eds., *Leisure and Society in Britain* (London: Allen Lane, 1973). The excitement of soccer football for both players and spectators is conveyed in Arthur Hopcraft, *The Football Man: People and Passions in Soccer* (London: Collins, 1968); Hunter Davies, *The Glory Game* (London: Weidenfeld and Nicolson, 1972); and Gerhard Vinnai, *Football Mania. The Players and the Fans: The Mass Psychology of Football*, trans. David Fernbach and Martin Gillard (London: Ocean Books, 1973). For the business side of the game, see Derek Dougan and Percy M. Young, *On the Spot: Football as a Profession* (Newton Abbot: Readers Union, 1975).

Nicolas Mason, *Football! The Story of All the World's Football Games* (London: Temple Smith, 1974), surveys the pervasive appeal of football in various forms throughout the world. The most popular form is soccer, as detailed in Martin Tyler, *Soccer: The World Game* (New York: St. Martin's, 1978). Probably the Latin Americans are the most rabid of all soccer enthusiasts. Until that story is told in a comprehensive fashion, one can learn much from two biographies of the Brazilian superstar, Pelé: Joe Marcus, *The World of Pelé* (New York: Mason/Charter, 1976), and François Theband, *Pelé*, trans. Leo Weinstein (New York: Harper & Row, 1975).

Jonathan Kolatch, *Sports, Politics, and Ideology in China* (New York: Jonathan David, 1972) is a reminder that sports since World War II stop at no East-West boundaries. Robert Whiting, *The Chrysanthemum and the Bat: Baseball Sumurai Style* (New York: Dodd, Mead, 1977), attends to baseball in Japan, and Richard Cashman and Michael McKernan, eds., *Sport in History: The Making of Modern Sporting History* (St. Lucia: University of Queensland Press, 1979), focuses primarily on Australian sports past and present.

The centrality of sports in the United States is fully documented in Frederick W. Cozens and Florence S. Stumpf, *Sports in American Life* (Chicago: University of Chicago Press, 1953); Robert H. Boyle, *Sport—Mirror of American Life* (Boston: Little, Brown, 1963); Robert Lipsyte, *Sportsworld: An American Dreamland* (New York: Quadrangle/New York Times, 1975); Paul Gardner, *Nice Guys Finish Last: Sport and American Life* (New York: Universe, 1975); James A. Michener, *Sports in America* (New York: Random House, 1976); Michael Novak, *The Joy of Sports: End Zones, Bases, Baskets, Balls, and the Consecration of the American Spirit* (New York: Basic Books, 1976); Edwin H. Cady, *The Big Game: College Sports and American Life* (Knoxville: University of Tennessee Press, 1978); Neil Isaacs, *Jock Culture, U.S.A.* (New York: Norton,

1978); and Richard Lipsky, *How We Play the Game: Why Sports Dominate American Life* (Boston: Beacon Press, 1981). For historical perspective, see William J. Baker and John M. Carroll, eds., *Sports in Modern America* (St. Louis: River City, 1981).

The story of American black athletes breaking the color barrier can be read in Edwin B. Henderson, *The Black Athlete—Emergence and Arrival* (New York: International Library of Negro History, 1968), and Art Rust, Jr., *"Get That Nigger Off the Field": A Sparkling Informal History of the Black Man in Baseball* (New York: Delacorte, 1976). For a first-hand memoir of the baseball break-through, see Jackie Robinson, *I Never Had It Made* (New York: Putnam's, 1972), which is best read beside a minor modern classic, Roger Kahn, *The Boys of Summer* (New York: Harper & Row, 1971). The persistence of racial discrimination, especially for black college athletes, provoked Jack Olsen to expose the problem in *The Black Athlete: A Shameful Story* (New York: Time-Life, 1968), and Harry Edwards to propose remedies in *The Revolt of the Black Athlete* (New York: Free Press, 1969).

For the emergence of women athletes, see Ellen W. Gerber, et. al., *The American Woman in Sport* (Reading, Mass.: Addison-Wesley, 1974); Carole A. Oglesby, ed., *Women and Sport: From Myth to Reality* (Philadelphia: Lea & Febiger, 1978); Stephanie L. Twin, ed., *Out of the Bleachers: Writings on Women and Sport* (Old Westbury, N.Y.: Feminist Press, 1979); and Janis Kaplan, *Women and Sports* (New York: Viking, 1979). For further information on women athletes, see Mary Lou Remley, *Women in Sport: A Guide to Information Sources* (Detroit: Gale, 1980).

American sport has expanded dramatically since World War II. On its geographical expansion, see Joseph J. Coniglio, *The Names in the Game: A History of the Movement of Sports Franchises* (New York: Vantage, 1978). Gary Davidson and Bill Libby, *Breaking the Game Wide Open* (New York: Atheneum, 1974), is a first-hand account of the entrepreneur who founded three new professional leagues. William O. Johnson, Jr., *The Super Spectator and the Electric Lilliputians* (Boston: Little, Brown, 1971), assesses the importance of television, the goose that lays the golden egg. For details on the growth of basketball, see Lewis Cole, *A Loose Game: The Sport and Business of Basketball* (Indiannapolis: Bobbs-Merrill, 1978); Leonard Koppett, *24 Seconds to Shoot: An Informal History of the National Basketball Association* (New York: Macmillan, 1968); and Ken Rappoport, *The Classic: The History of the NCAA Basketball Championship* (Mission, Kansas: NCAA, 1979). On golf and tennis, see Herb Graffis, *The PGA: The Official History of the Professional Golfers' Association of America* (New York: Crowell, 1975), and Rich Coster, *The Tennis Bubble: Big Money Tennis—How It Grew and Where It's Going* (New York: Quadrangle/New York Times, 1976).

As commercialism pervades both intercollegiate and professional sports in the United States, critics abound: Leonard Shecter, *The Jocks* (Indianapolis: Bobbs-Merrill, 1969); Joseph Durso, *The All-American Dollar: The Big Business of Sports* (Boston: Houghton Mifflin, 1971) and *The Sports Factory: An Investigation into College Sports* (New York: Quadrangle/New York Times, 1975); Paul Hoch, *Rip Off the Big Game: The Exploitation of Sports by the Power Elite* (Garden

City, N.Y.: Anchor, 1972); Glenn Dickey, *The Jock Empire: Its Rise and Deserved Fall* (Radnor, Pa.: Chilton, 1974); and Kenneth Denlinger and Leonard Shapiro, *Athletes for Sale* (New York: Crowell, 1975).

Violence comes under fire in Don Atyeo, *Blood and Guts: Violence in Sports* (New York: Paddington, 1979); Robert C. Yeager, *Seasons of Shame: The New Violence in Sports* (New York: McGraw-Hill, 1979); and John Underwood, *The Death of an American Game: The Crisis in Football* (Boston: Little, Brown, 1979). Behind much of the violence is the emphasis on winning at any cost, indicted by Thomas Tutko and William Bruns, *Winning is Everything and Other American Myths* (New York: Macmillan, 1976), and Martin Ralbovsky, *Lords of the Locker Room: The American Way of Coaching and Its Effects on Youth* (New York: Wyden, 1974).

Abuses provoke various schemes of reform, such as in Jack Scott, *The Athletic Revolution* (New York: Free Press, 1971), and John F. Rooney, Jr., *The Recruiting Game: Toward a New System of Intercollegiate Sports* (Lincoln: University of Nebraska Press, 1980). Regulations of government and law enter the picture in Roger G. Noll, ed., *Government and the Sports Business: Studies in the Regulation of Economic Activity* (Washington, D.C.: Brookings Institution, 1974); Lionel S. Sobel, *Professional Sports and the Law* (New York: Law-Acts Publishers, 1977); John C. Weistart and Cym H. Lowell, *The Law of Sports* (Indianapolis: Bobbs-Merrill, 1979); and Herb Appenzeller and Thomas Appenzeller, *Sports and the Courts* (Charlottesville, Va.: Michie, 1980). For one of the longest-contested issues in American courts, see Lee Lowenfish and Tony Lupien, *The Imperfect Diamond: The Story of Baseball's Reserve System and the Men Who Fought to Change It* (New York: Stein & Day, 1980).

Sports today concern not only lawyers but also literary critics. See Patrick Howarth, *Play Up and Play the Game: The Heroes of Popular Fiction* (London: Eyre Methuen, 1973); Wiley Lee Umphlett, *The Sporting Myth and the American Experience: Studies in Contemporary Fiction* (Lewisburg, Pa.: Bucknell Unviersity Press, 1975); Leverett T. Smith, Jr., *The American Dream and the National Game* (Bowling Green, Ohio: Bowling Green University Press, 1975); Henry B. Chapin, ed., *Sports in Literature* (New York: Longman, 1976); Robert J. Higgs and Neil Isaacs, eds., *The Sporting Spirit: Athletes in Literature and Life* (New York: Harcourt Brace Jovanovich, 1977); Tom Dodge, ed. *A Literature of Sports* (Lexington, Mass.: Heath, 1980); and Robert J. Higgs, *Laurel & Thorn: The Athlete in American Literature* (Lexington: University of Kentucky Press, 1981).

Sociologists of sport are also prolific. For examples of the sociologist's attempt to make sense of sports in the modern world, see John W. Loy, Jr., and G. S. Kenyon, eds., *Sport, Culture, and Society* (London: Macmillan, 1969); George H. Sage, ed., *Sport and American Society: Selected Readings* (Reading Mass.: Addison-Wesley, 1970); Eric Dunning, ed., *The Sociology of Sport: A Selection of Readings* (London: Cass, 1971); John T. Talamini and Charles H. Page, eds., *Sports and Society: An Anthology* (Boston: Little, Brown, 1972); Richard S. Gruneau and John G. Albinson, eds., *Canadian Sport: Sociological Perspectives* (Reading, Mass.: Addison-Wesley, 1976); and Jay J. Coakley, *Sport in Society: Issues and Controversies* (St. Louis: C. V. Mosby, 1978).

Especially valuable is the bibliography and appraisal of the issues concerning social scientists in Günther R. F. Lüschen and George H. Sage, eds., *Handbook of Social Science of Sport* (Champaign, Ill.: Stipes, 1981).

Representing an altogether different kind of literature is the recent emergence of athlete-authors: diarists such as Jerry Kramer, *Instant Replay: The Green Bay Diary of Jerry Kramer*, ed. Dick Schaap (Cleveland: World, 1969); Jim Bouton, *Ball Four*, ed. Leonard Shecter (New York: World, 1970); and Bill Bradley, *Life on the Run* (New York: Quadrangle, 1977); angry critics such as Dave Meggyesy, *Out of Their League* (Berkeley: Ramparts, 1970), and Gary Shaw, *Meat on the Hoof* (New York: St. Martin's, 1972); and mellow but perceptive retirees such as Bill Russell, *Second Wind: Memoirs of an Opinionated Man*, ed. Taylor Branch (New York: Randon House, 1979), and Arthur Ashe, *Off the Court*, ed. Neil Amdur (New York: New American Library, 1981).

To read these athletes in the context of the history of sports is to be reminded that Joseph Strutt got it right almost two hundred years ago: "In order to form a just estimation of the character of any particular people, it is absolutely necessary to investigate the Sports and Pastimes most generally prevalent among them."

INDEX